Revolutionizing the AI-Digital Landscape

This book investigates the growing influence of artificial intelligence in the marketing sphere, providing insights into how AI can be harnessed for developing more effective and efficient marketing strategies.

In addition, the book will also offer a comprehensive overview of the various digital marketing tools available to entrepreneurs, discussing their features, benefits, and potential drawbacks. This will help entrepreneurs make well-informed decisions when selecting the tools most suited to their needs and objectives. It is designed to help entrepreneurs develop and implement successful strategies, leveraging the latest tools and technologies to achieve their business goals.

As the digital landscape continues to evolve rapidly, this book aims to serve as a valuable resource for entrepreneurs looking to stay ahead of the curve and capitalize on new opportunities. The book's scope encompasses a wide range of topics, including customer experience, content marketing, AI strategy, and digital marketing tools.

Revolutionizing the AI-Digital Landscape

A Guide to Sustainable Emerging Technologies for Marketing Professionals

Edited by
Alex Khang, Pushan Kumar Dutta,
Sachin Gupta, Nishu Aayedee, and Sandeep Chatterjee

Routledge
Taylor & Francis Group

A PRODUCTIVITY PRESS BOOK

First published 2024
by Routledge
605 Third Avenue, New York, NY 10158

and by Routledge
4 Park Square, Milton Park, Abingdon, Oxon, OX14 4RN

Routledge is an imprint of the Taylor & Francis Group, an informa business

ISBN: 978-1-032-68831-2 (hbk)
ISBN: 978-1-032-68829-9 (pbk)
ISBN: 978-1-032-68830-5 (ebk)

DOI: 10.4324/9781032688305

Typeset in Garamond
by Deanta Global Publishing Services, Chennai, India

Contents

Preface

As the digital landscape continues to evolve rapidly, this book aims to serve as a valuable resource for entrepreneurs looking to stay ahead of the curve and capitalize on new opportunities. The scope of sustainable digital marketing for entrepreneurs encompasses a wide range of topics, including customer experience, content marketing, AI strategy, and digital marketing tools

By covering these diverse aspects, this book will equip readers with the knowledge and skills they need to thrive in the digital era. This book emphasizes the importance of an integrated approach to digital marketing for achieving success and highlights the various components that entrepreneurs need to consider as they develop and execute their strategies. The value is in its comprehensive approach to the subject matter, offering readers an in-depth understanding of various aspects of digital marketing and highlighting the importance of an integrated approach for achieving success. By providing actionable, and case studies, this book will help entrepreneurs develop effective strategies, make informed decisions, and ultimately drive growth.

This book will provide a thorough examination of the emerging trends and technologies in the digital marketing domain, exploring how these developments are impacting businesses and the way entrepreneurs can leverage them for growth. This book will delve into the role of customer experience in the modern marketing landscape, examining the strategies and tools that can help businesses memorable experiences for their customers. Additionally, the book will explore the ever-evolving field of content marketing, discussing the latest best practices, techniques, and innovations that are helping businesses reach and engage their target audiences more effectively. Furthermore, sustainable digital mMarketing for entrepreneurs will investigate the growing influence of artificial intelligence in the marketing sphere, providing insights into how AI can be harnessed for developing more effective and efficient marketing strategies.

This book targets a mixed audience of entrepreneurs, entrepreneurship starters, businesses, sales persons, staffs, directors, company leaders, company managers, project managers, recruiters, headhunting, professionals, students, scholars, lecturers, researchers, scientists, experts, and specialists in the any business and industry from different communities to share and contribute new ideas, strategies, methodologies, models, technologies, approaches, frameworks, theories, and practices to resolve the challenging issues associated AI with the leveraging of combating the six fields of Digital Marketing, Sustainability and Corporate Social Responsibility (CSR), Emerging Technology and Innovation, Entrepreneurship and Startups, Management and Leadership, and AI Applications for Business for developing a smart systems in the era of Industrial Revolution 4.0.

Happy reading!

Alex Khang, Pushan Kumar Dutta, Sachin Gupta, Nishu Ayedee, Sandeep Chatterjee

Acknowledgments

Revolutionizing the AI-Digital Landscape: A Guide to Sustainable Emerging Technologies for Marketing Professionals is based on the design and implementation of topics related to AI-Digital Landscape, Sustainable Emerging Technology, Artificial Intelligence, Blockchain, Data Analytics, AI-Enabled Digitization Tools, Digital Transformation Technologies, Customer Relationship Management, Enterprise Resource Planning, Social Media Marketing, Opportunities, Issues and Challenges of Cloud Computing Cybersecurity Technology, and Applications for Business Development and Strategy field in the the Era of the Industrial Revolution 4.0.

Planning and designing a book outline to introduce to readers across the globe is the passion and a noble goal of the editors. To be able to make ideas to a reality and the success of this book, the biggest reward belongs to the efforts, knowledge, skills, expertise, experiences, enthusiasm, collaboration, and trust of the contributors.

To all respected contributors, we really say big thanks for high-quality chapters that we received from our human resource managers, talent management leaders, experts, professors, scientists, engineers, scholars, Ph.D. candidates, postgraduate students, educators, and academic colleagues.

To all respected reviewers with whom we have had the opportunity to collaborate and monitor their hard work remotely, we acknowledge their tremendous support and valuable comments not only for the book but also for future book projects.

We also express our deep gratitude for all the pieces of discussion, advice, support, motivation, sharing, collaboration, and inspiration we received from our faculty, contributors, educators, professors, scientists, scholars, engineers, and academic colleagues.

Last but not least, we are really grateful to our publisher CRC Press (Taylor & Francis Group) for the wonderful support in making sure the timely processing of the manuscript and bringing out this book to the readers soonest.

Thank you, everyone.

Alex Khang, Pushan Kumar Dutta, Sachin Gupta, Nishu Ayedee, Sandeep Chatterjee

About the Editors

Alex Khang is a Professor in Information Technology, D.Sc. D.Litt., AI and Data scientist, AI and Data Science Research Center, Global Research Institute of Technology and Engineering, North Carolina, United States. He has more than 28 years of teaching and research experience in computer science and data science at the Universities of Science and Technology in Vietnam, India, and the United States. He has over 30 years of working experience as a software product manager, data engineer, AI engineer, cloud computing architect, solution architect, software architect, database expert in the foreign corporations of Germany, Sweden, the United States, Singapore, and multinationals. He has published 74 documents indexed Scopus, 52 authored books, two authored books (software development). He has published 31 edited books, 100 book chapters, and calling for book chapters for 11 edited books in the fields of AI Ecosystem.

Pushan Kumar Dutta is an accomplished Assistant Professor Grade III in Electronics and Communication Engineering Department at ASETK, Amity University Kolkata, India. He completed his Ph.D. from Jadavpur University in Kolkata in 2015, and subsequently pursued a post-doctorate with a full fellowship from Erasmus Mundus Association. In 2022, he delivered a keynote speech on the role of robotics in Data Science Europe, held in Belgrade, Serbia. Dr. Dutta is also a coordinator at Amity University Kolkata for sports and innovation competitions, leading students to participate in national competitions. He teaches classes on IoT, robotics, and first-year engineering, as well as PG Science level classes. He has an Indian copyright for his book titled *Innovative Digital Teaching and Learning for Professional Readiness* with registration number L-118639/2022.

Sachin Gupta has a brilliant academic record. He has earned his Doctorate degree (Ph.D.) from Department of Business Administration, University of Rajasthan, Jaipur, India. He completed his Dissertation Research during his M.Phil Degree on the topic "NGOs Role in developing economic condition of Rajasthan State," from Department of Business Administration, University of Rajasthan, Jaipur. He completed his Post Graduate Degrees specialties – One in Business Administration (Master of Commerce) from the Department of Business Administration, University of Rajasthan, Jaipur and another in Finance (MBA in Finance) from Rajasthan Technical University, Kota. He has served as Associate Professor and Head, Chairperson – Doctoral Research in JECRC University, Jaipur (Rajasthan), Assistant Professor Program- Coordinator MBA-Executive of FMS-The IIS University, Jaipur, visiting faculty in University Commerce College, University of Rajasthan, Jaipur, and visiting faculty in PTU (Master Somnath Technical College) for B.Sc and M.Sc Hotel Management Students. Currently, there are three research scholars working under him as registered Ph.D. students. He is so thankful to the education fraternity for the opportunities in the last 14 years and really looks forward to learning much more and achieving new horizons.

Nishu Ayedee is an Assistant Professor of Management in Bharati Vidyapeeth Institute of Management Studies and Research, New Delhi, India with a passion for quality research and collaboration. Currently serving as the Chief Marketing Officer at Confab 360 Degree, a company committed to building a comprehensive ecosystem by imparting quality research and promoting collaboration. She firmly believes that success rests on two pillars: Quality and Networking. She is also a dedicated educator, having completed several certifications in teaching and learning from Ramanujan College, University of Delhi. She recently completed the UGC-STRIDE Refresher Course on "Research Methodology: Research Ethics, Methods, Skills, Writing and Communication" held by Mizoram University, Aizawl-796004, Mizoram, India. With her extensive industry experience, commitment to quality research, and dedication to education, she is an asset to any publishing team.

Sandeep Chatterjee is a Supply Chain and Sustainability Leader with IBM Consulting with responsibility for engagements in supply chain, sustainability leveraging technology. Prior to IBM Consulting, he has worked with Deloitte, KPMG, Tata Motors, Lafarge, Infosys, and Oracle Consulting and his key strengths lie in the areas of supply chain management, business process reengineering, emerging countries enablement, network optimization, sustainability, ERP advisory across multiple industries and geographies. He holds an MBA from Indian Institute of Management, Kozhikode and a Bachelor of Engineering (Mechanical), Bengal Engineering and Science University, Shibpur (formerly Bengal Engineering College). He also teaches management students and has been part of the interview panel for various management entrances and corporate recruitments. Additionally, he belongs to the coveted MLE[SM] – Member of Leaders Excellence Group. Specialties: Supply Chain, Emerging Countries enablement, Business Process Reengineering, Oracle Application Implementation, Corporate Strategy, Sustainability, Supply Chain Network Optimization, ERP Footprint Review, Business Development, Solution Architecture, and Delivery Management.

List of Contributors

Nitisha Aggarwal
Institute of Informatics and Communication
University of Delhi
India

Ragimova Nazila Ali
Associate Professor
Azerbaijan State Oil and Industry University
Baku, Azerbaijan

Kyle Allison
Naveen Jindal School of Management
University of Texas at Dallas
Richardson, Texas, United States

Abuzarova Vusala Alyar
Educated Information Technologies
Azerbaijan State Oil and Industry University
Baku, Azerbaijan

Arpan Anand
Assistant Professor
Jaipuria Institute of Management
Noida, Uttar Pradesh, India

Zoran Ž. Avramović
Professor
Former RectorRector at Pan-European
University APEIRO
Beogradski Univerzitet, Romania
Faculty of Transport and Traffic Engineering
University of Belgrade
Belgrade, Serbia

Pretty Bhalla
Professor
Mittal School of Business
Lovely Professional University
Phagwara, India

Sharad Chaturvedi
Professor
Jaipuria Institute of Management
Indore, India

Pravin Chavan
Assistant Professor
Global Business School and
Research Centre
Dr. D.Y. Patil Vidyapeeth
Pune, India

Khurshudov Dursun
Azerbaijan University of Architecture and
Construction
Baku, Azerbaijan

Chandramowleeswaran Gnanasekaran
Assistant Professor
Department of Commerce
and Business Administration
VelTech Rangarajan
Dr. Sagunthala
R&D Institute of Science and
TechnologyAvadi
Chennai, India

Sonam Gour
Department of Computer Engineering
Poornima College of Engineering
Jaipur, Rajasthan, India

Manoj Govindaraj
Associate Professor
Department of Management Studies
VelTech Rangarajan Dr. Sagunthala R&D
Institute of Science and Technology
Avadi, Chennai, India

Rashmi Gujrat
Professor-Campus Director
KC Group of Institutions
Nawanshahr, Punjab, India

Vladimir Hahanov
School of Commerce, Finance and
Accountancy

Vugar Abdullayev Hajimahmud
Doctor of Technical Sciences
Associate Professor
Azerbaijan University of Architecture and
Construction
Baku
Azerbaijan

Md. Halimuzzaman
Ph.D. Scholar
School of Business
Galgotias University
Greater Noida
Uttar Pradesh, India

Kryshtal Halyna
Doctor of Economic Science
Professor, Head of the Department of Finance
Banking and Insurance
Interregional Academy of Personnel
Management
Kyiv, Ukraine

Cemalettin Hatipoğlu
Associate Professor
Department of Management Information
Systems
Bandirma Onyedi Eylül University
Bandırma/Balıkesir, Türkiye

Dhanashri Sanadkumar Havale
Associate Professor
MIMA Institute of Management
Pune, India

Le Thi Kim Hoa
Industrial University of Ho Chi Minh City
Ho Chi Minh City, Vietnam

Kalina Iryna
Doctor of Economic Science
Professor, Head of the Department of
Management
Interregional Academy of Personnel
Management
Kyiv, Ukraine

Rashad İsmibeyli
Associate Professor
Azerbaijan University of Architecture and
Construction
Baku, Azerbaijan

Asgarov Taleh Kamran
National Aviation Academy
Baku, Azerbaijan

Garima Kaneria
Assistant Professor
Department of Business Economics
Faculty of Commerce
The Maharaja Sayajirao University of Baroda
Vadodara, Gujarat, India

Christian Kaunert
Professor of International Security
Dublin City University
Dublin, Ireland

Jaskiran Kaur
Assistant Professor
Lovely Professional University
Phagwara, India

Alex Khang
Professor, D.Sc., D.Litt.,
AI and Data Scientist,
Department of AI and Data Science
Global Research Institute of Technology and
Engineering
Fort Raleigh, North Carolina

Bui Huy Khoi
Industrial University of Ho Chi Minh City
Ho Chi Minh City, Vietnam

Ajay Kumar
Assistant Professor
Sharda University
Greater Noida
Uttar Pradesh, India

Sanjeev Kumar
School of Hotel Management and Tourism
Lovely Professional University
Phagwara 144402, India

Jyoti Kumari
Research Scholar
Graphic Era (Deemed to be University)
Dehradun, India

Eugenia Litvinova
Doctor of Science
Professor of Computer Engineering Faculty
Design Automation Department
Kharkov National University of Radio
Electronics, Ukraine

Mariyappan M. S. R.
Professor and Dean – School of Management
VelTech Rangarajan Dr. Sagunthala R&D
Institute of Science and Technology
Avadi, Chennai, India

Geetika Madaan
Assistant Professor
University Centre for Research and
Development (UCRD)
Chandigarh University-140413, Punjab,
India.

Bhanu Pratap Singh Meena
Research Scholar, Graphic Era (Deemed to be
University)
Dehradun, India

Khushali A Mehta
Temporary Assistant Professor
Department of Business Economics
The Maharaja Sayajirao University of Baroda
Vadodara, Gujarat, India

Aditya Mishra
Student, B. Tech III Year
Department of Electronics and
Communications Engineering (ECE)
College of Technology and Engineering,
MPUAT, Udaipur, India

Amar Kumar Mishra
Professor, Graphic Era (Deemed to be
University)
Dehradun, India

Dinesh N.
Associate Professor and Programme
coordinator
OB and HR Area
CMS Business School
Jain Deemed to be University
Bangalore, India

Yitong Niu
School of Aeronautical Engineering
Anyang University
Anyang, China

Megha Ojha
Research Scholar
Graphic Era, (Deemed to be University)
Dehradun, India

Mariia Orel
Doctor of Science of Public
Administration
Professor at the Department of Public
Administration Interregional Academy of
Personnel Management (IAPM)
Kyiv, Ukraine

Periasamy P.
Associate Professor of Finance
Department of Management Studies
Saveetha College of Engineering
(Autonomous) Chennai 602105
Tamil Nadu, India

Amit Pundir
Maharaja Agrasen College
University of Delhi
Delhi, India

Adnan Raza
MCA Student
SOSS, CMR University
Bangalore, Karnataka, India

Sathish P.
Associate Professor
Department of Master of Computer
Applications
Nitte Meenakshi Institute of Technology
Bangalore
Bangalore, Karnataka, India

Geetika Jain Saxena
Maharaja Agrasen College
University of Delhi
Delhi, India

Asha Sharma
Assistant Professor
Department of Accountancy and Business
Statistics
University College of Commerce &
Management Studies
Mohanlal Sukhadia University
Udaipur (Rajasthan), India

Jaideep Sharma
Associate Professor
School of Business
Galgotias University
Greater Noida, Uttar Pradesh, India

Renu Sharma
Assistant Professor
Department of Business Administration
University College of Commerce &
Management Studies
Mohanlal Sukhadia University
Udaipur (Rajasthan), India

Rishi Sharma
School of Hotel Management and Tourism
Lovely Professional University
Phagwara 144402, India.

Archana Singh
Research Scholar
Graphic Era (Deemed to be University)
Dehradun, India

Bhupinder Singh
Professor
Sharda School of Law
Sharda University Greater Noida
India

Praveen Singh
Associate Professor
Graphic Era (Deemed to be University)
Dehradun, India

Sanjeet Singh
Professor
University Centre for Research and
DevelopmentChandigarh UniversityPunjab,
India

Sanjeev Singh
Institute of Informatics and Communication
University of Delhi, India

Pankaj A Tiwari
Assistant Professor
Department of Post Graduate Studies
St. Francis College
Koramangala, Bangalore, India

Triwiyanto
Department of Medical Electronics
Technology
Poltekkes Kemenkes Surabaya
Indonesia

Hayri Uygun
Doctorate
Ardesen Vocational School
Recep Tayyip Erdogan University
Rize, Turkey

Vajratiya Vajrobol
Institute of Informatics and Communication
University of Delhi
India

Sayeed Zafar
Chairperson
University of Business and Technology
Saudi Arabia

Chapter 1

The Landscape and Prospects of AI-Driven Applications in the Era of Digital Economy

Alex Khang, Vladimir Hahanov, Zoran Ž. Avramović,
Vugar Abdullayev Hajimahmud, Ragimova Nazila Ali,
Triwiyanto, Rashad İsmibeyli, Khurshudov Dursun,
Asgarov Taleh Kamran, and Yitong Niu

1.1 Introduction

Since the advent of artificial intelligence, a new path has been opened in the world of technology. This path was the basis for the creation of self-learning, working machines from these human-based machines. Artificial intelligence (AI) technology, which takes the human image as a role model, is currently the basis of many machines and systems – basically all the so-called "smart" technological tools.

Since the past centuries, the idea of making a machine that can think, make decisions, and "create" has existed based on human beings as a prototype, and finally today artificial intelligence technology continues its development on this basis. Already in the modern era, AI has begun to resemble a person in a real sense. In the history of AI technology, the idea of "Thinking Machines" put forward by Alan Turing has started to be realized and will probably complete its development as "Living Machines" in the near future. It should also be noted that AI-based robotics not only is based on human role models but also accepts other living beings as role models.

AI has many subsystems, some of which try to mimic humans more accurately and are more integrated. In particular, the subsystems of AI that take the human brain as a role model are: machine learning (ML), deep learning (DL), neural networks (NN), and natural language processing (NLP). AI-based technologies are also known as smart devices as mentioned, and other concepts are the types of smart applications. The definitions of both concepts are smart technologies and smart apps as below.

DOI: 10.4324/9781032688305-1

1.1.1 Smart Devices

Smart devices are AI-based devices and are smart electronic devices that can interact with both users and other smart devices. These devices can constantly exchange information both among themselves and with the user in the network environment. Smart devices are the main part of the Internet of Things (IoT) ecosystem. These devices accept commands given by users and assist users in simple daily activities. Smart devices mainly include smartphones, tablets, smartwatches, smart glasses, computers, etc. in terms of control. These devices can interact with other devices by connecting to the network and controlling them. For example, refrigerators, televisions, air conditioners, etc., which are part of smart home systems, can be remotely controlled by other small devices. In this respect, these mentioned devices are included in the range of smart devices. Smart devices are basically physical devices and they can perform virtual functions.

1.1.2 Smart Apps

Smart applications are AI-based applications that operate mainly in a virtual environment. The fact that they operate virtually, not physically, is the main factor that differentiates them from smart devices. On the other hand, like smart devices, they also rely on data, which is essential in the operation of smart devices. Smart applications act as virtual assistants, acting both locally and over the Internet. Currently, they are applied in a number of areas, and in the near future, they will be integrated into more areas. Smart apps are convenient and suitable to use (Khang & Muthmainnah et al., 2023).

As can be seen from the above descriptions, smart devices mainly represent hardware-based technologies, while smart applications, as the name suggests, represent software-based technologies. That is, while we can interact with smart devices in the physical environment, we can interact with smart applications only in the cyber environment.

1.2 Smart Applications

Smart apps are applications that use historical and real-time data from user interactions and other sources to make predictions and suggestions, providing personalized and adaptive user experiences (IntellApps, 2023). This definition of smart applications may seem relatively complicated, but there is a fairly simple way to understand it. Just look at smartphones – smartphones. So many of the apps on our smartphones these days are smart apps. These are available not only on smartphones but also on other electronic devices. That is, the small helper bots that we encounter on the sites – chatbots – belong to smart applications.

Smart applications are created as a result of the integration of a number of modern technologies. They are software that harness the power of various AI components such as ML, Big data analytics, NLP, DL, general intelligence, expert systems, robotics, etc. In general, these applications learn behavioral, contextual, and emotional patterns of the user in real time. The applications are designed to deliver predictive analytics, prescriptive analytics, transactional insights, and product insights to predict user needs and deliver them as relevant information, suggestions, or recommendations (Prerna, 2021). Smart applications help to make the processes that users perform on a daily basis in the cyber environment more convenient. Here are some Smart applications and their characteristics.

1.2.1 Google Assistant App

It is an intelligent virtual assistant developed by Google and announced at Google I/O in May 2016. Google Assistant offers voice commands, voice search, and voice-activated device control, allowing you to perform a number of tasks after saying "OK Google" or "Hey Google" (ELYSE, 2023). Opening applications, controlling smart devices (including wearable devices like smartwatches, etc.), reading notifications, scheduling appointments, sending messages, managing smart homes, and conducting real-time conversations can be done with Google Assistant.

1.2.2 Siri App

It is a built-in, voice-controlled personal assistant developed by Apple. It is available to Apple users; in simple terms, it is possible to talk to Siri, ask her questions, and ask her for help for many purposes. Siri is one of the most ideal voice assistants for users, and besides asking her about daily news, users can entrust Siri with many cyber environment processes that are done in daily life. Messaging, calling, using navigation, listening to music, controlling smart (home) devices, setting alarms, managing alert notifications, reading notifications, and setting timers, in short, at home, at work, and in sports, and on the go, Siri is always helping users as the most loyal virtual assistant everywhere. Siri is a highly advanced smart application.

1.2.3 Alexa App

Alexa was launched in 2014 as an artificial intelligence-powered virtual assistant solution developed by Amazon. Alexa is Amazon's cloud-based voice service available on more than 100 million devices from Amazon and third-party device manufacturers, and with Alexa, users can create natural voice experiences that offer customers a more intuitive way to interact with the technology they use every day. Alexa can communicate in English, German, French, Italian, Spanish, Portuguese, Japanese, Arabic, and Hindi.

1.2.4 Ada App

Ada Health is a digital health company that uses an AI-powered platform to help detect symptoms and offer treatment advice. This Berlin-based company has been operating since 2011. Ada is a global health company founded by doctors, scientists, and industry pioneers to create new opportunities for personal health (Ada, 2023). Ada's core system connects medical knowledge with smart technology to help all people actively manage their health and medical professionals to provide effective care (Khang & Medicine, 2023).

1.2.5 Cortana App

It is a personal virtual assistant provided by Microsoft. It was introduced in 2014. Cortana can help users find information faster, connect with other people faster, and more. Cortana, which continues to improve, has features similar to other virtual assistants (Cortana, 2023).

1.2.6 Generative AI App

Nowadays, the proliferation of AI technologies and generative AI applications has the potential to be a major game changer for most real-world business activities and services. Generative AI applications have enabled the creation of original-like contents by learning from huge existing data, and they have the power to revolutionize industries and transform the way of operations in organizations. By enabling the automation of various tasks that previously took much time for humans to perform, generative AI applications have the potential to reduce costs, avoid mistakes, ensure consistency, and increase efficiency and productivity, while opening up new opportunities to scale the business.

Since the explosion of generative AI applications, this technology seems to be a vital factor, not only for enterprises, but also for government organizations. They can make effective leverage of these intelligent technologies to gain a significant competitive advantage in the digital economy. With this tool, you'll be able to have new breakthroughs in the field that have the potential to drastically change the way we approach content creation and knowledge collection to support automating actions and monitoring activities, to manage tasks, to predict outcomes, to forecast risks, to support customers, and to make informed decisions that facilitate improving labor productivity and business efficiency in the digital world.

One of the famous generative AI apps is the ChatGPT app, which stands for Chat Generative Pre-trained Transformer. It is a large language model-based chatbot developed by OpenAI launched on November 30, 2022. It enables users to refine and steer a conversation towards a desired length, format, style, level of detail, and language (ChatGPT, 2022). ChatGPT technology is a language model that has the ability to interact with users in real time, providing prompt responses to their queries. It is a valuable tool in many assistant service and support applications for different business domains.

1.2.7 Benefits of Apps

For example, one of these applications, Cortana, is a virtual assistant, as we mentioned in the table. With this assistant provided by Microsoft, we can operate more comfortably in the cyber environment. Cortana basically responds when a user says "Hey Cortana" and when the user gives commands like "Hey Cortana, play music" or "Hey Cortana, open YouTube"; these processes are already performed by Cortana. This helps the user both in terms of time and in terms of not applying extra physical effort.

Overall, Siri, Google Assistant, Alexa, and Cortana act as virtual assistants, but Siri is generally more accurate in understanding speech and executing many other commands. These mentioned are some of the simplest processes that smart apps provide to users. So, smart apps are capable of much more.

From the above, it is clear that the main components of smart applications are especially ML, DL, and data analytics. Because, even in the simplest case, smart applications need to implement a certain decision-making process in order to perform the processes. So, these technologies that help in decision-making and have the characteristics of imitating humans and the human brain are the main helpers in this regard. When a person makes a decision, he first collects and reviews all the datasets that will affect his final decision. Then, he accepts the most optimal solution among the alternatives, i.e., the final result. Similarly, smart applications also perform the processes delegated to them in a similar manner to this process.

1.3 Features of Smart Apps

Key features of smart apps include:

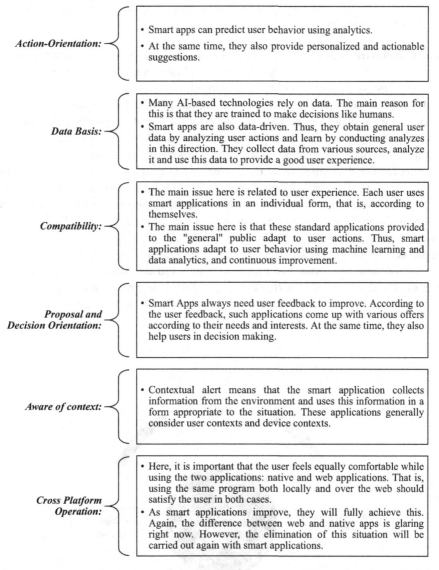

Action-Orientation:
- Smart apps can predict user behavior using analytics.
- At the same time, they also provide personalized and actionable suggestions.

Data Basis:
- Many AI-based technologies rely on data. The main reason for this is that they are trained to make decisions like humans.
- Smart apps are also data-driven. Thus, they obtain general user data by analyzing user actions and learn by conducting analyzes in this direction. They collect data from various sources, analyze it and use this data to provide a good user experience.

Compatibility:
- The main issue here is related to user experience. Each user uses smart applications in an individual form, that is, according to themselves.
- The main issue here is that these standard applications provided to the "general" public adapt to user actions. Thus, smart applications adapt to user behavior using machine learning and data analytics, and continuous improvement.

Proposal and Decision Orientation:
- Smart Apps always need user feedback to improve. According to the user feedback, such applications come up with various offers according to their needs and interests. At the same time, they also help users in decision making.

Aware of context:
- Contextual alert means that the smart application collects information from the environment and uses this information in a form appropriate to the situation. These applications generally consider user contexts and device contexts.

Cross Platform Operation:
- Here, it is important that the user feels equally comfortable while using the two applications: native and web applications. That is, using the same program both locally and over the web should satisfy the user in both cases.
- As smart applications improve, they will fully achieve this. Again, the difference between web and native apps is glaring right now. However, the elimination of this situation will be carried out again with smart applications.

The six features mentioned are the main features of smart apps. These foundational features are essential for improving smart apps, and they, in turn, are constantly being improved, and new features of smart apps are emerging.

1.3.1 Advantages of Smart Apps

The advantages of smart apps are related to their features as shown in Figure 1.1.

They are described below.

- **Smart Keyboard Inputs**: In the near future, users will use more voice commands. In this regard, one of the main advantages of smart applications is the ability to react to the user's voice and gestures, which is still being improved.
- **Time and cost savings**: The ability of smart applications to receive commands by voice, on the one hand, to make suggestions with the extensive use of ML and AI, allows users to save time. On the other hand, it helps to reduce the overall costs by reducing the risk of errors that users can make while making decisions by offering suggestions.
- **Support for the development of the sector**: It has a highly positive impact on the sector development of smart applications. This is the era of information and every sector continues to be data-driven. Smart applications affect the development of sectors such as business, healthcare, manufacturing, and education, and will play a central role in them in the near future.
- **Business help**: One of the sectors where smart applications are most widely used is business. The role of these applications in business growth and development is huge. As a result of their work with customer data, that is, the use of data and analytics, it helps business owners to achieve higher profits, and increase sales – the implementation of customer-oriented sales.

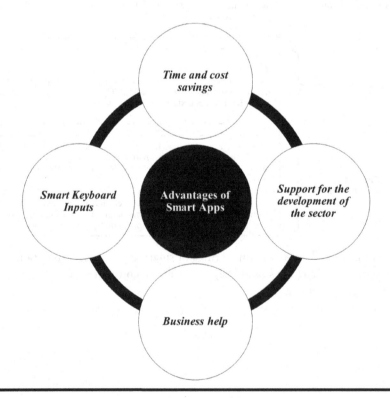

Figure 1.1 The advantages of smart apps.

1.3.2 Application Areas of Smart Applications

Smart applications are currently being used in many areas, including various fields such as business, health, education, and production, starting from everyday life. They are most commonly used in daily life.

1.3.2.1 Application of AI in Daily life

The area where smart applications are most used in everyday life. Users can use smart applications with the help of different types of tools. The most used tools are smartphones. The competition in the smartphone market causes these technologies to constantly evolve. On the other hand, the use of the Internet continues to grow, which creates a basis for smart applications.

Google Assistant, developed by Google and released to the public, and Siri, released by Apple, are smart applications that Android and iPhone users use in their daily lives. Through these, users are more comfortable in terms of both time and physical strength. In particular, these voice-operated applications not only carry out commands but can also communicate with the user. One of the main goals of these applications is to increase the ability to interact with users like real people through machine learning, natural language processing, and analytics.

Although we have mentioned only some of the main smart applications in the table above, smart applications are not limited to this. Recently, one of the indispensable applications of movie-loving users is Netflix. This smart application, which contains thousands of series and movies, analyzes user behavior and provides suitable suggestions to users. While these offerings are mostly in the movie or TV series industry, they also carry many of the same features as Netflix smart apps.

Today, many people continue to benefit as much from the Internet as they do from traditional ways of learning languages. At this point, one of the smart apps that users can use is the ELSA AI-based app. With this app, individuals can improve their English. ELSA operates with a large database and is constantly developing it.

The examples I mentioned above are AI-based applications that users use on a daily basis, and in turn, they are applied in various sectors. That is, every smart application has its impact on the development of different sectors. One of them is the business sector.

1.3.2.2 Application of AI in Business

The use of smart applications allows organizations to generate huge profits. In product-based companies, it can alert people about safety, thus reducing the chance of industrial accidents. These programs also have unique advantages for different sectors. Smart apps increase sales by evaluating and prioritizing leads and predicting winning opportunities (Webuters, 2020).

Especially in the business sector, which is a customer-oriented sector, smart applications allow organizations to achieve high efficiency by monitoring and analyzing customer behavior and using appropriate models. For example, the aforementioned Netflix smart app has generated revenue statistics for its organization with over 1 billion downloads and 230.8 million active users as of 2022, as shown in Figure 1.2.

At the same time, there are also a number of applications based on artificial intelligence, which include:

- ■ **Timely** – is an AI-based time tracking app. Scattered companies – useful for tracking employee hours in companies with multiple branches. It is used to record the working hours of employees working remotely, not only within

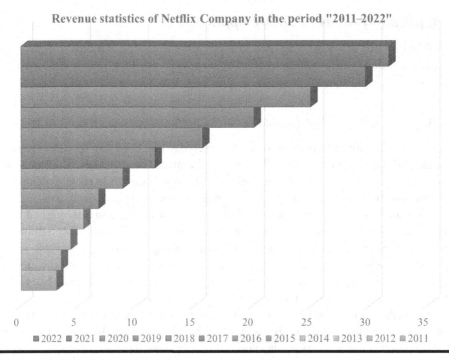

Revenue statistics of Netflix Company in the period "2011–2022"

0   5   10   15   20   25   30   35

■ 2022 ■ 2021 ■ 2020 ■ 2019 ■ 2018 ■ 2017 ■ 2016 ■ 2015 ■ 2014 ■ 2013 ■ 2012 ■ 2011

Figure 1.2   Statistics of the aforementioned Netflix smart app.

the branch. In short, a smart work schedule is organized with this AI-based application.

- ***Clara*** – This AI-based app also uses NLP and ML. It is mainly used for automatic replying of emails as well as for scheduling appointments. Clara, applied for planning, is used more and more by human resources in general and not only in the business sector.

- ***IBM Watson Assistant*** – Watson Assistant lets you create conversational interfaces across any app, device, or channel (Catalog, 2023). IBM Watson Assistant allows you to create and train Chatbots or AI assistants that allow you to interact with customers. It can be implemented in many CRM and sales departments to significantly enhance the customer experience (Vibhanshu & Margrish, 2021).

- ***Phrase AI*** – Phrase is a content authoring software that helps identify and categorize content opportunities based on search results. The software can be used to plan content and optimize it for SEO. Phrase AI helps you research, write, and optimize high-quality SEO content in minutes instead of hours (Frase, 2023) (Tom, 2023).

- ***Krisp*** – Krisp allows you to connect with customers in any way you want. From sales to customer support, Krisp keeps the workflow simple. More than just a chat app, Krisp can integrate with Slack, your emails, Messenger, Twitter, Telegram, SMS, and Line to centralize everything in one inbox (common). On the other hand, answering customer questions can be automated (with Chatbots, etc.), allowing for 24/7 customer service.

1.3.2.3 Application of AI in Healthcare

One of the areas where smart technologies are most widely applied, the Healthcare sector is increasingly integrated with technology. In this regard, the application of smart applications in the healthcare sector will also increase more and more. The healthcare sector is closely related to AI, ML, DL, and data analytics. AI and its sub-technologies are used in the healthcare decision-making process, data analysis, and image recognition. In the near future, smart applications can be widely applied in healthcare in terms of decision-making.

One of the most popular healthcare-based smart apps right now is the Ada Smart app. With this AI-based app, the user gets a customized report based on their symptoms. In more detail, the user tells Ada about their symptoms and answers questions asked by Ada to assess the symptoms and find out the cause. The application then analyzes the user's responses and presents them to the other party – the user – by creating a summary report of the cause of the symptoms. However, it should be noted that this application cannot completely replace a professional medical evaluation. On the other hand, it provides relatively more reliable results than the results of searches made in any search engine as the general information in Ada's database is reliable information.

1.3.2.4 Application of AI in Education

Smart applications have already started to be used in the education sector. Smart apps can be used to assess students, and understand their behavior and learning patterns, based on which a better and personalized learning model can be implemented in the education system. Smart apps can be used to provide learning assistance based on an individual's learning ability (Muthmainnah & Yakin et al., 2023).

1.3.2.5 Application of AI in Manufacturing

Artificial intelligence has a wide range of applications. One of these areas is the manufacturing industry. With the application of AI in production, traditional production begins to be replaced by intelligent production as shown in Figure 1.3. Even if this process is not yet complete, smart manufacturing continues to expand on a large scale, and in the near future, manufacturing, like many other sectors, may be fully automated.

1.3.2.6 Application of AI in Finance

AI is an effective tool for predicting and identifying trends of quick data analysis and can help individuals and businesses manage financial data efficiently by analyzing transactions, cash flow, budget, and accounting data to identify trends, issues, problems, and gaps for improvement. Many financial services are using AI-powered Chatbots to assist financial advisors as a knowledge resource that leverages the firm's internal repository of research and data. In the stock exchange sector, AI-powered apps can be used to help choose stocks, make predictions on market movement, optimize portfolios, manage risk, obtain personalized investment advice, manage trade entry and exit strategies, and automatically build a customized portfolio that meets specific investor criteria like risks.

1.3.3 Benefits of Smart Apps

One of the main goals of the application of artificial intelligence in production is the correct management of human labor and a more accurate assessment of many different issues such as

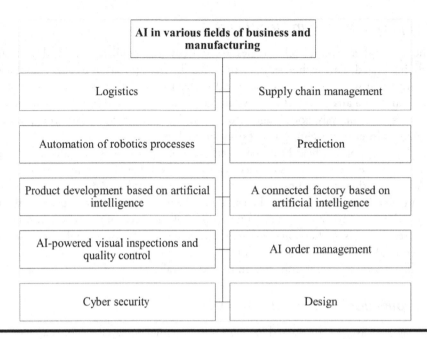

Figure 1.3   AI in business and manufacturing.

forecasting, analysis, and risk management. Branches of AI, especially ML and DL, are applied in prediction or forecasting:

■ *Prediction:* AI technology is used to solve existing problems and predict any future problems based on this. Any malfunctions that may occur in the future are predicted in advance in the equipment used in business or production.

■ *Quality control:* This again requires the application of AI in terms of monitoring and taking action on the quality of both equipment and manpower. So, especially with the application of Machine Vision technology, when any abnormality in the quality of the equipment occurs, it can be easily and quickly detected, which allows to quickly prevent the dangers that may occur in the subsequent work environment.

■ *Proper time management:* One of the main issues in product development is the proper analysis of that product, which again is related to data analysis. Data analysis will be done faster by intelligent systems, which will save time.

■ *Proper management of human resources:* This includes concepts such as time and risk management. The abovementioned is done by AI and the human workforce is focused only on more important tasks – the reduction of the labor force in the production sector, the improvement of human-centered systems, especially in the direction of decision-making, that is, there is a greater demand for human labor.

In short, it is more appropriate for people to be able to take the lead, and for other work to be done through smart technologies. However, it should also be noted that artificial intelligence-based technologies, which are constantly learning, will be able to implement the decision-making process on their own in the near future. Again, this will not lead to the complete withdrawal of human labor from the manufacturing sector, because the systems of the future will be human-centered systems.

1.4 Implementation of Smart Applications in Business and Production

Smart applications based on artificial intelligence have also opened the way to production, along with the application of artificial intelligence in production. The application of intelligent applications in manufacturing, which also corresponds to the application areas of artificial intelligence in manufacturing, is described in the following sections.

1.4.1 Control-monitoring Applications

Business or manufacturing managers use these types of smart applications to track planned workflows. Tracking applications visualizes the overall process flow. These generally include quality monitoring, manpower monitoring, time monitoring, cost monitoring.

1.4.2 Planning Applications

With planning applications, overall project planning – taking an order and turning it into a production order, planning the overall workflow, etc. – will be more convenient. Planning here covers all stages: Production planning (the design process mentioned earlier), time planning, production schedule planning, cost planning, test planning, etc.

1.4.3 Supply Chain Management Applications

A supply chain can be viewed as a network of raw material suppliers, manufacturing facilities, finished and unfinished goods inventories, warehouses and distribution centers, retail outlets or customers, materials, and information (Eli and Akene et al., 2021). The implementation of all these processes is automated through these applications. Automating the purchase of orders, the management of offers and costs, and the management of warehouse and logistics processes increases the efficiency and effectiveness of the manufacturing enterprise in terms of time, resources, and risk management. A properly managed supply chain system can significantly improve both efficiency and product quality, ultimately increasing customer satisfaction and profitability (Khang & Kali et al., 2023).

1.4.4 Proper Order Management Applications

The business process of production is customer-oriented. In other words, the customer is an important factor in the operation and sustainability of production. So, one of the most important issues in manufacturing, which is an order-oriented sector, is the proper management of orders. Proper management of the order covers all stages from its receipt to its full completion, and includes the previously mentioned ones – design, etc.

Receiving the order, visualizing it accordingly – preparing order schedules, putting forward requirements for the order, studying and considering the wishes of the customer, conducting active meetings with the customer during this time interval, planning resources (time, cost, etc.), etc. – and automating the correct management of the order are possible through smart applications. The implementation of the processes of receiving the order, relations with the customer, etc. in an automated form allows an increase in the efficiency of the enterprise both in terms of personnel resources and in terms of requirements such as time and cost.

1.4.5 Inventory Management Applications

Inventory refers to a set of equipment, supplies, etc., that belong to an enterprise, organization, department, etc. All imported and exported products can be monitored with manufacturing inventory control applications. In addition, not only the import and export but also the sorting and control of the products in the warehouse by type and serial number are carried out more easily. Accordingly, order management and convenient searches are carried out.

Each of the above-mentioned processes is interrelated, and any deviation that may occur in one of them will negatively affect the overall work process. In this regard, the automation of these processes and other similar processes, the prevention of human employee errors, the corresponding reduction of risks, and proper management of time and money resources allow for an increase in the efficiency and effectiveness of the enterprise (production in general) and has a positive effect on development. With the help of smart applications, not only the abovementioned, but also many small processes within them – generation of reports, etc. – are automated and proper management is carried out.

1.5 The Future of Smart Applications in the Digital Economy

The main desire of users is to create systems, machines, and programs that they can always use more comfortably. Visually, all systems with a simple working principle receive high reviews from users. The active use of the Internet in many parts of the world brings people (information, etc.) very close to resources. The main issue here is to reduce the use of large technologies to obtain these resources and to be able to do it with small technologies as well – for example, a computer or even a telephone.

The main goal of smart applications is to provide higher performance with a simpler user interface for existing users. Smart applications use the basic capabilities of artificial intelligence to fulfill the user's requirements, especially by reacting to voice commands. In addition, in the future, they will be able to function as a fully human model on smartphones. That is, he will be able to communicate with people at a high level, not only to follow orders.

The future of smart applications in the manufacturing industry is also related to their purpose. The main problems in the manufacturing industry are the proper utilization of time and raw materials, proper management of human labor, risks, planning, forecasting, implementation of a proper decision-making process, and many similar processes. Smart applications will ensure the automation and simple implementation of these processes using many capabilities of artificial intelligence technology (ML, DL, NLP, and data analytics). For this, smart applications must have a rich database (Pooja & Babasaheb et al., 2023).

1.6 Conclusions

Artificial intelligence-based applications provide a more convenient work environment by being applied in many different fields, as in people's daily lives. When creating smart applications, ML, DL, NLP, and data analytics, which are the main parts of AI technology, are applied in unity.

■ Smart applications can monitor and analyze user behavior, make appropriate offers, and make decisions. For this, the applications learn the behavioral, contextual, and emotional patterns of the user in real time.

- Key examples of smart apps are Siri, Alexa, Cortana, and Google Assistant. These are basically voice-activated virtual assistants that help users with many tasks and make everyday life easier.
- Smart apps incorporate several features of artificial intelligence.
- It is applied in a number of sectors such as health, business, manufacturing, and education.
- They are used in areas such as monitoring-control, forecasting, planning, order management, and inventory management in production.
- Smart applications continue to evolve with the development of artificial intelligence. It is possible to find more such applications in the near future because these applications provide users with a comfortable experience.
- Smart apps provide a personalized user experience with high adaptability.

The future prospects of AI-based smart apps in the digital transformation era hold great promise. AI-augmented technologies will allow managers to anticipate trends, maintain high rankings of business results, and create products and services that resonate more deeply with their customers. Nowadays, generative AI has ushered in a new era of assistance in digital transformation, offering unprecedented opportunities for businesses and managers. Basing on the partnership between AI solutions and human expertise is a significant aspect of staying at the forefront of digital transformation in the generative AI era. Moreover, by embracing AI-based technologies and applications, they can chart a course to success in the ever-evolving digital transformation landscape in every corner of life (Khang & Shah et al., 2023).

References

Ada Health. 2023. https://www.crunchbase.com/organization/adahealth

Catalog. 2023. IBM cloud. https://cloud.ibm.com/catalog/services/watson-assistant#about

ChatGPT. November 30, 2022. https://en.wikipedia.org/wiki/ChatGPT

Cortana. 2023. Experience AI-powered browsing with the new Bing built-in. https://www.microsoft.com/en-us/

Eli, T.M., Akene, A., and Ibhadode, O. 2021. "Supply chain management in a manufacturing industry." *Nigerian Journal of Engineering Science Research (NIJESR)*, 3(1), 48–62. https://sciendo.com/article/10.2478/jec-2021-0012

ELYSE BETTERS PICARO. April 16, 2023. What is Google assistant and what can it do? https://www.pocket-lint.com/apps/news/google/137722-what-is-google-assistant-how-does-it-work-and-which-devices-offer-it/

Frase. 2023. Smart AI for smarter SEO. https://www.frase.io/

IntellApps. 2023. The next generation of apps will be smarter and more contextual than ever before, intelligent apps: The next generation of applications. https://www.delaware.pro/en-lu/solutions/intelligent-apps

Khang, A. 2023. *AI and IoT-Based Technologies for Precision Medicine* (1st Ed.). IGI Global Press. ISBN: 9798369308769. https://doi.org/10.4018/979-8-3693-0876-9

Khang, A., Muthmainnah, M., Seraj, Prodhan Mahbub Ibna, Al Yakin, Ahmad, Obaid, Ahmad J., and Panda, Manas Ranjan. 2023. "AI-aided teaching model for the education 5.0 ecosystem." *AI-Based Technologies and Applications in the Era of the Metaverse* (1st Ed.). Page (83–104). IGI Global Press. https://doi.org/10.4018/978-1-6684-8851-5.ch004

Khang, A., Rath, Kali Charan, Satapathy, Suresh Kumar, Kumar, Amaresh, Das, Sudhansu Ranjan, and Panda, Manas Ranjan. 2023. "Enabling the future of manufacturing: Integration of robotics and IoT to smart factory infrastructure in industry 4.0." *AI-Based Technologies and Applications in the Era of the Metaverse* (1st Ed.). Page (25–50). IGI Global Press. https://doi.org/10.4018/978-1-6684-8851-5.ch002

Khang, A., Shah, V., and Rani, S. 2023. *AI-Based Technologies and Applications in the Era of the Metaverse* (1st Ed.). IGI Global Press. https://doi.org/10.4018/978-1-6684-8851-5

Muthmainnah, M., Khang, A., Seraj, Prodhan Mahbub Ibna, Al Yakin, Ahmad, Oteir, Ibrahim, and Alotaibi, Abdullah Nijr. 2023. "An innovative teaching model – The potential of metaverse for English learning." *AI-Based Technologies and Applications in the Era of the Metaverse* (1st Ed.). Page (105–126). IGI Global Press. https://doi.org/10.4018/978-1-6684-8851-5.ch005

Pooja, K., Jadhav, Babasaheb, Kulkarni, Ashish, Alex, Khang, and Kulkarni, Sagar. 2023. "The role of blockchain technology in metaverse ecosystem." *AI-Based Technologies and Applications in the Era of the Metaverse* (1st Ed.). Page (228–236). IGI Global Press. https://doi.org/10.4018/978-1-6684-8851-5.ch011

Prerna, Mahtani. January 13, 2021. What are intelligent apps? Features, examples & the future of I-Apps. https://itmunch.com/what-are-intelligent-apps-features-examples-the-future-of-i-apps/

Sarker, I.H., Hoque, M.M., Uddin, M.K., and Alsanoosy, T. 2020. "Mobile data science and intelligent apps: Concepts, AI-based modeling and research directions." *Mobile Networks and Applications*, 26, 285–303. https://link.springer.com/article/10.1007/s11036-020-01650-z

Tom, Kotze. 2023. Frase AI review – How good is it exactly? Featured image narrow content. https://www.contentellect.com/frase-ai-review

Vibhanshu, Dixit, and Margrish, Adya. February 25, 2021. 20 best AI apps for businesses to add to your toolkit this year. https://fireflies.ai/blog/best-ai-apps-for-business

Webuters. 2020. Intelligent apps (I – apps) – The future of mobile industry. https://www.webuters.com/intelligent-apps-the-future-of-mobile-industry

Chapter 2

Artificial Intelligence (AI) – Threat or Collaboration to Humanity in the 21st Century: Myth or Truth

Garima Kaneria and Khushali A Mehta

2.1 Introduction

Lately, the adoption of artificial intelligence (AI) has become very crucial in the era of digital technology. Since its beginning, it has given bullish and bearish trends, including in the hospitality industry (Citak & Weichbroth, 2021). To learn how innovation can be consolidated into a global economy, artificial intelligence must be taken into consideration. With the purpose of increasing people's standard of living, various AI-based technologies have been created to boost the economy.

To be more precise, the hospitality sector functions in a highly competitive climate that is filled with new technology. However, it is challenged by rising expenses. The company's ability to adapt to changing environment, their financial success, expand and change their services to meet the needs and demands of the customers. In order to improve customer service, the hospitality sector is utilizing technology like AI and robotics. These technological developments have been used to enhance the customer experience. Moreover, the expansion of AI in the hospitality industry has the potential to boost financial performance. As an instance, the hospitality sector gathers various data in different forms (Khanh & Khang et al., 2021).

To maintain competitive advantage and improve business performance, various organizations use AI-based technologies such as point of sale, Facebook, and line advertisements. As a result, AI and automation services offer a wide range of prospects for the hospitality industry to improve daily operations and ensure high-quality service to their customers.

DOI: 10.4324/9781032688305-2

2.2 Artificial Intelligence

The term artificial intelligence (AI) is comprised of two terms, artificial and intelligence, which are used to describe human-made objects and the capacity for independent thought, respectively. The replication of human intelligence by technology, especially computer systems, is known as AI. When it comes to carrying out certain duties, AI is incredibly efficient. Giving computers the ability to make wise decisions has resulted in more effective operations and has completely changed practically every dimension of the economy. Additionally, AI helps employees operate more efficiently, improving corporate outcomes. However, it also asks for the development of new competences and talents, from technological know-how to social and emotional intelligence to creative aptitudes. (https://blog.pressreader.com/hotels/is-artificial-intelligence-the-future-of-the -hospitality-industry)

In certain circumstances, AI may replace human expertise with technology, encouraging the hotel and tourism industries to recreate their organizational structures and operational procedures. Improved talent acquisition, development, deployment, and productivity in human resource management are the consequences of employing digital analytics and AI tools to manage and monitor the performance of human resources. There is a lot of interest in hospitality and tourism research to learn more about how AI technologies affect employee engagement, retention, and productivity because of the possible consequences for service quality and customer happiness. Therefore, AI is required in a variety of ways.

2.2.1 Significance of AI in the Hospitality Industry

In today's time, AI stands to be of enormous benefit to the hotel industry. Businesses are moving away from rule-based automated systems like chatbots in order to remain competitive and towards intelligent cognitive agents that can handle raw data, interact more naturally with humans, and continuously learn and improve. By merging AI technology with advanced analytical tools, the hotel industry has been providing customized services that create better value and memorable experiences for guests too. (https://blog.pressreader.com/hotels/is-artificial-intelligence-the-future -of-the-hospitality-industry)

Although the use of AI in the hospitality industry improves customer service, its applications are beyond interactions with guests. It serves in a number of operational areas that include allocation of resources, inventory control, and revenue management. With the help of AI, the hospitality sector is able to learn more about tastes, preferences, behavior, and trends of the customers. The degree of customization not only improves the client experience but also encourages continuous business and guest loyalty. AI has the ability to alter the hospitality sector at different levels. It begins from pre-stay marketing to post-stay elements like analytics and consumer feedback. AI also helps in analyzing the market trends, competitor pricing, and customer behavior. It also helps in optimizing the pricing strategies (Khang & Quantum, 2023).

In the hospitality sector, the guest experience is of prime focus and AI offers an opportunity to explore it at new levels. It enhances the client experience by incorporating chatbots and an automated room check-in system. This in turn increases the possibility that the visitors will come again in the future, leading to an increase in repeat reservations and improved customer loyalty. AI-based virtual assistants create customized recommendations, respond to visitor questions, and provide assistance. Each guest will have a more customized and interesting experience due to these systems' ability to comprehend their preferences, keep track of their previous encounters, and customize their responses accordingly.

It also reduces manual processes and improves operating efficiency, focusing on cost savings and allocation of resources. It facilitates an easy check-in system through face recognition technology and biometric thumb impressions. This helps in avoiding paperwork, reducing wastage of time, and eases the guest experience. The AI chatbot assistant provides 24/7 service by helping guests with various inquiries. It also focuses on learning feedback based on the services provided to customers and improving future interactions. For international guests, the chatbot translator makes it easy by not only recognizing the language but also translating the inquiries at the right time. It also helps to keep track of the energy consumption pattern and better energy usage and to enhance sustainability. These aspects not only serve senior citizens but also clients looking for customized services (AI and Robotics Technology in the Hospitality Industry: Current Applications and Future Trends. *Digital Transformation in Business and Society*).

2.2.2 Navigating the AI Landscape

The corporate environment is constantly changing. The forces of change we are currently facing, propelled by the development of AI, are presenting entrepreneurs with opportunities and problems never before seen. The secret to succeeding in this brave new world is to build resilient company models that can change, innovate, and endure.

2.2.2.1 Why Sustainability Is Important for Business

First and foremost, it's critical to understand the significance of sustainability in a company. The sustainability of a company model is crucial in today's global economy, which is defined by diminishing resources and growing social and environmental concerns. Sustainable company strategies try to balance making a profit and protecting the environment and social considerations. By developing resilience, lowering risk, and creating new opportunities, this comprehensive approach helps firms to generate value over the long term.

Additionally, it encourages entrepreneurs to contribute to the solutions to the world's issues rather than to the problems themselves. As far as the rise of AI is concerned, it has quickly become a disruptive force in the world of business. With unprecedented opportunities to boost productivity, efficiency, and innovation, AI is transforming how businesses run as technology continues to evolve at a dizzying pace.

Automation, predictive analytics, consumer segmentation, personalization, and many more tasks are made possible by AI. Businesses that use these skills can sharpen their competitive edge, improve decision-making, streamline processes, and improve customer experiences. However, there are difficulties with AI integration as well. Rapid change necessitates constant adaptation on the part of businesses in order to stay competitive. AI also poses ethical and social issues that companies must carefully handle. Companies utilizing AI must negotiate important issues such as algorithmic prejudice, job displacement, data security, and privacy concerns (Khang & Muthmainnah et al., 2023).

2.2.2.2 Adjusting to the AI Landscape

Entrepreneurs need to be adaptable, creative, and proactive given the rapid advancement of AI. Businesses must prepare for change, exploit opportunities, and steer clear of AI's potential hazards. In this situation, creating a sustainable business strategy requires several essential components:

1. Embrace Innovation: To realize the full potential of AI, businesses must constantly embrace and invest in innovation. This can entail implementing AI technology, creating fresh AI-based goods or services, or utilizing AI to improve current offerings.
2. Develop Ethical Habits: AI power comes with responsibility. Businesses must make sure that they utilize AI ethically and responsibly, preserving customer data, maintaining data security, and reducing the likelihood that AI systems will be biased.
3. Make workforce development a top priority. While AI may result in job displacement in some industries, it also opens up potential for new positions and skill sets. Businesses must spend money on employee training and development if they want to provide their staff with the skills they need to work with AI.
4. Encourage Collaboration: Business, technology, governmental, and other stakeholder collaboration can hasten the advancement and uptake of AI. Additionally, by working together, we can address social, ethical, and legal issues.
5. Remain Flexible: Flexibility is essential in the continually evolving AI field. Businesses must remain adaptable, change with the times, and be prepared to shift course as necessary.

2.2.3 The Risk Factors by AI

1. Privacy concern arises from the capacity of AI to analyze large amounts of personal data.
2. Dependency on AI includes the risk of over-dependency. This causes the loss of creativity, critical analyzing skills, and human intuition.
3. Workers may become stressed, which will affect their work efficiency and lead to loss of jobs. Based on the quality of work, it can also lead to competition between humans and robots.
4. It can be vulnerable to security and privacy threats, as AI-generated information drives the spread of wrong information.

2.3 Previous Research Supporting the Study

AI is a recent development that has the potential to enhance the influence of digital marketing on consumer behavior. Despite being a new technology, there are several disadvantages that can be avoided (Citak & Weichbroth, 2021). Due to the fact that India has the third-highest number of Internet users worldwide, businesses can increase their online marketing efforts. On the basis of useful customer insights gained using AI algorithms, they can target particular audiences.

The idea of using AI in marketing is a strategy for optimizing technological use to enhance the consumer experience (Khatri, 2021). In recent years, it has become more and more important for businesses to recognize and comprehend the demands and expectations of their customers in terms of goods and services. AI is used by marketers to process enormous volumes of data, carry out personalized sales, and satisfy client expectations. (Jain & Aggarwal, 2020). They are also able to increase campaign performance and return on investment due to their quicker understanding of customer needs. AI is anticipated to have a substantial impact on company models, sales processes, customer service alternatives, and consumer behavior in the future (Davenport, Guha, Grewal & Bressgott, 2020).

The impact of AI on marketing strategy; consumer behavior; and issues surrounding data privacy, bias, and ethics are three major areas that need to be examined. AI has already had an impact on marketing and will continue to do so in a substantial way. Moreover, there is still a lot to discover. AI approaches have continually proven worthwhile to implement in the hospitality sector for the benefit of customers. In the age of innovation, AI strategies in the hospitality sector are seen as modern machines to not only reduce dissatisfied clients but also to provide incentive services. As a result of the hospitality sector's adoption of cutting-edge technology and a high concentration of AI-based systems, travel firms have a fantastic chance to enhance their marketing, customer service, customer experience, and retention strategies (Bisoi, Mou & Samal, 2020).

Based on the above summary of previous studies, the present study is different in the following manner. The previous studies talk about AI in digital marketing, AI's influence on digital marketing on consumer behavior. This chapter attempts to talk about whether AI is a threat to humanity – a myth or truth with reference to the hospitality industry. It further continues to describe the risk factors associated with it. However, it also talks about adjusting the AI landscape for creating a sustainable business strategy. It also discusses the advantages and disadvantages of employability. It is further followed by how ChatGPT will affect employability. It describes that even if tasks and responsibilities are distributed between humans and machines based on the skills one has, a human touch can never be replaced by a new innovative technology.

2.4 ChatGPT Applications: Its Advantages and Disadvantages

This section is with reference to the Chat Generative Pre-trained Transformer introduced in November 2022: a newly introduced AI tool that gained importance. It provides the facilities of writing essays, articles, poems, and more. Basically, ChatGPT is an AI-based tool that generates helpful responses to users. To continue further, this section further talks about the merits and demerits of ChatGPT in reference to AI and employment. The merits are mentioned below.

2.4.1 Improves Travel Experience

When ChatGPT is merged with travel-related technologies and services such as travel-based services and sites for hotels, the overall experience gets better. It gives guests the opportunity to find out destination recommendations, travel advice, means of transportation, and specifics on the culture surrounding the area. It has the capacity to improve the overall accommodation and vacation experience. It also provides real-time information on weather conditions and local events. In order to provide a smooth experience to tourists, ChatGPT offers valuable information about local traditions and cultural norms.

2.4.2 Using for Accommodation Service

This point talks about the check-in and check-out process, emergency procedures, and sustainable guest behavior drafted with the aid of ChatGPT. It facilitates individualized recommendations for rooms, amenities, services, and activities.

2.4.3 For Training and Operating Efficiency

This segment talks about being capable of offering captivating job descriptions and interview questions that are specific to the company's policies and the sector. Throughout the entire employee onboarding process, chatbots can automate conversations. It covers the period during and following the procedure, providing important data about situations as part of automation. The users have access to laws, regulations, and other inquiries.

ChatGPT can optimize resource allocation by providing real-time data on room occupancy rates, cleaning crew status, VIP guest check-ins, and prepared rooms. In addition, it also assists with staffing levels, demand forecasts, lighting control, and the tracking of energy consumption in unoccupied spaces. It works as a useful training aid for recently hired employees. It provides solutions to common problems as well as scenario-based teaching.

2.4.4 For Digital Marketing

It assists in product creation; composes text, photos, and videos for marketing and sales purposes; assesses customer feedback; and increases sales. It assists in producing content more quickly, effectively, and possibly more efficiently than humans can do. This technology also assists marketers in researching and learning more about the opinions, thoughts, and feelings that consumers have towards advertisements and other commodities. It helps marketers to formulate ideas, offer customer services 24 hours a day, seven days a week, and improve the speed and accuracy of customer service.

2.4.5 For Multilingual Support

ChatGPT is supportive and comfortable with a wide range of languages. Hotels are able to help guests who don't speak English by offering real-time translation services. It can write programs and code since it is multilingual in computer languages. It has the ability to offer real-time translation services to hotels and ensure effective communication between international visitors and hotel employees. Hotels can successfully manage language barriers, improve customer satisfaction, and guarantee that every tourist, regardless of language proficiency, feels important and receives personalized service by utilizing ChatGPT for translation. The demerits are mentioned below.

2.4.5.1 Confined Context

Though ChatGPT is capable of analyzing and responding to a broad range of queries and cues, it lacks a comprehensive grasp of the questions context it causes to produce inaccurate and unnecessary responses.

2.4.5.2 Absence of Emotional Intelligence

Despite ChatGPT's ability in analyzing and assessing data, it lacks empathy and perspective due to its inability to comprehend human emotions. As a result, it becomes difficult to offer insightful responses on particular subjects.

2.4.5.3 Absence of Originality

ChatGPT isn't able to come up with unique ideas but it can solicit useful and pertinent information. Although it consolidates the pertinent data from several online sources, it won't be creative.

2.4.5.4 Dependency on the User and the Data

The data utilized by ChatGPT has a big impact on the quality of responses. Poor quality, old, and biased data would produce unsatisfactory results. In a similar vein, a low-quality response might result from a user failing to create a query and its output.

2.4.5.5 Has No Opinion

The thinking ability of humans is not the same as that of technology. Humans are different from chatbots only in the aspect of thinking beings. This is a challenge for ChatGPT; although it is capable of producing high-quality content, it is not able to offer individualized advice or solutions to social, political, or cultural difficulties.

2.4.6 How Will ChatGPT Affect Employability?

The employment has undergone a complete change, thanks to the introduction of AI and its subsidiary tools. But after November 2022, when ChatGPT was introduced, the concern still remains: how will it affect employability in the hotel industry? Is AI a threat to humanity, myth, or truth? These questions still remain unanswered. To put it in simple words, AI is a threat to humanity is not only a myth but truth too. This can be explained with the help of the points mentioned below.

2.4.6.1 Automated Client Support

With the use of ChatGPT, the hotel industry is able to reduce the dependency on customer service personnel by developing automated chatbots that can handle consumer inquiry queries.

2.4.6.2 Decreased Dependency on Interpreters

A multilingual chatbot called ChatGPT can be used for language translation, which helps to partially offset the need for human translators. However, it cannot take the place of the human element and may need human inspection to ensure accuracy.

2.4.6.3 An Increase in the Need of AI Experts

Expertise in software engineering, natural language processing, and machine learning is needed for the creation and implementation of AI language models like ChatGPT. Consequently, there will be a greater need for experts possessing these abilities.

2.4.6.4 Hiring Procedures

Companies can utilize ChatGPT to assist them in locating the best candidates for available positions throughout the recruitment process. Its ability to process natural language can be used to match candidates based on the knowledge and expertise needed for a certain position. It results in a quick recruitment process and is more effective, saving time and money in the process of identifying qualified applicants (Khang & AIoCF, 2024).

2.4.6.5 Fresh Employment and Prospects

Although ChatGPT's effects on the world labor market are still being felt, there is hope that they will simplify procedures, cut expenses, and open up new career prospects. However, as AI evolves further, there will be opportunities for new employment and career prospects in fields including software development, data analysis, programming, content creation, and AI research and

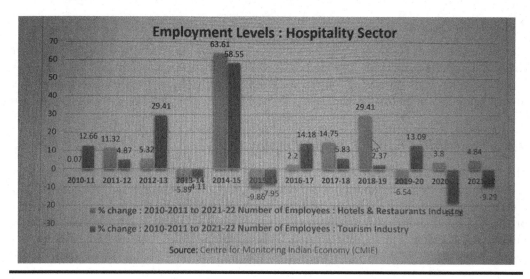

Figure 2.1   Chart of customer service, increasing operational capacity, and cutting expenses.

development. But at the same time it will reduce employability of customer representatives and others too.

2.5 Results and Discussion

A number of tourism and hospitality sectors, including the hotel and food and beverage industries, have already adopted AI technologies. The application of AI is a crucial and strategic component of economic growth. Additionally, AI-based technologies are evolving into digital assistants. They help hospitality organizations in a number of ways, including by enhancing customer service, increasing operational capacity, and cutting expenses as shown in Figure 2.1.

However, there are also problems associated with AI development, including employment loss in low-tech industries; control loss due to robot autonomy; and issues with safety, security, and privacy. The workforce and employment in the hospitality business are thus impacted by AI technology in a bad way as per the abovementioned figure.

2.6 Conclusion

The concept of AI is not new, as it came into existence way back in 1986. AI technologies have both bullish and bearish effects on employment in the hospitality sector. The hotel industry is embracing cutting-edge technology and a high degree of AI-based systems, giving travel firms a great chance to boost marketing, customer service, experience, and retention. It is useful since it allows marketers to access volumes of data, conduct personalized sales, and satisfy client expectations.

AI-based support can be utilized to enhance customer relationships by facilitating positive customer encounters. Organizations can choose better where to employ AI solutions in their value chain by understanding how AI can be used. To sum up, it's critical to concentrate on these technologies and use the right tactics to. Even if tasks are shared and distributed between humans and machines based on the skills one has, it is concluded that human touch can never be replaced by a new innovative technology.

AI and machine learning have the capability to alter the hotel industry at different levels (i.e., from planning, marketing, client acquisition to operation, guest experience, and facilities). It may impact staffing needs but also has the potential to create new job opportunities. Business in the future will be tech-driven and environmentally friendly, with AI taking center stage. Entrepreneurs can ensure they are not only a part of this future but also it is driving force by developing sustainable business models and adjusting to the changing AI landscape (Khang & Kali et al., 2023).

In addition to adapting to the shifting AI landscape, company owners must also make sure that their models are long-term. They will be able to take advantage of the enormous opportunities that AI offers while simultaneously contributing to the creation of a sustainable future. To sum up about ChatGPT, both pros and cons of ChatGPT are learned. It's also important to remember that AI cannot replace human intelligence and creativity, even though it may have an impact on the labor market around the world (Khang & Shah et al., 2023).

2.7 Suggestions

The suggestion of the study is to conduct empirical research on the long-term effects of AI and robotic technologies on actual behaviors and the risks to customers and employees. It is suggested to conduct study which is based on AI and its acceptance in the hospitality industry or other sectors. An interview approach to the study on focused groups such as business owners, marketers, and software application developers can help yield clear results. This will further help in implementing appropriate strategies to meet the expectations of clients. Further efforts should be dedicated towards conducting extensive empirical studies to further investigate the limitations that hinder the proper implementation of ChatGPT in the domain of hospitality (Khang & Rani et al., 2023).

References

Bisoi, S., Mou Roy, D. & Samal, A. (2020). Impact of artificial intelligence in the hospitality industry. *International Journal of Advanced Science and Technology*, 29(5), 4265–4275. https://www.researchgate.net/profile/Mou-Roy-2/publication/343180745_Impact_of_Artificial_Intelligence_in_the_Hospitality_Industry/links/5f1a9c8b92851cd5fa421ba3/Impact-of-Artificial-Intelligence-in-the-Hospitality-Industry.pdf

Citak, J., Owoc, M.L. & Weichbroth, P. (2021). A note on the applications of artificial intelligence in the hospitality industry: Preliminary results of a survey. *Procedia Computer Science*, 192, 4552–4559. https://www.sciencedirect.com/science/article/pii/S1877050921019724

Davenport, T., Guha, A., Grewal, D. & Bressgott, T. (2020). How artificial intelligence will change the future of marketing. *Journal of the Academy of Marketing Science*, 48(1), 24–42. https://link.springer.com/article/10.1007/s11747-019-00696-0

Jain, P. & Aggarwal, K. (2020). Transforming marketing with artificial intelligence. *International Research Journal of Engineering and Technology*, 7(7), 3964–3974. https://www.ingentaconnect.com/content/hsp/ama/2018/00000003/00000004/art00003

Khatri, M. (2021). How digital marketing along with artificial intelligence is transforming consumer behaviour? *International Journal for Research in Applied Science and Engineering Technology*, 9(7), 523–527. https://www.researchgate.net/profile/Manas-Khatri/publication/353156555_How_Digital_Marketing_along_with_Artificial_Intelligence_is_Transforming_Consumer_Behaviour

/links/60e9e76b1c28af34585e60e6/How-Digital-Marketing-along-with-Artificial-Intelligence-is
-Transforming-Consumer-Behaviour.pdf

Khang, A. (2023). *Applications and Principles of Quantum Computing* (1st Ed.). ISBN: 9798369311684. IGI Global Press. https://doi.org/10.4018/979-8-3693-1168-4

Khang, A. and AIoCF. (2024). *AI-Oriented Competency Framework for Talent Management in the Digital Economy: Models, Technologies, Applications, and Implementation* (1st Ed.). ISBN: 9781032576053. CRC Press. https://doi.org/10.1201/9781003440901

Khang, A., Muthmainnah, M., Seraj, Prodhan Mahbub Ibna, Al Yakin, Ahmad, Obaid, Ahmad J. & Panda, Manas Ranjan. (2023). AI-aided teaching model for the education 5.0 ecosystem. *AI-Based Technologies and Applications in the Era of the Metaverse* (1st Ed.). Page (83–104). IGI Global Press. https://doi.org/10.4018/978-1-6684-8851-5.ch004

Khang, A., Rani, S., Gujrati, R., Uygun, H. & Gupta, S.K. (2023). *Designing Workforce Management Systems for Industry 4.0: Data-Centric and AI-Enabled Approaches* (1st Ed.). CRC Press. https://doi.org/10.1201/9781003357070

Khang, A., Rath, Kali Charan, Satapathy, Suresh Kumar, Kumar, Amaresh, Das, Sudhansu Ranjan & Panda, Manas Ranjan. (2023). Enabling the future of manufacturing: Integration of robotics and IoT to smart factory infrastructure in industry 4.0. *AI-Based Technologies and Applications in the Era of the Metaverse* (1st Ed.). Page (25–50). IGI Global Press. https://doi.org/10.4018/978-1-6684-8851-5.ch002

Khang, A., Shah, V. & Rani, S. (2023). *AI-Based Technologies and Applications in the Era of the Metaverse* (1st Ed.). IGI Global Press. https://doi.org/10.4018/978-1-6684-8851-5

Khanh, H.H. & Khang, A. (2021). The role of artificial intelligence in Blockchain applications. *Reinventing Manufacturing and Business Processes through Artificial Intelligence*, 2 Page (20–40). CRC Press. https://doi.org/10.1201/9781003145011-2

Chapter 3

Embracing the Intelligent Future: AI and Digital Marketing Synergy

Jaskiran Kaur, Pretty Bhalla, Sanjeet Singh, and Geetika Madaan

3.1 Introduction

In the long run, artificial intelligence (AI) will be a crucial component of every business organization on the planet. Significant developments in the AI environment are reflected in the emerging trends in AI-driven automation. It is seen in the way that thoughts, interests, and investments in the area of enterprise adoption of AI have changed (Verma et al., 2021; Dimitrieska, 2018; Arsenijevic & Jovic, 2019). The ability of this technology to distinguish people and things has huge ramifications for several business applications. Facial recognition may be used to identify people for security purposes, while object detection can be used to separate and analyze photos. Artificial intelligence (AI) treats human photos like cookies, enabling more individualized services depending on client preferences. Facial recognition technology is being tested by several companies to identify client emotions and, as a result, offer the best product suggestions (Yang et al., 2021; Jain & Aggarwal, 2020).

In digital marketing, AI is largely concerned with lead conversion and user retention. With the use of perceptive AI Chatbots, clever email marketing, interactive site design, and other digital marketing services, it may point a user in the path that is consistent with the objectives of the company. The effect of AI on digital marketing is dependent on a number of things. A subset of AI called machine learning (ML) is concerned with programs for computers that retrieve data and utilize it to learn on their own. It gathers information from a variety of sources, including websites, menus, online reviews, and social media profiles. The information is then utilized by AI to create and distribute audience-relevant content. Deep online study of eateries and their patrons is made possible by AI technologies (Javaid & Haleem, 2020; Hermann, 2020; Siau & Yang, 2017). Businesses may make greater use of the data at hand and reach out to potential consumers with appealing advertising at more convenient times by using AI in their marketing strategies.

DOI: 10.4324/9781032688305-3

With AI for social media and digital platforms like Facebook and Instagram, digital marketing provides a clearly pleasant experience for customers. These systems carefully evaluate user data before leading customers to offerings that satisfy their needs. AI helps marketers spot and predict trends as well (Forrest & Hoanca, 2015; Dumitriu & Popescu, 2020). It keeps the business from overpaying on digital advertising and guarantees that the funds are utilized effectively. The term "computer vision" refers to a computer's capacity to identify individuals, groups, and scenes in visual data. A few applications include facial recognition, public safety, and security monitoring. Robots can forecast the future and take appropriate action in response to probable changes if computer vision and AI are correctly integrated (Wisetsri, 2021; Van Esch & Stewart, 2021, Yang & Siau, 2018).

Creating client profiles and understanding the customer journey process have been made easier by AI. It enables marketers to swiftly and simply deliver useful, customized content for the different customer profiles at every point of the marketing funnel and across all channels. AI technologies in digital marketing can evaluate what content is most likely to keep users returning to the site based on previous data. AI examines which clients are most likely to discontinue using a certain service and which qualities are common among discontinuers. This data allows marketers to plan their upcoming campaigns and put strategies in place that encourage customers to stick around (Saura et al., 2021; Stalidis et al., 2015; Gkikas & Theodoridis, 2019).

Digital marketing AI systems can go through the vast amount of online data to determine just what is needed to know to run the firm. They will outline information such as what pricing will generate the greatest conversions, the best time to post, the best subject line, etc. Marketers that are wise remain on top of all trends. AI systems simplify tasks and foster innovation and original thinking. Additionally, they increase value for the clients who profit (Mitic, 2019; Triberti et al., 2020). This chapter has looked at the need for AI in the marketing industry. We briefly discuss the numerous ways that AI is being used in various marketing fields. The report also examines further AI-based changes in the advertising and marketing sectors. The report also identifies and explores significant applications of AI in marketing (Khang & Shah et al., 2023).

For this research, relevant articles on AI in marketing were identified from Scopus, Google Scholar, ResearchGate, and other platforms. The theme of the study was developed after reviewing and reading the articles extracted from the above sources. The purpose of this chapter is to examine how AI is used in marketing. The precise uses of AI in various marketing segments and how they change marketing sectors are also looked at. Finally, important uses of AI in marketing have been illuminated, recognized, and analyzed.

3.2 Artificial Intelligence

AI is a branch of computer science that trains computers to understand and mimic human behavior and communication. A new intelligent computer that thinks, reacts, and completes tasks in a similar manner to people has been developed using AI and the data supplied. AI is capable of doing highly technical and specialized tasks like robotics (Khang & Kali et al., 2023), audio and image recognition, natural language processing (NLP), problem solving, etc. AI is a group of technologies that can carry out activities that require human intellect. These technologies can learn, behave, and perform like humans when used in conventional business procedures. Simulating human intelligence in robots helps us do business more quickly and for less money (Chintalapati & Pandey, 2022).

The goal of AI is to build intelligent machines that can think and behave just like people. It offers outstanding potential for a variety of sectors. Every sector listed is either afraid of or fascinated by AI's impending advent. AI is capable of developing intelligent machinery and gadgets that can behave and think like people. The next step in the industrial revolution has been named this technology. The majority of the issues of today are seen to have answers in AI and ML. AI may also help with problem prediction in the future. New industries, technologies, and surroundings can be produced through AI.

In a word, AI is the simulation of machine intelligence by human intellect. This may involve knowledge, logic, and – most significantly – the capacity for self-correction (Kaplan, 2021). AI has the capacity to assess, understand and decide. It is for data on current users and is used to forecast market trends and user behavior. Organizations all over the globe use it to fine-tune their sales and marketing strategies in order to boost sales. It is also known as data forecast. The majority of AI marketing apps now use ML, from personalizing product recommendations to aiding in identifying the most effective advertising channels, calculating churn rate or customer lifetime value, and creating superior client segments (Schiessl et al., 2022).

3.3 Artificial Intelligence in Marketing

A company's present content strategy may be complemented with AI, which is an intriguing and cutting-edge technology. This technology is a broad phrase that covers a variety of technologies, including computer vision, deep learning (DL), NLP, and ML. Because of its capacity to analyze data and offer analytical tools, ML has a huge influence on the digital marketing environment. Thus, it helps marketing teams carry out needs-based evaluations. By concentrating on other facets of digital marketing, businesses that employ AI solutions save time. AI is a rapidly developing field of technology with broad implications. As a result, using AI in digital marketing is encouraged to encourage innovation and boost productivity in the years to come (Frank, 2021).

To better classify and move clients to the next stage of their journey while offering the greatest experience, marketers may utilize AI to obtain deeper consumer insights. By carefully analyzing customer data and understanding what consumers really want, marketers may enhance ROI without spending money on futile initiatives. Additionally, they won't have to waste time watching boring advertisements that annoy customers (Peyravi et al., 2020). In a number of ways, AI will customize marketing. To better meet client needs, many businesses currently use AI to customize their websites, emails, social media postings, videos, and other resources. Automating tasks that formerly required human intelligence is one of AI's main objectives. Significant efficiency gains are possible due to the reduction in labor resources needed by an organization to complete a project or in the amount of time needed by a person to complete mundane tasks (Murgai, 2018; Khokar, 2019).

3.4 Objectives of the Study

To boost engagement and convince customers to convert or make a purchase, brands are personalizing marketing emails based on customer preferences and behaviors. Based on each recipient's lifecycle stage, AI automated the segmentation process and starts sending them individualized content through email, SMS, and in-app notifications. Existing cyberattack methods like spear phishing will be made more successful by using AI, and by removing labor constraints, more players will be able to carry them out.

Although AI is typically depicted as a threat to privacy, it may also help to maintain privacy, the ownership of private data, and the value of its derived assets. Policymakers will have to carefully evaluate how to regulate developing technology, finding a balance between the need to prevent malicious individuals from obtaining potent weapons and the need to prevent innovation from being stifled (Mikalef et al., 2021; Jones, 2018; Grandinetti, 2020). The following are the paper's main research aims: Briefly describe AI and why it is necessary in marketing. Also an attempt has been made to explore potential AI-based transformations for marketing sectors, identify and discuss major AI applications for marketing.

3.5 Research Methodology

As part of this literature-based review, reading a number of relevant books, blogs, and articles on AI for marketing was done. The writers then conducted a critical analysis of these works in light of the research problem. This literature study provides a thorough status on the investigation of the specific subject. The following conceptual concepts were looked at in this article as they pertain to the use of AI in marketing. The research topics are addressed in this chapter, which also offers a thorough explanation of AI in marketing.

3.6 Related Work

Figure 3.1 shows the many key marketing sectors of AI efforts. Targeting AI-based systems in marketing situations has required careful consideration of pricing, strategy and planning, product, promotion, and location management. Other factors, such as positioning, scenarios, and thinking models with regard to product design and end-user requirements, have been emphasized as crucial components of marketing for AI applications (Han et al., 2021; Ismagiloiva et al., 2020; Lai & Yu, 2021).

AI is used by marketers to boost customer demand. Integrated apps that take advantage of machine intelligence provide customers with a great user experience. It records every purchase,

Figure 3.1   Various categories of AI utilization within the marketing industry.

including the location and time it was made. It may examine the data and provide clients with personalized marketing messages. These notifications give tips and deals to raise a customer's average order value when they visit a nearby business (Rizvi et al., 2021). By utilizing an integrated strategy for system automation, marketing provides the business with a competitive edge. The AI marketing strategy has advantages in decision-making and client micromanagement. Data is essential for enhancing the patterns of content that ML systems propose to clients. The automated process for purchasing and selling online advertising is known as programmatic media bidding. These computer-based models use audience data, inherit ML characteristics, and provide pertinent adverts to potential customers (Karimova & Goby, 2021)

The danger of human mistake is decreased, audience data is effectively utilized, and display advertising is scaled, thanks to the employment of AI algorithms and ML. Ads that are pertinent to them or address their issues are more appealing to consumers. Marketers may make sure they are working with the proper core consumer groups who are most likely to act and respond favorably to the advertising in front of them by developing targeted ad campaigns for acceptable customers. By utilizing the digital superintelligence of AI models and algorithms, marketers may do this (Yau et al., 2021). Advertising targeting initiatives can benefit from AI's assistance for marketers. It can retarget prospects who have a better likelihood of converting by using ML to differentiate between purchasing, actual conversion, and exploring activity. One of the many incredible AI-driven solutions that helps monitor consumer in-store visits and correlate photographs to their social media accounts is facial recognition software. These cutting-edge technologies create a new level of tailored user experience when combined with AI-powered smart alerts, which deliver real-time discount offers and welcoming greetings to each visitor (Kose & Sert, 2016; Kreutzer et al., 2020; Ciuffo et al., 2019).

When used in conjunction with reliable market research data, AI is a powerful tool. This makes it possible for businesses to accomplish a variety of tasks. An essential component of this often utilized use case is the segmentation of target audiences. In this task, AI is noticeably quicker and more effective than humans (Puntoni et al., 2021). If companies go further, they may be able to make more individualized offers to their target markets that they are more likely to accept. With the rapid adoption of new technologies, many business titans have been inspired to push into more sophisticated and effective fields, where AI has established itself as the most practical. Organizations that have access to AI will have a higher chance of remaining one step ahead of the competition (Prentice et al., 2020a).

Marketers are better able to pinpoint which clients should be targeted and whether or not they should be included in the campaign. Customers will be more effectively matched to things they are likely to purchase, and unnecessary or out-of-stock items will be avoided. By offering each customer individualized information, offers, and outstanding customer service, brands can use AI to improve the customer experience. One strategy used by businesses using AI is predictive marketing analytics (Vladimirovich, 2020; Shovo, 2021).

AI can accurately and reliably forecast how performance will look in the future based on a variety of characteristics by accessing data from prior events. Making recommendations to people that are more meaningful requires an understanding of what they value most. But the majority of AI-based customization solutions work top–down and are built for a single person rather than an entire community. A significant technological development that will last for many years is the ability to utilize AI to predict the success of marketing activities and better customize user experiences (Ullal et al., 2020).

AI is causing conversational search queries and algorithms to change, which forces search engine marketers and content creators to adapt. AI can quickly produce more targeted marketing materials that have a higher conversion rate with customers while freeing up crucial human marketers' time in the area of marketing automation. Major social networks have fiercely resisted several tactics used by marketers using AI on social media. Customers may now ask customer service bots questions that do not need to be answered over the phone or in-depth human conversation.

Millions of people utilize disappearing messaging platforms to keep in touch with friends and businesses that want to engage with customers in more direct and personal ways. Thanks to the power of AI; brands can interact with people in distinctive and personal ways where audiences spend time online, particularly on social media (Kietzmann et al., 2018; Shaily & Emma, 2021; Andre et al., 2018).

Task management may benefit from additional products like HubSpot's software, which automates particular emails through a process. Although AI's low cost and high levels of efficiency are attractive, there are a lot of things that it can copy. To begin AI marketing, marketers need access to a lot of data. It can be challenging to work with vast volumes of data and deliver insights when marketing teams lack data science and AI competence (Ashima et al., 2021; Popkova & Gulzat, 2020). Enterprises should work with outside entities to launch initiatives and assist with data collection and analysis for AI system training and ongoing maintenance. As ML systems take in more data, they will develop the ability to make accurate, useful decisions. With the use of process intelligence technologies, organizations will be able to monitor and improve their processes in real time with greater accuracy and breadth (Zerfass et al., 2020).

This makes it possible for marketing teams to target the right channels affordably. Programmatic purchasing serves as an example of how ML may increase marketing flexibility to accommodate clients' shifting demands and preferences. Customers respond differently to communications across media; some may be moved by an emotional appeal, others by comedy, and still others by rationality. A more thorough user profile may be created using ML and AI, which can track which communications consumers have responded to (Chatterjee et al., 2020). Depending on the consumers' choices, marketing teams may then send them communications that are more tailored. The insights will be meaningless, and AI systems may make decisions that hurt marketing objectives, if the data is not harmonized and error-free. Before implementing AI marketing, marketing teams must collaborate with data management teams and other business lines to build data cleansing and data maintenance processes (Ghimire et al., 2020).

Computing tools that can do certain jobs instead of human intelligence are referred to as AI. The exponential expansion of database technology is eerily comparable to how quickly this technology is developing. Databases have developed into a vital component of the infrastructure supporting corporate applications (Prentice et al., 2020b). AI and big data are specifically related. "ML" AI Chatbots may be trained on data sets comprising text recordings of human conversations collected from messaging apps to comprehend what humans say and reply correctly. Recent advancements in AI development have mostly been driven by "ML." Massive data files can include patterns that the human eye is unable to recognize. Based purely on whatever Facebook postings a person liked, computer models can more correctly predict a person's personality qualities than their friends can (Javaid et al., 2021; Sestino & De Mauro, 2022; Zulaikha et al., 2020).

3.7 Several AI-Based Revolutions for the Marketing Industries

The marketing sector has seen a number of AI-based changes that have increased its effect and impressiveness. The many AIs employed to carry out the various intended functions for addressing the marketing problems in today's competitive and sophisticated level of marketing

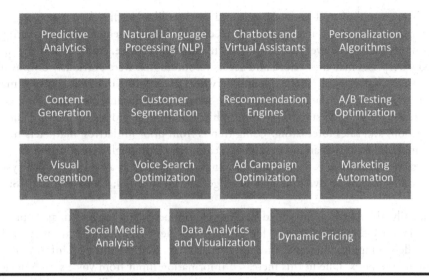

Figure 3.2   Transformations in the marketing industry driven by AI.

publicizing are illustrated in Figure 3.2. Additional inputs for implementing AI for managing market-level tactics include data collection, thorough market analysis, digitalization through AI strategies, thoughtful customer understanding, research, and need finalization in the market domain, among others.

AI technology may be used by marketers to recognize patterns and project them into the future. They may then choose who to target and how to distribute their money based on these details. Brands can spend less money on digital marketing and more time on tasks that are of high value. AI is essential to the success of every marketing effort, from the planning stage through the conversion and customer loyalty phases. Companies will therefore have a competitive edge if they fully exploit AI (Mikalef et al., 2019). It has proven possible to create machines that can mimic cognitive processes that are unique to the human mind, most notably learning and problem-solving. AI helps marketers in understanding the constantly evolving world of content marketing by evaluating user data and assisting marketers in making sense of user intent. AI may be used by marketers to create content for straightforward tales like stock updates and sports news (Hadiyati & Arizal, 2022).

Automating the search for software security may also be done with AI. Similar to how thieves search for unknown operating system weaknesses, software developers may utilize AI to evaluate security holes in their products. It is crucial to take into account the degree of openness necessary to comprehend why an AI platform made a given conclusion when choosing a tool. Marketing teams may obtain a clear report on why a certain decision was made and which data affected the decision based on the algorithm. In contrast, higher-level DL systems might not be able to offer conclusive reasoning (Siau, 2017; Dingus & Black, 2021; Guha et al., 2021). A useful new prediction tool is produced by AI algorithms learning from data, and the AI output may be distinguished from the initial training data. As a result, any assets must also be regulated in order to completely manage the data and its worth. Similar to how it is in any other business, the infrastructure that facilitates the gathering, storage, and analysis of big data should be viewed as an asset. Additionally, certain industries, like banking, have systemic effects and are significantly more important to protect because of third-party connections (Ribeiro & Reis, 2020).

In the background of well-known goods and services like Netflix, Amazon, Google, and so on, AI algorithms are always at work. But in recent years, AI has entered the marketing sector, helping businesses enhance every aspect of the customer experience. Additionally, medium- and small-sized enterprises may now afford and access resources that were previously only available to big corporations (Kupec et al., 2021). Neural networks are creating dynamic tools for marketers, enabling us to analyze big data sets that enable more insightful analysis, improving consumer behavior, creating and understanding more sophisticated buyer groups, marketing automation, content creation, and sales forecasting. Using trends from prior initiatives, marketers may utilize predictive analytics to anticipate the results of a campaign. Although neural networks have been present for some time, there is a larger need to analyze Big Data as a result of which systems are growing considerably more dynamic and intelligent (Mgiba, 2020; Dube et al., 2018; Hassan, 2021).

Additionally, the AI can interpret advertising requirements and suggest an appropriate target market. To identify the ideal audience for a certain business, algorithms examine user data like age, gender, demographics, interests, and other crucial data. On the Internet, information seekers now use many methods. Due to this increased information input from voice search devices, ML will grow more accurate in the upcoming years (Zeba et al., 2021). Similar to ML models, DL evaluates the validity of a prediction using more than a million data points. DL is a self-learning system, therefore no human input is necessary and the outcomes may be used right away. By adhering to specified themes and messaging, marketing campaigns spread the word about goods and services across a variety of media, pushing the top of the sales funnel and creating a pipeline for the company (Palanivelu & Vasanthi, 2020).

In order to make inferences and use a data-driven decision-making process, AI technology may aggregate and interpret data from numerous platforms. As power has passed from the industry to the customer, traditional marketing has undergone a drastic transformation. Systems created to collect, analyze, and utilize enormous volumes of corporate and consumer data are quickly gaining companies' interest and marketing budgets (Perez-Vega et al., 2021; Ammar et al., 2021). Marketers can now see what consumers feel, say, and think about their businesses, thanks to AI technologies. Similarly, with the abundance of social media at their disposal, marketers can genuinely comprehend how customers feel. With foresight, marketers may immediately alter messaging or branding for optimal efficacy using this data in real time. While there are many ways to optimize account-based marketing and digital advertising, AI solutions allow marketers to delve deeper for more in-depth knowledge and analysis (Ergen, 2021; Ameen et al., 2021; Wu et al., 2022; Dharmaputra et al., 2021).

From the period of assembly and marketing to the era of connection and intelligence, business conceptions have evolved (Maksimov et al., 2020; Gao & Zhang, 2020; Martin et al., 2020). The evolution of computer science has radically changed what ideas, innovations, and inventions mean today. Business models are developing further as a result. The idea of data processing has undergone a radical transformation because of the Internet of Things. These gadgets detect and record user interactions, which makes them smarter in addition to giving more access to customer data.

Additionally, since IoT technology research develops every day, organizations use it to analyze data gathered from IoT widgets for development and expansion. Productivity may improve a company's knowledge of the market and its clients. Product development can be more productive with the use of IoT devices (Caner & Bhatti, 2020; Guowei et al., 2021; Micu et al., 2018).

In the upcoming years, AI is anticipated to have a substantial influence on data security and transparency. Customers will want more openness as they become more aware of the volume of data that businesses obtain, how it is used, and how it is protected. Many businesses' email marketing strategies are optimized using AI-powered marketing technologies. In particular, they help them decide whether customized information or product suggestions to send to certain groups and when to send personalized emails. AI displays the most pertinent information at the most efficient moments. This technology can help with content planning, content reuse, and distribution optimization (Wang et al., 2020). It can also help discover top-performing material. Businesses already use automation, data analytics, and NLP. These three AI disciplines are increasing productivity and simplifying processes across several sectors (Khang & Abuzarova et al., 2023)."

3.8 Marketing Uses of Artificial Intelligence

Across a range of sectors, including finance, government, healthcare, entertainment, retail, and more, AI is used in marketing strategies. Different results are produced by each use case, such as better campaign performance, greater customer experiences, or more effective marketing operations. Marketers are addressing a variety of issues using AI through programmatic advertising (Khang & Medicine, 2023). ML is used by programmatic platforms to place bids on current ad space that is pertinent to target audiences. AI might also help eliminate errors in marketing processes (Sohrabpour et al., 2021; Grover et al., 2022).

AI is more efficient than humans at doing specific tasks as long as there is oversight and guidance. Since AI can significantly speed up marketing efforts, reduce costs, and increase efficiency, it is far more likely to produce a greater return on investment. This technology uses ML to make quick judgments based on campaign and consumer context and can analyze tactical data more quickly than humans. Team members are given more time to concentrate on strategic initiatives, which can then be utilized to direct AI-powered marketing. Instead of waiting until the conclusion of a campaign to make AI decisions, marketers may utilize real-time data to choose better media (Goyal, 2019; Sigirci, 2021). The important uses of AI applications for marketing are elaborated below:

- **Digital Marketing:** AI has a significant impact on this field. AI might be used by marketers to comprehend consumer behavior, behaviors, and indications. They are able to quickly and effectively target the appropriate approach to the appropriate person as a consequence. AI in marketing may help marketers swiftly process massive volumes of data from the web, emails, and social media. It may be used in conjunction with marketing automation to make data-driven decisions, meaningful interactions, and a positive impact on business results possible. AI marketing supports data collecting, consumer insight gathering, customer behavior prediction, and automated marketing decision-making.
- **Decreased human error:** AI has decreased human error, especially in the most crucial sector. Additionally, this technology can create and tailor information for multiple email formats that are appealing to the receivers. AI exists without a doubt to limit human contact and obviate the risk of human mistake. Many businesses are concerned about their employee's capacity to safeguard customer information and other crucial company data due to the regular data security concerns. By learning, adapting, and addressing an organization's cybersecurity needs, AI may help with a variety of problems. AI may replace a lot of the slash-and-burn resources that are often utilized to create and implement a marketing plan.
- **Connect business processes:** AI connects end-to-end business processes and provides a flawless experience by harnessing the power of information systems. When it comes to marketing outputs in businesses, marketers who take advantage of AI's potential excel. Marketing

professionals may develop and execute innovative marketing plans that are more individualized and human-centered, thanks to AI solutions. Customers are frequently thrilled by these strategies and become passionate brand advocates. The ability to influence customer micro-moments with technologies like AI may make interaction designs more enticing. The growing advantages of AI enable businesses to redefine marketing for a better user experience.

■ Examine enormous amounts of market data: AI is able to examine enormous amounts of market data and forecast the next move that a user is likely to make. It is capable of understanding trillions of search queries and helps to establish how likely a user is to make a purchase. AI also aids in detecting flaws and taking the right corrective action. The effects of AI and ML go well beyond the creation of straightforward tools. It significantly changes the way we run our business. Businesses are affected in such a way that it almost triples their productivity.

■ Deliver useful information: AI technologies simplify tasks by analyzing each new piece of data and providing clients with more pertinent information based on their preferences. It has to be viewed as a tool for directing marketing initiatives towards more ambitious goals. Marketers will surely benefit from AI's assistance in fusing cutting-edge technology with human intelligence to read, interpret, and engage with contemporary customers on an individual level through hyper-personalized, pertinent, and timely marketing. A website visitor's behavior is successfully analyzed by algorithms, which then instantaneously change and display personalized ad content. Data is continuously gathered and used to inform future changes to ad content. AI will enable sellers to concentrate more on outcomes and help their clients by utilizing personal and behavioral data. Psychographics will offer more thorough insights into the objectives, cravings, and spending habits affecting customers' decisions to use AI to pick a good or service.

■ Facilitate convenient customer service: AI helps us to provide customers with knowledgeable, straightforward, and convenient customer service at every stage of their journey. A flawless and ideal customer experience depends on it. The foundation of marketing automation strategies is the automation of routine marketing tasks and processes. Marketing automation, in particular, benefits greatly from AI applications. AI uses ML to acquire and analyze customer data in real time, applying the results on a large scale. AI facilitates the separation, organization, and prioritization of this data. Tools for marketing automation powered by AI are revolutionizing the field. By addressing demands that are changing in shape, including the desire for clients to receive hyper-personalized goods, next-generation platforms promise to strengthen marketing efforts.

■ Improved marketing automation tool: When AI is included in marketing automation systems, it helps marketers quickly discover qualified leads, create better nurturing strategies, and produce pertinent content. The best dynamic content emails, especially one-on-one ones, are those that employ contextual emails to amplify what the company says while also focusing on what subscribers want to hear. Depending on the geo-locations, psychographics, behavioral data, and insights of the subscribers, dynamic content tactics ensure that emails remain pertinent to them.

■ Reduce workload: While many of us are excellent at drawing insights from enormous volumes of data, the majority of us waste a lot of time trying to extract information from difficult data. AI might help in these situations by reducing burden and saving time. The use of AI in marketing through predictive analysis has the potential to have a significant impact on all of our marketing efforts. AI-powered predictive analysis can make a ton of value out of already-existing data. One of the most well-liked marketing uses of AI is predictive lead scoring. It is a fresh method of categorizing and evaluating leads. Marketers will keep utilizing the lead scoring method based on predictive algorithms.

■ Accelerates data processing: When compared to human contact, AI expedites data processing, ensures accuracy and security, and frees the team to concentrate on strategic objectives in order to develop successful AI-powered campaigns. AI can collect and monitor tactical data in real time, enabling marketers to respond now rather than waiting for campaigns to end. They may make better informed and unbiased decisions about what to do next based on the data-driven reports. AI may help with dull and repetitive tasks. It decreases the amount of time and employees needed to do such tasks while reducing errors to zero. The cost of hiring may be greatly decreased while using the talent already on hand to do more important tasks.

■ Make customer-centered decisions: Organizations may benefit greatly from the insights that AI collects for them in order to better understand their customers and make customer-centric decisions. By analyzing the vast amounts of online information on blogs, social media sites, etc., AI provides external market intelligence. Using billions of data points from AI technologies, marketers can swiftly create customer personas. They consist of in-person interactions, local specials, spending patterns, earlier encounters/communications, referral sources, and other elements.

■ Analyze customer data: ML may look at a client's millions of data points to determine the best times and days of the week to contact them, the recommended frequency, the content that most piques their interest, and which email themes and headers get the most clicks. Using advanced algorithms, a website experience may be tailored. After analyzing hundreds of data points on a single user, AI may give offers and information that are more appropriate for each type of user. Marketing is one of several industries where predictive models may be applied. These algorithms are able to predict the chance that a certain prospect will become a client. Additionally, they can reveal other details like the stated cost necessary to convert a consumer or which customers are more likely to make subsequent purchases.

■ Enhance stock control: AI may enhance stock control during periods of high demand and purchasing, automatically preventing customers from making irrational purchases and maximizing revenue for the company. Dynamic pricing and demand forecasting requirements vary for each firm. Depending on the activities performed and the types of clients serviced, a customized solution developed by a team or an outside vendor may be the best option for establishing a system that can achieve goals.

■ Customize shopping procedures: AI may create simulation models and modify shopping procedures by engaging with virtual assistants and offering recommendations based on ML technologies. AI is being used by many businesses to interact with their customers. Amazon uses AI to suggest products based on past purchases, views, and searches. These intelligent technologies are developing quickly and may soon be able to perform better than people in some capacities. Since AI has superior knowledge, data analysis, and input, it replaces humans in the task of identifying marketing trends. These may evaluate data to predict purchase trends and decisions of the target market with ease and can improve user experience to provide the audience with what they actually need.

■ Digital advertising: To ensure optimum performance, AI is widely utilized in digital advertising; it is applied across platforms like Facebook, Google, and Instagram to give the finest expertise. By assessing user data such as gender, age, interests, and other characteristics, relevant adverts are provided. AI technology may be used by marketers to spot microtrends and even predict trends. They will then be in a position to make tactical decisions. As a result, businesses may reduce the waste associated with digital advertising and guarantee that their investment generates the highest potential returns. Because AI makes use of the capabilities of IoT and linked devices, it has an impact on the future of digital marketing.

■ Better customer experience: Businesses and their marketing teams are increasingly using intelligent technology solutions to boost operational effectiveness and customer satisfaction. These platforms allow marketers to receive a more in-depth, comprehensive view of their target customers. The information acquired using this technique may then be used to increase conversions while also requiring less work from the marketing team.

■ Helping marketers: AI supports marketers in having effective client interactions. The most cutting-edge solutions for bridging the gap between the vast quantity of consumer data accessible and likely future actions are included in the AI marketing components. Big data has exploded as a result of the growth of digital media, giving marketers improved insight into their campaigns and the ability to transfer value across channels. Marketers now have a centralized platform for managing enormous amounts of data, thanks to efficient AI-powered technologies.

■ Increased income and client satisfaction: Each application provides benefits like lower risk, faster processing, happier customers, higher revenue, etc. AI platforms can quickly decide how to spend money across media channels, ensuring that customers are continually engaged and that campaigns are getting the most out of their budgets. AI can assist in sending clients individualized messages at the ideal moment in their lives. Using this technology, marketers may be able to spot clients who are in danger and offer them information that will persuade them to come back. With the help of AI-powered dashboards, it is possible to replicate successful strategies across channels and distribute funds effectively.

■ Creating a predictive model: AI-powered solutions may help with data collection, predictive model development, and testing and validation on actual consumers. Every customer may now receive customized, relevant emails, thanks to AI. Machine-learning algorithms may also help in spotting disengaged customer groups that are about to leave or switch to a competitor. The study of omnichannel events and the detection of falling customer involvement are made easier with the help of AI-powered churn prediction. To keep consumers interested, it may send emails, push alerts, and relevant offers. When tailored content production is combined with AI-powered churn prediction, more consumers are engaged, increasing lifetime value and income.

■ Discovering consumer preferences: Marketing teams may utilize AI to gain in-depth, individualized information about client preferences and unique demographic information. This makes it possible for marketers to create customized experiences based on the tastes of their customers. If a user would have read a headline without the image, for example, and how it influences future communications, marketing teams may utilize this data to build a more complete picture of the consumer.

■ Make better decisions: AI helps humans to get a greater understanding and, as a consequence, aids in improved decision-making by examining quantitative and qualitative data. Account managers and marketers can concentrate on more important decisions, including campaign strategy, thanks to AI in Google Ads. DL is a more complex subset of ML. Large data sets, including abstract and dispersed data, must be processed in order to find complicated patterns and correlations that may be utilized to analyze customer interactions and improve individual-focused marketing and ROI. Agencies may now utilize AI to examine data, forecast trends, and enhance the quality of their brand as it becomes more readily available. As a result, the way in which a firm approaches digital marketing is quickly changing. Utilizing AI, businesses may produce more creative, targeted marketing. The agency's digital marketing approach can boost sales while reducing costs by using AI.

■ Target audience: Businesses need to be aware of and cater to the requirements and expectations of their clients. AI marketing helps companies identify their target market so they can give each of their clients a more individualized experience. Conversion management solutions are elevated to new levels by AI. Marketers may now respond to complex strategic concerns by contrasting smart inbound communication with traditional KPIs. In the e-commerce, retail, and corporate areas, there is a rising focus on offering highly personalized and customized experiences as effectively as possible as customer expectations change with technology improvements.

■ Deliver the correct message at the right time: AI technologies help marketers better understand their current and potential clients, enabling them to send the appropriate message to the appropriate person at the appropriate time. Collecting information at each customer encounter is the only way to create a genuinely thorough profile. By expanding on these profiles, marketers may leverage AI technology to improve marketing efforts and create more customized content. For more creative and successful digital advertisements, AI can access the wealth of consumer data that is concealed in keyword searches, social profiles, and other online data.

■ Help companies: AI has a big part to play in helping businesses better understand their clients' demands and deliver a tailored user experience. By gathering information about customers' past purchases and social media activity, businesses may target and contact them more effectively. A big part of optimizing ad performance is AI technologies. In social media, AI technology is used to flag performance faults, advise best practices, and drive automated marketing. AI solutions can simultaneously improve targeting and ad budget, boosting effectiveness even in intricate campaigns.

The ideal method for forecasting customers and enhancing the customer journey through the integration of customer data is AI for marketing. Businesses now have a more substantial method to achieve this due to advances in AI. This technology can help businesses attract, nurture, and convert prospects more effectively, improve the customer journey, and design more effective marketing strategies (Alla-Cherif et al., 2021). By segmenting customers based on certain specializations, marketers employ AI to divide their clientele into important groups. AI content production controls machine-generated content and automated personalization for the client journey. We can better engage visitors and stay on top of their ideas, thanks to AI-powered content curation as it provides pertinent information and additional value while demonstrating domain knowledge. It can be used for a variety of things, such as customizing messaging and improving customer recommendations (Neuhofer et al., 2021; Brobbey et al., 2021; Varsha et al., 2021).

Customizing the features and content of a website or app using AI marketing apps is the first step in launching individualized marketing campaigns and stimulating significant customer interaction. AI Chatbots employ ML to continuously advance and become smarter. These provide customers with a more realistic experience since they are numerous, flexible, and intelligent. Organizations benefit from Chatbots because they are fantastic data-collecting tools that significantly reduce the need for staff and remove barriers.

Dynamic pricing modules are used by businesses to determine the best prices for their goods and services in order to maintain their competitiveness and quickly increase profitability. They are able to appropriately price their services, even for brief durations, thanks to AI-controlled dynamic pricing modules. It is one of the most successful AI marketing apps (Jo, 2020; Zhao et al., 2022; Rabby et al., 2021). AI is quite helpful when using retargeting strategies in marketing. Using ML and DL algorithms, AI continuously tracks customer behavior and purchase history to identify trends (Vinuesa et al., 2020; Xu et al., 2022; Jiang & Li, 2022; Wu et al., 2020).

3.9 Results and Discussion

AI has the ability to collect massive volumes of data in record speed due to iterative processing and algorithms that allow software to learn from patterns. AI's several subfields all function differently. The goal of ML is to understand how computers mimic or carry out human learning behaviors to acquire new information or abilities and reorganize pre-existing knowledge structures to continually enhance performance (Shaik, 2023). Because people's interests and fashions are always changing, AI can be useful. Even if basic variables like personality traits stay consistent, client personas may change gradually over time as trends change. AI automation may make it much simpler to organize all of this. Marketing teams can stay on top of rapidly evolving fads and trends to provide clients and potential consumers with material that is timely, relevant, and tailored to their needs.

AI has evolved into the ideal "enabler" for sales and marketing professionals. It exploits the enormous amounts of data that is already available. It automates the development of analytical models, unearths hidden information, and modifies program operations using cognitive reasoning. By incorporating all the data to produce a crucial mission-critical customer image in real time, ML enables marketers to complete the overall picture (Wu & Monfort, 2023). It uses algorithms to start data-driven activities and automated cognitive processes to tackle complicated data-rich situations. When patterns, trends, and insights are discovered, ML aids in their discovery and then automatically acts on them to produce micro-targeted ads (Nalbant & Aydin, 2023). Additionally, anticipating which prospects will convert and maximizing sales efforts helps to accelerate the entire sales funnel.

Large-scale data collection and analysis, customer insights, and rapid and effective decision-making are all made possible by AI in business. AI has the ability to push the limits of marketing when paired with big data, IoT, and the human brain. AI enables companies to gather data, carry out more thorough studies, and make decisions based on useful information consumption. The finest investment for a marketer's professional career may be AI. AI marketing relies heavily on DL (Rathore, 2023). It refers to the branch of ML that deals with algorithms modeled after the neural networks of the human brain. DL techniques "teach" computers how to comprehend user requests, text, pictures, and speech patterns. The computer then uses its expertise to offer pertinent, beneficial responses and solutions depending on the demands of the users. DL with AI enables businesses to adapt to customer needs more quickly and provide always-relevant, affecting content.

Data analysis and digital marketing tactics using AI are far more precise and efficient than those using humans. They make it possible to engage users, personalize their user experience, and boost eCommerce sales. User activity is gathered, analyzed, and forecasted by AI. Brands can target adverts based on customer preferences using this information. In terms of content marketing, AI is a very useful tool and may perhaps be the future of content creation. Before AI can operate automatically without human interaction, there is still considerable work to be done. Together, AI and people can dramatically save costs, improve effectiveness, and raise organizational production. The use of AI in traditionally structured analytics can provide a world of new opportunities. Recent applications include those that comprehend, explain, and forecast customer behaviors.

AI technologies examine massive data sets using cutting-edge computing power and sophisticated computer methodologies to glean insights from collected data. AI may aid email marketing initiatives by accelerating, enhancing, and streamlining the procedure. Prior to this, digital marketing strategists had doubts about AI's place in the field. The utility of AI, however, swiftly becomes the center of attention and a complex component of what it means to be a digital marketer as technology develops and marketing becomes more intuitive. AI solutions are already being adopted and used by a number of prosperous businesses as a part of their digital marketing strategy. In their digital marketing, several companies employ AI to direct customers to pertinent items and services. A customer's behavior may now be easily understood, thanks to advancements in ML. As a consequence, the equipment's rapid, predictive behavior aids marketers in using the gathered data to make wise judgments and address any issues in the future.

AI algorithms are far better than humans at creating email subject lines using natural language generation. This is done by figuring out a brand's voice through the data it gathers and training the AI with. AI with DL capabilities creates email text that appeals to target audiences, people, and client groups. To enhance conversions and engagement, this invention may customize email content suggestions on an individual basis. Business and marketing are using ML and AI. With the use of these tools, decision-makers can extract insightful information from vast volumes of data, enabling businesses to anticipate new trends. Businesses can optimize their product mix and forecast trends with the use of AI, which may assist them in navigating and assess the fast-moving market variations.

The capacity to swiftly and efficiently respond to information about client wants and preferences is essential to modern marketing. AI has gained popularity among marketing stakeholders as a result of its capacity to make judgments based on data in real time. When deciding how to incorporate AI into their campaigns and processes, marketers must exercise caution. AI tool development and use are still in their infancy. As a result, when introducing AI into marketing, a few issues need to be taken into account. AI does not know which tasks should be completed to achieve marketing objectives. It will need time and education to learn about the objectives of the business, the preferences of the consumers, historical trends, and the general environment (Khang & Muthmainnah et al., 2023).

Marketing departments must ensure that companies use consumer data legally and ethically. This presents a problem for AI. Without being specifically designed to adhere to certain legal standards, the technologies may go beyond what is allowed when using consumer data for personalization. Although AI in marketing is expanding, there are still considerable challenges. AI is made to sort through enormous amounts of data and perform various computations. In order to execute computations quickly, ML and DL as AI components require reliable hardware and a sizable computational capacity. For students, researchers, and fans of technology, AI is no longer a novel idea. However, very few people are aware of the potential and advantages of AI.

There are also huge competency gaps when it comes to AI. These skill inequalities are widening rather than closing. Despite a slight rise in interest in AI, data science courses that focus on AI development have become increasingly prevalent. To enable any business to enter AI, more bright people will be needed. AI is still a relatively new technology for many people. It will be challenging for them to believe in AI. If people do not comprehend how AI algorithms produce judgments, they are difficult to trust. Imagine supposing high-quality, timely, and representative data were not used to train AI systems. In that instance, the instrument's utility will be decreased since the tool will make poor judgments that are not in line with user preferences. Consumers and regulatory agencies are putting pressure on corporations to change how they use personal data.

3.10 Conclusion

AI describes methods that let robots carry out mental tasks that call for human intellect. These involve interaction with the environment, learning, and thinking. Two of the most well-known AI methods are ML and DL. In order to cultivate customer engagement and loyalty, AI may provide a more customized brand experience. To enhance the user experience, marketers deploy language-based AI as sales tools, payment processors, and engagement managers. Customers may now rely on Chatbots to complete the purchasing process for them rather than having to figure it out on their own.

Language-based AI is advancing quickly, "learning" from past usage and automatically fine-tuning to produce an even better experience the following time. Recognizing pertinent material that consumers desire to read, may help advertisers. With the use of AI, it is now feasible to personalize information through observation, data collecting, and analysis. By assisting marketers with email campaigns, this technology in digital marketing enables them to optimize outcomes. One of the digital marketing services that assist in reaching the target audience at the appropriate time and ensuring appropriate conversion tactics is email marketing. The main benefit of AI in marketing is data analysis. With the help of this technology, enormous volumes of data will be analyzed to give marketers practical and useful insights (Khang, 2023).

3.11 Future Scope of Work

AI may be used by marketers to assess customer trends and patterns, predict outcomes, and optimize advertising. To predict future trends, it makes use of data, statistical algorithms, and cutting-edge AI technologies. AI systems learn how to improve their results and provide the best answers over time as they study additional data. Massive volumes of previous consumer data may be analyzed by AI-powered ML algorithms to determine which adverts are suitable for customers and at what point of the purchase process. By exploiting trends and data, AI will provide marketers with the optimization advantages of releasing content at the ideal time. In order to detect patterns in data that will help you make better judgments in the future, ML is a technique that employs observations or data, such as direct experience or instruction. By enabling computers to learn autonomously and on their own, without human guidance or aid, ML seeks to make it possible for systems to adapt their behavior (Khang & Quantum, 2023).

Future marketers will be able to employ AI to customize consumer experiences and construct marketing analytics strategies to target prospective clients. Each time a customer or prospect interacts with a product or solution, a record of that contact is kept and utilized to enhance the good or service in the future. There will come a better moment for marketers to begin experimenting with AI tactics to aid them in producing highly customized client experiences. Marketers should invest time and money to test new ideas and make sure their marketing organization is prepared for ongoing success both now and in the future because AI is expected to continue developing across all sectors and segments (Khang & Kali, 2023).

References

Allal-Chérif, O., Simón-Moya, V., & Ballester, A. C. C. (2021). Intelligent purchasing: How artificial intelligence can redefine the purchasing function. *Journal of Business Research*, 124, 69–76. https://www.sciencedirect.com/science/article/pii/S0148296320308031

Ameen, N., Tarhini, A., Reppel, A., & Anand, A. (2021). Customer experiences in the age of artificial intelligence. *Computers in Human Behavior*, 114, 106548. https://www.sciencedirect.com/science/article/pii/S0747563220302983

Ammar, M., Haleem, A., Javaid, M., Walia, R., & Bahl, S. (2021). Improving material quality management and manufacturing organizations system through Industry 4.0 technologies. *Materials Today: Proceedings*, 45, 5089–5096. https://www.sciencedirect.com/science/article/pii/S2214785321006775

André, Q., Carmon, Z., Wertenbroch, K., Crum, A., Frank, D., Goldstein, W., & Yang, H. (2018). Consumer choice and autonomy in the age of artificial intelligence and big data. *Customer Needs and Solutions*, 5, 28–37. https://link.springer.com/article/10.1007/s40547-017-0085-8

Arsenijevic, U., & Jovic, M. (2019, September). Artificial intelligence marketing: Chatbots. In *2019 International Conference on Artificial Intelligence: Applications and Innovations (IC-AIAI)* (pp. 19–193). IEEE. https://ieeexplore.ieee.org/abstract/document/9007330/

Ashima, R., Haleem, A., Bahl, S., Javaid, M., Mahla, S. K., & Singh, S. (2021). Automation and manufacturing of smart materials in Additive Manufacturing technologies using Internet of Things towards the adoption of Industry 4.0. *Materials Today: Proceedings*, 45, 5081–5088. https://www.sciencedirect.com/science/article/pii/S2214785321006751

Brobbey, E. E., Ankrah, E., & Kankam, P. K. (2021). The role of artificial intelligence in integrated marketing communications. A case study of Jumia Online Ghana. *Inkanyiso: Journal of Humanities and Social Sciences*, 13(1), 120–136. https://www.ajol.info/index.php/ijhss/article/view/212352

Caner, S., & Bhatti, F. (2020). A conceptual framework on defining businesses strategy for artificial intelligence. *Contemporary Management Research*, 16(3), 175–206. https://cmr-journal.org/article/view/19970

Chatterjee, S., Nguyen, B., Ghosh, S. K., Bhattacharjee, K. K., & Chaudhuri, S. (2020). Adoption of artificial intelligence integrated CRM system: An empirical study of Indian organizations. *The Bottom Line*, 33(4), 359–375. https://www.sciencedirect.com/science/article/pii/S0040162521002158

Ciuffo, J., Jones, S. S., & Groom, F. M. (2019). Artificial intelligence in marketing. In *Artificial Intelligence and Machine Learning for Business for Non-Engineers* (pp. 71–76). CRC Press, Taylor & Francis Group. https://www.google.com/books?hl=en&lr=&id=-BTADwAAQBAJ&oi=fnd&pg=PP1

Dharmaputra, R. T., Fernando, Y., Aryshandy, G., & Ikhsan, R. B. (2021, October). Artificial intelligence and electronic marketing outcomes: An empirical study. In *2021 3rd International Conference on Cybernetics and Intelligent System (ICORIS)* (pp. 1–6). IEEE. https://ieeexplore.ieee.org/abstract/document/9649533/

Dimitrieska, S., Stankovska, A., & Efremova, T. (2018). Artificial intelligence and marketing. *Entrepreneurship*, 6(2), 298–304. https://www.ceeol.com/search/article-detail?id=722192

Dingus, R., & Black, H. G. (2021). Choose your words carefully: An exercise to introduce artificial intelligence to the marketing classroom using tone analysis. *Marketing Education Review*, 31(2), 64–69. https://www.tandfonline.com/doi/abs/10.1080/10528008.2020.1843361

Dubé, L., Du, P., McRae, C., Sharma, N., Jayaraman, S., & Nie, J. Y. (2018). Convergent innovation in food through big data and artificial intelligence for societal-scale inclusive growth. *Technology Innovation Management Review*, 8(2). http://167.99.177.39/article/1139

Dumitriu, D., & Popescu, M. A. M. (2020). Artificial intelligence solutions for digital marketing. *Procedia Manufacturing*, 46, 630–636. https://www.sciencedirect.com/science/article/pii/S2351978920309689

Ergen, F. D. (2021). Artificial intelligence applications for event management and marketing. In *Impact of ICTs on Event Management and Marketing* (pp. 199–215). IGI Global. https://www.igi-global.com/chapter/artificial-intelligence-applications-for-event-management-and-marketing/267510

Forrest, E., & Hoanca, B. (2015). Artificial intelligence: Marketing's game changer. In *Trends and Innovations in Marketing Information Systems* (pp. 45–64). https://www.igi-global.com/chapter/artificial-intelligence/139907

Frank, B. (2021). Artificial intelligence-enabled environmental sustainability of products: Marketing benefits and their variation by consumer, location, and product types. *Journal of Cleaner Production*, 285, 125242. https://www.sciencedirect.com/science/article/pii/S0959652620352860

Gao, F., & Zhang, L. (2020, April). Application of artificial intelligence and big data technology in digital marketing. In *Proceedings of the 2020 2nd International Conference on Big Data and Artificial Intelligence* (pp. 270–272). https://dl.acm.org/doi/abs/10.1145/3436286.3436404

Ghimire, A., Thapa, S., Jha, A. K., Adhikari, S., & Kumar, A. (2020, October). Accelerating business growth with big data and artificial intelligence. In *2020 Fourth International Conference on I-SMAC (IoT in Social, Mobile, Analytics and Cloud) (I-SMAC)* (pp. 441–448). IEEE. https://ieeexplore.ieee.org/abstract/document/9243318/

Gkikas, D. C., & Theodoridis, P. K. (2019). Artificial intelligence (AI) impact on digital marketing research. In *Strategic Innovative Marketing and Tourism: 7th ICSIMAT, Athenian Riviera, Greece, 2018* (pp. 1251–1259). Springer International Publishing. https://link.springer.com/chapter/10.1007/978-3-030-12453-3_143

Goyal, M. (2019). Artificial intelligence: A tool for hyper personalization. *International Journal of 360 Management Review*, 7(1). https://www.sciencedirect.com/science/article/pii/S2666603022000136

Grandinetti, R. (2020). How artificial intelligence can change the core of marketing theory. *Innovative Marketing*, 16(2), 91–103. https://pdfs.semanticscholar.org/aacc/cfb5a35fb9cdd8da825c4bd12ff3acc427f2.pdf

Grover, P., Kar, A. K., & Dwivedi, Y. K. (2022). Understanding artificial intelligence adoption in operations management: Insights from the review of academic literature and social media discussions. *Annals of Operations Research*, 308(1–2), 177–213. https://link.springer.com/article/10.1007/s10479-020-03683-9

Guha, A., Grewal, D., Kopalle, P. K., Haenlein, M., Schneider, M. J., Jung, H., & Hawkins, G. (2021). How artificial intelligence will affect the future of retailing. *Journal of Retailing*, 97(1), 28–41. https://www.sciencedirect.com/science/article/pii/S0022435921000051

Guowei, Z., Wenli, G., Jiahui, L., Sifan, L., & Jinfeng, L. (2021). Artificial intelligence marketing: A research review and prospects. *Foreign Economics & Management*, 43(7), 86–96. https://qks.shufe.edu.cn/J/ArticleQuery/b540cccf-590d-4eb5-a5cc-800089843578

Hadiyati, H., & Arizal, N. (2022). Literasi Pemasaran Online Pada Anggota Kelompok Usaha Bersama Graha Permai Di Kelurahan Tuah Karya Kecamatan Tuah Madani. *Jurnal Pengabdian Kompetitif*, 1(2), 122–128. https://ejournal.kompetif.com/index.php/pengabdian_kompetif/article/view/1263

Han, R., Lam, H. K., Zhan, Y., Wang, Y., Dwivedi, Y. K., & Tan, K. H. (2021). Artificial intelligence in business-to-business marketing: A bibliometric analysis of current research status, development and future directions. *Industrial Management & Data Systems*, 121(12), 2467–2497. https://www.emerald.com/insight/content/doi/10.1108/IMDS-05-2021-0300/full/html

Hassan, A. (2021). The usage of artificial intelligence in digital marketing: A review. In *Applications of Artificial Intelligence in Business, Education and Healthcare* (pp. 357–383). https://link.springer.com/chapter/10.1007/978-3-030-72080-3_20

Hermann, E. (2022). Leveraging artificial intelligence in marketing for social good—An ethical perspective. *Journal of Business Ethics*, 179(1), 43–61. https://link.springer.com/article/10.1007/s10551-021-04843-y

Ismagiloiva, E., Dwivedi, Y., & Rana, N. (2020). Visualising the knowledge domain of artificial intelligence in marketing: A bibliometric analysis. In *Re-imagining Diffusion and Adoption of Information Technology and Systems: A Continuing Conversation: IFIP WG 8.6 International Conference on Transfer and Diffusion of IT, TDIT 2020, Tiruchirappalli, India, December 18–19, 2020, Proceedings, Part I* (pp. 43–53). Springer International Publishing. https://link.springer.com/chapter/10.1007/978-3-030-64849-7_5

Jain, P., & Aggarwal, K. (2020). Transforming marketing with artificial intelligence. *International Research Journal of Engineering and Technology*, 7(7), 3964–3976. https://www.ingentaconnect.com/content/hsp/ama/2018/00000003/00000004/art00003

Javaid, M., & Haleem, A. (2020). Critical components of Industry 5.0 towards a successful adoption in the field of manufacturing. *Journal of Industrial Integration and Management*, 5(3), 327–348. https://www .worldscientific.com/doi/abs/10.1142/S2424862220500141

Javaid, M., Haleem, A., Singh, R. P., & Suman, R. (2021). Significant applications of big data in Industry 4.0. *Journal of Industrial Integration and Management*, 6(4), 429–447. https://www.worldscientific .com/doi/abs/10.1142/S2424862221500135

Jiang, B., & Li, Y. (2022). Construction of educational model for computer majors in colleges and universities. *Wireless Communications and Mobile Computing*, 2022. https://www.hindawi.com/journals /wcmc/2022/6737202/

Jo, J. W. (2020). Case studies for insurance service marketing using Artificial Intelligence (AI) in the InsurTech industry. *Journal of Digital Convergence*, 18(10), 175–180. https://koreascience.kr/article/ JAKO202031064817390.page

Jones, V. K. (2018). Voice-activated change: Marketing in the age of artificial intelligence and virtual assistants. *Journal of Brand Strategy*, 7(3), 233–245. https://www.ingentaconnect.com/content/hsp/jbs /2018/00000007/00000003/art00005

Kaplan, A. (2021). Artificial intelligence, marketing, and the fourth industrial revolution: Criteria, concerns, cases. In *Handbook of Research on Applied AI for International Business and Marketing Applications* (pp. 1–13). IGI Global. https://www.igi-global.com/chapter/artificial-intelligence-marketing-and-the -fourth-industrial-revolution/261930

Karimova, G. Z., & Goby, V. P. (2021). The adaptation of anthropomorphism and archetypes for marketing artificial intelligence. *Journal of Consumer Marketing*, 38(2), 229–238. https://www.emerald.com /insight/content/doi/10.1108/JCM-04-2020-3785/full/html

Khang, A. (2023a). *Advanced Technologies and AI-Equipped IoT Applications in High-Tech Agriculture* (1st Ed.). IGI Global Press. https://doi.org/10.4018/978-1-6684-9231-4

Khang, A. (2023b). *Applications and Principles of Quantum Computing* (1st Ed.). IGI Global Press. ISBN: 9798369311684. https://doi.org/10.4018/979-8-3693-1168-4

Khang, A., & Rath, K. C. (2023). Quantum mechanics primer – Fundamentals and quantum computing. In *Applications and Principles of Quantum Computing* (1st Ed.). IGI Global Press. ISBN: 9798369311684. https://doi.org/10.4018/979-8-3693-1168-4-ch001

Khang, A., Muthmainnah, M., Seraj, P. M. I., Al Yakin, A., Obaid, A. J., & Panda, M. R. (2023). AI-Aided teaching model for the education 5.0 ecosystem. In *AI-Based Technologies and Applications in the Era of the Metaverse* (1st Ed., pp. 83–104). IGI Global Press. https://doi.org/10.4018/978-1-6684-8851-5 .ch004

Khang, A., Rath, K. C., Panda, S., Sree, P. K., & Panda, S. K. (2023). Revolutionizing agriculture: Exploring advanced technologies for plant protection in the agriculture sector. In *Handbook of Research on AI-Equipped IoT Applications in High-Tech Agriculture* (pp. 1–22). Copyright: © 2023. https://doi.org /10.4018/978-1-6684-9231-4.ch001

Khang, A., Rath, K. C., Satapathy, S. K., Kumar, A., Das, S. R., & Panda, M. R. (2023). Enabling the future of manufacturing: Integration of robotics and IoT to smart factory infrastructure in industry 4.0. In *AI-Based Technologies and Applications in the Era of the Metaverse* (1st Ed., pp. 25–50). IGI Global Press. https://doi.org/10.4018/978-1-6684-8851-5.ch002

Khang, A., Shah, V., & Rani, S. (2023). *AI-Based Technologies and Applications in the Era of the Metaverse* (1st Ed.). IGI Global Press. https://doi.org/10.4018/978-1-6684-8851-5

Khokhar, P. (2019). Evolution of artificial intelligence in marketing, comparison with traditional marketing. *Our Heritage*, 67(5), 375–389. https://papers.ssrn.com/sol3/papers.cfm?abstract_id=3557091

Kietzmann, J., Paschen, J., & Treen, E. (2018). Artificial intelligence in advertising: How marketers can leverage artificial intelligence along the consumer journey. *Journal of Advertising Research*, 58(3), 263– 267. https://www.journalofadvertisingresearch.com/content/58/3/263.short

Kose, U., & Sert, S. (2016). Intelligent content marketing with artificial intelligence. In *International Conference of Scientific Cooperation for Future* (No. 837–43). https://www.academia.edu/download /49071139/BILDIRI_TEK.pdf

Kreutzer, R. T., Sirrenberg, M., Kreutzer, R. T., & Sirrenberg, M. (2020). Fields of application of artificial intelligence—Customer service, marketing and sales. In *Understanding Artificial Intelligence:*

Fundamentals, Use Cases and Methods for a Corporate AI Journey (pp. 105–154). https://link.springer .com/chapter/10.1007/978-3-030-25271-7_4

Kupec, M., Jakubíková, D., & Kupec, V. (2021). Web personalization and artificial intelligence as tools for marketing communications. https://www.ceeol.com/search/article-detail?id=999643

Lai, Z., & Yu, L. (2021). Research on digital marketing communication talent cultivation in the era of artificial intelligence. In *Journal of Physics: Conference Series* (Vol. 1757, No. 1, p. 012040). IOP Publishing. https://iopscience.iop.org/article/10.1088/1742-6596/1757/1/012040/meta

Maksimov, M. I., Akulinin, F. V., Velikorossov, V. V., Mayorova, I. A., Zaharov, A. K., & Zhanguttina, G. O. (2020). Artificial intelligence and machine learning methods for solving snp tasks. *Journal of Advanced Research in Dynamical and Control Systems*, 12(6), 1312–1315. https://elibrary.ru/item.asp ?id=44028218

Martin, B. A., Jin, H. S., Wang, D., Nguyen, H., Zhan, K., & Wang, Y. X. (2020). The influence of consumer anthropomorphism on attitudes towards artificial intelligence trip advisors. *Journal of Hospitality and Tourism Management*, 44, 108–111. https://www.sciencedirect.com/science/article/pii /S1447677020301571

Mgiba, F. M. (2020). Artificial intelligence, marketing management, and ethics: Their effect on customer loyalty intentions: A conceptual study. *The Retail and Marketing Review*, 16(2), 18–35. https://journals .co.za/doi/abs/10.10520/ejc-irmr1-v16-n2-a3

Micu, A., Capatina, A., & Micu, A. E. (2018). Exploring artificial intelligence techniques' applicability in social media marketing. *Journal of Emerging Trends in Marketing and Management*, 1(1), 156–165. https://www .researchgate.net/profile/Alex-Capatina/publication/328838515_Exploring_Artificial_Intelligence _Techniques'_Applicability_in_Social_Media_Marketing/links/5c1510034585157ac1c42633/ Exploring-Artificial-Intelligence-Techniques-Applicability-in-Social-Media-Marketing.pdf

Mikalef, P., Conboy, K., & Krogstie, J. (2021). Artificial intelligence as an enabler of B2B marketing: A dynamic capabilities micro-foundations approach. *Industrial Marketing Management*, 98, 80–92. https://www.sciencedirect.com/science/article/pii/S0019850121001486

Mikalef, P., Fjørtoft, S. O., & Torvatn, H. Y. (2019). Developing an artificial intelligence capability: A theoretical framework for business value. In *Business Information Systems Workshops: BIS 2019 International Workshops*, Seville, Spain, June 26–28, 2019. Revised Papers 22 (pp. 409–416). Springer International Publishing. https://link.springer.com/chapter/10.1007/978-3-030-36691-9_34

Mitić, V. (2019). Benefits of artificial intelligence and machine learning in marketing. In *Sinteza 2019-International Scientific Conference on Information Technology and Data Related Research* (pp. 472–477). Singidunum University. https://portal.sinteza.singidunum.ac.rs/paper/704

Murgai, A. (2018). Transforming digital marketing with artificial intelligence. *International Journal of Latest Technology in Engineering, Management & Applied Science*, 7(4), 259–262. https://fardapaper.ir/moha-vaha/uploads/2019/09/Fardapaper-Transforming-Digital-Marketing-with-Artificial-Intelligence.pdf

Nalbant, K. G., & Aydin, S. (2023). Development and transformation in digital marketing and branding with artificial intelligence and digital technologies dynamics in the Metaverse universe. *Journal of Metaverse*, 3(1), 9–18. https://dergipark.org.tr/en/pub/jmv/issue/72588/1148015?trk=organization _guest_main-feed-card_feed-article-content

Neuhofer, B., Magnus, B., & Celuch, K. (2021). The impact of artificial intelligence on event experiences: A scenario technique approach. *Electronic Markets*, 31, 601–617. https://link.springer.com/article/10 .1007/s12525-020-00433-4

Palanivelu, V. R., & Vasanthi, B. (2020). Role of artificial intelligence in business transformation. *International Journal of Advanced Science and Technology*, 29(4), 392–400. https://ejournal.lucp.net /index.php/ijrtbt/article/view/748

Perez-Vega, R., Kaartemo, V., Lages, C. R., Razavi, N. B., & Männistö, J. (2021). Reshaping the contexts of online customer engagement behavior via artificial intelligence: A conceptual framework. *Journal of Business Research*, 129, 902–910. https://www.sciencedirect.com/science/article/pii/ S0148296320307463

Peyravi, B., Nekrošienė, J., & Lobanova, L. (2020). Revolutionised technologies for marketing: Theoretical review with focus on artificial intelligence. *Business: Theory and Practice*, 21(2), 827–834. https://www .ceeol.com/search/article-detail?id=951005

Popkova, E. G., & Gulzat, K. (2020). Technological revolution in the 21 st century: Digital society vs. artificial intelligence. In *The 21st Century from the Positions of Modern Science: Intellectual, Digital and Innovative Aspects* (pp. 339–345). Springer International Publishing. https://link.springer.com/chapter/10.1007/978-3-030-32015-7_38

Prentice, C., Dominique Lopes, S., & Wang, X. (2020a). Emotional intelligence or artificial intelligence–an employee perspective. *Journal of Hospitality Marketing & Management*, 29(4), 377–403. https://www.tandfonline.com/doi/abs/10.1080/19368623.2019.1647124

Prentice, C., Dominique Lopes, S., & Wang, X. (2020b). The impact of artificial intelligence and employee service quality on customer satisfaction and loyalty. *Journal of Hospitality Marketing & Management*, 29(7), 739–756. https://www.tandfonline.com/doi/abs/10.1080/19368623.2020.1722304

Puntoni, S., Reczek, R. W., Giesler, M., & Botti, S. (2021). Consumers and artificial intelligence: An experiential perspective. *Journal of Marketing*, 85(1), 131–151. https://journals.sagepub.com/doi/abs/10.1177/0022242920953847

Rabby, F., Chimhundu, R., & Hassan, R. (2021). Artificial intelligence in digital marketing influences consumer behaviour: A review and theoretical foundation for future research. *Academy of Marketing Studies Journal*, 25(5), 1–7. https://www.academia.edu/download/68927976/Artificial_Intelligence_In_Digital_Marketing_Influences_Consumer_Behaviour_A_Review.pdf

Rathore, B. (2023). Digital transformation 4.0: Integration of artificial intelligence & metaverse in marketing. *Eduzone: International Peer Reviewed/Refereed Multidisciplinary Journal*, 12(1), 42–48. https://www.eduzonejournal.com/index.php/eiprmj/article/view/248

Ribeiro, T., & Reis, J. L. (2020). Artificial intelligence applied to digital marketing. In *Trends and Innovations in Information Systems and Technologies: Volume 2* (pp. 158–169). Springer International Publishing. https://link.springer.com/chapter/10.1007/978-3-030-45691-7_15

Rizvi, A. T., Haleem, A., Bahl, S., & Javaid, M. (2021). Artificial intelligence (AI) and its applications in Indian manufacturing: A review. *Current Advances in Mechanical Engineering: Select Proceedings of ICRAMERD*, 2020, 825–835. https://link.springer.com/chapter/10.1007/978-981-33-4795-3_76

Saura, J. R., Ribeiro-Soriano, D., & Palacios-Marqués, D. (2021). Setting B2B digital marketing in artificial intelligence-based CRMs: A review and directions for future research. *Industrial Marketing Management*, 98, 161–178. https://www.sciencedirect.com/science/article/pii/S0019850121001772

Schiessl, D., Dias, H. B. A., & Korelo, J. C. (2022). Artificial intelligence in marketing: A network analysis and future agenda. *Journal of Marketing Analytics*, 10(3), 207–218. https://link.springer.com/article/10.1057/s41270-021-00143-6

Sestino, A., & De Mauro, A. (2022). Leveraging artificial intelligence in business: Implications, applications and methods. *Technology Analysis & Strategic Management*, 34(1), 16–29. https://www.tandfonline.com/doi/abs/10.1080/09537325.2021.1883583

Shah, D., & Shay, E. (2019). *Handbook of Advances in Marketing in an Era of Disruptions: Essays in Honour of Jagdish N. Sheth. Mathura Road.* https://doi.org/10.1201/9781032688305

Shaik, M. (2023). Impact of artificial intelligence on marketing. *East Asian Journal of Multidisciplinary Research*, 2(3), 993–1004. https://journal.formosapublisher.org/index.php/eajmr/article/view/3112

Shaily, S. A., & Emma, N. N. (2021). Integration of artificial intelligence marketing to get brand recognition for social business. *International Review of Management and Marketing*, 11(4), 29.

Shovo, N. (2021). Marketing with artificial intelligence and predicting consumer choice. *Artificial Intelligence in Society*, 1(1), 6–18. https://pdfs.semanticscholar.org/9b47/0c9d6262612028e4342525d905274b664708.pdf

Siau, K. (2017, August). Impact of artificial intelligence, robotics, and automation on higher education. In *23rd Americas Conference on Information Systems (AMCIS 2017)* (p. 63). Association for Information Systems (AIS). https://scholars.cityu.edu.hk/en/publications/publication(e68960c5-d212-4752-b38b-13340b121609).html

Siau, K. L., & Yang, Y. (2017). Impact of artificial intelligence, robotics, and machine learning on sales and marketing. https://aisel.aisnet.org/cgi/viewcontent.cgi?article=1047&context=mwais2017

Sığırcı, Ö. (2021). Artificial intelligence in marketing: A review of consumer-AI interactions. In *Handbook of Research on Applied Data Science and Artificial Intelligence in Business and Industry* (pp. 342–365). https://www.igi-global.com/chapter/artificial-intelligence-in-marketing/284988

Sohrabpour, V., Oghazi, P., Toorajipour, R., & Nazarpour, A. (2021). Export sales forecasting using artificial intelligence. *Technological Forecasting and Social Change*, 163, 120480. https://www.sciencedirect.com/science/article/pii/S0040162520313068

Stalidis, G., Karapistolis, D., & Vafeiadis, A. (2015). Marketing decision support using artificial intelligence and knowledge modeling: Application to tourist destination management. *Procedia-Social and Behavioral Sciences*, 175, 106–113. https://www.sciencedirect.com/science/article/pii/S1877042815012409

Triberti, S., Durosini, I., Curigliano, G., & Pravettoni, G. (2020). Is explanation a marketing problem? The quest for trust in artificial intelligence and two conflicting solutions. *Public Health Genomics*, 23(1–2), 2–5. https://karger.com/phg/article/23/1-2/2/272912

Ullal, M. S., Hawaldar, I. T., Suhan, M., & Joseph, N. (2020). The effect of artificial intelligence on the sales graph in Indian market. *Entrepreneurship and Sustainability Issues*, 7(4), 2940–2954. https://papers.ssrn.com/sol3/papers.cfm?abstract_id=3636772

Van Esch, P., & Stewart Black, J. (2021). Artificial intelligence (AI): Revolutionizing digital marketing. *Australasian Marketing Journal*, 29(3), 199–203. https://journals.sagepub.com/doi/abs/10.1177/18393349211037684

Varsha, P. S., Akter, S., Kumar, A., Gochhait, S., & Patagundi, B. (2021). The impact of artificial intelligence on branding: A bibliometric analysis (1982–2019). *Journal of Global Information Management (JGIM)*, 29(4), 221–246. https://www.igi-global.com/article/the-impact-of-artificial-intelligence-on-branding/278776

Verma, S., Sharma, R., Deb, S., & Maitra, D. (2021). Artificial intelligence in marketing: Systematic review and future research direction. *International Journal of Information Management Data Insights*, 1(1), 100002. https://www.sciencedirect.com/science/article/pii/S2667096820300021

Vinuesa, R., Azizpour, H., Leite, I., Balaam, M., Dignum, V., Domisch, S., & Fuso Nerini, F. (2020). The role of artificial intelligence in achieving the Sustainable Development Goals. *Nature Communications*, 11(1), 1–10. https://www.nature.com/articles/s41467-019-14108-y)

Vladimirovich, K. M. (2020). Future marketing in B2B segment: Integrating artificial intelligence into sales management. *International Journal of Innovative Technologies in Economy*, 4(31). https://rsglobal.pl/index.php/ijite/article/view/1584

Wang, R., Luo, J., & Huang, S. S. (2020). Developing an artificial intelligence framework for online destination image photos identification. *Journal of Destination Marketing & Management*, 18, 100512. https://www.sciencedirect.com/science/article/pii/S2212571X20301347

Wisetsri, W. (2021). Systematic analysis and future research directions in artificial intelligence for marketing. *Turkish Journal of Computer and Mathematics Education (TURCOMAT)*, 12(11), 43–55. https://www.turcomat.org/index.php/turkbilmat/article/view/5825

Wu, C. W., & Monfort, A. (2023). Role of artificial intelligence in marketing strategies and performance. *Psychology & Marketing*, 40(3), 484–496. https://doi.org/10.1201/9781032688305

Wu, F., Lu, C., Zhu, M., Chen, H., Zhu, J., Yu, K., & Pan, Y. (2020). Towards a new generation of artificial intelligence in China. *Nature Machine Intelligence*, 2(6), 312–316. https://www.nature.com/articles/s42256-020-0183-4

Wu, L., Dodoo, N. A., Wen, T. J., & Ke, L. (2022). Understanding Twitter conversations about artificial intelligence in advertising based on natural language processing. *International Journal of Advertising*, 41(4), 685–702. https://www.tandfonline.com/doi/abs/10.1080/02650487.2021.1920218

Xu, Z., Lv, Z., Li, J., & Shi, A. (2022). A novel approach for predicting water demand with complex patterns based on ensemble learning. *Water Resources Management*, 36(11), 4293–4312. https://link.springer.com/article/10.1007/s11269-022-03255-5

Yang, X., Li, H., Ni, L., & Li, T. (2021). Application of artificial intelligence in precision marketing. *Journal of Organizational and End User Computing (JOEUC)*, 33(4), 209–219. https://www.igi-global.com/article/application-of-artificial-intelligence-in-precision-marketing/280496

Yang, Y., & Siau, K. L. (2018). A qualitative research on marketing and sales in the artificial intelligence age. https://www.researchgate.net/profile/Keng-Siau-2/publication/325934359_A_Qualitative_Research_on_Marketing_and_Sales_in_the_Artificial_Intelligence_Age/links/5b9733644585153a532634e3/A-Qualitative-Research-on-Marketing-and-Sales-in-the-Artificial-Intelligence-Age.pdf

Yau, K. L. A., Saad, N. M., & Chong, Y. W. (2021). Artificial intelligence marketing (AIM) for enhancing customer relationships. *Applied Sciences*, 11(18), 8562. https://www.mdpi.com/2076-3417/11/18/8562

Zerfass, A., Hagelstein, J., & Tench, R. (2020). Artificial intelligence in communication management: A cross-national study on adoption and knowledge, impact, challenges and risks. *Journal of Communication Management*, 24(4), 377–389. https://www.emerald.com/insight/content/doi/10.1108/JCOM-10-2019-0137/full/html

Zhao, H., Lyu, F., & Luo, Y. (2022). Research on the effect of online marketing based on multimodel fusion and artificial intelligence in the context of big data. *Security and Communication Networks*, 2022, 1–9. https://www.hindawi.com/journals/scn/2022/1516543/

Zulaikha, S., Mohamed, H., Kurniawati, M., Rusgianto, S., & Rusmita, S. A. (2020). Customer predictive analytics using artificial intelligence. *The Singapore Economic Review*, 1–12. https://www.worldscientific.com/doi/abs/10.1142/S0217590820480021

Chapter 4

Role of Government Participation in Social Media Usage and the Impact of e-Government Ecosystem

Manoj Govindaraj, Chandramowleeswaran Gnanasekaran, and Mariyappan M. S. R.

4.1 Introduction

Information and Communication Technology (ICT) helps governments build the infrastructures necessary to carry out public policy effectively. Since ICT can accommodate a wide range of services for the public in a relatively short time, the Indonesian government views it as a crucial resource in running public services. The growing importance of providing government services to the public has contributed to the widespread use of ICT in this sector. However, the government is still faced with the difficulty of putting ICT to use in ways that provide good public service. This was discovered by looking at the widespread need for meeting various public service interests and problem-solving.

In order to meet the needs of its citizens, the government at the time made use of e-government, one of the ICT products. The core concept behind e-government is the provision of government services through digital means. Electronic government (e-government) can be used to increase the efficacy of existing information management systems and public service developments. Public sector e-government aims to connect the public with government, businesses, and nonprofits to improve service delivery and foster collaboration. e-Government increases the likelihood of citizens having faith in government decision-making and working with officials to shape new policies, data, and services. e-Government is a powerful force in public policy because of the efficient and effective communication between the government and the people.

One tool used to involve more people in shaping public policy is electronic government. The success of the policy instruments is evidenced by the growing interest in and use of e-government.

DOI: 10.4324/9781032688305-4

Deliberative policy theory argues that in order for a public policy to be successful, it must have input from a wide variety of interested parties. For this to happen, it will be necessary to earn the confidence of a number of interested parties, chief among them the local populace. A model for trust-based deliberative policy-making has been established. It shows the importance of trust in the implementation of government programs. Earning the public's confidence in the actions of their government is difficult. As a result, it is crucial to investigate strategies for boosting confidence in e-government as a method of implementing policies after careful consideration.

Getting the public to trust the government again is a difficult task. In this highly technical era, the challenge for the government is how to best use social media to promote e-government (electronic government). Its prevalence means it has the potential to influence public opinion in a variety of ways. Due to the proliferation of bad content about the government on social media platforms, it is becoming more difficult to promote a favorable image of e-government socialization in order to boost citizen engagement.

A lack of good governance in the management of e-government is a predictor of citizens' inability to participate actively in government affairs. According to Mansoor (2021), public confidence in government policies is dependent on the quality of governance exercised during the implementation of e-government initiatives. Deliberative policy-making can be attained through factors like social media, good governance, and trust; yet, this study revealed shortcomings in the application of e-government as an instrument of government policy.

4.2 Background of the Study

Social media platforms offer governments a direct channel for citizen engagement and participation. By studying the impact of government participation on social media, we can identify effective strategies for fostering meaningful interactions, soliciting public opinions, and involving citizens in decision-making processes. This can lead to increased citizen empowerment, trust, and legitimacy in government actions.

In the era of misinformation and fake news, studying social media usage in e-government becomes crucial. Governments can leverage social media platforms to counter misinformation, disseminate accurate information, and engage in fact-based communication. By understanding the impact of government participation, we can develop strategies to build trust, combat disinformation, and ensure citizens have access to reliable information.

Research on social media usage in e-government provides valuable insights for policymakers, government officials, and practitioners. It can inform the development of guidelines, policies, and frameworks for effective government participation on social media. Additionally, it can help identify challenges, risks, and opportunities associated with social media usage in e-government, leading to informed decision-making and improved practices.

To address this knowledge vacuum, this research explains the role of e-government involvement that draws on deliberative policy ideas and incorporates social media, good governance, and trust. The public sees the use of social media features as important for reaching out to them and boosting the openness of e-government management. As a result, confidence in the government and its online services is growing. Mansoor (2021) argues that the rise in public trust makes it imperative for the government to use social media to communicate.

Good governance can be defined as the interplay between responsibility, accountability, and openness to the needs of those governed. When it comes to running the government's administration, the three principles of good governance are crucial, and this includes incorporating them into e-government policy. Beshi and Kaur (2020) argue that e-government can expand if there is more openness and accountability in government operations and policies. Thirdly, trust is essential for the government to encourage public involvement in all public policy (Lee and Park 2016). As a result, more people in a community will get involved in e-government initiatives if they have faith in the government's policies and programs. Participation in e-government can be anticipated with the help of a deliberative policy-based model that incorporates the three factors of social media, good governance, and trust.

The objective of the study on "Social Media Usage in e-Government: Role of Government Participation and Its Impact" is to study the relationship between government participation on social media platforms and its impact on e-government practices, with the aim of understanding the motivations, strategies, challenges, and outcomes of government engagement on social media, and providing recommendations for maximizing the benefits and addressing potential risks associated with social media usage in e-government.

Overall, studying social media usage in e-government, with a focus on government participation and its impact, allows us to harness the potential of social media platforms to enhance e-governance, promote citizen engagement, strengthen transparency, and improve public service delivery. By understanding the dynamics between government participation and social media usage, we can shape effective strategies that leverage these platforms for the benefit of citizens and society as a whole.

4.3 Literature Review

According to Abu-Shanab (2015), "open government" is a recent concept that has gained a lot of attention in academic circles. Some overlap exists between the primary dimensions of open government and their respective signals. This research seeks to dissect the three pillars of open government into their component parts by conducting a comprehensive literature review. The next phase involves compiling a summary of the core ideas found in the literature and relating them to the aforementioned criteria. The final goal of this endeavor is to attempt a synthesis of the concepts involved along four primary axes. These are the proposed parameters: values of openness, honesty, teamwork, and individual agency.

Aisha et al. (2015): Overall, the study supported the importance of sharing information via social media and other forms of modern communication technology in the wake of natural disasters. Victims of the floods in Malaysia are disproportionately likely to use WhatsApp, a popular mobile messaging service in the country. During the floods, it saw heavy use, and its primary function was to disseminate information. Since many flood victims were also forced to temporarily relocate, it's likely that they went without the usual means of communication, such as the media. The convenience and speed of mobile phones make them a potential game-changer as a means of communication for those affected by the flood. Since the majority of respondents were under the age of 35, it stands to reason that they are also among the most adept users of modern communication tools and are more likely to have adopted their use for a variety of reasons, including information exchange.

Song and Lee (2016) found out in their study that governments are embracing social media to expand citizens' access to government and government officials, as well as to facilitate citizens' engagement with and participation in government. Using data from the Pew Research Center's 2009 national e-government survey, this study concludes that: (1) trust in government is positively related to perceptions of government transparency; (2) perceptions of government transparency are positively related to trust in government; and (3) perceptions of government transparency mediate the relationship between use of government social media and trust in government. These results show that using social media to increase government openness is a successful strategy for boosting citizens' faith in their government.

Allcott and Gentzkow (2017): Social media has recently become a major source of anxiety. When compared to traditional media technologies, the architecture of social media platforms like Facebook is radically different. Users are able to share information with one another without substantial vetting, fact-checking, or editorial judgment from a central authority.

This research by Sanina et al. (2017) was motivated by the realization that the theoretical literature on enhancing government's communication with business audiences has paid scant consideration to the technical (or formal) organization of the communicative process. This research provides a quantitative evaluation of the advantages of employing multiple channels of communication simultaneously. It does this by introducing the idea of "communicative result" as a means of evaluating effectiveness. It goes even further by contrasting the channels' technical parameters in terms of dependability, speed, and efficiency. It examines how cultural differences can affect the efficacy of various forms of communication. A data-driven methodology is presented for assessing and improving government communication channels within the context of distinct national and cultural contexts.

Zha et al. (2018): Users with low information processing capacity have been overwhelmed by social media, making task-information fit an urgent concern. Understanding the informational influence mechanisms that contribute to the success of dual-route persuasion and attitude modification is the focus of the elaboration likelihood model (ELM).

Androutsopoulou et al. (2019): The long-standing problem of poor communication between the public and government may finally be solved thanks to this new digital communication channel. However, government practitioners should take great care in constructing the necessary "knowledge base" of these sophisticated Chatbots, which must include all the crucial records, as well as pertinent internal data from their functional IS, and possibly pertinent social media, pertaining to the spectrum of topics and subjects each Chatbot is expected to handle.

Djerf and Pierre (2019): This study examined the most-watched AMR-related videos on YouTube during the years 2016 and 2018. The study compared the engagement topics voiced in comments to the themes presented in journalistic and popular science videos. The most popular AMR videos on YouTube are high-quality instructional popular scientific documentaries. Based on a qualitative examination of 3,049 comments, we can identify seven primary types of deep interaction, such as emotional outpourings, accusations, and pleas for change. The results of this research make it clear that journalism plays a significant role on YouTube by sparking conversations about social and political responsibility.

Mergel and Haug (2019): Citizens' expectations of governments' abilities to provide high-value, real-time digital services are shifting in response to digital transformation initiatives outside the public sector. Governments are shifting their approach in order to meet the evolving needs of their citizens and to comply with supranational agreements that call for greater openness, interoperability, and citizen satisfaction in public service delivery.

Hariguna et al. (2019): They studied the relationship between social media engagement and the DeLone and McLean Variables for Information System Success Model. This study looks into what influences people's decisions to join in on a social media activity that has already been proposed for study. The experimental outcomes of this study accomplish two goals and make major pledges. To begin with, many e-government research projects overlook the effects of information dissemination operations via social media. This research demonstrates that public satisfaction impacts people's propensity to get involved in activities when information is disseminated via social media.

Beshi and Kaur (2020): According to the results of this research, open government practices at the municipal level are crucial. Why? Because citizens need clear details to assess and monitor the government's performance and to plan for the future. Especially, it is evident that the government accomplishes nothing for the public if it does not explain to the people what it does. After all, the information citizens receive about their government affects their attitude, whether favorable or bad. Because of these worries, democratic leaders around the world are prioritizing the topic of transparency in an effort to remove government secrecy and increase public trust in the government (Khang & Kali et al., 2023).

Arshad and Khurram (2020): This research took an empirical look at the link between citizens' online political engagement and the quality of information offered by a government agency via social media. It investigates the mediating effect of openness, trust, and responsiveness to address the why and how concerns raised by the existence of this connection. Results also indicate that citizens' trust in government agencies is related to the quality of information provided by those agencies via social media. When it comes to people's involvement in politics online, faith in agency was a weak predictor, but perceived responsiveness was a negative one. Furthermore, the connection between an agency's provision of high-quality information via social media and people's online political activity was dampened by trust in agency and perceived responsiveness.

The findings showed a connection between strong governance practices and public confidence in government, both immediately and indirectly through Perceived government response on COVID-19 (PGRC). Similarly, Government agency's provision of quality information on social media (GQS) was found to interact with PGRC to increase citizens' faith in their government. This research aimed to fill in some of the blanks left by the paucity of literature on how governments used ICT to reap benefits from social media and communicate with citizens on a broad scale during the COVID-19 pandemic. In addition, the current analysis provides helpful strategic and practical suggestions for organizations and politicians (Mansoor, 2021).

4.4 Overview of the Increasing Use of Social Media in e-Government

Government participation in social media interactions plays a crucial role in shaping public opinion, fostering transparency and accountability, and facilitating democratic participation. Here are some key reasons highlighting the importance of government involvement in social media interactions:

1. Enhancing Citizen Engagement: Social media platforms have become essential channels for citizens to connect with their governments. By actively participating in social media discussions, governments can directly engage with their constituents, listen to their concerns, and address their grievances. It allows for a more inclusive and participatory democracy, where citizens have a platform to voice their opinions and actively contribute to policy-making processes.

2. Promoting Transparency and Accountability: Social media platforms offer governments an opportunity to share information and updates directly with the public. By providing real-time updates, government agencies can enhance transparency, keeping citizens informed about their activities, policies, and decisions. This transparency fosters public trust and ensures that governments remain accountable for their actions.

3. Disseminating Information Rapidly: Social media enables governments to quickly disseminate information during emergencies, crises, or public health events (Khang & Rana et al., 2023). Governments can utilize these platforms to provide timely alerts, safety guidelines, and other critical information to ensure public safety. Direct communication through social media allows for rapid information sharing, helping to mitigate misinformation and facilitating effective emergency responses.

4. Bridge the Gap with the Younger Generation: Social media is particularly popular among younger demographics, who are often underrepresented in traditional political processes. By actively participating in social media interactions, governments can bridge the generational gap, reaching out to young citizens, and engaging them in civic discussions. This helps in creating a more inclusive democracy and encourages young people to become active participants in the political process.

5. Monitoring Public Sentiment: Social media platforms provide a vast amount of real-time data on public sentiment and opinions. By actively monitoring and analyzing these conversations, governments can gain valuable insights into the needs, concerns, and preferences of their citizens. This data can inform policy decisions, help to identify emerging issues, and guide effective communication strategies.

6. Combating Misinformation and Disinformation: Social media has also become a breeding ground for misinformation and disinformation campaigns. Governments can play a crucial role in countering such false narratives by actively participating in social media interactions. By providing accurate information, clarifying misconceptions, and debunking falsehoods, governments can help promote reliable sources of information and protect the public from the harmful effects of misinformation.

The mediating role of government participation in social media usage for e-government refers to how government engagement on social media platforms facilitates the effective implementation of e-government initiatives. Here are some key points highlighting this mediating role:

1. Communication and Information Dissemination: Government participation in social media allows for direct communication with citizens, enabling the dissemination of information related to e-government services, policies, and initiatives. Through social media, governments can reach a wider audience, provide updates, and address queries or concerns. This facilitates the efficient delivery of e-government services and ensures that citizens are well-informed about available digital services.

2. Feedback and Citizen Engagement: Social media platforms offer a two-way communication channel that allows citizens to provide feedback, suggestions, and concerns regarding e-government initiatives. Government participation in social media interactions enables direct engagement with citizens, promoting active participation and collaboration. By actively listening to citizen feedback, governments can refine their e-government strategies, improve service delivery, and address any issues that arise.

3. Building Trust and Credibility: Government participation in social media fosters transparency and accountability, which is vital for building trust and credibility in e-government initiatives. Through social media interactions, governments can share success stories, showcase the benefits of e-government services, and address any skepticism or doubts. By actively engaging with citizens on social media, governments can establish themselves as reliable providers of digital services and reinforce trust in e-government.

4. Awareness and Adoption of e-Government Services: Government participation in social media helps raise awareness about the availability and benefits of e-government services. By leveraging social media platforms, governments can effectively promote and educate citizens about the convenience, efficiency, and accessibility of digital services. This can lead to increased adoption of e-government services, reducing the digital divide and ensuring that more citizens benefit from the advantages of digital governance.

5. Mitigating Challenges and Facilitating Innovation: Social media platforms provide governments with valuable insights into citizens' needs, concerns, and expectations regarding e-government services. Government participation in social media interactions allows them to identify and address challenges or barriers faced by citizens in using digital services. Moreover, governments can tap into the collective intelligence of social media users to gather innovative ideas and suggestions for enhancing e-government initiatives.

6. Collaborative Policy Development: Social media offers a platform for governments to engage citizens in collaborative policy development processes related to e-government. By soliciting input and involving citizens in decision-making through social media platforms, governments can ensure that e-government initiatives align with the needs and aspirations of the public. This participatory approach enhances the effectiveness and relevance of e-government services.

4.5 e-Government and Social Media

e-Government, also known as electronic government, refers to the use of information and communication technologies (ICTs) by government organizations to enhance the delivery of public services, improve governance processes, and foster citizen engagement. It encompasses the digital transformation of traditional governmental functions and the utilization of technology to streamline administrative processes, facilitate communication, and promote transparency and efficiency in the public sector.

The concept of e-government revolves around leveraging ICTs to transform the way governments interact with citizens, businesses, and other governmental entities. It involves the integration of various digital tools and platforms, such as websites, mobile applications, online portals, and social media, to enable the delivery of government services, access to information, and participation in decision-making.

4.5.1 The State of Digital India in 2023

At the beginning of 2023, 48.7% of Indian residents had access to the Internet, making 692.0 million Indians Internet users. In January 2023, 32.8% of India's total population was among the country's 467.0 million social media users. There were 1.10 billion active cellular mobile connections in India as of early 2023, or around 77.0% of the country's entire population.

In January of 2023, 692 million people in India were online. As of the beginning of the year 2023, 48.7% of Indian citizens had access to the Internet at home. According to Kepios, the number of Indian Internet users did not change between 2022 and 2023. According to these statistics, as of the beginning of 2023, 51.3% of the Indian population was still offline, with 730 million individuals not having Internet access.

However, due to the difficulties in collecting and analyzing data from Internet users, studies are typically not ready for publication for several months. This means that the most up-to-date estimates of Internet usage consistently underestimate the true picture, and that actual adoption and growth may be higher than indicated. For further information, please review our detailed data notes.

According to Ookla's published data, Indian Internet users in early 2023 may have anticipated the following download and upload speeds. The average speed of a cellular network-based mobile Internet connection is 18.26 Mbps. The average speed of a fixed Internet connection is 49.09 Mbps. According to Ookla's findings, in the year leading up to the beginning of 2023, the median mobile Internet connection speed in India climbed by 3.87 Mbps (+26.9%). According to Ookla's numbers, however, the average download speed of a fixed Internet connection in India grew by 3.6%, or 1.69 Mbps, during the same time frame.

The Digital India initiative encompasses nine key pillars, namely, Broadband Highways, Universal Access to Mobile Connectivity, Public Internet Access Program, e-governance: Reforming Government through Technology, e-Kranti – Electronic Delivery of Services, Information for All, Electronics Manufacturing, IT for Jobs, and Early Harvest Programs. Each of these topics represents a multifaceted program that spans various Ministries and Departments. In the mid-1990s, India's e-governance programs expanded to cover a greater range of sectors and focused more on providing services directly to individual citizens. Some of the government's largest ICT projects were the computerization of railways and land records, among others, with a primary emphasis on the creation of information systems.

Later, many governments launched comprehensive, standalone initiatives to improve residents' access to government services by way of the Internet. Despite focusing on the public, these e-governance initiatives were not as effective as had been hoped. Isolated and less participatory systems exposed significant inadequacies that were impeding widespread implementation of e-governance across all spheres of government, as shown in Figure 4.1. They highlighted the need for a more thorough design and implementation of the infrastructure needed to develop a more connected government, address interoperability challenges that need to be addressed, etc.

4.5.2 India's Social Media Data for the Year 2023

As of January 2023, 467 million Indians were active on social media platforms. In fact, there has been no obvious decline in total social media use, and in almost all countries, social media use continues to expand, according to an examination of numerous data sources from reliable third parties like GWI and data.ai. Therefore, readers should not use these discrepancies to mean that fewer people are using social media, but rather as "corrections" to the statistics.

At the turn of the 22nd century, 32.8% of India's total population was active on social media; however, this figure may not be representative of actual people (for more information, see our data comments). As of the beginning of 2023, there were 398.0 million users aged 18 and up on social media in India, which is equivalent to 40.2% of the total population aged 18 and up in that country, according to data disclosed in the ad planning tools of main social media platforms. In addition, as of January 2023, 67.5% of all Internet users in India (regardless of age) were active on at least one social networking platform. In 2014, just 26.5% of Indian social media users were women, while 73.5% were men. India has the world's largest population and the second-highest number of Internet users, making its Internet market both lucrative and fiercely contested. Despite the fact that just 43% of the population has access to the Internet, there is a large social media user base that apparently spends 2.6 hours per day on these sites.

There were approximately 470.1 million monthly active social media users in India in 2022, with a year-over-year growth rate of 4.2%. About one-third of the world's population is represented

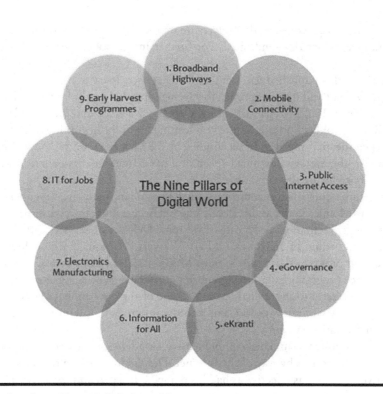

Figure 4.1 **The nine pillars of digital world.**

here as shown in Figure 4.2. These individuals log an average of 2.6 hours each week on social media and utilize 8.6 different services.

Data from 2022 indicates that WhatsApp has the greatest user population in India among the social media sites owned by Meta. This is followed by Instagram and Facebook. A large number of users is not, however, an indicator of popularity. According to a January 2023 study of consumer attitudes in India performed by AXIS My India, 35% of respondents said that Facebook was their preferred social media site.

In 2022, a three-person grievance redressal committee was established by India's Ministry of Electronics and Information Technology (MEIT), which was a significant development given the opposition from tech corporations. After the committee is established, social media businesses are obligated to follow the government's content moderation recommendations, which is often interpreted as the government trying to assert control over social media platforms.

Government can play a significant role as a mediating factor in social media usage. As social media platforms have gained prominence and influence in society, governments around the world have recognized the need to regulate and manage their impact. Here are some ways in which governments can mediate social media usage:

Governments can develop policies and regulations to govern social media platforms and users. These policies can address issues such as data privacy, cybersecurity, hate speech, fake news, online harassment, and intellectual property rights. By establishing clear guidelines and rules, governments aim to protect the interests and well-being of individuals and society at large.

Governments may have mechanisms in place to moderate and regulate content on social media platforms. They can set guidelines for platform operators to ensure that content aligns with legal

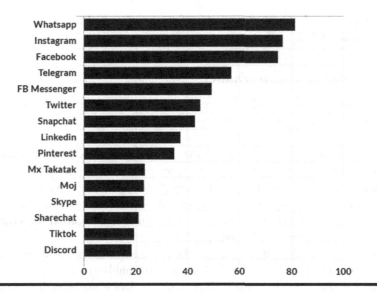

Figure 4.2 Indian social media users were women and men.

and ethical standards. Governments may also enforce censorship measures in certain cases to address national security concerns or prevent the spread of harmful or illegal content.

Governments can enact laws and regulations to safeguard the privacy and personal data of social media users. They can establish frameworks that require social media platforms to implement robust data protection measures, obtain user consent, and provide transparency in data collection and usage practices. Governments may also establish regulatory bodies to oversee compliance with data protection laws.

Governments can play a role in promoting digital literacy and educating citizens about responsible social media usage. They can develop programs and initiatives to raise awareness about the risks and benefits of social media, online etiquette, critical thinking skills, and digital citizenship. By empowering individuals with the necessary knowledge and skills, governments aim to promote responsible and informed use of social media (Khang & Rani et al., 2023).

Social media platforms operate globally, and their impact extends beyond national boundaries. Governments can engage in international cooperation and collaboration to address cross-border issues related to social media, such as cybercrime, hate speech, and misinformation. Through partnerships and agreements, governments can work together to develop common frameworks and guidelines for regulating social media usage.

Governments have a role in ensuring equitable access to social media and digital technologies. They can implement policies and initiatives to bridge the digital divide, making social media and Internet access more accessible to marginalized communities and underserved areas. This includes initiatives to improve Internet infrastructure, reduce connectivity costs, and promote digital inclusion.

4.6 Benefits and Challenges of e-Governance

The degree to which governments interfere with citizens' use of social media may be impacted by cultural, political, and legal considerations, and so differs from country to country. It is always tricky to strike a balance between the necessity for regulation and the values of free expression, privacy, and technological advancement.

4.6.1 Advantages of e-Governance

Governments should ensure the public interest is safeguarded while also encouraging a free and flourishing online community as shown in Figure 4.3.

- **Speed:** Technology has facilitated quicker means of interaction. The Internet, regular phones, and cell phones have all helped to speed up the communication process.
- **Cost Reduction:** The majority of government funds is allocated to cover the price of office supplies. The constant high cost of paper-based communication tools like paper, printers, computers, etc. The government can save money on communication costs due to the widespread use of the Internet and mobile phones.
- **Transparency:** The use of ICT increases the openness of the political process. The government's records would be fully searchable online. The public has access to the data whenever they like. But this can only occur if all government data is made publicly accessible online. The current system of government provides enough opportunity for information withholding. Using ICT, we can make all of this data accessible online, where it can't be hidden.
- **Accountability:** When government is held accountable, transparency in the system is essential. A government that is accountable to its citizens is one that answers to them. It's the responsibility of the government to account for its actions. A responsible government is one that is held accountable.
- **Convenience**: e-Government brings public services to citizens on their schedule and their venue.
- **Improved Customer Service**: e-Government allows for the redeployment of resources from back-end processing to the front line of customer service.
- **Increased Access to Information**: e-Government helps citizens feel more in control of their lives since it increases their access to government information, which can then be used as a reliable resource for making decisions that directly affect them.

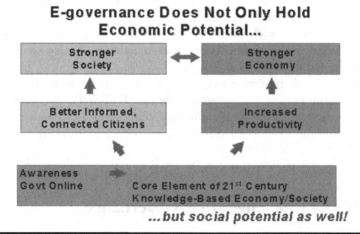

Figure 4.3 Benefits of e-governance.

4.6.2 Challenges in e-Governance

There are many things that could stand in the way of e-government being put into action. Security concerns, citizens' unequal access to IT, prohibitive startup costs for e-government solutions, and reluctance to adapt are just a few of the roadblocks that stand in the way of full deployment. Trust, aversion to change, the digital gap, cost, and privacy and security concerns have all been named as obstacles.

4.6.2.1 Trust

Trust can be understood in two ways: as an evaluation of the present circumstances, or as a dispositional quality. There must be two types of trust for e-government to be used for public administration. The first is that the user must have faith in, familiarity with, and trust in the technology being used. Having faith in one's government is the second pillar of trust. A system's ability to detect and prevent fraudulent transactions must be weighed against the cost that additional checks may place on honest users. The loss of a computer carrying sensitive data on service veterans has recently put that data at risk. Users' faith and confidence in government processes might be damaged by incidents like this. Trust and monetary security are the two major barriers to the widespread use of e-government services.

4.6.2.2 Resistance to Change

In the long run, the majority of a population will get exposed to an innovation, but the rate of exposure will vary between the early adopters and the laggards, according to the innovation diffusion theory. Many citizens' reservations about switching from a paper to a Web-based method for dealing with their government can be attributed to the resistance to change phenomena.

There may be varying opinions on the best way to handle financial transactions among citizens, workers, and enterprises. In spite of this, governmental bodies and public policy administrators must account for the shifts that occur as a result of ICT adoption. One way to lessen the opposition to the new systems is by educating about them. Leaders and managers can benefit greatly from adopting the new method as soon as possible.

4.6.2.3 Digital Divide

The term "digital divide" is used to describe the gap between people who have access to information technology and those who do not. The existence of the digital divide can be explained by a variety of factors, including social, economic, infrastructure, and ethnolinguistic indices. Low income and lack of access to technology go hand in hand. As the digital divide is bridged, e-government can be implemented more widely. The digital gap has several roots, not the least of which is economic hardship. Lack of public education is another possible contributor. Some of the most financially secure citizens are unaware of e-governance's potential. One and only visit to that service delivery channel can be aided by raising awareness. The system's design must be such that it produces the desired results if it is to ensure continued use. Simplifying processes to provide tangible benefits and providing clear rules can increase their uptake by end users and decrease their reliance on intermediaries.

4.6.2.4 Cost

In nations like India, where the majority of the population lives below the poverty line, the high price of implementing e-governance is a major barrier. It doesn't appear that elected officials and politicians care much about adopting e-governance.

4.6.2.5 Privacy and Security

e-Government stakeholders will have the option of having no access, limited access, or full access to a Web service; however, when personal sensitive data is present, the formation of the security access policy is a much more complex process with legal consideration. Protecting individuals' privacy is a top priority as more government functions move online. It might be difficult to move forward with initiatives that require access to private information like financial or medical records when there are no established security policies and standards in place.

Overcoming these implementation challenges requires a comprehensive approach that encompasses technological investments, capacity building, policy development, stakeholder engagement, and ongoing evaluation. Governments must be proactive in addressing these difficulties to leverage social media's potential for enhancing citizen engagement, transparency, and accountability in e-government practices. Collaboration with relevant stakeholders, learning from best practices, and adapting strategies to local contexts can help overcome implementation hurdles.

4.7 Introduction to Social Media

The term "social media" encompasses all the various sites and programs that encourage users to build online communities and share and discuss various forms of media created by those communities' members. The Internet has changed the way individuals talk to one another and share information. Some of the most well-known examples of social media sites are Facebook, Twitter, Instagram, LinkedIn, YouTube, and Snapchat, although there are many more.

4.7.1 Role in Transforming Communication

Social media has had a profound impact on communication, bringing about significant transformations in various aspects. Here are some key ways in which social media has transformed communication. Social media plays a significant role in fostering citizen engagement and participation in various ways. Here are some key aspects highlighting its significance.

1. Accessible Platform: Social media provides an accessible platform for citizens to engage and participate in public discussions. It breaks down barriers of entry, allowing individuals to share their opinions, ideas, and concerns on a wide range of topics. Citizens can actively participate in conversations, join online communities, and contribute to public discourse without the need for traditional gatekeepers or intermediaries.
2. Democratization of Voice: Social media has democratized the ability to have a voice and be heard. It empowers individuals to express their thoughts, experiences, and perspectives, irrespective of their social status, geographical location, or background. Citizen engagement on social media allows marginalized groups, who might have been historically underrepresented or ignored, to have a platform to advocate for their rights, share their stories, and seek justice.

3. Amplification of Issues: Social media enables citizens to amplify their concerns and raise awareness about important issues. Through sharing, retweeting, and tagging, information and campaigns can quickly reach a wider audience. This has proven to be particularly effective in mobilizing support for social causes, grassroots movements, and humanitarian initiatives. Social media campaigns have helped shed light on pressing issues and create momentum for change.

4. Real-time Feedback and Interaction: Social media allows citizens to engage directly with policymakers, government officials, and public figures. It provides a platform for real-time feedback, enabling citizens to express their opinions, seek clarifications, and ask questions. This direct interaction fosters a sense of transparency, accountability, and responsiveness in governance and public administration.

5. Collaborative Problem Solving: Social media facilitates collaborative problem-solving by connecting citizens with shared interests or concerns. It allows for the formation of online communities, advocacy groups, and grassroots movements that work together to address common challenges. Citizens can share resources, exchange ideas, and pool their efforts to find innovative solutions, driving positive change at both local and global levels.

6. Information Sharing and Awareness: Social media platforms serve as powerful tools for sharing information and raising awareness about important issues. Citizens can access a diverse range of perspectives, news articles, research studies, and expert opinions on social media. This empowers individuals to stay informed, make informed decisions, and engage in informed discussions on matters that affect them and their communities.

7. Civic Mobilization and Activism: Social media has played a significant role in mobilizing citizens for various civic causes and activism. It has been instrumental in organizing protests, rallies, and demonstrations, as well as coordinating relief efforts during times of crisis. Platforms such as Facebook, Twitter, and Instagram have been used to galvanize public support, mobilize volunteers, and amplify the voices of citizens fighting for social justice and equality.

Social media's significance in fostering citizen engagement and participation lies in its ability to provide an accessible platform, amplify citizen voices, raise awareness, facilitate real-time feedback, promote collaborative problem-solving, and mobilize citizens for social causes. It has transformed the way citizens engage with each other, policymakers, and institutions, enabling a more inclusive and participatory democracy.

4.7.2 Government Participation in Social Media

The term "social media" refers to a range of Internet-based tools, platforms, and cultural practices that facilitate the exchange of ideas and information. It boils down to talking with one another. When compared to mainstream media like newspapers, television, and radio, social media serves a distinct purpose. The government and the people have a two-way conversation through social media. This means that the level of control typically associated with traditional media is giving way to a more in-depth interaction with the audience. When used thoughtfully and carefully, social media can increase public trust in government by fostering greater transparency, fostering an interactive relationship with the public, and fostering a stronger sense of ownership over government policy and services.

The applications of social media are diverse and numerous. Social media can act as an internal communications tool for the government to promote coordination across government agencies or even inside a single agency, bring attention to specific concerns, increase credibility with targeted audiences, involve Oman in policy consultation, or serve as a means of engagement with government agencies. The basics of social media: There are five main social media platforms. (1) Social networks, a catchall word for online platforms that facilitate communication and collaboration between users. (2) Communication is usually casual and conducted solely online. (3) Websites like Facebook and Twitter are good examples. (4) Online communities where users can upload, share, and view multimedia content. Users can share their own material, see media shared by others, and leave comments. You can see this on sites like YouTube and Flickr.

Blog, an abbreviation for "web log," refers to online diaries. A blog is a type of content management website that displays postings in reverse chronological order and encourages user interaction in the form of comments. Popular content management systems (CMS) for blogs include Blogger and WordPress. Wikis are web-based software that facilitate collaborative website development and maintenance. Wikipedia is the prime illustration of this. (5) Forums, software used on the Internet to host group conversations on a certain topic.

4.7.2.1 The Impact of e-Government on Governance Has Been Significant

1. Enhanced Efficiency and Cost Savings: e-Government has streamlined administrative processes, reduced paperwork, and improved the speed and accuracy of service delivery. This has resulted in cost savings for governments and increased operational efficiency.
2. Improved Service Delivery: e-Government has made public services more accessible, convenient, and citizen-centric. It has enabled 24/7 availability of services, reduced waiting times, and provided personalized and tailored services to citizens.
3. Transparency and Accountability: e-Government has increased transparency by providing access to government information, policies, and decision-making processes. Citizens can monitor government activities, track spending, and hold officials accountable for their actions. Digital records and audit trails enhance transparency and traceability in governance.
4. Citizen Engagement and Participation: e-Government has facilitated active citizen engagement through online platforms, enabling citizens to participate in decision-making processes, provide feedback, and contribute to policy development. It has transformed governance into a more inclusive and participatory process.
5. Data-Driven Decision Making: e-Government has generated vast amounts of data that can be analyzed to inform evidence-based decision-making. Governments can utilize data analytics to gain insights, identify trends, and make informed policy choices.
6. Economic Development and Innovation: e-Government has stimulated economic growth by creating a favorable business environment, encouraging entrepreneurship, and attracting investments. It has promoted innovation in the public sector and the development of a digital economy.

4.7.2.2 Top of Form Bottom of Form National e-Governance Plan

Many efforts have been made throughout the years by both state and federal governments to usher in the era of e-government. There have been ongoing initiatives at many different levels to streamline the delivery of public services and make them easier to obtain.

India's e-government projects have progressed beyond simple departmental computerization to more nuanced concepts like citizen-centricity, service orientation, and transparency. The progressive e-governance approach of the country was heavily influenced by the lessons learned from past e-governance initiatives. It has been taken into account that a programmatic approach, based on a shared vision and set of guiding principles, is necessary to expedite the rollout of e-governance across all tiers of government. This strategy has the potential to convey a unified picture of government to the public while also reducing costs by allowing for the sharing of core and support infrastructure and the adoption of common standards.

The National e-Governance Plan (NeGP) is a comprehensive strategy for advancing e-government across the United States. This concept is driving the development of a vast nationwide infrastructure that will eventually reach even the most outlying settlements, and the widespread digitalization of records to facilitate quick, trustworthy online access. According to NeGP's Vision Statement, the ultimate goal is to improve access to government services for local residents. To meet the basic needs of the average person, the government should "make all Government services accessible to the common man in his locality, through common service delivery outlets, and ensure efficiency, transparency, and reliability of such services at affordable costs."

The National e-Governance Plan (NeGP), which consists of 27 mission mode projects (MMPs) and 8 components, was authorized by the government on May 18, 2006. There were originally 27 mission mode projects (MMPs), but in 2011, four new ones were added in the areas of health, education, public distribution system (PDS), and postal service (Posts). All of NeGP's big-picture ideas, strategies, components, implementation methods, and management structures have been green-lighted by the government. However, the green light for NeGP does not guarantee funding for all the MMPs and their constituent parts. To better achieve the goals of the NeGP, the MMP categories already established or continuing projects would receive appropriate enhancements from the relevant Central Ministries, State Ministries, and State Departments.

Several policy initiatives and projects have been launched to build out e-government's fundamental and auxiliary systems. Middleware gateways, such as the National e-Governance Service Delivery Gateway (NSDG), the State e-Governance Service Delivery Gateway (SSDG), and the Mobile e-Governance Service Delivery Gateway (MSDG), are also essential parts of the core infrastructure. Standardization in areas such as metadata, interoperability, enterprise architecture, information security, and social media engagement are also crucial pillars of support. e-Pramana is a new authentication framework, and G-I cloud will provide cloud computing advantages to e-government activities.

4.7.2.3 Mediating Factors in Social Media Usage

In the term "e-Governance", e stands for "electronic." That's why using Information and Communications Technology(ICT) to carry out the functions and achieve the results of governance is what e-governance is all about. Equal access to public services and the advantages of economic growth are an essential part of good governance, which also involves protecting the legal rights of all individuals. Good governance also guarantees that the government will be open and honest in its dealings, accountable for its actions, and responsive to citizens' needs in a timely manner.

To achieve this goal, however, the government must first undergo fundamental transformations in its own operations, philosophy, laws, norms, and interactions with the public. An increase in government capability and public education on e-government is also needed.

ICT allows for the effective storage and retrieval of data, the instantaneous transmission of information, the processing of information and data at a faster rate than earlier manual systems, the acceleration of governmental processes, the rapid and prudent adoption of policy, greater transparency and accountability, and the enforcement of policy. It also aids in expanding the government's sphere of influence, both physically and socially.

The establishment of NICNET, India's national satellite-based computer network, in 1987 provided the primary impetus for the country's transition to e-government. Soon after, the National Informatics Centre's District Information System (DISNIC) plan was unveiled to provide free hardware and software to the state governments in order to computerize all district offices across the country. By 1990, all regional offices had been connected to NICNET via the state capitals. Many e-government programs have since been formed at the federal and state levels, thanks to the proliferation of computers, telephones, and Internet access in the intervening years.

4.8 Future Directions and Suggestions

The incorporation of social media into public relations plans is on the rise as a means for local governments to shape coverage of their actions in the media. Citizens' trust in their government rises when the media portrays it favorably (Gross & Aday, &, 2009). Since negative media coverage of governments has been on the rise in recent decades (Khang & Shah et al., 2023), local governments can improve their image and legitimacy by using social media to foster better communication and relationships with their constituents and the official media.

Lee (2012) similarly emphasizes the important and changing role of public relations and external communications in the context of government. Public relations, according to Lee (2012), is inherent to good public administration, whether for program implementation, public support, democratic accountability, public policy development, or agency power, and that success in this area now depends on high levels of constant communication, making use of constantly evolving technologies and social media. First, people's daily lives are increasingly dominated by social media; second, public administration is largely defined in terms of communications, for the purpose of educating and informing citizens; and third, communications enable government to fulfill its mission and be accountable to its constituents, as outlined by Lee, Neeley, and Stewart (2012).

The government has adopted the following measures to improve data governance, which will help the country's economy and society. The Open Government Data platform was intended to simplify data exchange and stimulate innovation over non-personal data. There are around 5.65 million datasets available in over 12,800 catalogs. There have been 93.5 million downloads made possible via the service.

API Setu is a platform designed to make it easier for different systems to share and use information. More than a thousand different companies are using the platform. To maximize the effectiveness of data-led governance and public service delivery and to catalyze data-based research and innovation, MeitY has drafted the National Data Governance Framework Policy. This policy outline is currently being polished. On May 26, 2022, MeitY posted for comment the first draft of the National Data Governance Framework Policy. The government has already taken the required steps to address data privacy and security concerns by enforcing the Information Technology (IT) Act, 2000, which includes data privacy and security rules.

4.9 To Improve e-Governance through Social Media, Here Are Some Suggestions

The government needs to create official social media accounts. Governments should keep a close eye on social media in order to hear out citizen complaints, ideas, and concerns. They should be responsive and accountable to the people they serve by answering questions and having substantive dialogue with them. This encourages civic engagement and strengthens public faith in government.

Publicize the word about government programs and services by spreading the word on social media. Permit applications, healthcare enrollment, and tax returns are only a few examples of the governmental services that should be frequently promoted and explained by the government. This facilitates citizen awareness of and engagement with government services.

In terms of crisis communication and emergency response, social media may be incredibly useful. During times of crisis, such as those caused by natural disasters or outbreaks of a contagious disease, governments should make use of social media to quickly and accurately distribute information. This gives the populace the direction and guidance they need to stay safe and healthy.

Governments can utilize social media to collect input from citizens and conduct surveys on a variety of policies and initiatives by asking for responses from the general public. Governments may improve their decision-making processes and guarantee that policies are in line with citizen requirements by soliciting comments and viewpoints from the public. Citizen feedback can be collected and analyzed with the help of online polls, surveys, and comment sections.

To address societal problems, social media can serve as a forum for crowdsourcing ideas and approaches. Through social media, governments can invite citizens to offer their suggestions, ideas, and creative solutions. This not only gets people involved in the government, but it also uses the wisdom of the crowds to solve difficult issues.

Campaigns to educate the public can make use of social media's widespread reach and low production costs. The government can use social media to spread information about health, environmental protection, voting rights, and citizens' obligations to their communities. Effective campaigns can encourage people to alter their behavior in constructive ways and provide them with the tools they need to become engaged participants in government. Infographics and data visualizations allow governments to deliver complex data and information in digestible ways that are widely shared on social media. The increased public understanding and use of government data, reports, and records is a boon to openness and evidence-based policymaking (Khang and Abuzarova et al., 2023).

Social media influencers, NGOs, and community groups can help governments spread their messages to a wider audience by working together with the relevant authorities. Governments can improve information dissemination, initiative promotion, and citizen engagement by forming partnerships with influential influencers. Officials in the government should undergo frequent training on social media use, covering topics such as best practices, ethical issues, and communication methods. This ensures that public servants have the knowledge and abilities they need to have productive conversations with the people they represent.

Putting these ideas into practice can help governments harness the potential of social media to improve e-governance, increase transparency, increase citizen engagement, and encourage more citizen participation in decision-making.

4.10 Conclusion

The connection, collaboration, and community features of social media have the ability to ensure broad-based consultation, and they can help organizations shorten the consultation process and obtain rapid input on services provided. If agencies want to make good use of this social medium, they need to first establish what they hope to achieve through it; then they need to choose the platforms that will be used for engagement; establish ground rules for engagement; develop a communication strategy to reach a wide audience; and, if all of this proves successful, integrate social media into the mainstream engagement process.

Governments at all levels, from the federal to the state and local, are making use of this medium, including the Indian government. But this is a dynamic and evolving domain, and the success of such efforts will depend on continual participation and the flexibility to respond to an ever-changing circumstance. In the recent decade, the Internet and other forms of communication have become more widely available in India, offering a glimmer of hope to the country's population as they struggle to overcome poverty, corruption, regional disparities, and high unemployment rates. The slow speed at which projects are completed, along with pushback from government staff and citizens, has not produced the anticipated outcome. In conclusion, the evolution of e-government has brought about substantial changes in governance. It has improved efficiency, service delivery, transparency, and citizen participation. e-Government has transformed governance practices, making them more accessible, inclusive, and responsive to citizen needs.

References

Abu-Shanab, E. A. (2015). Reengineering the open government concept: An empirical support for a proposed model. *Government Information Quarterly*, 32(4), 453–463. https://doi.org/10.1016/j.giq.2015.07.002.

Aisha, T. S., Wok, S., Manaf, A. M. A., & Ismail, R. (2015). Exploring the use of social media during the 2014 flood in Malaysia. *Procedia – Social and Behavioral Sciences*, 211(September), 931–937. https://doi.org/10.1016/j.sbspro.2015.11.123

Allcott, H., & Gentzkow, M. (2017). Social media and fake news in the 2016 election. *Journal of Economic Perspectives*, 31(2), 211–236. https://doi.org/10.1257/jep.31.2.211

Androutsopoulou, A., Karacapilidis, N., Loukis, E., & Charalabidis, Y. (2019). Transforming the communication between citizens and government through AI-guided chatbots. *Government Information Quarterly*, 36(2), 358–367. https://doi.org/10.1016/j.giq.2018.10.001

Arshad, S., & Khurram, S. (2020). Can government's presence on social media stimulate citizens' online political participation? Investigating the influence of transparency, trust, and responsiveness. *Government Information Quarterly*, 37(3), 101486. https://doi.org/10.1016/j.giq.2020.101486

Basak, E., & Calisir, F. (2015). An empirical study on factors affecting continuance intention of using Facebook. *Computers in Human Behavior*, 48, 181–189. https://doi.org/10.1016/j.chb.2015.01.055

Baur, A. W. (2017). Harnessing the social web to enhance insights into people's opinions in business, government and public administration. *Information Systems Frontiers*, 19(2), 231–251. https://doi.org/10.1016/j.chb.2015.01.055

Beshi, T. D., & Kaur, R. (2020). Public trust in local government: Explaining the role of good governance practices. *Public Organization Review*, 20(2), 337–350. https://doi.org/10.1007/s11115-019-00444-6

Chun, S., & Luna Reyes, L. F. (2012). Social media in government. *Government Information Quarterly*, 29(4), 441–445. https://doi.org/10.1016/j.giq.2012.07.003

Criado, J. I., Sandoval-Almazan, R., & Gil-Garcia, J. R. (2013). Government innovation through social media. *Government Information Quarterly*, 30(4), 319–326. https://doi.org/10.1016/j.giq.2013.10.003

Djerf-Pierre, M., & Pierre, J. (2019). Mediatised local government: Social media activity and media strategies among local government officials 1989–2010. *Media and Governance*, 77–100. https://doi.org/10.1332/030557315X14434624683411

Dwivedi, Y. K., Rana, N. P., Tajvidi, M., Lal, B., Sahu, G. P., & Gupta, A. (2017). Exploring the role of social media in e-government. *Proceedings of the 10th International Conference on Theory and Practice of Electronic Governance*. https://doi.org/10.1145/3047273.3047374

Gross, K., Brewer, P. R., & Aday, S. (2009). Confidence in government and emotional responses to terrorism after September 11, 2001. *American Politics Research*, 37(1), 107–128. https://doi.org/10.1177/1532673X08319954

Hariguna, T., Rahardja, U., Aini, Q., & Nurfaizah. (2019). Effect of social media activities to determinants public participate intention of e-government. *Procedia Computer Science*, 161, 233–241. https://doi.org/10.1016/j.procs.2019.11.119

Hung, S. Y., Chen, K., & Su, Y. K. (2019). The effect of communication and social motives on E-government services through social media groups. *Behaviour and Information Technology*, 3001(May), 1–17. https://doi.org/10.1080/0144929X.2019.1610907

Karakiza, M. (2015). The impact of social media in the public sector. *Procedia – Social and Behavioral Sciences*, 175, 384–392. https://doi.org/10.1016/j.sbspro.2015.01.1214

Khan, G. F., Yoon, H. Y., & Park, H. W. (2014). Social media communication strategies of government agencies: Twitter use in Korea and the USA. *Asian Journal of Communication*, 24(1), 60–78. https://doi.org/10.1080/01292986.2013.851723

Khang, A. (2023). *AI and IoT-Based Technologies for Precision Medicine* (1st Ed.). IGI Global Press. ISBN: 9798369308769. https://doi.org/10.4018/979-8-3693-0876-9

Khang, A., Abdullayev, V. A., Alyar, A. V., Khalilov, M., & Murad, B.. (2023). AI-aided data analytics tools and applications for the healthcare sector. In *AI and IoT-Based Technologies for Precision Medicine* (1st Ed.). IGI Global Press. ISBN: 9798369308769. https://doi.org/10.4018/979-8-3693-0876-9.ch018

Khang, A., Muthmainnah, M., Seraj, P. M. I., Al Yakin, A., Obaid, A. J., & Panda, M. R. (2023). AI-aided teaching model for the education 5.0 ecosystem. In *AI-Based Technologies and Applications in the Era of the Metaverse* (1st Ed., pp. 83–104). IGI Global Press. https://doi.org/10.4018/978-1-6684-8851-5.ch004

Khang, A., Rana, G., Tailor, R. K., & Hajimahmud, V. A. (2023). *Data-Centric AI Solutions and Emerging Technologies in the Healthcare Ecosystem* (1st Ed.). CRC Press. https://doi.org/10.1201/9781003356189

Khang, A., Rani, S., Gujrati, R., Uygun, H., & Gupta, S. K. (2023). *Designing Workforce Management Systems for Industry 4.0: Data-Centric and AI-Enabled Approaches* (1st Ed.). CRC Press. https://doi.org/10.1201/9781003357070

Khang, A., Rath, K. C., Satapathy, S. K., Kumar, A., Das, S. R., & Panda, M. R. (2023). Enabling the future of manufacturing: Integration of robotics and IoT to smart factory infrastructure in industry 4.0. In *AI-Based Technologies and Applications in the Era of the Metaverse* (1st Ed., pp. 25–50). IGI Global Press. https://doi.org/10.4018/978-1-6684-8851-5.ch002

Khang, A., Shah, V., & Rani, S. (2023). *AI-Based Technologies and Applications in the Era of the Metaverse* (1st Ed.). IGI Global Press. https://doi.org/10.4018/978-1-6684-8851-5

Mansoor, M. (2021). Citizens' trust in government as a function of good governance and government agency's provision of quality information on social media during COVID-19. *Government Information Quarterly*, 38(4), 1–14. https://doi.org/10.1016/j.giq.2021.101597

Mergel, I. (2019). Digital service teams in government. *Government Information Quarterly*, 36(4), 101389. https://doi.org/10.1016/j.giq.2019.07.001

Mergel, I., Edelmann, N., & Haug, N. (2019). Defining digital transformation: Results from expert interviews. *Government Information Quarterly*, 36(4), 101385. https://doi.org/10.1016/j.giq.2019.06.002

Park, M. J., Kang, D., Rho, J. J., & Lee, D. H. (2016). Policy role of social media in developing public trust: Twitter communication with government leaders. *Public Management Review*, 18(9), 1265–1288. https://doi.org/10.1016/j.giq.2021.101597

Panagiotopoulos, P., Bigdeli, A. Z., & Sams, S. (2014). Citizen-government collaboration on social media: The case of Twitter in the 2011 riots in England. *Government Information Quarterly*, 31(3), 349–357. http://dx.doi.org/10.1016/j.giq.2013.10.014

Porumbescu, G. A., Cucciniello, M., & Gil-Garcia, J. R. (2020). Accounting for citizens when explaining open government effectiveness. *Government Information Quarterly*, 37(2). https://doi.org/10.1016/j.giq.2019.101451

Rahman, N. A. A., Hassan, M. S. H., Osman, M. N., & Waheed, M. (2017). Research on the state of social media studies in Malaysia: 2004–2015. *Jurnal Komunikasi: Malaysian Journal of Communication*, 33(4), 38–55. https://doi.org/10.17576/JKMJC-2017-3304-03

Sanina, A., Balashov, A., Rubtcova, M., & Satinsky, D. M. (2017). The effectiveness of communication channels in government and business communication. *Information Polity*, 22(4), 251–266. https://doi.org/10.3233/IP-170415

Song, C., & Lee, J. (2016). Citizens use of social media in government, perceived transparency, and trust in government. *Public Performance and Management Review*, 39(2), 430–453. https://doi.org/10.1080/15309576.2015.1108798

Vicente, M. R., & Novo, A. (2014). An empirical analysis of E-participation. The role of social networks and e-government over citizens' online engagement. *Government Information Quarterly*, 31(3), 379–387. https://doi.org/10.1016/j.giq.2013.12.006

Wok, S., & Mohamed, S. (2017). Internet and social media in Malaysia: Development, challenges and potentials. In *The Evolution of Media Communication*. https://doi.org/10.5772/intechopen.68848

Zha, X., Yang, H., Yan, Y., Liu, K., & Huang, C. (2018). Exploring the effect of social media information quality, source credibility and reputation on informational fit-to-task: Moderating role of focused immersion. *Computers in Human Behavior*, 79, 227–237. https://psycnet.apa.org/doi/10.1016/j.chb.2017.10.038

Chapter 5

Unlocking Growth: The Synergy of Marketing Analytics and Operations

Sharad Chaturvedi, Arpan Anand, and Ajay Kumar

5.1 Introduction

One of the primary challenges in the field of operational research pertains to the notion of achieving alignment among the many functional units within an organization. The notion of alignment has inherent challenges due to its often lack of precise definition or coherence, making it arduous to implement in practice. In a broader sense, the alignment of the various functional units within a firm can be characterized as the harmonization or compatibility of the strategic objectives, organizational structures, and operational approaches of these units with one another.

Nevertheless, the concept of alignment can be seen from various perspectives, such as a strategy issue, a procedural challenge, or a difficulty related to the utilization of capabilities. The current state of affairs has resulted in the absence of a singular prevailing paradigm for organizational alignment. This study adheres to the conceptualization proposed by Nadler and Tushman, positing that organizational alignment can be characterized as the degree to which the strategies, processes, and capabilities of a particular functional unit within an organization align with those of one or more additional functional units. This alignment facilitates the organization's ability to act cohesively and effectively leverage its existing resources. The alignment of an organization can serve as a significant competitive advantage for the firm, enabling it to enhance its responsiveness to dynamic conditions and optimize resource utilization. Additionally, research has demonstrated that it leads to enhanced financial outcomes.

The reciprocal relationship between marketing analytics and operations in the present business landscape has become a keystone for companies looking to prosper in an era defined by data-driven decision-making and digital transformation. To get deep insights into customer behavior, market trends, and campaign performance, merging these two disciplines helps organizations not only to get deep insights into customer behavior but also to execute marketing strategies with unique precision and efficiency. Marketing analytics and operations have ascended to a position of

DOI: 10.4324/9781032688305-5

essential relevance, offering enterprises a competitive edge that can make the difference between market leadership and stagnation. This intricate relationship has become a defining factor that distinguishes organizations, offering a competitive edge that can make the difference between market leadership and stagnation.

However, this rising differentiation is accompanied by plenty of issues and opportunities. The constantly increasing technical environment, the variety of data sources, and the quest for real-time insights create intimidating impediments. Yet, they also present possibilities for innovation and strategic gain. In this chapter, we understand the delicate interplay between marketing analytics and operations. The following sections will probe into the varied qualities of each subject, study their confluence, and give practical insights into harnessing their potential and how organizations navigate this dynamic landscape to attain sustainable growth and competitiveness.

5.1.1 The Fundamentals of Marketing Analytics

The systematic process of gathering, analyzing, interpreting, and utilizing data for marketing analytics is to make informed decisions about marketing strategies and campaigns. In the contemporary corporate environment, it serves as a pivotal point by enabling businesses to gain crucial insights into consumer behavior, market trends, and the success of marketing initiatives. Marketing analytics turns that data into useful intelligence and goes beyond merely compiling data; it helps marketing professionals to plan campaigns, allocate resources wisely, and ultimately spur business growth.

The growth of marketing analytics in the IT and AI age has been nothing short of world-shattering. Decision-making in the early days of marketing often relied on expert opinion, intuition, and derisory facts. However, the advent of the internet, social media, and e-commerce platforms shepherded an era of data wealth. Today, marketing analytics is at the center of commercial operations, fueled by sophisticated technologies and robust data collection approaches. The digital age has brought forth an unparalleled influx of data, allowing firms a multitude of chances to enhance their marketing tactics, tailor client experiences, and optimize return on investment (ROI) (Kannan & Li, 2017). This evolution emphasizes the indispensability of marketing analytics in modern corporate processes.

5.1.2 Key Marketing Metrics

In the world of marketing analytics, certain key performance metrics hold a prominent role in driving decision-making and evaluating the efficacy of marketing operations. Among these critical measures are return on investment (ROI), customer lifetime value (CLV), and conversion rates. Each of these measures offers distinct insights into different parts of a marketing campaign's performance and helps to provide a holistic knowledge of how marketing investments influence business outcomes.

The profitability of marketing operations is usually assessed by return on investment (ROI). It is calculated by deducting the cost of the marketing campaign from the income earned and then dividing the result by the incurred campaign's cost. ROI provides a clear indicator of how successfully marketing dollars are being spent. A positive ROI implies that the campaign is generating more income than it costs, whereas a negative ROI suggests that the effort is not delivering a favorable return. ROI is crucial in resource allocation decisions, enabling marketers to prioritize and invest in projects that have the best potential for profitability.

Client lifetime value (CLV) is another essential measure that focuses on the long-term value of a client. CLV indicates the overall revenue a business may expect to collect from a customer during their whole relationship. It is determined by multiplying the average purchase value, the average purchase frequency, and the average client lifespan. CLV is crucial because it underlines the importance of client retention and relationship-building in marketing efforts. A greater CLV suggests that customers are not just making repeat purchases but are also staying loyal to the brand, making them more valuable to the business over time.

Conversion rates assess the efficacy of marketing efforts in turning prospects into consumers. They are often given as a percentage and are derived by dividing the number of conversions (e.g., website sign-ups, sales, or downloads) by the total number of visitors or leads. Conversion rates assist marketers in measuring the efficacy of their sales funnel and discovering areas that may require modification. High conversion rates show that a campaign is successful in persuading potential customers to take the intended action, whereas poor conversion rates signal the need for adjustments in language, design, or targeting.

These vital marketing metrics, ROI, CLV, and conversion rates, play a pivotal role in evaluating the impact of marketing efforts and directing strategic decisions. By learning how to compute and interpret these indicators, marketers can tweak their campaigns, manage resources more efficiently, and ultimately achieve sustainable growth for their enterprises.

5.2 Integrating Marketing and Operations

Integrating marketing operations is a significant endeavor for firms wanting to streamline their marketing efforts and maximize productivity. It requires aligning multiple marketing departments, processes, and technologies to work impeccably together. A worldwide consumer products company may amalgamate its marketing operations by centralizing its customer data, permitting marketing teams across different locations to access and feat customer insights for targeted campaigns. Such integration adds to increasing collaboration and standardization in marketing efforts, and also strengthens the ability to track and quantify the influence of campaigns, thereby improving overall marketing performance.

5.2.1 The Role of Marketing and Operations

Planning, execution, and management of all marketing processes are part of marketing operations and include resources to deliver activities inside a company. It plays a decisive role in performing marketing strategies by ensuring that effective and efficient marketing campaigns are executed. Marketing operations incorporate several functions, including campaign management, budgeting, resource allocation, project management, and the coordination of cross-functional teams. The main focus is to optimize the operational facets of marketing to fulfill marketing goals and objectives. By restructuring marketing operations, firms can lift their ability to acclimate to changing market conditions, optimize the allocation of resources, and eventually achieve improved marketing performance (Workman et al., 2018).

In order to create a coherent and strategic approach, the alignment of marketing operations with business goals is very critical. To successfully implement marketing plans, companies must confirm that their marketing operations are aligned with broader business objectives. This enables the measurement of marketing ROI and gives a chance to organizations to change their marketing activities in response to changing market dynamics and client preferences, thereby retaining competitiveness in the market (Workman et al., 2018).

5.2.2 Role of Technology in Optimizing Marketing Operations

Extensive expansion and transformation in technology in recent years have witnessed their crucial role in optimizing marketing operations. Customer relationship management (CRM) solutions are at the vanguard of this paradigm, providing a single repository for customer data and interactions. CRM technologies, such as Salesforce and HubSpot, enable marketing teams to efficiently manage customer connections, track customer interactions, and segment audiences for tailored marketing efforts (Jambulingam et al., 2018). By combining customer data and facilitating communication, CRM systems boost collaboration across marketing, sales, and customer support teams, resulting in improved customer engagement and more effective operations.

Marketing automation tools offer another crucial component of the marketing technology stack (Maxwell et al., 2018). These solutions, typified by platforms like Marketo and Pardot, automate repetitive marketing processes such as email marketing, lead nurturing, and campaign management. Marketing automation not only saves time and minimizes manual work but also enables a more personalized and timely connection with prospects and customers. By automating lead scoring and nurturing workflows, marketing teams can focus on high-value activities and improve marketing operations to deliver the right message to the right audience at the right time, eventually driving higher conversion rates and revenue.

In addition to CRM and marketing automation, analytics tools are crucial for marketers to make data-driven decisions and streamline operations. Advanced analytics tools like Google Analytics and Adobe Analytics provide insights into website performance, user activity, and campaign efficacy. These tools enable marketing professionals to measure key performance indicators (KPIs), track ROI, and discover areas for development.

5.2.3 Analytics in Planning and Execution of Marketing Operations

Campaign strategy and execution are key to the success of marketing activities in today's dynamic business context. Recent literature highlights the necessity of extensive planning as the cornerstone for effective campaigns. Research emphasizes the relevance of data-driven insights in influencing campaign strategy. It demonstrates how advanced analytics and customer data are crucial in identifying target audiences, improving messaging, and optimizing channel selection. Furthermore, study underlines the need to integrate digital and traditional marketing channels in campaign design. This integrated strategy enables businesses to build cohesive and multichannel experiences for customers, resulting in more impactful campaigns.

Executing marketing initiatives in a continually shifting digital economy demands adaptability and agility. Recent literature implies that successful execution hinges on real-time monitoring and reactivity. Research by Patroni et al. (2022) emphasizes the need for constant monitoring of key performance indicators (KPIs) during campaign execution. It underlines the usefulness of marketing automation and AI-driven solutions in making real-time adjustments to campaign aspects such as ad placements, targeting parameters, and content based on data-driven insights. Additionally, a study by Ooi et al. (2021) recommends leveraging social media and influencer marketing in campaign execution. They find that engaging with influencers who agree with brand values can considerably boost campaign reach and engagement, especially among younger audiences.

Together, these recent studies underline the need for data-driven planning and agile execution tactics to achieve the best results in modern marketing efforts.

5.3 The Synergy of Marketing Analytics and Operations

The synergy between marketing analytics and operations is a major driver of success in current marketing undertakings. A recent study underlines the rising importance of this integration. For example, a study by Troisi et al. (2021) and Awani et al. (2021) stresses how marketing analytics enables operations by offering data-driven insights that boost decision-making processes. This information enables more precise resource allocation, individualized client experiences, and the optimization of marketing initiatives. Adoption of data-driven marketing (DDM) and strategies that businesses can use to increase shareholder value through "customer centricity" (Grandhi et al., 2021). Moreover, marketing analytics and operations may collaboratively streamline supply chain and inventory management, ensuring that marketing efforts correspond with product availability. This synergy not only promotes the effectiveness of marketing operations but also improves overall consumer satisfaction and loyalty, ultimately leading to higher returns on investment.

5.3.1 *Bridging the Gap*

The historical separation between marketing analytics and operations within firms has been a chronic difficulty. This division sometimes originated from disparities in their objectives, methods, and methodologies. Marketing analytics largely focused on collecting insights from data to analyze consumer behavior, market trends, and campaign performance. This department was more focused on strategic decision-making, frequently working in isolation from the day-to-day operational duties.

On the other hand, marketing operations were responsible for executing marketing plans, managing budgets, and coordinating the logistical components of campaigns. This operational job was frequently perceived as more tactical and focused on the efficient execution of marketing activities. The gap between these two responsibilities resulted in a lack of alignment, with analytics teams delivering significant insights that operations teams may not have fully leveraged in real-time decision-making. This gap inhibited the agility and reactivity required to adapt to quickly changing market conditions.

Aligning marketing analytics with operations offers numerous key benefits that can strengthen decision-making processes. When marketing analytics and operations operate in unison, operations teams may receive real-time data-driven insights. Patroni et al. (2022), demonstrated the significance of real-time marketing analytics in making fast alterations to campaigns, ad placements, and viewer direction. This coordination enables quicker reactions to market changes, enhancing campaign performance and client engagement. Capabilities of operations when combined with the analytical strengths of marketing analytics, business may improve resource allocation. Marketing analytics can categorize which marketing channels and initiatives deliver the highest ROI, while operations squads may efficiently distribute budgets and resources accordingly. This placement ensures that funds are directed with strategic objectives and have a higher likelihood of success.

When marketing analytics impacts operational decisions, companies are likely to deliver more personalized and relevant experiences to their consumers. Marketing analytics can provide insights into customer preferences and behaviors, allowing operational teams to adjust messaging and services accordingly. This configuration promotes customer contentment and loyalty. The harmonization of marketing analytics and operations improves dealings and reduces inadequacies. Marketing initiatives can be executed with better precision and coordination, minimizing the probability of errors and overspending. This operational efficiency leads to cost savings and higher ROI on marketing spending.

5.3.2 Data-Driven Marketing Operations

Marketing operations can harness the power of analytics to boost efficiency and performance in numerous ways. For instance, analytics can be utilized to optimize marketing workflows and resource allocation. Cao et al. (2019) conducted a survey of 221 firm managers in the United Kingdom and found that the benefits of using marketing analytics have shown a positive effect on both product development management and marketing decision-making. When a company uses AI on the strength of the marketing analytics platform, the performance of sensing, seizing, and reconfiguring improves (Hossain et al., 2022). By examining data on the time taken to accomplish different tasks within a campaign, they can discover areas for improvement and optimize their processes. This data-driven optimization approach can result in faster time-to-market for campaigns, eventually leading to cost savings and boosted competitiveness. According to Cao et al. (2022), the results show that using big data has a good impact on applying marketing analytics, which in turn has an impact on brand management, customer relationship management, product development management, brand planning, and marketing implementation inside the company.

Inventory and supply chain management are critical for marketing operations in industries such as e-commerce and retail business. By reviewing past sales data and market patterns, marketing operations teams can make data-driven decisions regarding when and how much to refill products. This eliminates overstocking or understocking, ensuring that products are available when customers require them, thus boosting customer happiness and operational efficiency.

Data-driven decision-making is at the foundation of modern marketing operations. For instance, assume a scenario in which a marketing operations team is responsible for handling digital advertising campaigns. Through the use of analytics tools, they may continuously analyze key performance indicators (KPIs) such as click-through rates, conversion rates, and return on ad spend (ROAS). If the data suggests that a certain ad creative or location is underperforming, the team can make real-time adjustments. For example, they may opt to reallocate the budget to higher-performing channels, modify ad copy, or target a new audience segment to boost campaign performance (Patroni et al., 2022).

Another example is marketing operations in content production. Content marketing is an important component of many marketing strategies, and analytics may influence content generation and dissemination. They can inspect the efficacy of content pieces, finding which themes, formats, and distribution channels resonate most with their target audience. If analytics suggest that video material creates better engagement compared to written pieces, the team can alter their content strategy accordingly, generating more video content to maximize audience engagement and ROI.

5.3.3 Continuous Improvement through Feedback Loops

Feedback loops between analytics and operations are critical for firms aiming to optimize their marketing strategy and operations. These loops offer a constant flow of information that enables data-driven decision-making and adaptation. Feedback loops enable marketing operations to continuously learn from data and adapt plans accordingly. For example, if analytics suggest that a certain advertising channel is not producing the intended results, operations teams might reallocate money to more effective channels or adjust campaign parameters. This incremental enhancement is vital in the ever-evolving world of digital marketing (Patroni et al., 2022).

Rapid responsiveness to changing market conditions is vital for enterprises. By developing feedback loops, marketing operations may quickly adjust to emerging trends or shifts in customer behavior. Insights obtained through feedback loops govern resource allocation, ensuring that marketing funds are directed towards plans and approaches that yield the highest ROI. This optimization leads to cost savings and more efficient use of resources. Input loops can also incorporate customer input and sentiment analysis. Organizations can use this data to adjust their marketing strategies and processes, aligning them more closely with customer preferences and expectations (Patroni et al., 2022). Top management increases the impact of big data analytics-skilled staff members and facilitates sense-making to advance the direction of data-driven decision-making (Johnson et al., 2021). Data-driven insights enable firms to personalize their marketing activities.

Insights from feedback loops can discover operational inefficiencies. Marketing operations can use this information to optimize procedures, cut expenses, and increase the overall efficiency of their marketing campaigns. As market conditions vary, firms can adapt their plans and operations based on real-time knowledge. For instance, if feedback reveals a shift in customer behavior, marketing operations might pivot their campaigns to accommodate these changes successfully (Patroni et al., 2022).

5.4 AI Tools and Technologies in Marketing and Operations

Within the domain of marketing and operations, Artificial Intelligence (AI) has emerged as a significant catalyst, fundamentally altering the manner in which organizations interact with clients and enhance their internal operations. By utilizing advanced artificial intelligence techniques and technologies, organizations are now able to analyze extensive volumes of data in order to acquire priceless insights into customer behavior and preferences. Machine learning algorithms facilitate the application of predictive analytics, granting marketers the ability to forecast trends and anticipate client requirements. Consequently, marketers may customize their plans to achieve optimal outcomes.

Additionally, the utilization of AI-powered Chatbots and virtual assistants has revolutionized the field of customer care by providing immediate and tailored solutions, hence augmenting overall client satisfaction. In the field of operations, the implementation of artificial intelligence (AI)-powered automation has proven to be highly effective in optimizing processes by minimizing the need for manual intervention and mitigating the occurrence of errors. AI algorithms play a crucial role in various aspects of business operations, ranging from demand forecasting to supply chain management. These algorithms effectively analyze patterns and factors, enabling decision-makers to make well-informed choices. Consequently, the integration of AI algorithms ensures the smooth functioning of operations inside an organization.

As organizations progressively incorporate artificial intelligence (AI) tools into their marketing and operational strategies, they are not only augmenting operational effectiveness but also reshaping the benchmarks for customer experiences in the digital era.

5.4.1 AI Tools Used In Marketing Analytics

There are several AI tools and technologies that can be used in marketing analytics to help businesses make data-driven decisions and optimize their marketing strategies. Here are some key AI tools commonly used in marketing analytics:

- **Marketing Automation Platforms:** Tools like HubSpot, Marketo, and Pardot use AI algorithms to automate marketing tasks, segment leads, and personalize content to improve engagement and conversions.
- **Customer Relationship Management (CRM) Systems:** CRM systems like Salesforce and Microsoft Dynamics often incorporate AI features for lead scoring, predictive analytics, and customer segmentation.
- **Predictive Analytics:** Tools such as RapidMiner and IBM Watson Studio enable marketers to predict future trends and customer behavior based on historical data, allowing for more informed decision-making.
- **Chatbots and Virtual Assistants:** AI-powered Chatbots like Intercom and Drift can engage with customers in real time, answer their queries, and gather valuable data for marketing teams.
- **Natural Language Processing (NLP) Tools:** NLP tools like MonkeyLearn and TextBlob can analyze customer reviews, social media mentions, and other text data to extract insights and perform sentiment analysis.
- **Data Analytics Platforms:** Tools like Google Analytics and Adobe Analytics leverage AI to provide deeper insights into website and app traffic, user behavior, and conversion rates.
- **A/B Testing Tools:** Platforms such as Optimizely and VWO use AI algorithms to optimize A/B tests automatically and identify winning variations faster.
- **Personalization Engines:** AI-driven personalization engines like Dynamic Yield and Evergage analyze user behavior to deliver personalized content and product recommendations.
- **Social Media Analytics:** Tools like Hootsuite and Sprout Social use AI to track social media trends, monitor brand mentions, and analyze social media engagement.
- **Email Marketing Optimization:** AI-powered email marketing platforms like Mailchimp and SendGrid use predictive analytics to optimize email send times, subject lines, and content to improve open and click-through rates.
- **Marketing Attribution Models:** AI-based attribution models like Google Attribution help marketers understand the impact of various marketing channels on conversions and ROI.
- **Competitive Analysis Tools:** Tools like SEMrush and Moz use AI to provide insights into competitors' online strategies, keyword rankings, and backlink profiles.
- **Content Recommendation Engines:** AI-driven content recommendation engines, like Outbrain and Taboola, suggest relevant articles and content to website visitors, increasing engagement.
- **Customer Segmentation:** AI algorithms help segment customers based on their behavior, preferences, and demographics, allowing marketers to tailor their campaigns more effectively.
- **Voice Search Optimization:** As voice search grows, AI tools like Amazon Alexa Skills Kit and Google Assistant can help optimize content for voice search queries.
- **Image and Video Analysis:** AI tools like Clarifai and Rekognition can analyze images and videos for content recognition, sentiment analysis, and object detection.
- **Marketing Analytics Dashboards:** AI-powered analytics platforms like Datorama and Tableau use AI to provide real-time insights and visualizations for better decision-making.

It's important to note that while these AI tools can provide valuable insights and automation capabilities, they should be integrated into a broader marketing strategy and used in

5.4.1.1 Exploring User Analytics Capabilities: A Comparative Study of Top Five Marketing Analytics Tools

In the ever-evolving landscape of digital marketing, choosing the right analytics tool is paramount. In this section, we delve into a comparative analysis of the top five marketing analytics tools, exploring their user analytics capabilities and shedding light on their unique features and advantages.

- **HubSpot:** HubSpot offers robust user analytics, including tracking website visitors, form submissions, and email interactions. It provides detailed information about individual contacts, their behavior on your website, and their engagement with marketing materials. Users can create custom reports and dashboards to analyze user data and measure the effectiveness of marketing campaigns.
- **Google Analytics:** It excels in web analytics and user tracking. It provides comprehensive insights into website traffic, user demographics, source/medium data, and user behavior. Users can track conversions, goal completions, and e-commerce transactions, allowing for in-depth analysis of user interactions.
- **Salesforce Marketing Cloud:** It offers user tracking and engagement analytics as part of its suite. It allows users to monitor email opens, clicks, and engagement metrics, providing insights into email marketing performance. The platform's CRM integration enables tracking of customer journeys and interactions across multiple channels.
- **IBM Watson Marketing:** Itg leverages AI and machine learning for advanced user analytics. It provides predictive analytics to understand user behavior and predict future actions. The platform offers customer segmentation based on AI-driven insights, enabling targeted marketing efforts.
- **Marketo:** It offers user analytics and engagement tracking within its marketing automation platform. Users can track email opens, clicks, landing page visits, and lead scoring to gauge user interest. It provides lead tracking and scoring, allowing marketers to prioritize and engage with leads effectively.

Here's the comparison of the top five marketing analytics tools on some major attributes shown in Table 5.1.

In summary, while all these tools offer various levels of user analytics capabilities, the choice depends on the specific needs and objectives of your marketing efforts. Google Analytics stands out for web analytics, while HubSpot, Salesforce Marketing Cloud, IBM Watson Marketing, and Marketo provide comprehensive user tracking and engagement analytics within their marketing automation and CRM platforms.

5.4.2 AI Tools Used in Operations Analytics

AI tools are increasingly being used in operations analytics to optimize processes, improve efficiency, and make data-driven decisions. Some of the AI tools widely used in operations analytics are as follows:

Table 5.1 Comparison of the Top Five Marketing Analytics Tools on Major Attributes

Attribute	HubSpot	Google Analytics	Salesforce Marketing Cloud	IBM Watson Marketing	Marketo
Type	Marketing automation	Web analytics	Marketing automation	AI-Enhanced marketing	Marketing automation
Customer Segmentation	Yes	Limited	Yes	Yes	Yes
Predictive Analytics	Yes	No	Yes	Yes	Yes
Personalization	Yes	Limited	Yes	Yes	Yes
Integration	Wide range of integrations	Integration with Google	Salesforce integration	Integrates with IBM tools	Extensive integrations
Ease of Use	User-friendly	User-friendly	User-friendly	Moderate	User-friendly
Pricing	Varies based on features	Free and paid versions	Custom pricing	Custom pricing	Custom pricing
Reporting	Robust reporting features	Strong reporting options	Comprehensive reporting	Advanced reporting tools	Extensive reporting
AI Capabilities	Limited AI features	No AI features	AI-enhanced marketing	Advanced AI and machine learning	Limited AI features

- **Predictive Maintenance Tools:** AI-powered predictive maintenance platforms like IBM Watson IoT and Uptake can analyze sensor data from equipment and machinery to predict when maintenance is needed, reducing downtime and costs.
- **Supply Chain Optimization:** AI-based supply chain optimization tools, such as Llamasoft and Kinaxis, use algorithms to optimize inventory management, demand forecasting, and logistics, ensuring efficient operations.
- **Quality Control and Assurance:** AI-driven quality control tools like Cognex and Sight Machine use computer vision to inspect products for defects and maintain quality standards.
- **Demand Forecasting:** AI-powered demand forecasting tools like DemandWorks and Forecastly use machine learning to predict future demand for products, helping companies manage inventory more efficiently.
- **Energy Management:** AI tools like Grid4C and Verdigris analyze energy consumption data to optimize energy usage in buildings and industrial processes, reducing costs and environmental impact.
- **Process Automation:** Robotic Process Automation (RPA) tools like UiPath and Automation Anywhere use AI algorithms to automate repetitive tasks and streamline business processes.
- **Production Scheduling:** AI-based production scheduling tools like Preactor and PlanetTogether optimize production schedules to minimize lead times and maximize resource utilization.
- **Workforce Optimization:** Workforce management platforms like Verint and Nice Systems use AI to optimize workforce scheduling, improve customer service, and manage employee performance.
- **Quality Assurance in Customer Service:** AI-powered Chatbots and virtual assistants, like Intercom and ChatGPT, can provide automated customer support and analyze customer interactions for quality assurance.
- **Inventory Management:** AI-driven inventory management tools, such as Llamasoft Inventory Guru and Lokad, optimize inventory levels, reducing carrying costs while ensuring product availability.
- **Facility Management:** AI tools like IBM TRIRIGA and Planon use predictive analytics to optimize facility maintenance, space utilization, and resource allocation.
- **Asset Tracking:** AI-based asset tracking solutions, like Mojix and RFgen, use RFID and IoT technologies to track and manage assets efficiently.
- **Process Monitoring:** AI tools can monitor and analyze manufacturing and industrial processes in real time, detecting anomalies and optimizing operations for improved efficiency and safety.
- **Transportation and Fleet Management:** AI-driven transportation management systems, like MercuryGate and JDA Software, optimize routing, scheduling, and logistics for efficient transportation operations.
- **Procurement and Vendor Management:** AI tools can analyze vendor performance, assess supplier risk, and optimize procurement processes to reduce costs and improve supplier relationships.

These AI tools are instrumental in operations analytics, helping organizations across various industries streamline their operations, reduce costs, enhance quality, and stay competitive in today's data-driven business landscape. Here's the comparison of the top five operations analytics tools on some major attributes shown in Table 5.2.

Table 5.2 Comparison of the Top Five Operations Analytics Tools on Major Attributes

Attribute	IBM Watson	Google Cloud AI	Microsoft Azure AI	AWS AI Services	OpenAI (GPT-3)
Type	AI and ML platform	AI and ML platform	AI and ML platform	AI and ML services	AI API (GPT-3)
Ease of Use	Requires technical expertise	User-friendly	User-friendly	User-friendly	User-friendly
Customization	Highly customizable	Supports custom models	Supports custom models	Customizable with SageMaker	Limited customization
Integration	Integrates with various platforms	Integrates with Google Cloud	Integrates with Azure services	Integrates with AWS services	Offers API for integration
AI Capabilities	Advanced AI, NLP, and ML	Strong NLP and ML	Strong NLP, CV, and SR	Robust AI capabilities	Powerful NLP and generation
Use Cases	Healthcare, finance, and more	e-Commerce, healthcare, etc. (Khang & Medicine, 2023)	Healthcare, finance, etc. (Khang & Abuzarova et al., 2023)	e-Commerce, healthcare, etc.	Content generation, NLP

Critically evaluating the top five AI tools for Marketing and Operations Analytics as outlined in Table 5.3, this section delves into an in-depth comparative analysis. Each tool is scrutinized for its unique user analytics capabilities, allowing readers to grasp the distinct strengths and applications of these cutting-edge technologies. By exploring these tools in detail, we aim to provide a comprehensive understanding, enabling businesses and professionals to make informed decisions regarding their marketing and operational strategies.

Let's navigate through the intricate world of AI-driven analytics, deciphering the features that set these tools apart in reshaping the future of digital marketing and operational efficiency. See the comparison of the top five AI tools for marketing analytics and operations analytics shown in Table 5.3.

5.5 Conclusion

There exists a vital need to combine marketing analytics and operations within firms. It highlights the ancient difference that has frequently existed between these functions and the issues it brings. Historically, marketing analytics and operations have operated in silos with discrete objectives and approaches, hindering effective collaboration and decision-making. At the same time, bridging the gap between analytics and operations is vital for modern marketing success, giving benefits such as real-time decision-making, resource optimization, increased customer experiences, and overall operational efficiency. Establishing feedback loops between analytics and operations is critical. These loops help firms to continuously learn from data, adjust strategy, and respond to market dynamics with agility. Data-driven decision-making is at the basis of marketing operations. Insights from analytics inform resource allocation, customization efforts, content optimization, and increases in operational efficiency.

The integration of marketing analytics and operations creates a substantial growth opportunity for firms. By properly combining these functions, businesses can lead to more efficient resource allocation, ensuring that marketing funds are focused towards tactics with the highest ROI. Organizations can better understand and respond to customer preferences and behaviors, resulting in more tailored and effective marketing efforts that resonate with target audiences. Streamlining marketing processes based on data-driven insights reduces costs and boosts operational efficiency, freeing up resources for innovation and growth projects. The capacity to react fast to changing market conditions and consumer behavior enables firms to stay competitive and grab emerging possibilities for growth.

Looking ahead, various developments and problems in the field of marketing analytics and operations are expected. The usage of artificial intelligence and automation in marketing analytics and operations is projected to rise. As the digital landscape continues to grow, organizations will confront the challenge of integrating data and processes across many channels and touchpoints for a seamless customer experience. Maintaining data quality and ensuring data correctness will be crucial to drawing useful insights and making educated decisions. In conclusion, the effective coupling of marketing analytics and operations is a potent method for firms to unlock growth, enhance customer experiences, and increase operational efficiency. Embracing emerging trends and addressing obstacles will be vital for staying competitive in the ever-evolving landscape of modern marketing.

The emergence of marketing-operations alignment as a concept can be attributed to the industrial transformations seen during the 1970s and 1980s. This period was characterized by heightened competition among manufacturers, which rendered the traditional manufacturing-centric

Table 5.3   Comparison of the Top Five Marketing Analytics and Operations Analytics AI Tools

Tool	Marketing analytics features	Operations analytics features	AI Integration	Notable benefits
Google Analytics 360	User behavior tracking	N/A	AI-driven insights and recommendations	Comprehensive website and app performance analysis
	Demographics and acquisition analysis		Advanced segmentation	Integration with Google Ads for campaign analysis
	Custom reporting and dashboards			User-friendly interface for non-technical users
Adobe Analytics	Real-time data tracking	N/A	Predictive analytics	Deep insights into customer journeys and engagement
	Customer journey analysis		Customer segmentation	Integration with Adobe Marketing Cloud for automation
	Cross-device and cross-channel tracking			A/B testing and personalization for marketing optimization
IBM Watson Analytics	Data visualization and storytelling	Predictive maintenance for machinery	Machine learning models	Enhanced decision-making through data-driven insights
	Predictive analytics	Inventory optimization	Natural language query	Data preparation and cleansing for improved accuracy
	Automated data preparation	Supply chain analysis	Automated data discovery	AI-driven anomaly detection for operational efficiency
Tableau	Interactive data exploration and visualization	N/A	Integrations with AI platforms	Real-time data analytics with a user-friendly interface
	Ad-hoc analysis and reporting		AI-powered data connectors	Collaboration and sharing for team collaboration
	Integration with various data sources			Scalability for handling large datasets
Domo	Real-time data monitoring and alerts	Inventory and supply chain tracking	Predictive analytics	Unified platform for marketing and operational insights
	Integration with marketing automation tools	Employee performance tracking	AI-driven anomaly detection	Cross-functional insights for informed decision-making
	Data blending and transformation	Financial analytics and forecasting	Natural language processing	Collaboration features for data-driven teams

design and sales approach less efficacious. Nevertheless, its development has been gradual. The recognition of marketing-operations alignment as a source of competitive advantage became evident throughout the late 1980s and late 1990s. However, it was not until the early 2000s that the initial exploratory studies investigating the practical implementation of marketing operations alignment in organizations were conducted. The pace of development has remained sluggish during the interim period, as there is still a lack of empirical evidence regarding actual firm practices, the effects on the firm, and the appropriate resolution of challenges such as resource conflicts and purpose conflicts.

The limited advancement in this area can be attributed, at least in part, to the absence of a robust theoretical framework for the alignment between marketing and operations. The phenomenon of aligning marketing and operations has been the subject of extensive discourse, with several labels such as fit, interface, and cooperation being used. However, a comprehensive theoretical framework explaining the origins of marketing-operations alignment and the factors that shape its priorities and practices has yet to be established. Additionally, there exist other constraints, such as the absence of a reliable metric that can be utilized to evaluate the alignment between marketing and operations.

The present study aimed to address the existing gap in the literature by employing configuration theory and incorporating relevant theoretical and empirical findings from prior research. The study was established with the intention of serving as a dual-purpose framework, facilitating external examination of the company's horizontal alignment while also functioning as an internal analytical instrument. The aforementioned background is inherently constrained as it has not undergone empirical testing.

The empirical literature on marketing-operations alignment is further constrained by its limitations. Hence, there exists a potential avenue to enhance our comprehension of the alignment between marketing and operations by employing this model in empirical investigations. This would facilitate a more comprehensive comprehension of the alignment between marketing and operations, both in practical terms and in terms of theoretical development of the suggested model.

5.5.1 Theoretical and Practical Contributions

The existing body of knowledge on the alignment between marketing and operations is now characterized by fragmentation across several academic disciplines, resulting in subtle variations in concepts and models. Although many of these variations have fundamental similarities, differences in nomenclature and underlying causal mechanisms contribute to the overall fragmentation. The absence of uniformity in this context indicates that the establishment of a harmonious relationship between marketing and operational departments inside an organization, a practice that has been evolving since the 1970s, has progressed at a far faster rate than its theoretical foundation.

This study presents a theoretical framework for consolidating and integrating previous research on marketing-operations alignment, as well as related concepts, by incorporating an integrated process model within the context of the alignment point proposed by Parente (1998). The research presented in this study offers a valuable contribution to the field of practice by bringing forth the importance of marketing-operations alignment. This chapter is based on real-world organizational practices and can be utilized by strategic managers to assess the effectiveness of their current alignment practices. Additionally, it can help identify areas where implementation gaps may exist or guide the implementation of new alignment practices.

The primary finding of this study with regard to practical implementation is that the alignment between marketing and operations is not a natural outcome, particularly within a hierarchical departmental organizational framework. Managers are required to consciously opt for the establishment of formal, and perhaps informal, communication and decision channels. These channels facilitate the coordination of marketing and operations decision-making and activities across strategic, operational, and tactical levels.

5.5.2 *Future Research*

In light of the current study's findings, it is recommended that further research be conducted to further investigate and expand upon the identified themes and patterns. Simultaneously, it is evident from case studies that organizations are encountering challenges in effectively aligning their marketing and operations functional units. Consequently, they may experience negative consequences due to the presence of inefficient and fragmented coordination and alignment mechanisms. The lack of progress in theoretical development has hindered the empirical investigation of alignment inside organizations in a broad sense. Consequently, this obstacle prevents companies from effectively applying organizational strategies derived from academic literature. Therefore, it is crucial for organizations to enhance their comprehension and execution of the alignment process by reinforcing the theoretical elucidation of marketing-operations alignment.

In summary, it is evident that further efforts are required to address the issue of aligning marketing and operations, as this area has been characterized by limited attention from both academic and organizational perspectives. In the field of operations research, there is a lack of consensus over the best practices and a failure to establish a single theoretical model or construct. However, there has been a certain degree of redundancy in the existing literature on organizational alignment, since it has been explored through many notions such as coordination and fit. Unfortunately, this body of knowledge has not been unified or integrated into a cohesive theoretical framework. The lack of actual research on the topic has hindered its progress (Khang & Shah et al., 2023).

There are several other areas that warrant further investigation. One of the most prominent concerns pertains to the absence of empirical substantiation about the mechanisms and rationales behind firms' implementation of organizational alignment within diverse functional units, as well as the associated costs and benefits. So far, the majority of research conducted in this area has primarily consisted of limited-scale surveys or case studies. In-depth case studies of organizations have the potential to offer additional empirical support for the alignment of functional units and their various manifestations, hence contributing to the advancement of theoretical frameworks. The current state of research necessitates a re-examination of the fundamental principles underlying the concept of marketing-operations alignment, as well as a renewed emphasis on the development of theoretical frameworks (Khang & Kali et al., 2023).

References

Awan, U., Shamim, S., Khan, Z., Zia, N. U., Shariq, S. M., & Khan, M. N. (2021). Big data analytics capability and decision-making: The role of data-driven insight on circular economy performance. *Technological Forecasting and Social Change*, 168, 120766. https://doi.org/10.1016/j.techfore.2021.120766

Cao, G., Duan, Y., & El Banna, A. (2019). A dynamic capability view of marketing analytics: Evidence from UK firms. *Industrial Marketing Management*, 76, 72–83. https://doi.org/10.1016/j.indmarman.2018.08.002

Cao, G., Tian, N., & Blankson, C. (2022). Big data, marketing analytics, and firm marketing capabilities. *Journal of Computer Information Systems*, 62(3), 442–451. https://doi.org/10.1080/08874417.2020.1842270

Grandhi, B., Patwa, N., & Saleem, K. (2021). Data-driven marketing for growth and profitability. *EuroMed Journal of Business*, 16(4), 381–398. https://doi.org/10.1108/EMJB-09-2018-0054

Hossain, M. A., Agnihotri, R., Rushan, M. R. I., Rahman, M. S., & Sumi, S. F. (2022). Marketing analytics capability, artificial intelligence adoption, and firms' competitive advantage: Evidence from the manufacturing industry. *Industrial Marketing Management*, 106, 240–255. https://doi.org/10.1016/j.indmarman.2022.08.017

Jambulingam, T., Joshi, M. P., & Kathuria, R. (2018). Competitive analysis of CRM strategies using analytic hierarchy process. *Management Dynamics*, 18(1), Article 1, 1–22. https://doi.org/10.57198/2583-4932.1036

Kannan, P. K., & Li, H. (2017). Digital marketing: A framework, review and research agenda. *International Journal of Research in Marketing*, 34(1), 22–45. https://doi.org/10.1016/j.ijresmar.2016.11.006

Khang, A. (2023). *AI and IoT-Based Technologies for Precision Medicine* (1st Ed.). IGI Global Press. ISBN: 9798369308769. https://doi.org/10.4018/979-8-3693-0876-9

Khang, A., Abdullayev, V. A., Alyar, A. V., Khalilov, M., & Murad, B. (2023). AI-aided data analytics tools and applications for the healthcare sector. In *AI and IoT-Based Technologies for Precision Medicine* (1st Ed.). IGI Global Press. ISBN: 9798369308769. https://doi.org/10.4018/979-8-3693-0876-9.ch018

Khang, A., Rath, K. C., Satapathy, S. K., Kumar, A., Das, S. R., & Panda, M. R. (2023). Enabling the future of manufacturing: Integration of robotics and IoT to smart factory infrastructure in industry 4.0. In *AI-Based Technologies and Applications in the Era of the Metaverse* (1st Ed., pp. 25–50). IGI Global Press. https://doi.org/10.4018/978-1-6684-8851-5.ch002

Khang, A., Shah, V., & Rani, S. (2023). *AI-Based Technologies and Applications in the Era of the Metaverse* (1st Ed.). IGI Global Press. https://doi.org/10.4018/978-1-6684-8851-5

Liang, X., Li, G., Zhang, H., Nolan, E., & Chen, F. (2022). Firm performance and marketing analytics in the Chinese context: A contingency model. *Journal of Business Research*, 141, 589–599. https://doi.org/10.1016/j.jbusres.2021.11.061

Maxwell, S., & Khan, A. M. (2018). Electronic Customer Relationship Management (E-CRM): A study of its role, influence & benefits to E-Commerce. *Management Dynamics*, 18(1), Article 4, 43–51. https://doi.org/10.57198/2583-4932.1039

Ooi, K. B., Lee, V. H., Hew, J. J., Leong, L. Y., Tan, G. W. H., & Lim, A. F. (2023). Social media influencers: An effective marketing approach?. *Journal of Business Research*, 160, 113773.

Parente, D. H. (1998). Across the manufacturing-marketing interface: Classification of significant research. *International Journal of Operations & Production Management*, 18(12), 1205–1222. https://doi.org/10.1108/01443579810236638.

Patroni, J., von Briel, F., & Recker, J. (2022). Unpacking the social media–driven innovation capability: How consumer conversations turn into organizational innovations. *Information & Management*, 59(3), 103267. https://doi.org/10.1016/j.im.2020.103267

Troisi, O., Maione, G., Grimaldi, M., & Loia, F. (2020). Growth hacking: Insights on data-driven decision-making from three firms. *Industrial Marketing Management*, 90, 538–557. https://doi.org/10.1016/j.indmarman.2019.08.005

Workman Jr, J. P., Homburg, C., & Gruner, K. (1998). Marketing organization: An integrative framework of dimensions and determinants. *Journal of Marketing*, 62(3), 21–41. https://doi.org/10.2307/1251741

Chapter 6

Transforming SEO in the Era of Generative AI: Challenges, Opportunities, and Future Prospects

Vajratiya Vajrobol, Nitisha Aggarwal, Geetika Jain Saxena, Sanjeev Singh, and Amit Pundir

6.1 Introduction

The rapid changing of deep learning models, exemplified by GPT-3 (Generative Pre-trained Transformer 3), has ushered in an era of generative artificial intelligence (GAI). This transformative development knows no bounds and offers groundbreaking opportunities across a multitude of sectors. GPT-3, as a shining aspect of GAI, has emerged as a cornerstone in the fusion of technology and human-like text generation. It catalyzes innovations that have redefined the landscape for numerous industries.

From revolutionizing content creation and enhancing customer support to transforming healthcare, education, legal services, and more, GPT-3 and its generative AI counterparts are reshaping the world as we know it (Khang & Medicine, 2023). In this exploration, we dive into the impact of GPT-3 and its generative AI counterparts across a diverse range of industries, like SEO. They automate content creation through natural language generation, reduce the effort required for content marketing, and improve organic search rankings. For instance, Google ranks web pages based on various factors such as keywords, backlinks, content quality, and user experience in search engine optimization (SEO). Websites and businesses employ SEO strategies to optimize their online presence and enhance their position in Google's search results.

AI tools are now streamlining the SEO process. They facilitate keyword research, enhance user experiences through Chatbots and personalization, and provide data-driven insights for SEO strategy. With the capability to generate scalable and consistently high-quality content, professionals working in SEO can maintain a fresh and relevant online presence that pleases both search

DOI: 10.4324/9781032688305-6

engines and users (Ooi et al., 2023; Zelch et al., 2023; Lv, 2023). This synergy between GAI and SEO represents a significant step forward, where AI-powered content generation and optimization are harmonizing to create a more effective and efficient online presence. It's a testament to how technology continues to reshape and redefine our approach to various industries, transcending the boundaries of what was previously possible.

Generative AI has made some improvements possible, one of which is content creation. The generation of content has been transformed by AI-driven solutions because it is the lifeblood of SEO. Businesses and content producers can now automate the creation process of high-quality, relevant, and keyword-rich content, thanks to tools like GPT-3 and its successors. These AI models can create content such as articles, product descriptions, and even social media posts, saving SEO specialists' time and money (Mayahi & Vidrih, 2022; Cao et al., 2023).

In addition to increasing process efficiency, AI content producers have sparked concerns regarding the legitimacy and originality of content. There is constant discussion over the value of human creativity and emotional resonance in writing, despite the fact that these AI technologies can produce text that is intelligible and grammatically correct. For SEO experts, finding the ideal balance between content produced by humans and by AI continues to be difficult (Korneeva et al., 2023).

Generative AI is crucial for language processing and intent recognition in addition to content production. In order to understand the intricacies of language and produce more accurate search results, search engines are increasingly depending on AI (Ma, 2023). Since knowing user intent is significant n creating better content for search engines, this advancement has a big impact on SEO. SEO experts can more successfully customize their campaigns as AI systems get better at identifying user intent, ensuring that content is aligned with the audience's particular requirements and inquiries (Yuniarthe, 2017; Rismay, 2023).

There are several difficulties and moral issues that must be resolved along with the enormous opportunities that generative AI presents to the SEO industry. Concerns regarding plagiarism, openness, and the possibility of information manipulation are raised by AI-generated content (Boddu et al., 2022). Ongoing vigilance is needed to address issues including the requirement for transparent disclosure when information is AI-generated and the prohibition of content that is generated by AI being utilized deceptively (Kirkby et al., 2023). Additionally, biases can still affect AI systems, and this holds true for search results (Howard & Borenstein et al., 2018). A crucial ethical issue is ensuring that search algorithms are impartial and support diversity and inclusivity. To reduce bias and ensure fair representation in search results, SEO experts and search engine providers must work together to design policies and procedures. On the other hand, the prospects for generative AI in SEO look bright in the future. AI has the ability to improve search result personalization and user experience even more as it develops. Future SEO tactics will be built on the capacity to deliver information that is specifically customized to user intent.

This chapter begins with an introductory section, setting the stage for the discussion. It then delves into the intricacies of generative AI and its relationship with SEO, highlighting the evolving landscape of search engine optimization. This chapter explores the significant impact of AI in content creation, emphasizing its role in evolving the digital content landscape. Furthermore, it delves into the critical aspect of intent recognition and language, showcasing how AI plays a vital role in understanding user needs and search queries. Ethical considerations are also thoroughly examined, shedding light on the ethical challenges and responsibilities associated with using AI in SEO practices.

This chapter looks ahead, offering insights into the future prospects of SEO in the generative AI era and discussing the potential transformations and advancements. It then wraps up by providing practical recommendations for businesses and SEO professionals, offering valuable guidance in navigating this AI-driven SEO landscape. Finally, the article concludes by summarizing the key takeaways and insights presented throughout the discussion as shown in Figure 6.1.

6.2 Understanding Generative AI in SEO

GAI has transformed digital marketing in recent years, especially in the area of search engine optimization (SEO) (Mandapuram et al., 2020; Mondal et al., 2023). The capabilities, constraints, and applicability of generative AI to SEO strategies are highlighted in this section's thorough description of the technology. We explore the capabilities of natural language processing (NLP) models, such as GPT-3, in understanding user intent, producing high-quality content, and eventually boosting search engine ranks (Deepika et al., 2020; Shah et al., 2023).

6.2.1 Generative AI and Its Capabilities

A term of artificial intelligence known as "generative AI" excels at creating content, whether it takes the form of writing, graphics, or even code. The outcome of deep learning models, such as OpenAI's GPT-3 (Generative Pre-trained Transformer 3), is one of the most significant advances in generative AI. These models have already been trained on enormous datasets, which enable them to comprehend and produce language that is remarkably fluent, coherent, and human-like (Floridi & Chiriatti, 2020).

The application of generative AI to SEO is revolutionary. It can automatically create content that is enhanced for particular keywords and user intent while also being grammatically and contextually correct (Ventayen, 2023). By streamlining the content development process,

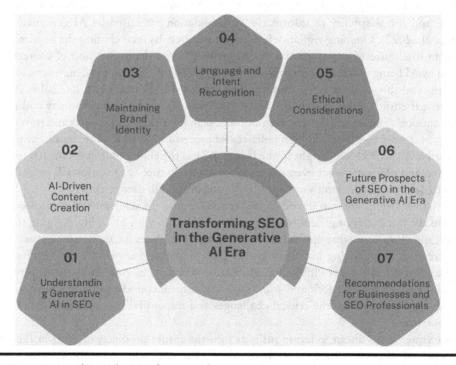

Figure 6.1 Generative AI in SEO framework.

SEO specialists can conserve time and resources while still producing high-quality material. Additionally, AI can produce content at scale, aiding websites in maintaining freshness and keeping their blogs, product descriptions, and landing pages up-to-date.

6.2.2 Limitations of Generative AI

Generative AI has inherent limitations despite its many capabilities. These restrictions mostly concern things like authenticity and inventiveness. AI-generated work is frequently seen as lacking the emotional complexity, originality, and nuance that a human author can offer. It can produce language that is intelligible and culturally appropriate, but it cannot produce content that is truly original or emotionally compelling (Corizzo & Leal-Arenas, 2023; Rahmeh, 2023). Concerns exist around the possibility of an excessive reliance on content produced by AI. To maintain an authentic and engaging online presence for their audience, SEO practitioners must carefully balance the usage of AI-generated content with content authored by humans. A great SEO strategy depends on finding the appropriate balance.

6.2.3 Relevance to SEO Techniques

The application of GAI to SEO strategies has many facets. NLP and user intent recognition are included in content generation. In the current SEO environment, search engines have improved their ability to comprehend and rank content depending on user intent. In this process, GAI is crucial. To capture what people are looking for and match their queries with the most pertinent material, search engines use AI algorithms. SEO experts can modify their content to better match user intent as AI models get better at comprehending the subtleties of human language. This means that the content must successfully address the underlying user inquiries in addition to being relevant to particular keywords.

In conclusion, Generative AI is a game-changing force in SEO, powered by deep learning models like GPT-3. SEO techniques are changing due to their strengths in content development, language processing, and user intent identification (Sarikaya et al., 2014; Wu et al., 2020). Even if it allows for unparalleled size and efficiency in content creation, there are still restrictions on originality and authenticity. To ensure authenticity and relevance, SEO experts must use generative AI sparingly, balancing it with human-generated content. In the changing world of digital marketing, the interaction of generative AI with SEO has enormous potential to improve user experience and boost search engine rankings.

6.3 AI-Driven Content Creation

AI-powered content-generating tools have become a disruptive force in the constantly changing world of search engine optimization (SEO), presenting a multitude of advantages and difficulties for SEO specialists. The advantages and drawbacks of AI-generated content are explored in this section, including increased productivity, personalized user experiences, potential plagiarism issues, content quality, and the vital matter of maintaining brand identity.

6.3.1 AI-Generated Content Advantages

AI-generated content offers several advantages in the context of SEO as described in these sub-sections:

6.3.1.1 Efficiency

Notably, AI-driven content creation, exemplified by models like GPT-3, excels in efficiency. These AI models can generate huge amounts of content at a pace far exceeding that of human writers. This efficiency empowers SEO specialists to excel in their content efforts, ensuring a continuous flow of fresh and relevant material for their websites.

6.3.1.2 Personalized User Experiences

AI-generated content can be tailored to each user's preferences and search criteria. This personalization results in more engaging and relevant information, leading to increased user satisfaction and improved conversion rates. AI achieves this by analyzing behavior and user data, enabling it to understand user intent and generate content that meets their needs.

6.3.1.3 Reduce Human Bias

AI-generated content is less prone to human biases. While human writers may unintentionally inject their perspectives or biases into content, AI can generate content that is more neutral and objective, which is essential for maintaining an unbiased and fair online presence.

6.3.1.4 Multilingual Capabilities

AI models have the capacity to generate content in multiple languages. This is a significant advantage for websites with a global audience, as it enables them to produce content that caters to diverse linguistic demographics.

6.3.1.5 Reduced Labor Costs

AI content generation can significantly reduce labor costs. It automates many of the repetitive or time-consuming tasks associated with content creation, allowing organizations to allocate resources more efficiently.

6.3.1.6 Automating Repetitive or Time-Consuming Tasks

AI is adept at automating routine tasks, such as generating product descriptions, meta tags, or content for similar product variations. This frees up human resources to focus on more strategic and creative aspects of SEO. These advantages collectively lead to a more efficient, user-centric, and cost-effective approach to SEO, making AI-generated content an invaluable asset for businesses looking to enhance their online presence and search engine rankings.

6.3.2 Challenges and Worries

6.3.2.1 Plagiarism and Originality

When employing AI to generate material, plagiarism and duplicate content might be a problem. Text is generated using AI models like GPT-3, which is the foundation of many AI content generators, using Internet data patterns. As a result, the possibility of accidental plagiarism exists.

Dehouche (2021) emphasizes how crucial it is for content producers to confirm the authenticity of AI-generated content before posting.

6.3.2.2 Content Quality

It's true that AI-generated content may have difficulty while creating extremely original, emotionally impactful, or profoundly nuanced content. While AI can produce grammatically correct and culturally suitable content, Noy and Zhang (2023) stated that it might not always provide truly creative, interesting, or thought-provoking stuff. Additionally, AI-generated information could occasionally experience hallucinations or yield erroneous results, which might affect its dependability and quality.

6.3.2.3 Concerns with Data Security and Privacy

Since AI-generated content frequently uses enormous datasets, privacy and data security issues may arise. There is some chance that AI-generated material may unintentionally reveal private information if these datasets contain sensitive or personal data. To reduce these dangers, appropriate data security and anonymization techniques are essential.

6.3.2.4 Lack of Creativity

Despite its strength, AI is fundamentally constrained by the data it was trained on. Focusing on originality and creativity, AI models frequently rely on patterns and examples from previously published content. To make sure that AI-generated material is interesting and original, getting around this restriction is a huge problem.

6.3.2.5 AI Models with Bias

Biases found in training data can be inherited by AI models. AI-generated material may reflect these prejudices, which could reinforce preconceptions or result in unfair and biased information. Fairness, diversity, and equity must be ensured in AI-generated material, which calls for careful oversight, moral principles, and bias mitigation techniques.

6.3.2.6 Concerns about Ethics and Transparency

Concerns about ethics and transparency are also raised by using AI in content generation. Users should be mindful when dealing with AI-generated material, and content producers need to make sure that the AI technologies used to create the content are properly credited and transparent. To overcome these obstacles, a mix of human control, thorough AI model training, moral standards, and ongoing monitoring is needed. Recognizing AI's limitations is essential, as is working to expand its capabilities while upholding the highest ethical and quality standards.

6.4 Maintaining Brand Identity

When deploying AI-generated content, maintaining brand identity and voice is essential. Although AI can help with content generation, it must be consistent with the brand's values, tone, and messaging. To make sure that AI-generated content connects with the company and its target audience, human monitoring is crucial. For SEO experts, maintaining a balance between AI's effectiveness and a brand's distinct personality is a significant difficulty (Ma, 2021). While effective, AI-generated material should not be seen as a replacement for humans. The best strategy for SEO experts is to use AI as an additional tool. Human content creators may now concentrate on more imaginative and strategic areas of content development because AI can handle regular, data-driven activities like creating product descriptions or optimizing meta tags.

In conclusion, AI-driven content generation is becoming more common in the SEO sector and offers a number of advantages in terms of effectiveness and customized user experiences. The necessity to uphold content quality and brand identification, as well as potential issues with plagiarism, poses some difficulties. SEO specialists must use AI wisely, incorporating it into their content strategy while maintaining the distinctive human touch that makes their business stand out and appeal to their audience. The secret to a fruitful and all-encompassing SEO strategy is the dynamic interaction of AI and human innovation.

6.5 Language and Intent Recognition

Generative AI is excellent at deciphering human intent and natural language, which has implications for semantic search, keyword research, and content optimization. We examine how AI affects keyword selection, long-tail keyword targeting, and the user experience via tailored search results.

6.5.1 Recognizing Language and Intent

The way search engine optimization (SEO) specialists handle keyword research, content optimization, and semantic search has been substantially impacted by the new era of natural language understanding and user intent recognition brought about by generative AI. This section explores how AI's capability in language processing affects keyword selection and long-tail keyword targeting, and how personalized search results improve user experience (Cohen & Queen, 2023).

6.5.2 Keywords Techniques

The conventional method of keyword research has been revolutionized by AI-driven language models like GPT-3. Instead of relying simply on exact match keywords, SEO specialists may now employ AI to explore the motivation behind user requests. This change from a keyword-centric to an intent-centric strategy enables the development of content that more effectively meets user demands. SEO professionals may now research a wider range of relevant keywords and phrases because of AI's capacity to recognize semantic correlations between words and phrases. This broader keyword approach makes sure that the content is not only thoroughly optimized for a particular keyword but also for related topics and user intent (Reisenbichle et al., 2022).

6.5.3 Targeting Long-Tail Keywords

Long-tail keywords, which are often lengthier and more detailed search queries, have become increasingly popular as a result of AI's ability to recognize language and intent. Today, SEO experts may find and target a wide variety of long-tail keywords that correspond to the precise queries and purpose of the user (Rismay, 2023). Long-tail keywords frequently have lower search volume but are much more specialized, bringing in more qualified traffic. These complex long-tail keywords can be found with the help of AI, allowing websites to attract customers with targeted demands.

6.5.4 Improved User Experience

The improvement of user experience is one of the most important effects of AI-driven language and intent recognition. In terms of AI algorithms, search engines can interpret the purpose of a user's query and deliver more search results that are relevant. These customized results consider the user's previous interactions with the website, location, and search history. This results in better user happiness, more pertinent search results, and perhaps even increased engagement and conversion rates. Customers receive content that is customized to their preferences, making their online experience more engaging and satisfying (Cheng, 2020). Additionally, conversational search inquiries, voice search optimization, and the insertion of more intricate and context-aware questions are all made possible by AI's grasp of natural language. Understanding and using conversational language is a crucial component of SEO as voice-activated devices grow more prevalent.

Finally, the language and intent recognition capabilities of generative AI have revolutionized SEO tactics. A new age in digital marketing has begun with the transition from keyword-centric to intent-centric SEO methods, the growing emphasis on long-tail keywords, and the improvement of the user experience through personalized search results. With the ability to produce more thorough and user-focused content, SEO specialists are better able to adapt their techniques to the changing environment of AI-powered search engines and enhance users' entire online experiences.

6.6 Ethical Considerations

A variety of ethical issues, including content creation, ownership, biases, and the veracity of AI-generated information, are raised by the incorporation of generative AI into SEO. We examine these ethical issues in this part and offer recommendations for the proper and moral application of AI to SEO techniques.

6.6.1 Ownership and Attribution of the Content

The question of content ownership and credit is one of the main ethical considerations when using AI-generated content in SEO. The content is created by AI tools, but it is monitored and used by humans. It is important that the AI system receives sufficient credit, showing that the content was produced with AI assistance. By keeping the audience informed of the source of the content, transparency preserves credibility (Israel & Amer, 2023). Furthermore, ethical standards ought to address the problem of content that unintentionally infringes on copyright or other intellectual property rights. SEO experts need to make sure that AI-generated material doesn't violate anyone else's intellectual property, and they should keep a close eye out for any potential infractions.

6.6.2 AI-Generated Content Bias

Large datasets that could be biased are used to train generative AI models. AI-generated content may contain these biases, which could cause problems with justice and representation.

SEO specialists must take action to reduce prejudices in the material they provide and make sure it is inclusive and culturally sensitive (Fang et al., 2023). The necessity to examine and edit AI-generated content to get rid of any unintentional biases should be emphasized in ethical guidelines. Maintaining variety and inclusivity in a material is crucial in preventing the spread of stereotypes or the favoring of some groups over others.

6.6.3 Credibility of Information Produced by AI

The prevalence of AI-generated content raises questions regarding the veracity and quality of the data. It is the job of SEO experts to guarantee the veracity and accuracy of AI-generated content. This calls for fact-checking the data and, when necessary, identifying reliable sources (Lee et al., 2020).

Balancing between the effectiveness of AI-generated content and the veracity of the data displayed is also essential. SEO experts should put quality over quantity, making sure that the content meets high standards of reliability and correctness.

6.6.4 Ethics Principles for Responsible Use of AI

The following rules should be followed by SEO practitioners in order to handle these ethical issues:

- **Transparency:** Clearly state when content is AI-generated and give credit to the AI tool that produced it.
- **Information Review:** To guarantee that AI-generated information complies with moral and exemplary standards, it should be regularly reviewed and edited to eliminate biases.
- **Fact-checking**: Check the veracity of information produced by AI, citing reliable sources when appropriate.
- **Diversity and Inclusivity**: Make an effort to produce content that is inclusive, sensitive to cultural differences, and devoid of prejudice.
- **Intellectual Property Compliance:** Ensure that content produced by AI does not violate copyrights or other intellectual property rights.
- **User Education**: Inform users of the function AI plays in content production and any potential drawbacks.
- **Maintaining Human Monitoring** throughout the content development process will help to uphold moral and professional standards.

In conclusion, using generative AI in SEO raises ethical questions about content ownership, biases, and the reliability of information. SEO specialists can utilize the power of AI while upholding moral and responsible standards by adhering to ethical standards that prioritize transparency, content assessment, fact-checking, diversity, and intellectual property compliance as shown in Figure 6.2.

6.7 Future Prospects of SEO in the Generative AI Era

We look to the future and imagine a world where AI-aided SEO methods bring about radical changes as the incorporation of GAI reshapes the search engine optimization (SEO) field. We

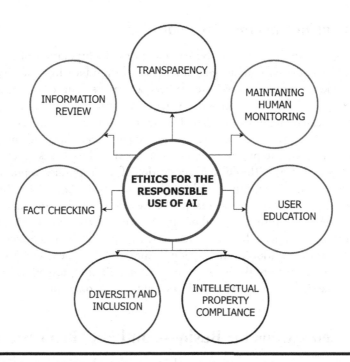

Figure 6.2 Ethics for responsible use of AI.

examine the possible advantages of AI-augmented SEO in this area, including better user experiences, predictive SEO analytics, and higher search engine rankings.

6.7.1 Improved User Experience

A new era of individualized and user-focused SEO is predicted to be ushered in by GAI. The nuanced purpose behind search queries can be understood by search engines with AI algorithms, resulting in more individualized search results. Users receive content specifically tailored to their requirements and interests, which is based on past data and user behavior. SEO experts can generate content that connects more deeply with their target audiences as AI continues to enhance its grasp of user intent for better user experiences and possibly increased engagement and conversion rates.

6.7.2 Utilizing Predictive SEO Analytics

Predictive analytics contributed by AI is what will shape SEO in the upcoming future. Large-scale datasets can be analyzed by machine learning (ML) algorithms to predict trends, user behavior changes, and adjustments to search engine algorithms. Professionals can proactively adjust their strategy using predictive SEO analytics, ensuring that their material remains pertinent and in line with changing user intent. This dynamic method of SEO promotes quicker decision-making and shortens the period between changes in SEO strategy and the emergence of new trends.

Predictive analytics driven by AI also have the potential to anticipate changes in search engine algorithms, assisting in proactive content optimization. In order to ensure that their material is not only optimized for current rankings but also well-prepared for future search engine requirements, SEO specialists can remain ahead of algorithm adjustments.

6.7.3 Search Engine Ranking Has Improved

Boosted search engine rankings are possible, thanks to the incorporation of generative AI into SEO. The ability of AI-driven content generation tools to produce high-quality, keyword-rich content at scale makes it simpler for websites to keep a steady stream of timely information. AI can help websites achieve these requirements by generating valuable and often updated content, which is something search engines appreciate. Furthermore, more accurate content optimization is possible, thanks to AI's capacity to comprehend user intent, semantics, and context. This makes it possible for SEO specialists to produce content that exactly fits what customers are looking for, improving organic search ranks. The efficient application of AI techniques to produce content that appeals to both search engine algorithms and people represents the future of SEO.

In conclusion, improved user experiences, predictive SEO analytics, and higher search engine rankings characterize SEO's future possibilities in the generative AI era. By delivering personalized and user-centric content, enabling quick responses to new trends, and preserving high search engine ranks through the creation of high-quality content, AI-augmented SEO tactics have the potential to completely transform the industry. In the dynamic and prosperous future of the ever-evolving digital marketing industry, AI and SEO's combination offers promise.

6.8 Recommendations for Business and SEO Professionals

We offer actionable advice for companies and SEO experts looking to enhance the power of AI in their SEO strategy in light of the transformational potential of generative AI in SEO. These suggestions include using AI tools, user intent analysis, keyword research, and content creation.

6.8.1 Adopt AI in Content Creator

- Use AI-powered content-generating technologies to generate content that is effective and scalable.
- Maintain a balance between content produced by humans and AI to ensure originality and creativity.
- Invest in human monitoring to check the quality and brand identity of AI-generated content.

6.8.2 Rethink Keyword Strategies

Focus on understanding the user intent behind search queries rather than utilizing a keyword-centric approach that is keyword-centric.

- Apply AI to find semantic connections between keywords and phrases, thus broadening keyword strategy.
- Look into targeting long-tail keywords to get more targeted and qualified traffic.

6.8.3 Prioritize User Intent Analysis

- Use AI models to learn about user intent and then modify content to meet their needs.
- Constantly assess user intent and revise content tactics as necessary.
- Make an investment in AI solutions that offer data and insights on user behavior and intent in real time.

6.8.4 Use AI Tools for Analytics and Insights

- Use AI-driven analytics tools to foresee user behavior changes, discover upcoming possibilities, and forecast trends.
- Make use of predictive SEO analytics to proactively modify SEO tactics in response to changing trends and modifications to search engine algorithms.
- Take into account AI techniques for real-time content optimization and monitoring to meet search engine standards.

6.8.5 Prioritize Ethical AI Use

- Encourage content transparency by making it clear when it was produced using AI.
- Check for biases and alter AI-generated content to guarantee inclusion.
- Verify facts to preserve the veracity and accuracy of content produced by AI.

6.8.6 Invest in AI Education and Training

- Assure that SEO specialists have received thorough training in AI technology and its SEO applications.
- Keep your knowledge and abilities up to date for developing fields of AI and SEO.

6.8.7 Keep up with AI Developments

Keep up with the most recent advancements in SEO applications. Continually be updated with new AI models, tools, and implementing best practices.

6.8.8 Promote Cross-Functional Teams

- To fully utilize the power of AI in SEO, promote cooperation among content producers, SEO experts, and data analysts.
- Create cross-functional teams to fill the gap between the implementation of an SEO strategy and AI knowledge.

6.8.9 Continuously Monitor and Adjust

In conclusion, adopting generative AI for content creation, switching to intent-centric keyword strategies, prioritizing user intent analysis, deploying AI tools for analytics, and supporting ethical AI utilization are all necessary for the successful integration of generative AI in SEO tactics. We have to:

- Consistently evaluate the effectiveness of AI-enhanced SEO tactics and make data-driven changes.
- Adopt an adaptable culture to keep up with the changing AI world.

SEO specialists and businesses must make educational and training investments, stay current on AI developments, encourage collaboration, and foster a culture of constant observation and adaptation. These suggestions offer a road map for responsibly and successfully navigating the constantly changing world of AI and SEO (Khang & Muthmainnah et al., 2023).

6.9 Conclusions

In this exploration of the consequences of generative AI (GAI) on SEO, we have revealed the transformative potential of this technology. It is evident that GAI has the capacity to revolutionize SEO practices, particularly in content creation, search engine rankings, and user experiences. While embracing AI offers numerous advantages, the critical importance of ethical considerations cannot be overstated. In concluding our discussion, we emphasize the need for SEO professionals and businesses to adopt responsible AI practices to remain at the forefront of SEO in the generative AI era (Khang & Shah et al., 2023).

Generative AI, powered by deep learning models like GPT-3, has redefined the traditional approach to content creation in SEO. AI-driven content generation tools have emerged as efficient and scalable solutions, enabling businesses to meet the increasing demand for fresh, relevant, and keyword-rich content. This has not only improved efficiency but also paved the way for more personalized user experiences through content tailored to specific user intent.

The future prospects of SEO in the Generative AI era hold great promise. AI-augmented strategies will allow SEO professionals to anticipate trends, maintain high search engine rankings, and create content that resonates more deeply with their audience. It is a landscape where the synergy between AI and human creativity drives success. However, amidst these advancements, ethical considerations take center stage. Content ownership, potential biases, and content credibility must be closely monitored. By following ethical guidelines that prioritize transparency, content quality, and inclusivity, businesses and SEO professionals can apply the power of AI while maintaining the trust of their audience.

In conclusion, generative AI has ushered in a new era for SEO, offering unprecedented opportunities for businesses and SEO professionals. By responsibly embracing AI and upholding ethical standards, they can chart a course to success in the ever-evolving SEO landscape. The partnership between AI and human expertise is a significant aspect to staying at the forefront of SEO in the generative AI era (Khang & Kali et al., 2023).

References

Boddu, R. S. K., Santoki, A. A., Khurana, S., Koli, P. V., Rai, R., & Agrawal, A. (2022). An analysis to understand the role of machine learning, robotics and artificial intelligence in digital marketing. *Materials Today: Proceedings*, 56, 2288–2292.

Cao, Y., Li, S., Liu, Y., Yan, Z., Dai, Y., Yu, P. S., & Sun, L. (2023). A comprehensive survey of AI-generated content (AIGC): A history of generative AI from GAN to CHATGPT. arXiv preprint arXiv:2303.04226.

Cheng, Y., & Jiang, H. (2020). How do AI-driven Chatbots impact user experience? Examining gratifications, perceived privacy risk, satisfaction, loyalty, and continued use. *Journal of Broadcasting & Electronic Media*, 64(4), 592–614. https://www.tandfonline.com/doi/abs/10.1080/08838151.2020 .1834296

Cohen, S., & Queen, D. (2023). Generative artificial intelligence community of practice for research. *International Wound Journal*, 20(6), 1817. https://www.ncbi.nlm.nih.gov/pmc/articles/PMC10333021/

Corizzo, R., & Leal-Arenas, S. (2023). One-class learning for AI-generated essay detection. *Applied Sciences*, 13(13), 7901. https://www.mdpi.com/2076-3417/13/13/7901

Deepika, K., Tilekya, V., Mamatha, J., & Subetha, T. (2020, August). Jollity Chatbot-a contextual AI assistant. In *2020 Third International Conference on Smart Systems and Inventive Technology (ICSSIT)* (pp. 1196–1200). IEEE. https://ieeexplore.ieee.org/abstract/document/9214076/

Dehouche, N. (2021). Plagiarism in the age of massive Generative Pre-trained Transformers (GPT-3). *Ethics in Science and Environmental Politics*, 21, 17–23. https://www.int-res.com/abstracts/esep/v21/p17-23/

Fang, X., Che, S., Mao, M., Zhang, H., Zhao, M., & Zhao, X. (2023). Bias of AI-generated content: An examination of news produced by large language models. arXiv preprint arXiv:2309.09825. https://arxiv.org/abs/2309.09825

Floridi, L., & Chiriatti, M. (2020). GPT-3: Its nature, scope, limits, and consequences. *Minds and Machines*, 30, 681–694. https://link.springer.com/article/10.1007/s11023-020-09548-1

Howard, A., & Borenstein, J. (2018). The ugly truth about ourselves and our robot creations: The problem of bias and social inequity. *Science and Engineering Ethics*, 24, 1521–1536. https://link.springer.com/article/10.1007/s11948-017-9975-2

Israel, M. J., & Amer, A. (2023). Rethinking data infrastructure and its ethical implications in the face of automated digital content generation. *AI and Ethics*, 3(2), 427–439. https://link.springer.com/article/10.1007/s43681-022-00169-1

Khang, A. (2023). *AI and IoT-Based Technologies for Precision Medicine* (1st Ed.). IGI Global Press. ISBN: 9798369308769. https://doi.org/10.4018/979-8-3693-0876-9

Khang, A., Muthmainnah, M., Seraj, P. M. I., Al Yakin, A., Obaid, A. J., & Panda, M. R. (2023). AI-aided teaching model for the education 5.0 ecosystem. In *AI-Based Technologies and Applications in the Era of the Metaverse* (1st Ed., pp. 83–104). IGI Global Press. https://doi.org/10.4018/978-1-6684-8851-5.ch004

Khang, A., Rath, K. C., Satapathy, S. K., Kumar, A., Das, S. R., & Panda, M. R. (2023). Enabling the future of manufacturing: Integration of robotics and IoT to smart factory infrastructure in industry 4.0. In *AI-Based Technologies and Applications in the Era of the Metaverse* (1st Ed., pp. 25–50). IGI Global Press. https://doi.org/10.4018/978-1-6684-8851-5.ch002

Khang, A., Shah, V., & Rani, S. (2023). *AI-Based Technologies and Applications in the Era of the Metaverse* (1st Ed.). IGI Global Press. https://doi.org/10.4018/978-1-6684-8851-5

Kirkby, A., Baumgarth, C., & Henseler, J. (2023). To disclose or not disclose, is no longer the question–effect of AI-disclosed brand voice on brand authenticity and attitude. *Journal of Product & Brand Management*. https://www.emerald.com/insight/content/doi/10.1108/JPBM-02-2022-3864/full/html

Korneeva, E., Salge, T. O., Teubner, T., & Antons, D. (2023). Tracing the legitimacy of artificial intelligence: A longitudinal analysis of media discourse. *Technological Forecasting and Social Change*, 192, 122467. https://www.sciencedirect.com/science/article/pii/S004016252300152X

Lee, S., Nah, S., Chung, D. S., & Kim, J. (2020). Predicting ai news credibility: Communicative or social capital or both?. *Communication Studies*, 71(3), 428–447. https://www.tandfonline.com/doi/abs/10.1080/10510974.2020.1779769

Lv, Z. (2023). Generative artificial intelligence in the metaverse era. *Cognitive Robotics*. https://www.sciencedirect.com/science/article/pii/S2667241323000198

Ma, C. (2023). ChatGPT and generative AI in IT processes. NYU SPS Applied Analytics Laboratory. http://archive.nyu.edu/handle/2451/69530

Ma, L. (2021, October). Research on brand digital Development and Design Method in intelligent Era. In *2021 2nd International Conference on Intelligent Design (ICID)* (pp. 234–237). IEEE. https://ieeexplore.ieee.org/abstract/document/9681576/

Mandapuram, M., Gutlapalli, S. S., Reddy, M., & Bodepudi, A. (2020). Application of artificial intelligence (AI) technologies to accelerate market segmentation. *Global Disclosure of Economics and Business*, 9(2), 141–150. https://i-proclaim.my/journals/inde6.php/gdeb/article/view/662

Mayahi, S., & Vidrih, M. (2022). The impact of generative AI on the future of visual content marketing. arXiv preprint arXiv:2211.12660.

Mondal, S., Das, S., & Vrana, V. G. (2023). How to bell the cat? A theoretical review of generative artificial intelligence towards digital disruption in all walks of life. *Technologies*, 11(2), 44. https://www.mdpi.com/2227-7080/11/2/44

Noy, S., & Zhang, W. (2023). Experimental evidence on the productivity effects of generative artificial intelligence. Available at SSRN 4375283. https://papers.ssrn.com/sol3/papers.cfm?abstract_id=4375283

Ooi, K. B., Tan, G. W. H., Al-Emran, M., Al-Sharafi, M. A., Capatina, A., Chakraborty, A., & Wong, L. W. (2023). The potential of generative artificial intelligence across disciplines: Perspectives and future directions. *Journal of Computer Information Systems*, 1–32. https://www.tandfonline.com/doi/abs/10.1080/08874417.2023.2261010

Rahmeh, H. (2023). Digital verses versus inked poetry: Exploring readers' response to AI-generated and human-authored sonnets. *Scholars International Journal of Linguistics and Literature*, 6(9), 372–382. https://saudijournals.com/media/articles/SIJLL_69_372-382.pdf

Reisenbichler, M., Reutterer, T., Schweidel, D. A., & Dan, D. (2022). Frontiers: Supporting content marketing with natural language generation. *Marketing Science*, 41(3), 441–452. https://pubsonline.informs.org/doi/abs/10.1287/mksc.2022.1354

Rismay, C. (2023). The role of AI in modern SEO strategies. https://www.webdesignplusseo.com/the-role-of-ai-in-modern-seo-strategies/

Sarikaya, R., Hinton, G. E., & Deoras, A. (2014). Application of deep belief networks for natural language understanding. *IEEE/ACM Transactions on Audio, Speech, and Language Processing*, 22(4), 778–784. https://ieeexplore.ieee.org/abstract/document/6737243/

Shah, C., White, R. W., Andersen, R., Buscher, G., Counts, S., Das, S. S. S., & Yang, L. (2023). Using large language models to generate, validate, and apply user intent taxonomies. arXiv preprint arXiv:2309.13063. https://arxiv.org/abs/2309.13063

Ventayen, R. J. M. (2023). OpenAI ChatGPT generated results: Similarity index of artificial intelligence-based contents. Available at SSRN 4332664. https://papers.ssrn.com/sol3/papers.cfm?abstract_id=4332664

Wu, C. S., Hoi, S., Socher, R., & Xiong, C. (2020). TOD-BERT: Pre-trained natural language understanding for task-oriented dialogue. arXiv preprint. https://arxiv.org/abs/2004.06871

Yuniarthe, Y. (2017, September). Application of artificial intelligence (AI) in search engine optimization (SEO). In *2017 International Conference on Soft Computing, Intelligent System and Information Technology (ICSIIT)* (pp. 96–101). IEEE. https://ieeexplore.ieee.org/abstract/document/8262550/

Zelch, I., Hagen, M., & Potthast, M. (2023). Commercialized generative AI: A critical study of the feasibility and ethics of generating native advertising using large language models in conversational web search. arXiv preprint arXiv:2310.04892.

Chapter 7

The Power of Consistency: Building Long-term Success with Content Marketing

Pretty Bhalla, Jaskiran Kaur, and Sayeed Zafar

7.1 Introduction

A content marketing strategy is a comprehensive plan for producing and disseminating content to expand your audience and accomplish a range of commercial objectives. Examples of content marketing include:

- Blog posts
- Emails
- Newsletters
- Social media posts
- Podcasts
- Ebooks
- Videos.

The goal is to send the right message to current and potential customers. A content plan, often called a "content calendar," is a documented strategy that will assist in organizing your distribution timetable.

7.2 Why Have a Content Marketing Strategy?

A content marketing strategy facilitates the establishment of precise objectives, unambiguous success measurements, and procedures for targeted improvement. This works better than creating stuff randomly and hoping it works. Actually, a defined approach is possessed by 80% of marketers

DOI: 10.4324/9781032688305-7

who achieve remarkable success with content marketing. Other benefits of a content marketing plan include:

- **Increased Internet Visibility**: You may draw in more business by posting on a regular basis. Provide informative, practical information that tackles the problems faced by consumers.
- **More Leads:** A successful content marketing plan may generate leads in addition to visitors.
- **Greater Authority**: People in your field will see you as an authoritative figure more and more when you contribute helpful material over time.
- **Higher Levels of Client Engagement:** Repeat business comes from loyal consumers. Interact with others who leave comments or reply to your posts.
- **Greater Budget**: It will probably be simpler to request a larger marketing budget in the future if you can demonstrate your marketing success.

7.3 Five Elements of a Powerful Content Marketing Strategy

An effective content marketing strategy should have these five core elements to be successful, as shown in Figure 7.1.

- Audience personas
- Positioning and brand storytelling
- Content marketing mission

Figure 7.1 Six components of content marketing strategy.

- Business case
- An action plan.

7.3.1 Audience Personas

Telling the narrative of your brand is challenging if you don't know who will be hearing it. Because of this, deciding on the target audience should be the first step. To that end, below are several methods: Take a survey of your current clientele, investigate market trends, choose who you don't want to target, and keep an eye on whoever your rivals are focusing on as shown in Figure 7.2.

7.3.2 Brand Story and Positioning

A brand narrative is an overview of the background, goals, and core values of a business. Choosing the appropriate themes and ideas to cover in your content may be made easier by clearly defining your brand narrative. This helps in determining the best course for a content marketing plan. Your story should focus on:

- The hero of the story (your customer) and their goals and challenges
- Your brand's personality
- The purpose of branding and key brand values
- The way products and content can help reinforce all the above and empower your hero
- Keeping your brand's story in mind when making content will create a consistent experience for your audience and build the right image on all content marketing channels.

Figure 7.2   Audience personas.

Here are some questions to help you brainstorm your brand story and positioning in the market:

- Who are my existing and potential customers? What are their goals?
- Who are my top competitors? How do they market their brands?
- What is my brand's unique value?
- What problems does my product solve?
- What makes my product a better choice over my competitors?

You can also use this free brand storytelling template to complete this step and document your efforts. This step can be especially beneficial for small businesses and startups that can leverage their unique backgrounds and identities.

7.3.3 Content Marketing Mission Statement and Owned Media Value Proposition

Any digital marketing platforms under control are considered owned media, such as social media or your website. Define owned media's value proposition to present the company as a reliable content creator.

7.3.3.1 Stated Differently

What distinct value does the material associated with your brand offer? (This should be different from the material of your rivals.) This will assist you in developing a content marketing plan that distinguishes you from other businesses. The content marketing mission statement is a crucial component of a business plan. It should include a synopsis of content creation goals and details about who will find value in it. Make sure that the content marketing mission statement includes the following elements:

- **Your Audience**: Who are you creating content for?
- **The Benefit**: What information or answers will you provide?
- **The Outcome:** How will your content help your audience achieve their goals?

7.3.3.2 For Example

A software company's mission statement be our content is where digital marketing managers find multimedia information about SEO and content marketing so they can help their companies grow via organic channels as shown in Figure 7.3.

7.3.4 Business Case and Content Marketing Goals

Providing value to the audience is an integral part of a successful content marketing plan. But in addition to attracting new readers and followers, content marketing should drive the business forward. Creating a documented business case will help you or your team better understand the benefits, costs, and risks of implementing a content marketing strategy for any company. A business case is a project management document that outlines why particular tasks should be executed and how their benefits outweigh their costs.

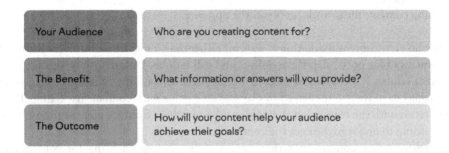

Figure 7.3   Mission statement of content in digital marketing managers.

To get started, identify the business goals the company needs to achieve and figure out how content marketing will bring the company closer to those goals. Additionally, what resources are required to invest in your content strategy? And what results do you want to generate? This will allow us to come up with a firm budget for content creation and marketing.

7.3.5 Action Plan

Finally, add main content marketing campaigns and projects to the content plan. Using a formal content plan will help you think through each content marketing strategy step individually. Make sure to cover the following while content planning:

- Choose content topics for each campaign.
- Determine which content formats you will produce.
- Pick the channels for content distribution.

Key elements to include in the calendar are:

- Topics or keywords
- Target dates
- Headlines
- Categories or clusters
- Content formats
- Target personas
- Success metrics.

To decide on your optimal content formats and channels, there is a need to look at historical content performance and further analyze the audience.

7.4 Long-Term Content Strategy

It's no secret that content is time-consuming. However, some marketers are so focused on whittling down that time, on cutting corners just to "get something out," that they ultimately end up losing out. What do they lose? The power inherent in high-quality content helps to:

- Rank on Google
- Build trust with consumers
- Earn leads
- Convert leads
- Rushing content, meanwhile, gets you the opposite.

Marketers who view content marketing as a sprint rather than a marathon think they can write 20 short, low-quality blog posts, slap them online, and call it done. Unfortunately, this is a recipe for major content failure. For content to succeed – truly succeed, with the rankings, engaged readers, and conversions to prove it – they need to play the long game with content marketing. They need to come to terms with the realization that it may take anywhere from six months to a year (or even longer, according to one study) to get the content ranking well.

Why focusing on a content marathon, not a sprint, is a good thing for your marketing? Consider a footrace for a second: It's harsh, isn't it? If someone really needs speed to win a footrace, style and technique are less necessary (at least until they become a professional track runner, when form and style become quite vital). As a result, the best runner in the group isn't always the victor of a footrace. That winner would probably burn out at the start of a 10-kilometer race, right? This is to exemplify, Why focusing on a content marathon, not a sprint, is a good thing for your marketing?

What the same thing applies to content? While anyone can sprint in a general direction towards the finish line with crappy content and poorly thoughtout content strategies, not every marketer can devise an effective, long-term strategy for consistently ranking well with content. This is the main reason that the long-term content strategy is so much better than a short-term content strategy. In addition to being more sustainable, the long-term approach is also wiser and more fully thoughtout.

In the words of Tim Ferriss, there will always be a need for high quality, and there will always be a need for long form. While short-term content strategies seek to produce instant and short-lived results, long-term content strategies allow marketers to bond with their audiences, build their voice, provide real value, and rank in an authentic and sustainable way. Because of this, marketers who create long-term content strategies often publish more effective content, build bigger audiences, and garner more shares across the board.

7.5 10 Reasons Long-Term Content Strategy is Better

7.5.1 It's a Better Use of Money and Resources

Imagine going on a diet to lose weight. For two weeks, you eat only whole, clean foods and you exercise for two hours a day. You feel great and – hey! – You lose weight. At the end of those two weeks, however, you stop exercising and go right back to your old diet habits.

What happens? Of course, you gain all the weight back, and the guise of physical fitness takes a nosedive. Not surprisingly, the same thing happens with content. Regardless of what we are doing, content marketing takes money and resources. If you're paying someone to flood our accounts with content for two weeks and then laying off strategy entirely, you can bet not only will the strategy be ineffective, but it will also be a waste of money and resources. Instead, you are much better off allocating resources to a long-term content strategy that will build readers over time and help maintain steady levels of traffic and clicks over months or years. Instead of wasting resources, this funnels them right back into the company and ensures that we are building value while also establishing a solid foundation of lasting, relevant content.

7.5.2 Long-Term Content Engages Readers

To keep readers interested and engaged for an extended period, the need is to offer them comprehensive, in-depth content that helps them address their concerns and solve problems. And that means long content, in terms of word count per article. Don't think just because at present we live in an age where attention spans are short that long-form content won't do well. In fact, it's quite the opposite. An Orbit Media survey found that bloggers who write longer posts (anything over 1,500 words) get better results. Why does long-form content perform so well as part of a long-term content strategy? In addition to providing outstanding value for readers, long-form content also allows the company to build authority and establish dominance by showcasing knowledge on relevant topics in the industry.

7.5.3 Content Changes All the Time

As search engines and reader's progress, the demand for quality, informed, relevant content increases all the time. Because of this, a long-term content strategy is the best possible weapon. Designed to insulate marketers against change and help them maintain their traffic and readership despite changing SEO, content, and marketing requirements, long-term content marketing allows space for the strategy to absorb and adapt to changing trends. This ensures more effective content and a more adaptive strategy that doesn't have to scramble to keep up.

7.5.4 Long-Term Content Is Synonymous with Cornerstone Content

Every good house needs a solid foundation, and every good marketing strategy needs cornerstone content to provide long-lasting value and relevance to readers. Cornerstone content is long-term content that might not draw a huge number of clicks right off the bat but remains valuable for months or years after the publishing date. Think of it as a down payment toward your own business.

In fact, if you look at some wonderful, powerful, and impactful blogs, you'll notice most of the most popular blog posts were written up to two years ago. How's that for an effective long-term strategy? In contrast, short-term content strategies are largely aimed at ranking well for a specific keyword or phrase, so they all but neglect cornerstone content entirely. Unfortunately, this leads to a less valuable and less relevant website for users of all types. For attracting long-term clicks and ensuring that a website's readers are engaged, entertained, and consuming value always, cornerstone content becomes more of an essential than a luxury.

7.5.5 Long-Term Content Doesn't Turn Off with A Hard Sell

In today's marketing environment, there is virtually nothing customers hate more than being hard sold. Nobody wants to know why they can't live without your product or why it's critical for them to "buy now!" Often, these approaches simply alienate customers and make it harder for your company to sell products naturally. Unfortunately, the hard sell is often a tone taken by short-term content. Because short-term content is insistent by nature, it's tough to engineer it so it doesn't push on your customers.

As a result, short-term content strategies run a high risk of alienating customers and making it more difficult to sell your product. Long-term content strategies, on the other hand, do not do such thing. Because they're not designed to elicit an immediate response from readers, they seek to provide value and relevance rather than insistence and immediacy. In other words, they succeed in explaining a problem, helping the audience handle the problem, and then inviting them to engage in a discussion about the problem. This, in turn, is a fantastic way to nurture long-term customer relationships and ensure that the company continues to meet the needs of its clients.

7.5.6 Long-Term Content Strategy Is an Effective Way to Approach Current Events

Do you think writing about trending news and industry events makes you a short-term content strategist? Think again. The trending content-focused blogs are extremely important, and it's a mistake to think of this as only a short-term strategy. In fact, trending news can be critical to long-term strategy, and can help establish the website as the source for up-to-date and relevant industry news. When the focus is on using trending, to-the-minute news pieces as a way to enhance and strengthen the long-term content strategy, it's easy to see how to improve brand presence and boost the business overall.

7.5.7 Long-Term Content Promotes Itself

Failing to promote the content is one of the most dangerous mistakes in the entire content marketing industry and, unfortunately, it's one many marketers make. While short-term content needs aggressive promotion to succeed, long-term content essentially promotes itself. When we create high-quality, in-depth, well-researched, long-term content and push it out to the followers, it's easy to rank well for the chosen keyword. Because long-term content is meant to garner clicks and shares over time, it's a great way to build steady, long-term rankings that can boost the placement and improve standing over time.

7.5.8 Long-Term Content Is Good Content

One of the differences between long-term content and short-term content comes down to priority and intention. Generally, people who commit to the pursuit and development of content for the long term are much more in love with content. While all types of content are important, creating good long-term content requires a different mindset and series of priorities than creating short-term content. Because of this, long-term content strategies often boast better content that caters more effectively to readers.

7.5.9 Long-Term Content Effectively Builds an Audience

When it comes to building an audience, don't aim for the largest audience possible. This will result in a massive but unengaged group of followers. Instead, build an audience of people who are genuinely interested in the concept and the content and will engage with it actively when it comes out. This is one of the areas in which long-term content strategy is so powerful. Fewer people have the attention span for long-term (or long-form) content today, and by making it a large part of the content strategy, we can build a better audience and earn more qualified leads.

7.5.10 Long-Term Content Is Best for SEO

SEO is a complex mix of strategies that companies need to succeed online. In addition to optimizing content correctly, companies that want to use good SEO also need to ensure their content is high-quality, relevant, and useful to their readers. While this can be difficult with a short-term content strategy, a long-term content strategy suits the goal quite nicely.

7.6 Statistic of Investment or Cost for Content Marketing in Enterprise

Content marketing is an expensive endeavor, regardless of its efficacy and popularity. A significant financial commitment is required to create your content marketing plan, regardless of whether you want to employ pricey marketing tools, pay content writers, or place paid media advertisements. The cost for content marketing depends upon strategy and can be segmented based on the value addition process in content marketing.

- Content planning and governance
- Content creation
- Content promotion
- Content analytics, optimization, and lead generation.

The governance style and the way in which the work is assigned by the content marketing team will determine the total cost of content marketing. As a channel, content marketing functions in sales, customer service, and product marketing departments of an organization. When a content writer produces sales enablement material, the sales team should also bear some of the expenses in addition to the content marketing team. When examining your content marketing expenses, take these elements into account as they are not insignificant. Several types of people can be involved in your content marketing team, and the costs of each content writer will vary depending on:

- Their experience
- Their skills
- Their location.

Since it would be hard to compute all of these factors, additional titles—such as "content marketing specialist," who often work for a content manager—as well as writers, copywriters, and other titles that are unique to content may be used to simplify this computation. According to Glassdoor, the average yearly compensation for a content marketing manager in the United States and the United Kingdom is $56,779 and $35,372, respectively. The following wages are shown in other nations:

- Canada: C$56,187 per year
- Germany: €49,310 per year
- India: ₹623,262/year.

7.7 AI-Powered Content Creation and Strategy

Content created by a machine is referred to as AI content production. These days, written content, such as blog entries, articles, and marketing copy, is often referred to as AI content generation. However, AI is also beginning to show promise in the production of audio and video. AI gets instructions, settings, or descriptions from humans. The material is generated by the machine in a matter of seconds or minutes. Because of this, you can often generate a large volume of information much more quickly than you could if you relied only on human writers or content producers. The AI tool you use to actually create AI-powered content is all that is meant to be understood when we discuss using AI for content development. These tools are quite powerful. Some people compose blog entries. Others create advertisement content or email subject lines. Even AI tools for content creation exist that will write anything on any subject for you. Nowadays, the majority of the best content creation tools concentrate on writing content.

7.8 The Best AI-Powered Content Generation and Strategy Tools

Which AI technologies, therefore, should be really used to produce content and develop more intelligent content strategies? After studying dozens of AI-powered marketing and sales solutions, a few that are mentioned below are among the greatest to look at.

7.8.1 HubSpot – AI-Powered Content Strategy

HubSpot's Content Strategy tool leverages machine learning to assist marketers in identifying high-performing content ideas and expeditiously validating those concepts. The program makes recommendations for subject clusters to investigate based on relevancy and competitiveness. Additionally, it automatically does competitive analysis on such subjects to see if they are worthwhile. As a consequence, creating effective content marketing campaigns requires less guessing and less labor, thanks to machine-assisted content strategy.

7.8.2 Concurred – AI Content Personalization

Concurred shows advertisers precisely what subjects generate engagement and what to write about next by using artificial intelligence and machine learning. The end product is an AI-driven content strategy platform that tracks the effectiveness of content marketing and automates tasks like subject research, content audits, data-driven content brief generation, and content promotion. All things considered, it's merely a more intelligent method of creating and planning content (Khang Abuzarova et al., 2023).

7.8.3 BrightEdge – AI-Powered Enterprise SEO

Search intent detection, optimal content production, and performance assessment are all combined into one cohesive system by BrightEdge, a pioneer in SEO and content performance marketing globally. Using artificial intelligence and machine learning, the solution finds out what people are looking for, helps create content that revolves around those phrases, and helps develop a content strategy to draw in more visitors and customers.

7.8.4 Crayon – AI-Powered Competitive Intelligence Software

When creating content marketing strategies, lack of fresh ideas can be a major time waster, as anyone who has hit a creative wall can attest. Crayon uses artificial intelligence and machine learning to give you competitive intelligence on exactly what your competitors are doing online. You'll be able to see how the main pages of a company's website change over time, which in turn reveals insights about their content marketing strategy, targeting, and messaging. This kind of information can be a goldmine of ideas for our content marketing efforts. Just search for the top competitors or brands we admire using Crayon, and get ready for a torrent of inspiration.

7.8.5 MarketMuse – AI Content Planning and Optimization

MarketMuse assists you in developing a content marketing strategy by using machine learning and artificial intelligence. The tool is going to tell you just the phrases you should aim for in order to compete in certain subject areas. It will also highlight subjects that you may need to focus on if you want to master them. The outcome? Artificial intelligence (AI)-driven SEO insights and suggestions that help direct your whole team and content development process.

7.8.6 Acrolinx – AI-Powered Content Governance

Major corporate brands may enhance the quality of their content generation at scale with the aid of Acrolinx, a platform for content strategy alignment. No matter who is creating the material, the tool employs advanced artificial intelligence that was created in one of Germany's leading artificial intelligence research labs to "read" it and ensure that it adheres to brand requirements. This entails evaluating and making improvements in hundreds of areas, such as content on-brandness, acceptable language and style, and tone of voice. Regardless of size or language of communication, the outcome is consistent, powerful content production across teams.

7.8.7 Cobomba – AI-Powered Content Intelligence

A content intelligence tool called Cobomba assists marketers in tailoring their message, content strategy, and marketing communications to consumers more effectively. With Cobomba, you can monitor your content analytics over time and track success at a large scale. Additionally, it provides astute advice on how to raise the efficacy of material (Khang & Shah et al., 2023).

7.8.8 Frase – AI-Powered Answer Bot

Frase creates outline briefings on various search queries using machine learning and artificial intelligence. It also has an AI-powered response chatbot that leverages your website's content to respond to inquiries from users. The chatbot interprets user inquiries using natural language processing (NLP) and then presents content on your website that provides pertinent responses.

It is possible to create and plan material more intelligently thanks to these two characteristics. With the help of the outlines, you can produce content more quickly by automatically summarizing articles and extracting pertinent data. The user queries that the response bot has gathered can also be used to guide your future writing. Any content marketer or content producer can create more intelligent content with the help of Frase's artificial intelligence and machine learning capabilities (Khang & Kali et al., 2023).

7.8.9 Automated Insights – Content Automation

Using natural language generation (NLG), Automated Insights is an AI content production platform that creates tales. You may create templates using the tool to convert data into content. After creating the template, you may use the AI tool to generate a written story by running a spreadsheet through it. With Automated Insights, you can create content automatically for a variety of use cases, including press releases, reports, and data-driven narratives that content writers may later refine.

7.8.10 HyperWrite – AI Writer

NLG is used by HyperWrite to compose whole phrases and paragraphs for you. With this tool, you may compose whole articles or simply start working on your next piece of content. Based on our own testing, we have found the tool to be entirely unique and mostly factually correct.

7.8.11 Jasper – AI Writer

Jasper creates short-form content for blogs, emails, landing pages, and social media platforms using AI. When you give Jasper an instruction, it will generate hundreds of short-form content ideas to help you get your next article started.

7.9 Case Study

7.9.1 Canva's Design Challenge Campaign

The well-known graphic design tool from Canva makes it simpler for influencers, brands, and artists worldwide to produce content. It started a weekly competition in 2022 where users could win some delicious rewards, such as a paid yearly subscription to Canva. Images for the #CanvaDesignChallenge must be distinctive, imaginative, and sometimes "out there." A group of Canva employees evaluates entries. At the conclusion of the week, they choose their top five. Visit Canva's Instagram page to see previous weekly winners or have a look at one of the challenges (Khang & Muthmainnah et al., 2023).

7.9.2 Learning from Canva case

It's the ideal illustration of how to foster user-generated content (UGC). With the hashtag #CanvaDesignChallenge, Canva has accumulated 36,000 posts since its introduction. Its crew no longer has to work very hard to decide what material to post on Instagram. Furthermore, Canva – a pioneer in creativity – allows its users to take on the role of experts. Canva pushes content producers to innovate and think outside the box. Additionally, it is creating a community of producers eager to use the tool and showcase their abilities as shown in Figure 7.4. How might the material produced by your brand benefit your audience in the same way?

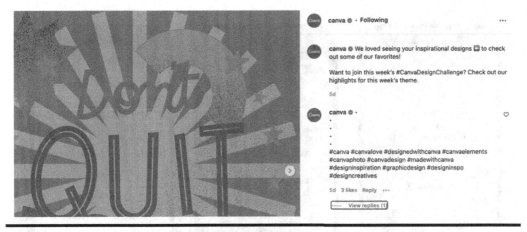

Figure 7.4 Mission statement of content in digital marketing managers.

7.9.3 Spotify Wrapped 2022

Among the most well-known instances of content marketing is Spotify Wrapped. This immersive marketing effort was initiated by the music streaming service back in 2016. Over 188 million people were Spotify customers as of 2022. That amounted to only 100 million in 2019. It's reasonable to argue that Spotify Wrapped greatly increased the number of users on the streaming service. Listeners may see their year-end data "Wrapped" up nicely for the holidays with this feature. Metrics such as the number of minutes listened, top musicians, and other interesting information specific to them are eagerly anticipated by users.

7.9.4 Learning from Sopity Case

Spotify Wrapped appeals to people's need to feel special while also being very shareable on social media. Even more companies are trying to run year-end marketing campaigns based on user data. When executed properly, immersive experiences may provide remarkable results, as shown in Figure 7.5.

7.10 Conclusion

Although it may first appear simpler to approach content as a sprint rather than a marathon, doing so will only cause your content to stagnate. Thought, time, and effort go into creating excellent, results-driven content. Content doesn't operate in the short term by nature; thus, it requires dedication to a long-term plan.

Your long-term objectives and plan will ultimately pay off with larger dividends and a better return on investment (ROI) if you put in the necessary time and effort. That results in time well spent. In the field of content marketing, consistency is crucial, as "the power of consistency: building long-term success with content marketing" emphasizes. To sum up, this book highlights a few important lessons:

■ **Consistency Is Key:** The main takeaway from the book is that content marketing requires consistency above all else. Building trust, credibility, and a devoted following takes time and consistent, high-quality content development.

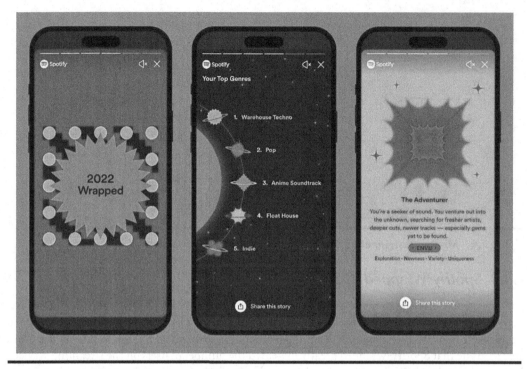

Figure 7.5 The advantage of user data is that you get to create something beneficial and marketable.

- **Content Quality Is Important**: Maintaining good content quality is just as crucial as maintaining consistency. Creating worthwhile and captivating material consistently is the key to long-term success.
- **Long-term Viewpoint**: Content marketing is a marathon, not a sprint. It's essential to have a long-term view and stick to your content strategy if you want to see benefits that last.
- **Knowing Your Audience:** It's essential to have a thorough awareness of the intended audience. Building enduring connections and increasing engagement need information that is specifically tailored to their needs and tastes.
- **Evolution and Adaptation:** Recognize how crucial it is to keep up with market developments and modify the content strategy as necessary. Be adaptable; what works now may not work tomorrow.
- **Measurement and Analysis**: It's critical to routinely measure and assess how well the material is doing. This data-driven method aids in plan optimization and effort refinement.
- **Developing a Brand:** One of the most effective ways to develop and strengthen your brand is via consistent content marketing. It aids in developing a unique personality that appeals to the intended market.

In a world where consumer behavior and digital surroundings are always evolving, "the power of consistency" serves as a useful reminder that content marketing is more than just passing trends or quick wins. It's all about the long game, where patience, hard effort, and tenacity are ultimately what lead to continuous success. Therefore, we should make consistency our guiding principle if we want to thrive in content marketing. If we do this, we will be well on our way to long-term, sustainable success (Aakansha & Adhishree et al., 2023).

References

Khang A., Abdullayev V. A., Alyar A. V., Khalilov M., Murad B. "AI-Aided Data Analytics Tools and Applications for the Healthcare Sector." *AI and IoT-Based Technologies for Precision Medicine.* (1st Ed.) (2023). IGI Global Press. ISBN: 9798369308769. https://doi.org/10.4018/979-8-3693-0876-9.ch018

Khang A., Muthmainnah M., Seraj P. M. I., Al Yakin A., Obaid A. J., Panda, M. R. "AI-Aided Teaching Model for the Education 5.0 Ecosystem." *AI-Based Technologies and Applications in the Era of the Metaverse.* (1st Ed.) (2023). Page (83–104). IGI Global Press. https://doi.org/10.4018/978-1-6684-8851-5.ch004

Khang A., Rath K. C., Satapathy S. K., Kumar A., Das S. R., Panda M. R. "Enabling the Future of Manufacturing: Integration of Robotics and IoT to Smart Factory Infrastructure in Industry 4.0." *AI-Based Technologies and Applications in the Era of the Metaverse.* (1st Ed.) (2023). Page (25–50). IGI Global Press. https://doi.org/10.4018/978-1-6684-8851-5.ch002

Khang A., Shah V., Rani S. *AI-Based Technologies and Applications in the Era of the Metaverse* (1st Ed.). (2023). IGI Global Press. https://doi.org/10.4018/978-1-6684-8851-5

Saxena A. C., Ojha A., Sobti D., Khang A. "Artificial Intelligence (AI) Centric Model in Metaverse Ecosystem." *AI-Based Technologies and Applications in the Era of the Metaverse.* (1st Ed.) (2023). Page (1–24). IGI Global Press. https://doi.org/10.4018/978-1-6684-8851-5.ch001

Chapter 8

Influence of Artificial Intelligence Competencies on Business Value: B2B Marketing Capabilities Context

Pankaj A. Tiwari and Alex Khang

8.1 Introduction

Progressively, the existence of a huge amount of information on digital devices has shaped a revived significance of artificial intelligence (AI) across various domains as the need for AI deployment to enhance competitiveness by organizations in the dynamic environment. AI is not recognized by senior management as a fundamental competency that companies should drive in the long term to remain competitive (Mikalef et al., 2021). One of the potential areas of AI usage within internal operations for an organization is business-to-business (B2B) marketing.

To strengthen the offerings of B2B marketing, intelligent solutions are required in the dynamic business environment to overcome the substantial informational complexity and for decision-making. Considering this view, the potential of AI can be applied to transform conventional activities to process large amounts of information and offer business understandings to primary stakeholders (Shin & Kang, 2022). Moreover, applications based on AI have been recommended to facilitate the automation of many manual business processes to overcome business-driven blockages and improve day-to-day business-oriented operational efficiency.

Even though the use of artificial intelligence can improve business-to-business marketing undertakings, a significant number of companies continue to be reluctant to leverage AI-specific funds to bring business value. Existing literature (such as Collins et al., 2021) argues that AI investments need thorough orientation with organizational maneuvers. Alternatively, it is notable that AI is observed as a substantial enabler for organizations and their key operations by improving appropriate AI applications.

DOI: 10.4324/9781032688305-8

Prior research has argued on AI adoption, and the way organizations should strategically prepare for AI deployment to have a competitive advantage. To date, there is a limited understanding of this. The research objective of this study is to assess how the B2B context can reduce the failed deployment of AI within organizational operations. Additionally, there are a few significant barriers to the adoption and application of AI in businesses that transcend technical difficulties. The study also aims to investigate the value of AI adoption, which makes it more difficult to implement important organizational (Rana & Khang et al., 2021).

However, a survey carried out by McKinsey recently emphasized the usage of AI related to optimizing services in organizations and processes that relate to B2B marketing. However, there were still various challenges related to achieving business value based on AI reserves, particularly in determining a business requirement-setting for the artificial intelligence-based capability that might be continuously implemented. This study supports the core competency theory by Prahalad (1993) in order to fill the identified research gap and to generate an understanding of AI use in organizations. The following research inquiries are consequently endeavored to be answered by this study:

- Research Question 1: In what ways do AI competencies influence business value?
- Research Question 2: How do AI competencies translate into business value?

8.2 Review of Literature

8.2.1 Business-to-Business Marketing Capabilities

Businesses engaged in B2B transactions must establish dependable connections with their customers. Consequently, links and inter-organizational interactions are key components of B2B marketing. B2C marketing prioritizes public relations and brand building, while the complex interactions built into B2B marketing necessitate increased credibility and confidence between consumers and suppliers. In a B2B context, customers are usually treated individually, while consumer marketing targets many customers who do not necessarily require individual treatment. But in each case, know-how in marketing is essential for an enterprise to succeed.

The capabilities of marketing (MC) are described as the ability of an organization to perform tasks using the assets that a business has dedicated to accomplishing its goals (Herhausen et al., 2020). As per Guo et al. (2018), the ability of an organization to efficiently arrange and deploy resources to forge a long-lasting competitive edge is improved by its marketing competencies. Consequently, MC is a comprehensive amalgamation of organizational abilities and assets that are specific to the firm and extremely challenging for rivals to reproduce. Previous studies have divided MC into different classes, viz. inward, outward, and traversing. External competencies arise from within the organizational arrangement and fit into various functions, while external competencies come from the marketplace and aid businesses in understanding their clients and rivals.

Finally, holistic integration encompasses the organization's processes inside as well as outside, comprehending the organization's internal business processes and the market. Thus, comprehensive marketing skills link mutually in–out and out-in abilities. Santos-Vijande et al. (2012) noted that "when [a company] claims that it has all kinds of capabilities, it can be assumed that they have developed internal and external capabilities in the past." These skills involve forming and implementing marketing tactics, policies, and programs (Khang & AIoCF.17, 2024).

Both internal and external processes drive the implementation and utilization of AI-based marketing. In this study, we investigate B2B marketing opportunities using comprehensive attributes. In particular, the integrated functions such as implementation, planning, and management of information within marketing are selected in this study. Information management within marketing is the capacity of an organization to obtain and explore significant knowledge from various sponsors to develop efficient programs.

Marketing planning ability anticipates changes in the market environment and responds strategically to them, which further contributes to the achievement of organizational goals. Finally, marketing execution capability refers to the implementation, management, and evaluation of marketing. An arising argument about whether artificial intelligence is affecting businesses' B2B marketing has emerged in recent years. A growing body of research indicates that firms involved in B2B marketing are quickly integrating AI into their operations by streamlining or enhancing crucial activities (Rusthollkarhu et al., 2022). This body of research and practical experiences from the business world demonstrate the way AI might improve client comprehension, better customization and design accuracy, and better customer experience.

As a result, there are wide subjective arguments about the probable use of AI in business-to-business marketing operations based on various technical expertise. In order to examine such diverse applications of artificial intelligence, researchers have underlined that it is crucial for enterprises to build AI competencies (Lundin & Kindström, 2023). Earlier studies recommend that the use of artificial intelligence in B2B marketing can help businesses to influence a wider range of targeted customers, by improving the efficiency of current maneuvers but also unlocking opportunities with novel ideas.

8.2.2 Artificial Intelligence-Based Competencies

Artificial intelligence is a subfield of computer science with a long history. Although AI has historically been largely confined to the theoretical realm, recent advances in information generation and data processing have enabled AI to advance from concept to application. The advances in technology that comprise the idea of artificial intelligence have been presented in a variety of forms and serve primarily as techniques to address challenging issues that take a while to resolve, and secondly, as a system that replicates behavioral and psychological processes in humans, and in other words, as intelligent computer agents (Khang & Rani et al., 2023).

Artificial intelligence (AI) systems are created and evolved is one of its tenets to work according to predefined requirements based on available information and knowledge (Paschen et al., 2020). The requirement emphasizes the way AI systems may draw deductions from analyzing information and acquiring knowledge from previous encounters using machine learning. Machine learning-based artificial intelligence algorithms can adapt the way they process to take into account newly obtained information. Thus, the main difference from other prior decision-making or assistance methods is that such algorithms have inherent adaptability because these methods adapt on the basis of novel feedback.

Despite the most recent major advancements in artificial intelligence (AI) systems, several companies still find it difficult to utilize them effectively (Collins et al., 2021). An increasing body of literature on the subject highlights that the context of organizations is largely to blame for the difficulties in fully utilizing AI's capabilities. Parallel to this, a few well-known firms have successfully incorporated artificial intelligence into their daily operations and discovered ways to make such technology an avenue of financial gain. Such cases showed how the instrumentation of artificial intelligence can be established as a primary competence of the firm, bringing substantial structural benefits.

The AI competency concept, consequently, expands traditional thinking about merely evolving AI-based systems to include their design and implementation within organizational environments to facilitate value creation. In order to make a distinction between basic technologies (AI technologies) and fundamental abilities (AI competencies), the study of artificial intelligence (AI) reflects an extensive lineage of academic research. As a result, AI's proficiency includes not only the technology supporting it or the technical know-how necessary to use it efficiently but also the creative fusion of such innovations, organizational expertise, and frameworks into a unified environment.

Latest surveys and research on the use of AI among leading organizations emphasize that the capability to extract business value is indeed related to the capability to integrate AI into innovative developments. Therefore, the creative organization and assembly of artificial intelligence technologies in a business improvement way requires the existence of artificial intelligence expertise. Based on previous information systems literature, the concept of AI expertise is defined (Collins et al., 2021). It contends that AI competencies should have three key traits in accordance with the framework of abilities put forth by Prahalad (1993).

Firstly, it is important to have the technical ability to manage technology and have the potential to differentiate from the competition effectively and efficiently. Secondly, this should support various business functions and encompass a set of processes. Thirdly, competitors must be challenging to reproduce, which necessitates an emphasis on ongoing exploration and proactivity. Together, each of these components supports the development of AI expertise.

8.2.3 Business Value

The notion of "business value" is frequently used in financial management and economics. It is used generally for an extended period to determine the business's well-being and incorporate several ideals. While conducting the literature research, it was discovered that professionals only consider the commercial value of the business process when converting beneficial outcomes into monetary value (by translating the valuable work products). In the economic sciences, business value is not offered as a concept.

Organizations devote a significant amount of time and effort to enhance long-term business results by executing IT projects that deliver value to the business. Outlining company value is a common deliberation that can be defined in several ways based on the environment, objective, and purpose. Business value, on the other hand, is an intuitive notion that includes various types of values that represent an organization's health and well-being. The supposed utilization value, which is explicitly assessed by the user who utilizes the offerings, and the valuation, depending on the amount charged, are the two types of business values (Khang & Medicine, 2023).

Many studies examine the company's value from diverse viewpoints. To ensure an organization's competitiveness, all views concur on accounting for both perceived utilization value and valuation. It is proposed that when making decisions, organizations should appraise both pros and cons. In addition, organizations always work to increase the beneficial aspects of decision-making and reduce the drawbacks (Ghasemaghaei, 2020). According to Schwartz (2017), using a single metric to measure business value is incorrect. Organizations should evaluate a set of indicators to reflect the business, most of which may or may not be quantified, to fulfill the demands of the project sponsors. Khurum et al. (2013) focused on the economic benefit of IT development. They argued that the drivers for success in IT firms are their abilities to build and render a project that meets the needs of customers and offers value, leading to success in business. As a result, business value is as diverse as the organization itself (Gregor et al., 2006).

8.3 Theoretical Background

To address the stated research questions, this chapter draws on the core competency theory (Prahalad, 1993) and proposes a theoretical framework for the use of artificial intelligence within the limits of the organization, following the central principles of the theory. In particular, it is argued that the concept of AI capability as an essential competence of firms emphasizes the necessity for an innovative and appropriate application of AI. The theory recommends that AI expertise can be developed by organizations that can achieve a competitive advantage over their competitors.

Since AI implementations are customized, several entities within an organization need to collaborate holistically to complete business operations that are difficult to imitate and produce value. The conceptual framework and corresponding hypotheses built on this concept contend that AI knowledge can improve business-to-business marketing opportunities in the next section.

8.4 Hypotheses Development and Conceptual Framework

As per the available literature and theoretical support, it is argued that competencies for AI are significant for organizations to realize business success. The three underlying pillars of AI competencies, such as infrastructure for an organization, ability to span the business, and proactiveness, enhance B2B marketing capabilities. Also, these are substantial in achieving business value. Thus, it is proposed that the impact of AI-based competencies on business value is direct (Figure 8.1)

The effectiveness of marketing activities is based on market research conducted by the organization. When conducting market research, an organization needs to consider market developments, consumers, rivals, and various other significant parties into account. Information may be gathered for market research from a variety of resources (such as reports from within and outside

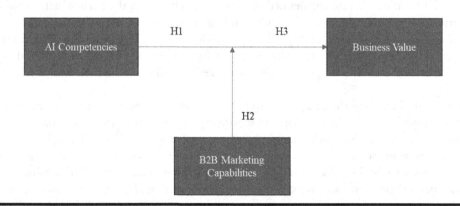

Figure 8.1 Summarizes the hypotheses and the conceptual framework.

the company, social networking sites, etc.). Analyzing these different types of information and distinguishing information requires AI skills. The use of artificial intelligence technologies in marketplace investigation and decision support can aid organizations in making more informed choices (Khang & AIoCF, 2024).

Previous findings often combined marketing abilities with business success. For instance, Mariadoss et al. (2011) argued that capabilities related to marketing influence technical as well as nontechnical improvements, which influence the competitive advantage of an organization resulting in business value. Whereas Morgan et al. (2009) established a direct effect of marketing capability on organizational performance and, in turn, business success. Kamboj and Rahman (2015) argued that marketing capability has a compelling impact on business success and value. Information management in marketing is to be considered as the ability to obtain and examine significant information from various sponsors to develop efficient marketing tactics (Cavazos-Arroyo & Puente-Diaz, 2019).

Consequently, enhanced market information management can offer managers the latest data when required. It can furthermore benefit managers by serving customers to increase customer satisfaction, company revenue, and productivity. An organization can make decisions that increase productivity and overall performance by integrating marketing intelligence management technologies driven by AI. In addition, the information created with the help of artificial intelligence technologies can offer novel insights, and thus, the business can find innovative opportunities and generate ideas for the market faster than competitors.

Marketing planning relates to the adeptness to foresee changes in the market environment and strategically respond to them, which further contributes to the achievement of long-term goals and objectives. An organization can connect its diverse resources and develop successful marketing strategies by using comprehensive marketing planning. In today's highly competitive environment, predicting and proactively responding to ever-shifting markets is essential. In today's unpredictable economy, a business will fail if the appropriate actions are not taken in a timely manner. AI-based marketing planning can present several options by taking into account past market data, rivals, all parties involved, and industry trends, amongst other factors. To remain competitive in the marketplace and increase profitability, innovative organizations innovate and investigate various approaches to operation (Ravichandran, 2018).

Finally, marketing execution capability refers to the implementation, management, and evaluation of marketing approaches. Marketing planning is about organizing fluctuating markets, while marketing execution relates to performing operations and assigning resources. To constantly adapt to the marketplace and achieve success in business, it is necessary to evaluate and realize different marketing tactics. Acting as needed can improve operational, financial, and marketing results. Utilizing artificial intelligence technological advances, the organization may make decisions against rivals efficiently and rapidly, which will improve the efficiency and effectiveness of the organization (Wamba-Taguimdje et al., 2020). Additionally, more successful businesses may pool resources to execute novel marketing strategies that complement their business models, or even update their current business plans in response to marketing activity evaluations. Hence, proposed:

- H1: AI competencies have a substantial influence on business value.
- H2: B2B information management capabilities have a substantial influence on business value.
- H3: The B2B marketing capabilities moderate the association between AI competencies and business value.

8.5 Research Methodology

8.5.1 Sampling

For the hypothesis analysis, a sample size of 137 data points was collected. To assess the effects of AI Competencies and B2B marketing capabilities on business value, technology organizations were chosen for the study. In total, approximately 300 respondents were emailed to answer a questionnaire based on Google Forms. The data cleansing and analysis process involved thoroughly validating each response and considering the participants from the targeted organizations (Hair et al., 2011). The rate of response to the survey was 26.8%. There were no significant differences (alpha 5%) among the earlier and subsequent responses (Podsakoff et al., 2003). Participants in various positions/roles were contacted to reduce the bias risk as per the common-method variance to assess the study variables.

8.5.2 Sample and Respondents' Characteristics

As the chart shown in Figure 8.2 indicates the sample attributes, most of the respondents, were from a firm size between 101 and 200 employees and belonged to director/senior vice president roles considering 2 to 3 years of overall AI experience in IT organizations.

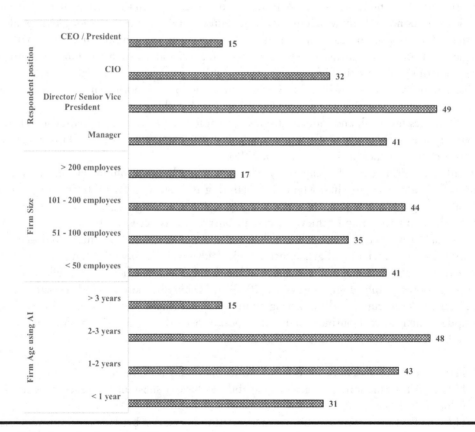

Figure 8.2 Sample characteristics.

8.5.3 Study Variables

The measures were constructed on multiple-item scales as reviewed from the information system literature and the latest studies performed. Some of the items were rephrased and altered to fit into the scope of the present research. Three domain experts relating to the sample organization were inquired to evaluate measures (Hair et al., 2011), and a pilot test was carried out to validate the appropriate meaning to the respondent (Nunnally, 1978). Using partial confirmatory factor analysis (PCFA), the validity of all item scales was confirmed, followed by confirmatory factor analysis (CFA).

The PCFA was conducted to examine all items loaded in one factor. Cronbach's alpha (α) values appropriate values were found to be greater than 0.7 for the scale reliability. A confirmatory factor analysis (CFA) was performed to validate the measurement model and is considered satisfactory at CMIN/DF = 2.837, CFI = 0.924, RMSEA = 0.069, and SRMR = 0.031 (Guide & Ketokivi, 2015; Hu & Bentler, 1999).

The independent variable AI Competence is assessed with the help of a 13-item scale (α = 0.798) recommended by Lu and Ramamurthy (2011). The dependent variable **Business Value** is determined by applying a 9-item scale (α = 0.875) established by Gregor et al. (2006). The moderating variable of B2B marketing capabilities is calculated using nine items (α = 0.882), as suggested by Vorhies and Morgan (2005). The control variable used in the study is *firm size*, which is one of the important metrics of business value and is evaluated with a scale reformed by Mikalef and Gupta (2021) and denoted by the natural logarithm of the average number of employees.

8.6 Research Outcomes

This study adds value to information systems literature and different practices by examining the moderation effect of B2B marketing capabilities on AI competence and business value in IT organizations using descriptive statistics as shown in Table 8.1.

Table 8.1 indicates the descriptive statistics with the mean and standard deviation values along with the correlation between different study variables.

Table 8.1 Descriptive Statistics

		Variables	0	1	2
		Mean	3.574	3.152	3.043
		Std. Dev.	1.153	1.318	1.233
		Reliability	0.875	0.798	0.882
Kendall's tau-b	0	Business value	1		
	1	AI Competencies	0.563***	1	
	2	B2B market capabilities	0.435***	0.374***	1
Spearman's rho	0	Business value	1		
	1	AI competencies	0.634***	1	
	2	B2B market capabilities	0.597***	0.469***	1

*** Correlation is significant at the 0.01 level (2 tailed)

8.7 Ordinal Regression Method for Moderation Analysis

The association between ordinal outcome variables is examined in the current study, i.e., business value, artificial intelligence competence, and B2B marketing capabilities. An ordinal, categorical, and five-point Likert scale was used for assessing the study variables. The ordinal categorical results could not be assumed to be normal or to have homogeneous variance. The ordinal regression method was used because it requires the assumption of parallel lines across each stage of the categorical outcome rather than constant variance and normality (Tiwari et al., 2021; Norusis, 2008). Prior to running the regression analysis, diagnostic tests were conducted to check for any violations of preconceived notions. None of the variables had values that were missing. Additionally, the SPSS tool was used to analyze the findings using the ordinal regression method, as shown in Table 8.2.

Table 8.2 represents the outcomes of the ordinal regression method used for data analysis. To quantify the independent variable's direct influence on business value, Model 1 established artificial intelligence competencies ($B = .838$, $p < 0.001$) along with the control variable, i.e., firm size ($B = .121$, $p < 0.001$). Model 1 shows the significant direct impacts of artificial intelligence competencies on business value and explains 50.2% of the variation using the Cox and Snell pseudo-R^2.

The moderating variable B2B marketing competencies ($B = .312$, $p < 0.001$) is included in Model 2 along with the independent variable artificial intelligence competencies ($B = .568$, $p < 0.001$). Similarly, the variables in Model 2 explained a 59.7% variation in business value. Model 3 introduced the interaction between artificial intelligence (AI) Competencies ($B = .245$, $p < 0.001$)

Table 8.2 Ordinal Regression Analysis

Variables	Business value					
	Model 1		Model 2		Model 3	
Control variable						
Firm size	0.125***	0.011	0.112***	0.021	0.026***	0.012
Independent variable						
AI competencies	0.838***	0.016	0.568***	0.017	0.245***	0.089
Moderating variable						
B2B marketing capabilities			0.312***	0.034	0.178***	0.076
Interaction						
AI competencies *B2B marketing capabilities					0.313***	0.086
-2 log likelihood	447.768		452.771		472.771	
Likelihood ratio (chi-square)	87.256***		113.636***		125.283***	
Pesudo R^2 Cox and Snell	0.532		0.598		0.659	

Notes: N = 137 1. Unstandardized regression coefficients and standard errors are shown.

****Significance at the 0.001 level (2-tailed).*

and B2B marketing capabilities (B = .178, p < 0.001). Model 3 described a 63.3% variation in business value. The variation inflation factor (VIF) was found with a value of 2.16.

8.8 Discussion of the Research Findings

In the present chapter, it is recognized whether AI enables organizations to achieve B2B performance and, if so, by what means. This chapter builds a theory of core competencies to conceptualize AI competencies that are outside the technical aspects of AI. By applying the same concept, it is argued that businesses that can encourage AI expertise will achieve business value through their B2B activities. It is argued that AI capabilities enable businesses to foster business-to-business marketing along with planning and application. The hypothesized relationships were investigated the ordinal regression method based on the responses of 137 technology professionals.

8.9 Conclusion

Based on studies investigating the importance of artificial intelligence, the objective of this research was to recognize the conditions where artificial intelligence can create organizational business value. To respond to the research inquiry, the concept of an artifact of artificial intelligence on the theory of core competencies was referred to. Therefore, it is focused on AI expertise from the perspective of an organization's key capability that can give organizations a competitive advantage.

AI expertise is therefore not only viewed from a technical perspective but includes management's ability to innovatively visualize efforts that add business value and include the capacity to explore novel AI usage through experimentation. This method views AI proficiency as a core competency that businesses should work to develop rather than merely a group of additional abilities that can assist tasks.

By emphasizing the unique way these AI competencies are produced and retained in businesses, conceptualizing AI competency in this way highlights its importance. This strategy has the implication that each organization must develop these AI competencies in a particular way based on a variety of factors, including the industry, organizational history, organizational culture, and factors describing the business setting. This study's conclusion regarding how AI competencies benefit enterprises is another significant discovery. Research has shown that enhancing B2B marketing capabilities could potentially impact organizational performance.

This research emphasizes how changeable AI competencies are and how they may be applied to various organizational tasks that may be made possible or improved by various AI techniques. This study notably illustrated the potential benefits of B2B marketing, a crucial component of every company's operation. Organizations get an edge over rivals by expediting such procedures through the focused deployment of AI solutions. As they include intricate and constantly changing scenarios, B2B marketing functions present many chances for the application of AI (Khang & Kali et al., 2023).

AI can rapidly analyze data and deliver pertinent insights in these circumstances. Additionally, artificial intelligence can be used to automate many tasks related to B2B marketing activities or to improve the collaboration between humans and artificial intelligence. The most interesting finding from the empirical investigation is that not all forms of B2B marketing abilities are equally impacted by AI competencies. It is found that the scope of implementation options is smaller than managing the marketing information. This is likely attributed to the simple fact that knowledge management tasks are simpler to integrate with AI in B2B scenarios than implementation operations.

Consequently, AI implementation in certain functions is even more difficult, which can give organizations a competitive advantage. It is additionally emphasized that businesses that can have excellent B2B marketing execution capabilities also have superior business outcomes. The main premises of the core competency theory, which state that businesses can achieve a competitive advantage by developing a distinct and challenging-to-imitate skill, are supported by this research. Furthermore, the findings demonstrate that, although AI can generate value through the three B2B marketing options, those channels are not the only ones to create overall value.

8.10 Study Limitations and Recommendations for Future Research

The importance of AI insights to enhance B2B marketing capabilities and eventually organizational performance has been emphasized in this research, but it has some limits. First, despite the processes through which AI competencies enhance B2B marketing capabilities in this study report, the chosen methodology only allows for inferred causality and makes major impact assumptions. There are likely to be fundamentally different approaches to leverage AI knowledge to better B2B marketing in various firms, nevertheless, given the sample from technology organizations (Rana & Khang et al., 2021).

Such findings may not highlight challenges for other industries or a specific type of AI application. Also, this study is based on a survey-based approach, which limits data collection in a limited timeframe. By itself, the impact of AI expertise on business-to-business marketing opportunities may be spurious because of delayed causes. To better observe the impact of AI abilities on business phenomena, future research can choose a delayed approach to collecting performance-based evidence or, instead, employ objective-based performance methods. Finally, while these findings emphasize the scope and systems of AI in transforming B2B marketing opportunities, they also encourage future research to find how such effects can be interpreted into practical relevance (Khang & Shah et al., 2023).

Although this research is an eminent step in defining the manner AI is organized in companies and the mechanisms for value creation, further research is needed on identifiable forms of AI applications and challenges to implement. Since the influence of AI competencies on business value is moderated by the B2B capabilities mentioned above, this suggests that there are additional ways that AI can offer value that this study did not cover. The significance of such interventions for subsequent studies is shown by the degree to which B2B marketing features promote business value outcomes (Khang & Muthmainnah et al., 2023).

References

Cavazos-Arroyo, J., & Puente-Diaz, R. (2019). The influence of marketing capability in Mexican social enterprises. *Sustainability*, 11(17), 4668. https://doi.org/10.3390/su11174668

Collins, C., Dennehy, D., Conboy, K., & Mikalef, P. (2021). Artificial intelligence in information systems research: A systematic literature review and research agenda. *International Journal of Information Management*, 60, Article 102383. https://doi.org/10.1016/j.ijinfomgt.2021.102383

Ghasemaghaei, M. (2020). The role of positive and negative valence factors on the impact of bigness of data on big data analytics usage. *International Journal of Information Management*, 50, 395–404. https://doi.org/10.1016/j.ijinfomgt.2018.12.011

Gregor, S., Martin, M., Fernandez, W., Stern, S., & Vitale, M. (2006). The transformational dimension in the realization of business value from information technology. *The Journal of Strategic Information Systems*, 15(3), 249–270. https://doi.org/10.1016/j.jsis.2006.04.001

Guide Jr, V. D. R., & Ketokivi, M. (2015). Notes from the editors: Redefining some methodological criteria for the journal. *Journal of Operations Management*, 37(1), v–viii. https://doi.org/10.1016/j.jom.2017.05.001

Guo, Z., & Dong, B. (2018). Comparing the impact of different marketing capabilities: Empirical evidence from B2B firms in China. *Journal of Business Research*, 93, 79–89. https://doi.org/10.1016/j.jbusres.2018.04.010

Hair, J. F., Ringle, C. M., & Sarstedt, M. (2011). PLS-SEM: Indeed a silver bullet. *Journal of Marketing Theory and Practice*, 19(2), 139–152. https://doi.org/10.2753/MTP1069-6679190202

Herhausen, D., Mioˇceviˊc, D., Morgan, R. E., & Kleijnen, M. H. (2020). The digital marketing capabilities gap. *Industrial Marketing Management*, 90, 276–290. https://doi.org/10.2753/MTP1069-6679190202

Hu, L. T., & Bentler, P. M. (1999). Cutoff criteria for fit indexes in covariance structure analysis: Conventional criteria versus new alternatives. *Structural Equation Modeling: A Multidisciplinary Journal*, 6(1), 1–55. https://doi.org/10.1080/10705519909540118

Kamboj, S., & Rahman, Z. (2015). Marketing capabilities and firm performance: Literature review and future research agenda. *International Journal of Productivity and Performance Management*, 64(8), 1041–1067. https://doi.org/10.1108/IJPPM-08-2014-0117

Khang, A. (2023). *AI and IoT-Based Technologies for Precision Medicine* (1st Ed.). IGI Global Press. ISBN: 9798369308769. https://doi.org/10.4018/979-8-3693-0876-9

Khang, A., & AIoCF. (2024). *AI-Oriented Competency Framework for Talent Management in the Digital Economy: Models, Technologies, Applications, and Implementation* (1st Ed.). CRC Press. ISBN: 9781032576053. https://doi.org/10.1201/9781003440901

Khang, A., & AIoCF.17. (2024). Design and modelling of AI-Oriented Competency Framework (AIoCF) for information technology sector. *AI-Oriented Competency Framework for Talent Management in the Digital Economy: Models, Technologies, Applications, and Implementation* (1st Ed.) CRC Press. ISBN: 9781032576053. https://doi.org/10.1201/9781003440901-17

Khang, A., Muthmainnah, M., Seraj, P. M. I., Al Yakin, A., Obaid, A. J., & Panda, M. R. (2023). AI-aided teaching model for the education 5.0 ecosystem. In *AI-Based Technologies and Applications in the Era of the Metaverse* (1st Ed.) Page (83–104). IGI Global Press. https://doi.org/10.4018/978-1-6684-8851-5.ch004

Khang, A., Rath, K. C., Satapathy, S. K., Kumar, A., Das, S. R., & Panda, M. R. (2023). Enabling the future of manufacturing: Integration of robotics and IoT to smart factory infrastructure in industry 4.0. *AI-Based Technologies and Applications in the Era of the Metaverse* (1st Ed.). Page (25–50). IGI Global Press. https://doi.org/10.4018/978-1-6684-8851-5.ch002

Khang, A., Shah, V., & Rani, S. (2023). *AI-Based Technologies and Applications in the Era of the Metaverse* (1st Ed.). IGI Global Press. https://doi.org/10.4018/978-1-6684-8851-5

Khurum, M., Gorschek, T., & Wilson, M. (2013). The software value map— An exhaustive collection of value aspects for the development of software intensive products. *Journal of Software: Evolution and Process*, 25(7), 711–741. https://doi.org/10.1002/smr.1560

Lu, Y., & (Ram) Ramamurthy, K. (2011). Understanding the link between information technology capability and organizational agility: An empirical examination. *MIS Quarterly*, 931–954. https://doi.org/10.2307/41409967

Lundin, L., & Kindstrom, D. (2023). Digitalizing customer journeys in B2B markets. *Journal of Business Research*, 157, Article 113639. https://doi.org/10.1016/j.jbusres.208.113639

Mariadoss, B. J., Tansuhaj, P. S., & Mouri, N. (2011). Marketing capabilities and innovation-based strategies for environmental sustainability: An exploratory investigation of B2B firms. *Industrial Marketing Management*, 40(8), 1305–1318. https://doi.org/10.1016/j.indmarman.2011.10.006

Mikalef, P., & Gupta, M. (2021). Artificial intelligence capability: Conceptualization, measurement calibration, and empirical study on its impact on organizational creativity and firm performance. *Information & Management*, Online. https://doi.org/10.1016/j.im.2021.103434

Morgan, N. A., Vorhies, D. W., & Mason, C. H. (2009). Market orientation, marketing capabilities, and firm performance. *Strategic Management Journal*, 30(8), 909–920. https://doi.org/10.1002/smj.764

Norusis, M. (2008). *SPSS 16.0 Statistical Procedures Companion*. Prentice Hall Press. https://dl.acm.org/doi/abs/10.5555/1628756

Nunnally, J. C. (1978). An overview of psychological measurement. *Clinical Diagnosis of Mental Disorders: A Handbook* Page (97–146). https://doi.org/10.1007/978-1-4684-2490-4_4

Paschen, J., Wilson, M., & Ferreira, J. J. (2020). Collaborative intelligence: How human and artificial intelligence create value along the B2B sales funnel. *Business Horizons*, 63(3), 403–414. https://doi.org10.1016/j.bushor.2020.01.003

Podsakoff, P. M., MacKenzie, S. B., Lee, J. Y., & Podsakoff, N. P. (2003). Common method biases in behavioral research: A critical review of the literature and recommended remedies. *Journal of Applied Psychology*, 88(5), 879. https://doi.org/10.1037/0021-9010.88.5.879

Prahalad, C. K. (1993). The role of core competencies in the corporation. *Research Technology Management*, 36(6), 40–47. https://doi.org/10.1080/08956308.1993.11670940

Rana, G., Khang, A., Sharma, R., Goel, A. K., & Dubey, A. K. (2021). *Reinventing Manufacturing and Business Processes through Artificial Intelligence* (1st Ed.). CRC Press. https://doi.org/10.1201/9781003145011

Ravichandran, T. (2018). Exploring the relationships between IT competence, innovation capacity and organizational agility. *The Journal of Strategic Information Systems*, 27(1), 22–42. https://doi.org/10.1016/j.jsis.2017.07.002

Rusthollkarhu, S., Toukola, S., Aarikka-Stenroos, L., & Mahlamaki, T. (2022). Managing B2B customer journeys in digital era: Four management activities with artificial intelligence-empowered tools. *Industrial Marketing Management*, 104, 241–257. https://doi.org/10.1016/j.indmarman.208.04.014

Santos-Vijande, L., Sanzo-Pérez, M., Trespalacios Gutiérrez, J., & Rodríguez, N. (2012). Marketing capabilities development in small and medium enterprises: Implications for performance. *Journal of CENTRUM Cathedra: The Business and Economics Research Journal*, 5(1), 24–42. https://ssrn.com/abstract=2018367

Schwartz, M. (2017). *A Seat at the Table and the Art of Business Value. It Revolution*. EBook: Schwartz. https://www.google.com/books?hl=en&lr=&id=J6x-DwAAQBAJ&oi=fnd&pg=PT7

Shin, S., & Kang, J. (2022). Structural features and diffusion patterns of Gartner hype cycle for artificial intelligence using social network analysis. *Journal of Intelligence and Information Systems*, 28(1), 107–129. https://doi.org/10.13088/jiis.208.28.1.107

Tiwari, P., & Suresha, B. (2021). Moderating role of project innovativeness on project flexibility, project risk, project performance, and business success in financial services. *Global Journal of Flexible Systems Management*, 22(3), 179–196. https://doi.org/10.1007/s40171-021-00270-0

Vorhies, D. W., & Morgan, N. A. (2005). Benchmarking marketing capabilities for sustainable competitive advantage. *Journal of Marketing*, 69(1), 80–94. https://doi.org/10.1509/jmkg.69.1.80.55505

Wamba-Taguimdje, S. L., Fosso Wamba, S., Kala Kamdjoug, J. R., & Tchatchouang Wanko, C. E. (2020). Influence of artificial intelligence (AI) on firm performance: The business value of AI-based transformation projects. *Business Process Management Journal*, 26(7), 1893–1924. https://doi.org/10.1108/BPMJ-10-2019-0411

Chapter 9

Challenges Hindering Women's Involvement in the Hospitality Industry as Entrepreneurs in the Era of Digital Economy

Jyoti Kumari, Praveen Singh, Amar Kumar Mishra,
Bhanu Pratap Singh Meena, Archana Singh, and Megha Ojha

9.1 Introduction

One in five women throughout the world intends to launch a business, and many of them are successful business owners. Even though women own and operate successful businesses, there are still significant inequities in the prospects for business startups and expansion. Their enterprises are typically smaller than those operated by males, concentrated in industries with little room for value addition, and over-represented in the unofficial sector of the economy. These difficulties are made worse by the caregiving responsibilities of women, which put additional strain on their time, workloads, and well-being. They are also made worse by unfavorable institutional environments, which may lead to unequal access to land and decision-making positions as well as insufficient social protection coverage.

The act of starting a firm to make money using one's creativity and business acumen while simultaneously taking on all the associated risks is known as entrepreneurship. Technical excellence, inventiveness, initiative, excellent judgment, intelligence, leadership qualities, electricity, proper opinion, originality, objectivity, and authenticity are important attributes of prosperous entrepreneurs.

One of the key elements in the economic development of any country is believed to be entrepreneurship. It has long been believed that entrepreneurs play a crucial role in launching and sustaining socioeconomic progress. There is evidence to support the idea that nations with

DOI: 10.4324/9781032688305-9

a proportionately higher percentage of entrepreneurs in their population have progressed more quickly than nations with a lower share.

Tact and emotional stability, cooperation, strong tolerance, and the capacity to take risks are essential to the growth and development of our nation. Entrepreneurs are responsible for shaping the economy through developing new resources, opportunities, goods, and services. Women entrepreneurs are actively participating in the business world and contributing significantly to society. Today's women are highly motivated and empowered. They do take part in all these initiatives to raise our nation's economic standing and promote economic growth. Women entrepreneurs are described as women who establish, plan, and run a business. Entrepreneurs are women who create, launch, or adopt a business activity.

The Government of India defines a woman entrepreneur as "a woman who owns and controls an enterprise with a minimum financial interest of 51% of the capital and provides at least 51% of the employment created in the enterprise to women." Entrepreneurs of all genders may experience comparable difficulties in their business endeavors, but women suffer extra gender-based obstacles that restrict their access to opportunities and resources.

In response to these difficulties, the International Labor Organization's Women's Entrepreneurship Development (ILO-WED) program works with stakeholders to ensure that enterprise initiatives consider gender dynamics and inequalities in their conception and implementation. ILO-WED aims to address current gender imbalances in enterprise development through approaches targeted specifically at women. The curriculum uses a variety of tried-and-true methods and techniques to assist aspiring and seasoned female company owners in starting, running, and expanding their enterprises.

9.2 Main Areas of Focus

The ILO-WED initiative promotes and uses the techniques and incomes to afford full interventions to enhance ladies' entrepreneurship in these important areas:

- Enabling Situation for Women's Free Enterprise Development: ILO-WED endeavors to remove some of the structural barriers that women tycoons face by comprehending and establishing the prerequisites for their enhanced accessibility to resources and opportunities.
- Financial and business development services: ILO-WED supports service providers in adopting more environmentally friendly business models while working to improve the accessibility, relevance, and gender sensitivity of service provision for entrepreneurs.
- ILO-WED promotes the delivery of focused guidance and post-training modes that enhance women's enterprise executives' interactive and monetary abilities. Training and Post-Training Support for Women Entrepreneurs, the ILO has built the training over time, tried, tested, and tailored them to national situations while creating and maintaining a network of extremely dedicated trainers.

9.2.1 List of Indian Government Programs to Empower Women

1. Udhyogni Scheme
2. Cent Kalyani Scheme
3. Mahila Udhyam Nidhi Scheme
4. Women Entrepreneurship Platform

5. Bharatiya Mahila Bank Business Loan
6. Mudra Yojana Scheme
7. Dena Shakti Scheme.

9.2.2 Women's Government Investment Programs

Along with the Employees' Provident Fund (EPF), the Electric Kisan Vikas Patra Scheme, tax-advantaged unit-linked insurance plans (ULIPs), National Saving Certificates (NSCs), Sukanya Samriddhi Schemes (SSY), and the most recent small savings program, Mahila Samman Savings Certificates, there are also several other savings programs.

9.3 Review of Literature

Self-leadership plays a significant role in the entrepreneurial intention of individuals, particularly women entrepreneurs. According to Fiernaningsih et al. (2023), self-leadership directly contributes to entrepreneurial intention. Self-leadership entails an introspective process where people are actively motivated to bring about the desired changes, advancements, and novel behaviors. This self-leadership-based motivation fuels the intent behind the innovative enterprise.

Other psychological elements can affect entrepreneurial intention in addition to self-leadership. According to Alshebami (2022), people who have a high internal locus of control are more likely to succeed in establishing entrepreneurial behavior, intention, and venture development. In particular, during bad or difficult circumstances, those with a greater internal locus of control are more likely to handle problems positively and discover significant solutions to roadblocks.

Furthermore, entrepreneurial resilience plays a crucial role in managing the connection relating to business self-efficacy and the continuation of business activities during challenging and adverse times (Alshebami, 2022). The effect of business resilience during serious and contrary times is still an underexplored area in literature. Sighting how entrepreneurial resilience can moderate the relationship between self-efficacy and business purpose is essential for supporting women entrepreneurs in overcoming challenges and sustaining their entrepreneurial activities.

Overall, the combination of self-leadership, entrepreneurial mindset, and internal center of control resilience contributes to the desire for entrepreneurship among female business owners. These psychological factors empower women to take initiative, overcome obstacles, and persist in their entrepreneurial endeavors. By fostering self-leadership skills, promoting an internal locus of control, and providing support for building entrepreneurial resilience, policymakers and organizations can create an enabling environment for women entrepreneurs to thrive and succeed. The study looked at how well cyber self-leadership teaching promoted leads' self-leadership abilities and practices with recovery. A controlled experiment that wasn't random. Self-reported self-leadership skills and rescue encounters are measured using standardized questionnaires. (Krampitz, 2023)

This book teaches strategies to embody and integrate your leadership style into your daily life, empowering you to make powerful decisions and tackle leadership challenges. Strategies to embody personal leadership, increase energy and make powerful decisions, Jensand Bergstein (2023). The study found that self-leadership can be understood by elementary school students with some encouragement and adjustment in teaching style, and live approach method used in the research Abdul (2023)

Entrepreneurial intention refers to an individual's desire and motivation to start their own business or engage in entrepreneurial activities. The quantitative-based study used a structured questionnaire for data collection (Tan, 2021). The paper does not provide information about the challenges related to entrepreneurial intention (Khang Rana et al., 2023), but only shares ibliometric analysis, bibliographic couplings, co-citation, and co-occurrences analysis (Víctor Alfaro-García, 2022). The obstacles preventing women from becoming entrepreneurs in the hospitality sector include work-family conflicts, a lack of sociocultural support, restricted access to capital, and regulatory restrictions. A quantitative approach and a snowball sampling method have been used in this method (Rimsha 2022).

Women business owners in South Africa face challenges that include poor educational levels, a lack of funding, gender inequity, an absence of sponsors from stakeholders, and a lack of technical know-how. The authors advise and encourage women to take the lead and engage in entrepreneurship in the tourism sector, where stakeholder funding is essential for attaining economic growth. The writers of the paper use a thorough biography review exploration to assess the potential and problems facing female financiers in South Africa's tourist sector through analyses of documentary reviews (Vikelwa, 2017). The paper provides an overview of the factors affecting females' career evolution in hotel activity and explores the mechanisms hospitality companies adopt to address the issue. In this paper, the writers examined whether women are avoided from progressing in their professions by causes involving the business advance of females in the hotel business as stated by academics in several parts of the world (Lynette, 2022)

South African women entrepreneurs confront obstacles such as poor educational levels, a lack of financial resources, gender inequality, insufficient stakeholder support, and limited technical abilities (Vikelwa, 2017). This paper provides an overview of the factors affecting women's career progression in the hotel industry and explores mechanisms hospitality companies adopt to address the issue (Ranjith, 2018). This paper investigates the challenges preventing women chefs from reaching top positions in the culinary industry and suggests measures to overcome them. In this article, the authors investigate the challenges preventing women chefs from reaching the top positions in the kitchen of a hotel, identify measures to overcome them, and suggest measures to prepare women for leadership positions and find ways to overcome the barriers that may exist to women's career advancement (Usha, 2015)

To examine women managers' perceptions of factors that facilitate and constrain their career advancement and determine whether there are any notable differences among them, a profile of women managers in the Indian hospitality industry has been provided. This profile includes information about their positions and an investigation into the challenges they have faced throughout their careers (Vidya, 2012).

The paper discusses the hindrances to female career development in the hotel industry but does not specifically address women's involvement as entrepreneurs. The presence of female managers in two Accor hotel networks, Tap Hotel, and Formula in this article (38% of managers) raises questions regarding career paths within these low-cost hotel chains (Nathalie, 2009). The study focuses on barriers to business development for women in the hospitality sector in Oman but does not specifically address challenges for women as entrepreneurs in the industry. A questionnaire was administered to women employees: Analysis of data using the chi-square test (Nupur, 2013).

The text does not provide specific information about challenges hindering women's involvement in the hospitality industry as entrepreneurs. For example, the authors found that women working in this area are proactive; they are taking responsibility for their career opportunities rather than relying so much on their companies; while not completely erased, barriers to women's advancement appear to be slowly but surely coming down (Bonnie, 2001). The paper does not specifically mention industrial and geographical gaps in the study of social support and work-life conflict in the hotel industry. Literature research and questionnaire method: Work-family conflict scale and family, work conflict scale. Manxiao (2016) the paper does not specifically mention the challenges faced by women in the hospitality industry as entrepreneurs (Swati, 2018).

The authors of this essay examine the significance of cultural practices and other factors that affect the growth of female entrepreneurship in this review of the literature on women's entrepreneurship, which focuses on the major barriers that prevent women from starting businesses in developing nations (Dennis, 2014). The research found that women in hotel management face barriers such as work-family conflict and organizational culture that hinder their career progression. The online survey and follow-up interviews methodology has been used in this paper (Shelagh, 2009). Moreover,(Lan, 1999) the paper focuses on the barriers that prevent middle-level female managers in Singapore hotels from advancing to executive positions. Study of the universal report of feminine hotel executives in Singapore. Examination of difficulties preventing middle-level managers from increasing.

9.4 Major Challenges Faced by Women Entrepreneurs

9.4.1 Homes and Family

Indian women feel deeply connected to their homes and family. They are expected to handle all household chores and to keep an eye on the family's members. They are involved with family jobs; therefore, they spend a lot of time and effort taking care of their husband, children, and in-laws. In such a situation, it might be difficult to concentrate and manage a business effectively.

9.4.2 Socio-cultural Barriers

Women may occasionally face obstacles to advancement and success due to the customs and traditions that are widespread in Indian civilizations. Castes and religions dominate our society, which hurts female business owners. In rural sections, they face significantly more societal challenges. They are often met with suspicion.

9.4.3 Male-Dominated Society

The fact that our society promotes gender equality, male superiority still holds sway. Males and females do not share the same rights. Their decision to go into the company needs the family head's approval, who is typically a male member. Historically, men have been linked to entrepreneurship. Each of them prevents the growth of female-owned businesses.

9.4.4 Illiteracy or Low Level of Education

In the area of education, women in India remain far behind. Even after more than 77 years of freedom, many women still lack access to education. When compared to their male counterparts, women who are educated receive either a lesser or insufficient education because of early marriage, home responsibilities, and poverty. Most female business owners lack sufficient education, which prevents them from learning about new technologies, production techniques, marketing strategies, networking opportunities, and other government initiatives that could help them advance in management (Khang & Muthmainnah et al., 2023).

9.4.5 Dearth of Financial Assistance

Women business owners struggle greatly to raise and meet the company's financial needs. Due to their lower creditworthiness, reserves, creditors, and financial societies are averse to offering fiscal aid to female debtors. They also experience monetary hurdles because of the blockage of funds in direct items, inventories, working in progress, and terminated possessions, and the failure to receive payments from clients.

9.4.6 Lack of Technical Knowledge

Management has evolved into a specialized profession carried out only by effective managers. Women business owners occasionally struggle to do managerial tasks like organizing, regulating, directing, inspiring, recruiting, coordinating, and leading an organization. As a result, ladies' poor management abilities have made it hard for them to run their businesses (Khang & Kali, 2023).

9.4.7 Marketing Skills

The majority of women are unable to run around for marketing, distribution, and money collection, hence they must rely on middlemen for these tasks. Middle-aged males often take advantage of them while pretending to be helpful. They labor to increase their profit margin, which results in lower sales and profits for female business owners.

9.4.8 Entrepreneurial Skill

For female business owners, a problem is the lack of entrepreneurial ability. They don't have a lot of entrepreneurial skills. Even after joining numerous entrepreneurship education programs, womanlike tycoons still battle to deal with the risks and issues that can arise while working in an organization.

9.4.9 Lack of Self-Confidence

Due to their innate characteristics, female entrepreneurs lack the self-confidence that is required for successfully operating a business. Striking a balance between running their family and their business takes a lot of effort. People may have to compromise their entrepreneurial instinct to achieve stability between the two, which results harm to potential business (Khang & Rani et al., 2023).

9.4.10 Mobility Constraints

Women's mobility in India is highly restricted and has become a worry due to traditional standards and subpar driving skills. Still viewed with mistrust are requests for a place to work late at night and moving alone. When dealing with males who show them extra interest outside of work-related matters, inexperienced women can feel uneasy (Khang & Hajimahmud et al., 2023).

9.5 Suggestions to Overcome the Challenges

■ Women entrepreneurs should receive distinct financial assistance from the government so they won't have any problems starting their businesses.

- Special infrastructure facilities should be made available to assist women in starting their businesses quickly and easily.
- Women entrepreneurs should receive specialized training to improve their entrepreneurial skills and abilities that support them in running their businesses daily.
- To encourage and urge more women to pursue such jobs, it is important to recognize and honor top-ranking female entrepreneurs.
- Better educational facilities should be made available beginning in elementary school and continuing through higher education and several occupational studies.
- All cities should establish Women Entrepreneurs' Guidance Cells to address issues with day-to-day operations, including production, marketing, and distribution issues.
- To assist female entrepreneurs in starting their businesses and obtaining quick permission for various legal procedures, several legal laws and regulations for the establishment of an enterprise by women need to be clarified.
- Most essentially, it is necessary for women to leave their homes with the backing of family members. When they are aware that their family is supporting their decisions, they can produce more effectively.
- Fairs, exhibitions, and workshops organized for female entrepreneurs will enable them to network with one another and discuss ideas and challenges. Additionally, it will offer direction to emerging female entrepreneurs who may learn from and benefit from their more seasoned peers.
- Making provisions for marketing and sales help to prevent middlemen from taking advantage of female entrepreneurs.

9.6 Conclusion

Women lack the courage to lead their enterprises in difficult situations. Women can acquire ownership in the company by eradicating male domination. Additionally, women have higher intentions to pursue self-leadership activities as a result of the implementation of gender-based equality. Since there are fewer and fewer women entering the tourist and hospitality industries as entrepreneurs, these methods strengthen the decision-making authority to address managerial issues and foster the emergence of new entrepreneurial formation for economic growth. To provide a conceptual model of women's entrepreneurial activity that is well-organized, this research contributes new insights to the literature. The findings also outline the practical ramifications and offer guidance for further research (Khang & Shah et al., 2023).

The entrepreneurial mindsets of women have a significant impact on their entrepreneurial goals. Women's ambitions to start businesses are not significantly impacted by business education or entrepreneurial training. Age and family history are negatively correlated with an entrepreneurial bent. Business experience, the need for more money, the want for stability, the desire for prestige, self-efficacy, a willingness to take risks, and cultural views are all positively correlated with the desire to launch a business. Research on female entrepreneurs is conducted all over the world. Involvement levels and business performance differ between cultures. Men might exaggerate their capacity for entrepreneurship. Women do not necessarily lack confidence despite having lower self-efficacy. There is a lack of knowledge regarding learning motivation and competencies as they relate to female entrepreneurs' company performance (Khang & Muthmainnah et al., 2023).

The suggested conceptual model can advance academic understanding and help governments develop skill-building plans for female entrepreneurs. Technology can be utilized to create teams of female entrepreneurs. Technology-based networking and mentoring can be a starting point. Female entrepreneurs' intentions are strengthened by psychological assistance. Gender preconceptions and barriers can be overcome through same-gender group mentorship. There is a lack of knowledge regarding learning motivation and competencies as they relate to female entrepreneurs' company performance. The suggested conceptual model can advance academic understanding and help governments develop skill-building plans for female entrepreneurs (Khang & Quantum, 2023).

References

Ariyanto Hadji, M., Maigo, R. Z. G., Aditya Eka S., M. R., Rahmat, A., & Hutagalung, R. (2022). Responsibility and discipline self to practice self-leadership in reaching ideals in Sd Negeri 5 Tilongkabila Indonesia. *British Journal of Global Ecology and Sustainable Development*, *11*, 46–53. https://www.journalzone.org/index.php/bjgesd/article/view/174

Aiko, D. M. (2014). What drives women out of Entrepreneurship? The joint role of culture and access to finance. *DBA Africa Management Review*, *4*(2). https://papers.ssrn.com/sol3/papers.cfm?abstract_id=1749845

Akinyi, O. L., Wadongo, B., & Omondi, R. K. (2022). The challenges in the provision of informal hospitality services to socio-economic well-being of women entrepreneurs in Kenya. *Journal of Hospitality and Tourism Management*, *5*(1), 25–43. https://doi.org/10.53819/81018102t6005

Bergstein, J., Lassalle, J., & Ritter, F. (2023). *Self-Empowered Leadership*. München: Vahlen. ISBN print: 978-3-8006-6945-5.

Bosse, N., & Guégnard, C. (2009, April). Projects, careers and resistances in hotels. In *27th International Labour Process Conference "Work Matters"*. https://shs.hal.science/halshs-00380637/

Khalid, R., Raza, M., Sawangchai, A., & Raza, H. (2022). The challenges to women's entrepreneurial involvement in the hospitality industry. *Journal of Liberty and International Affairs*, *8*(3), 220–240. https://doi.org/10.47305/JLIA2283220k

Khang, A. (2023). *Applications and Principles of Quantum Computing* (1st Ed.). IGI Global Press. ISBN: 9798369311684. https://doi.org/10.4018/979-8-3693-1168-4

Khang, A., & Rath, K. C. (2023). Quantum mechanics primer – Fundamentals and quantum computing. *Applications and Principles of Quantum Computing* (1st Ed.). IGI Global Press. ISBN: 9798369311684. https://doi.org/10.4018/979-8-3693-1168-4-ch001

Khang, A., Alyar, A. V., Khalilov, M., Murad, B., & Litvinova, E. (2023). Introduction to quantum computing and its integration applications. *Applications and Principles of Quantum Computing* (1st Ed.). IGI Global Press. ISBN: 9798369311684. https://doi.org/10.4018/979-8-3693-1168-4-ch002

Khang, A., Muthmainnah, M., Seraj, P. M. I., Al Yakin, A., Obaid, A. J., & Panda, M. R. (2023). AI-aided teaching model for the education 5.0 ecosystem. *AI-Based Technologies and Applications in the Era of the Metaverse* (1st Ed., pp. 83–104). IGI Global Press. https://doi.org/10.4018/978-1-6684-8851-5.ch004

Khang, A., Rana, G., Tailor, R. K., & Hajimahmud, V. A. (2023). *Data-Centric AI Solutions and Emerging Technologies in the Healthcare Ecosystem* (1st Ed.). CRC Press. https://doi.org/10.1201/9781003356189

Khang, A., Rani, S., Gujrati, R., Uygun, H., & Gupta, S. K. (2023). *Designing Workforce Management Systems for Industry 4.0: Data-Centric and AI-Enabled Approaches* (1st Ed.). CRC Press. https://doi.org/10.1201/9781003357070

Khang, A., Shah, V., & Rani, S. (2023). *AI-Based Technologies and Applications in the Era of the Metaverse* (1st Ed.). IGI Global Press. https://doi.org/10.4018/978-1-6684-8851-5

Kowang, T. O., Apandi, S. Z. B. A., Hee, O. C., Fei, G. C., Saadon, M. S. I., & Othman, M. R. (2021). Undergraduates entrepreneurial intention: Holistic determinants matter. *International Journal of Evaluation and Research in Education*, *10*(1), 57–64. https://eric.ed.gov/?id=EJ1285728

Krampitz, J., Tenschert, J., Furtner, M., Simon, J., & Glaser, J. (2023). Effectiveness of online self-leadership training on leaders' self-leadership skills and recovery experiences. *Journal of Workplace Learning*, *35*(9), 66–85. https://doi.org/10.1108/JWL-10-2022-0125

Kumara, Y. R. (2018). Career development of women in the hotel industry: An overview. *Journal of Applied and Natural Science, 10*(1), 330–338. http://journals.ansfoundation.org/index.php/jans/article/view /1626

Li, L., & Wang Leung, R. (1999). Female managers in Asian hotels: Profile and career challenges. *International Journal of Contemporary Hospitality Management, 13*(4), 189–196. https://www.emerald .com/insight/content/doi/10.1108/09596110110389511/full/html

Mooney, S., & Ryan, I. (2009). A woman's place in hotel management: Upstairs or downstairs?. *Gender in Management: An International Journal, 24*(3), 195–210. https://www.emerald.com/insight/content/ doi/10.1108/17542410910950877/full/html

Nomnga, V. J. (2017). Unlocking the potential of women entrepreneurs in the tourism and hospitality industry in the Eastern Cape Province, South Africa. *Journal of Economics and Behavioral Studies, 9*(4(J)), 6–13. https://doi.org/10.22610/jebs.v9i4(J).1817

Panda, S. (2018). Constraints faced by women entrepreneurs in developing countries: Review and ranking. *Gender in Management: An International Journal, 33*(4), 315–331. https://www.emerald.com/insight/ content/doi/10.1108/GM-01-2017-0003/full/html

Patwardhan, V., & Venkatachalam, V. B. (2012). A study on career management issues of women managers in Indian Hospitality Industry. *JOHAR, 7*(1), 67. https://search.proquest.com/openview/a2700a9 2bb6499ebff9ac42ebc2a4d21/1?pq-origsite=gscholar&cbl=2030935

Usha, D. (2015). Women chefs in the Indian hospitality industry: Challenges and strategies. *Golden Research Thoughts, 4*(7). https://www.cabdirect.org/cabdirect/abstract/20153122594

Zhou, X., & Wen, B. (2016). An empirical study about the impact of work-family conflict on female staff's career development in hotels. *Journal of Sustainable Development, 9*(5), 100–109. https://pdfs.semanticscholar.org/f7b8/994a8ce5192ea816a26eee4d7782ab3a41cb.pdf

Zopiatis, A., Lambertides, N., Savva, C. S., & Theocharous, A. L. (2019). Hospitality education and finance courses: An 'inconvenient' relationship?. *Journal of Hospitality, Leisure, Sport & Tourism Education, 24*, 63–69. https://www.sciencedirect.com/science/article/pii/S1473837618302041

Chapter 10

The Impact of Technology on Educational Sustainability in the Tourism Industry

Rishi Sharma and Sanjeev Kumar

10.1 Introduction

Incorporating sustainability into tourism education through technology can have many beneficial benefits. When tourism education was initially introduced, it was taught as a trade school subject (Airey & Tribe, 2005), but as it developed, it was conducted with more academic complexity. It indicates that the purpose of tourist education is to reconcile the need for tourism growth with the broader goal of controlling tourism (Nayak & Padhye, 2018). More thorough research is required on the sector than simply producing qualified graduates who can work in the tourist industry. These tendencies and advances will help the tourist industry's education become more lasting and significant as technology develops (Dhiraj & Kumar, 2023).

Educational institutions may better prepare upcoming tourism professionals with the information and abilities required to advance sustainability and spur constructive change by utilizing technology (Dhiraj & Kumar, 2023). Virtual reality (VR) has been applied in a variety of fields, such as education (Bower et al., 2020), medicine (Yang et al., 2017), marketing (Pestek & Sarvan, 2021), and tourism (Choi et al., 2020). The digital revolution's impact on tourism, which may account for one in 11 employments globally by 2025, may have the most significant societal impact.

Some tourism jobs may become obsolete, thanks to intelligent technology, while others will change significantly. Higher education institutions (HEIs) must, in this situation, adapt their tourism education curricula to stay up with the ongoing digital revolution, especially in the tourist business (Angelico, 2020). Digitalization has taken the top spot in the nation's higher education institutions and public sectors. According to Adukaite et al. (2016), the tourist and educational sectors have grown considerably due to the digital revolution's increased social and economic development prospects (Wirtz et al., 2019)

DOI: 10.4324/9781032688305-10

Current digital technologies for teaching and learning have yet to be wholly adopted and utilized in the educational sector. Teachers, scholars, and administrators have been forced to make quick, creative decisions about how students will continue to learn through online courses due to the abrupt shift to online education, particularly after COVID-19. The usage of virtual audio programs, tutorials, video conferencing equipment, and e-learning software has significantly expanded (Haiduwa et al., 2022). Despite educational and technological developments, most of today's tourist education is still delivered conventionally. The learning environment, methodology, and curriculum have all evolved and been redefined over time. However, the necessary revolutionary changes have yet to occur in a world of innovation and upheaval. It's also important to point out that the tourist business has seen most of its innovation efforts arise online (Kumar et al., 2023).

Technology may improve sustainability education in the travel and tourism industry in several ways. It will lower the environmental impact; thanks to technology, learning remotely and getting an online education is now possible, eliminating the need for students to travel to courses or training sessions. As a result, there will be less of an environmental impact from transportation-related carbon emissions. Technology helps the tourist industry's education sector minimize its overall carbon footprint by offering virtual learning opportunities.

Education professionals, students, and business leaders may all benefit from collaboration and knowledge sharing. Online forums, discussion boards, and social media networks offer venues for exchanging thoughts, stories, and creative tourist solutions. In the community of tourist education, collaborative learning stimulates the adoption of sustainable practices and fosters information sharing. Real-time updates on sustainable practices enable the transmission of up-to-date information on sustainable tourism practices. Current research, case studies, and best practices in sustainable tourism may be accessed instantly through educational portals. It guarantees that learners are armed with the most up-to-date information and techniques for addressing the sector's environmental and social concerns.

In data-driven decision-making, the tourism sector can gather and analyze sustainability-related data. Educational institutions may evaluate how tourist activities affect the environment, pinpoint areas for improvement, and make wise choices to advance sustainability using data analytics. Virtual reality (VR), although not a brand-new term like "humanoid robots" (Kazandzhieva & Filipova, 2019), offers several advantages for the tourism sector (Tussyadiah, 2020). Education professionals and students can monitor progress and assess the success of sustainability programs, thanks to technology's facilitation of monitoring and reporting methods.

Virtual experiments and simulations of modern technologies, such as virtual reality (VR) and augmented reality (AR), may provide engaging educational opportunities (Aini, 2020). Without traveling, students may explore locations, comprehend local cultures, and learn about sustainable tourism practices through virtual tours, simulations, and interactive courses. It lessens the adverse effects of tourism-related education on the environment while giving students beneficial hands-on learning experiences (Khang & Rana et al., 2023).

10.2 Leveraging Digital Transformations

Leveraging digital transformations refers to the strategic use and integration of digital technologies to drive positive and meaningful changes in an organization's processes, operations, products, services, and overall business model (Saarikko et al., 2020). It involves adopting and implementing digital solutions that can improve efficiency, enhance customer experiences, increase innovation, and gain a competitive advantage in the market (Solberg et al., 2020). The needs and expectations of customers should drive digital transformation. Understanding customer pain points and preferences will help develop digital solutions that deliver personalized and seamless experiences. It will also embrace data analytics to gather insights from various sources, including customer interactions, operational processes, and market trends (Kretschmer & Khashabi, 2020).

Data-driven decision-making allows organizations to identify opportunities for improvement and make informed choices. It can improve efficiency, reduce errors, and free-up resources for more strategic initiatives (Brunetti et al., 2020). Omni-channel engagement offers a consistent experience across multiple channels, such as websites, mobile apps, social media, and in-person interactions. Omni-channel engagement ensures customers can interact with the organization seamlessly, regardless of the platform (Bhalla, 2014). Cloud-based solutions provide scalability, flexibility, and cost-effectiveness. Migrating data and applications to the cloud can improve accessibility, collaboration, and data security (Manser Payne et al., 2017). Employee empowerment digital transformations are successful when employees are empowered to embrace new technologies and processes and provided with training and support to help employees adapt to digital changes and encourage a culture of continuous learning (Alrasheedi et al., 2022).

Integrate emerging technologies and evaluate how their potential impact on the industry such as AI, IoT, blockchain, and others, can enhance your organization's offerings and operations (Mbunge, 2020). As organizations embrace digital solutions, security and compliance become crucial. Implement robust cybersecurity measures and ensure compliance with relevant regulations to protect customer data and maintain trust (Lin et al., 2015). Collaborate with technology providers, startups, and other industry partners to leverage their expertise and innovations.

Partnerships can accelerate digital transformations and open-up new opportunities. Digital transformations are ongoing processes, not one-time projects (Gannon-Leary et al., 2006). Encourage a culture of continuous improvement, where feedback is collected and digital initiatives are iterated upon to drive ongoing success. Successfully leveraging digital transformations requires a clear vision, a well-defined strategy, and a commitment to embracing change. Organizations that effectively incorporate digital technologies into their operations will be better positioned to thrive in the dynamic and competitive business landscape (Santamaría et al., 2021).

10.3 Role and Significance of Education Sustainability in the Tourism Sector

Online educational resources and courses may be accessed using digital learning platforms, which can be created and used. According to Boyle and Jenkins (2015), firms, local organizations, and universities increasingly include sustainability and (corporate) social responsibility in their tourism programs. As a result, there will be less demand for printed documents and physical infrastructure, resulting in less paper being used and a minor carbon impact. VR and AR technology may be utilized to develop immersive learning experiences in tourist education. Students may digitally visit tourist attractions, historical places, and natural marvels without traveling, lowering the carbon footprint associated with physical travel. Online collaboration and communication technologies make it easier for students, teachers, and specialists worldwide to communicate and work together in real time. Due to decreased physical travel required for academic objectives, corresponding greenhouse gas emissions are also reduced.

The environmental effect of travel is reduced because e-learning and webinars give travel industry employees access to ongoing education without requiring them to attend physical workshops or seminars. Sustainable travel tourism education courses may include sustainability ideas through content. Future tourism professionals may be better equipped to promote and engage in sustainable tourism by embracing sustainability principles and best practices. Energy-efficient procedures and green computer technology may reduce educational institutions' energy use and carbon footprint (Muthmainnah & Yakin et al., 2023).

Gamification has been increasingly incorporated into tourism education to make learning more engaging and interactive. It involves using game-like elements, such as quizzes, challenges, and rewards, to promote active learning (Wei et al., 2023). By utilizing gamification, educational institutions and tourism companies can foster a culture of continuous learning and knowledge retention, leading to a more sustainable and skilled workforce (Aguiar-Castillo et al., 2021) (Khang & Rani et al., 2023).

e-Learning technology has facilitated the development and distribution of various e-learning resources, including e-books, videos, and webinars (Logan et al., 2021). These resources can be updated and accessed easily, reducing the reliance on printed materials, which can be resource-intensive and environmentally harmful (Admiraal & Lockhorst, 2009). Sustainable practices technology plays a significant role in promoting sustainable tourism practices as shown in Figure 10.1. For instance, using intelligent systems for energy management, waste reduction, and resource optimization in hotels and tourist attractions has become more prevalent (Della Corte et al., 2019).

Collecting and analyzing data on tourism and sustainability are made possible through data analytics for sustainable decision-making. In light of the COVID-19 pandemic, concerns about the tourist industry's future have been sparked (Brouder et al., 2020). Making choices and

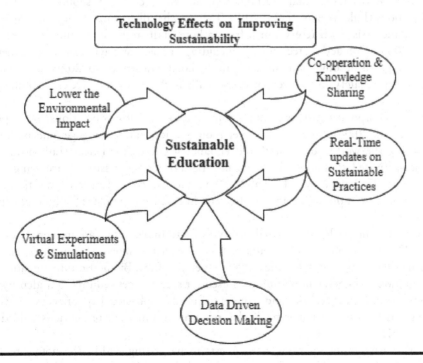

Figure 10.1　Components of sustainable education.

implementing regulations that support sustainability in the travel and tourist industry may be done using this data (Dubois & Dimanche, 2021). Initiatives like "Smart Campuses" employ technology to reduce trash, use resources efficiently, and use energy more sustainably. Online certification programs focusing on sustainable tourism practices may be easily created, thanks to technology (Hockings et al., 2020). Such certificates can aid in adopting more sustainable practices by tourist industry experts and enterprises. Technology may eliminate the need for actual travel through virtual conferences, webinars, and remote learning, reducing transportation-related carbon emissions in the travel, tourism, and education industries (Khang & Muthmainnah et al., 2023).

10.4 New Technologies and Tools for the Hotel Industry

The hotel industry is continuously evolving, and new technologies and tools are crucial in enhancing guest experiences, improving operational efficiency, and staying competitive in the market. Hotel mobile apps offer guests a seamless and personalized experience. Guests can use these apps to make reservations, check-in and out, access digital room keys, and request services. Nowadays new facial technology is used for opening guest rooms, which is found to be safer, more secure, and trust in hosital industry (Xu et al., 2021). Mobile check-in reduces wait times and allows guests to bypass the front desk, enhancing convenience and efficiency (Torres, 2018).

Internet of Things (IoT) devices and sensors enable the creation of intelligent rooms. Guests can control room settings like lighting, temperature, and entertainment through voice commands or mobile apps. IoT also facilitates energy management, predictive maintenance, and automated services, improving overall guest satisfaction and operational efficiency (Car et al., 2019). *AI-powered chatbots and virtual assistants provide instant customer support and personalized guest interactions (Lukanova & Ilieva, 2019). They can handle common inquiries, make recommendations, and assist with reservations, freeing hotel staff from more complex tasks (Pillai & Sivathanu, 2020). Contactless technology, including contactless payments, digital menus, and mobile ordering, has become more prevalent in the hotel industry (Hao, 2021). Contactless solutions improve guest safety and convenience, especially in the post-pandemic era (Mukherjee et al., 2021).

Hotels are incorporating robotics and automation to streamline operations and improve efficiency (Lee et al., 2021). Robots can deliver room service, handle luggage, and perform other tasks, reducing the workload for staff and enhancing guest experiences (Lukanova & Ilieva, 2019). Voice-activated assistants, like Amazon's Alexa or Google Assistant, are being integrated into hotel rooms (Buhalis & Moldavska, 2022). Guests can control various aspects of their stay using voice commands, providing a hands-free and interactive experience (Buhalis & Moldavska, 2021).

Augmented reality (AR) and virtual reality (VR) technologies create immersive experiences for guests. Hotels can offer virtual tours of their properties, showcase amenities, and provide AR-based navigation assistance for guests (Nayyar et al., 2018). Biometric authentication, such as facial recognition or fingerprint scanning, is used for secure access control and identity verification. Biometrics enhances security and reduces the need for physical keys or access cards. Digital signage systems are used in hotels to display relevant information, promotions, and directions (Kim et al., 2011).

Interactive wayfinding solutions assist guests in navigating within the hotel premises and nearby attractions (Chee, 2023). These new technologies and tools empower hotels to provide personalized experiences, streamline operations, and adapt to changing guest expectations. Embracing these innovations is essential for hotels to remain competitive and relevant in the ever-evolving hospitality industry.

10.5 Benefits and Drawbacks

Regarding promoting sustainability, using technology in the tourist industry's education sector offers both benefits and drawbacks. Here are some things to think about:

10.5.1 Benefits

1. *Resource Efficiency:* The use of digital textbooks, online resources, and e-learning platforms lessens the demand for paper-based materials, which results in less resource use and waste production. By deploying energy-efficient equipment and implementing cloud-based computing and storage solutions, technology may help reduce energy usage.
2. *Virtual Learning:* Thanks to technology, it is possible to participate in virtual learning activities like online classes and webinars, eliminating the need for physical travel and the resulting carbon emissions. Virtual platforms may offer immersive experiences, virtual tours, and interactive simulations to improve education without endangering the environment.
3. *Information Access:* Students and teachers in the tourism industry may easily access a wealth of current information on sustainable practices. It makes them better able to comprehend and apply sustainability ideas effectively.
4. *Networking and Collaboration:* With the advancement of technology, students and educators may interact and exchange ideas worldwide. They can interact with experts, practitioners, and fellow learners worldwide through online platforms, boosting knowledge sharing and encouraging the development of sustainable tourism practices.

10.5.2 Drawbacks

1. Electronic waste and energy consumption: The manufacture, usage, and disposal of technological gadgets may all contribute to electronic waste and energy consumption. Without effective management and recycling practices, the environmental impact of technology might jeopardize the education sector's overall sustainability aims (Khang & Kali et al., 2023).
2. Inequality in access to technology and the internet among students and educational institutions is known as the "*digital divide.*" Inequalities brought about by this digital gap may prevent certain people from taking advantage of technical improvements in sustainable tourism education.
3. Skills Gap: The rapid development of technology necessitates ongoing skill improvement. There is a chance that teachers will need to gain the necessary abilities to properly integrate sustainability principles into the curriculum as they may find it challenging to stay up with the most recent technology tools and platforms (Khang & AIoCF, 2024).
4. Technology Overuse: Using technology too much might prevent students from engaging in hands-on learning and other activities that are crucial for some areas of tourism education. Some skills, including hands-on training in the hospitality industry or fieldwork, might be taught only in some places.

10.6 The Potential for Sustainability in Tourism Education in the Future

Technology has a bright future in introducing sustainability to tourism-related education. Increased adoption of virtual reality (VR) and augmented reality (AR) technologies will advance and will be more frequently used in tourist education (Fitria, 2023). Students can participate in virtual field trips, explore digital recreations of popular tourist attractions, and practice making sustainable decisions in context. This immersive learning strategy encourages experiential learning while reducing the adverse effects of physical travel on the environment (Ivanova, 2018). Gamification for Sustainable Learning strategies is increasingly utilized to make sustainability education exciting and fun. Gamified learning applications (Aguiar-Castillo et al., 2021) and platforms may reward sustainable actions and challenges, motivating students to use sustainable practices in virtual and actual tourist settings as shown in Figure 10.2.

Education may encourage good change and propel sustainable behaviors by combining game components (Aguiar-Castillo et al., 2021). Blockchain for transparency and responsive tourists can increase accountability and transparency in the travel and tourism industry. It may be applied to monitor and validate supply chain data, sustainable business practices, and certifications. Blockchain-based platforms can encourage responsible travel by disseminating open data regarding the adverse effects of tourism on the environment and society (Machado et al., 2020).

The Internet of Things (IoT) and smart technology tools will be used to track and improve sustainable practices in the travel and tourism industry. In educational institutions and tourism destinations, smart sensors can monitor environmental indicators, water usage, trash management, and energy use. The gathering and analysis of real-time data will help decision-makers manage resources sustainably. The growth of online learning will continue to increase as it becomes a more flexible and long-lasting form of education.

Online learning will be improved and more effective because of developments in e-learning platforms, virtual classrooms, and interactive technologies (Lutfiani et al., 2021). By expanding online knowledge, conventional education will leave a smaller carbon footprint and require

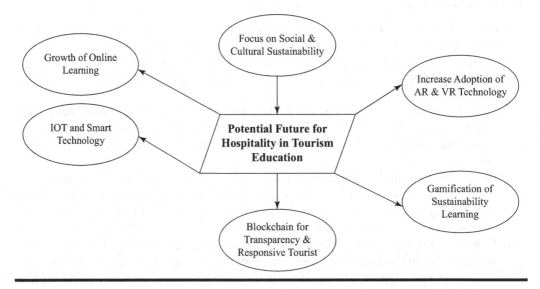

Figure 10.2 The potential for sustainability in tourism education in the future.

less physical travel. The focus on social and cultural sustainability technology will continue to emphasize the role of social and cultural sustainability in tourist education. Maintaining regional cultures, assisting local people, and fostering ethical and inclusive tourist practices will be highlighted on platforms and through materials (Nayyar et al., 2018). Collaboration and knowledge exchange made possible by technology will promote intercultural understanding and ethical travel practices.

The integration of artificial intelligence (AI) has the potential to have a significant impact on tourist industry sustainability education. Virtual assistants and chatbots with AI capabilities may offer individualized learning opportunities and respond to inquiries on eco-friendly practices (Short & Short, 2023), travel destinations, and cultural sensitivity (Kohnke et al., 2023). To establish successful sustainability policies, AI algorithms may also analyze extensive databases to find trends and patterns.

10.7 Limitations

Despite technology's enormous potential to support educational sustainability in the tourist sector, these constraints must be considered to realize its advantages and fully solve any possible drawbacks (Sterling, 2004). By acknowledging and resolving these limits, educational institutions may use technology's promise while guaranteeing inclusion, fairness, and sustainable practices in the tourism education industry. Although technology has typically influenced educational sustainability in the tourist business, several restrictions should be considered. These restrictions consist of the following:

1. Limited Human Contact and Experience Learning: Human contact and experience learning, essential for comprehending and putting sustainability in the tourist business into practice, may be lacking in technology-mediated education. Virtual ones cannot entirely replace real-world experiences but can enhance them. For complete sustainability education, balancing technology-based learning and practical experiences is crucial.
2. Quick Technological Breakthroughs: Educational institutions may need help to stay up with the newest tools and platforms due to the fast speed of technological breakthroughs. This necessitates ongoing investment, training, and curriculum change to successfully embrace developing technology. Institutions of higher learning should have plans to stay current and relevant in the face of quickly changing technologies.
3. Cultural and Contextual Considerations: Technology applications in the tourism sector should be made considering both culture and context. Unique sustainability issues and solutions arise in many cultures and locations. Technology-based education should be customized for local contexts, cultural values, and community needs to promote successful and respectful sustainability practices.
4. Disparities in Access and Infrastructure: Despite technological developments, therethere are still needs to be gaps in access to reliable internet connectivity and infrastructure, especially in rural or underdeveloped regions. Inequalities in educational possibilities can be caused by limited access to technology, which can impede the implementation of sustainable education projects.
5. Equity Concerns and the Digital Divide: The digital divide is the difference in access to technology between the two groups of people. Socioeconomic differences can worsen education inequalities, leading to uneven access to technology and online learning resources. It

is essential to eliminate these inequalities and guarantee that all students have fair access to technology.

10.8 Conclusion

In conclusion, technology substantially influences educational sustainability in the tourist industry and offers tremendous opportunities for improvement. Technology has transformed education delivery, becoming more open, inclusive, and environmentally sustainable. Educational institutions in the tourist industry may encourage sustainability and give aspiring professionals the information and abilities to responsibly navigate the sector's problems using various technological tools. Technology lessens the need for physical travel through e-learning and online education platforms, reducing carbon emissions and helping to create a more sustainable learning environment (Khang & Shah et al., 2023).

Students may visit places and learn about sustainable practices without taking an actual trip, thanks to virtual reality and augmented reality technology, which offer immersive experiences that imitate real-world tourism circumstances. Educational institutions in the tourism sector may play a significant role in determining a more sustainable and responsible future for the business by embracing technology and incorporating sustainable practices into their curricula. Educators and students may help preserve natural and cultural heritage, lessen environmental damage, and promote ethical tourist practices that will benefit current and future generations using technology effectively (Khang & Quantum, 2023).

References

Admiraal, W., & Lockhorst, D. (2009). E-learning in small and medium-sized enterprises across Europe: Attitudes towards technology, learning and training. *International Small Business Journal, 27*(6), 743–767. https://journals.sagepub.com/doi/abs/10.1177/0266242609344244

Adukaite, A., Van Zyl, I., & Cantoni, L. (2016). The role of digital technology in tourism education: A case study of South African secondary schools. *Journal of Hospitality, Leisure, Sport & Tourism Education, 19*, 54–65. https://www.sciencedirect.com/science/article/pii/S1473837616300363

Aguiar-Castillo, L., Clavijo-Rodriguez, A., Hernández-López, L., De Saa-Pérez, P., & Pérez-Jiménez, R. (2021). Gamification and deep learning approaches in higher education. *Journal of Hospitality, Leisure, Sport & Tourism Education, 29*, 100290. https://www.sciencedirect.com/science/article/pii/S1473837620302264

Aini, Q. (2020). Digitalization of smart student assessment quality in era 4.0. *International Journal of Advanced Trends in Computer Science and Engineering, 9*(1.2), 257–265. https://doi.org/10.30534/ijatcse/2020/3891.22020

Airey, D., & Tribe, J. (2005). Issues for the future. In *An international handbook of tourism education* (pp. 501–506). https://www.academia.edu/download/6741595/filepages_from_chapter_35.pdf

Alrasheedi, N. S., Sammon, D., & McCarthy, S. (2022). Understanding the characteristics of workforce transformation in a digital transformation context. *Journal of Decision Systems, 31*(sup1), 362–383. https://www.tandfonline.com/doi/abs/10.1080/12460125.2022.2073636

Angelico, T. (2020). Educational inequality and the pandemic in Australia: Time to shift the educational paradigm. *International Studies in Educational Administration, 48*(1), 46–53. http://cceam.net/wp-content/uploads/2020/07/ISEA-2020-Vol-48-No.-I.pdf#page=52

Bhalla, R. (2014). The omnichannel customer experience: Driving engagement through digitization. *Journal of Digital & Social Media Marketing, 1*(4), 365–372. https://www.ingentaconnect.com/content/hsp/jdsmm/2014/00000001/00000004/art00008

Bhatti, M. A., & Nawaz, M. A. (2020). The impacts of tourism risk management, IT adoption, agility and resilience on the sustainable tourism supply chain performance of Maldives' tourism industry. *IRASD Journal of Management*, *2*(2), 100–108. https://journals.internationalrasd.org/index.php/jom/article/view/161

Bower, M., DeWitt, D., & Lai, J. W. (2020). Reasons associated with preservice teachers' intention to use immersive virtual reality in education. *British Journal of Educational Technology*, *51*(6), 2215–2233. https://bera-journals.onlinelibrary.wiley.com/doi/abs/10.1111/bjet.13009

Boyle, J., & Jenkins, J. (2015). Open legal educational materials: The frequently asked questions. *Washington Journal of Law, Technology & Arts*, *11*, 13. https://heinonline.org/hol-cgi-bin/get_pdf.cgi?handle=hein.journals/washjolta11&section=4

Brouder, P., Teoh, S., Salazar, N. B., Mostafanezhad, M., Pung, J. M., Lapointe, D., Higgins Desbiolles, F., Haywood, M., Hall, C. M., & Clausen, H. B. (2020). Reflections and discussions: Tourism matters in the new normal post-COVID-19. *Tourism Geographies*, *22*(3), 735–746. https://www.tandfonline.com/doi/full/10.1080/14616688.2020.1770325

Brunetti, F., Matt, D. T., Bonfanti, A., De Longhi, A., Pedrini, G., & Orzes, G. (2020). Digital transformation challenges: Strategies emerging from a multi-stakeholder approach. *The TQM Journal*, *32*(4), 697–724. https://www.emerald.com/insight/content/doi/10.1108/TQM-12-2019-0309/full/html

Buhalis, D., & Moldavska, I. (2021). *In-room voice-based AI digital assistants transforming on-site hotel services and guests' experiences* (pp. 30–44). https://link.springer.com/chapter/10.1007/978-3-030-65785-7_3

Buhalis, D., & Moldavska, I. (2022). Voice assistants in hospitality: Using artificial intelligence for customer service. *Journal of Hospitality and Tourism Technology*, *13*(3), 386–403. https://www.emerald.com/insight/content/doi/10.1108/JHTT-03-2021-0104/full/html

Car, T., Stifanich, L. P., & Šimunić, M. (2019). Internet of Things (IoT) in tourism and hospitality: Opportunities and challenges. *Tourism in South East Europe*, *5*, 163–175. https://www.academia.edu/download/66894304/293-internet-of-things-iot-in-tourism-and-hospitality-opportunities-and-challenges.pdf

Chee, S. Y. (2023). Navigating the twilight years: Supporting older adults' orientation and wayfinding in senior living facilities. *Archives of Gerontology and Geriatrics*, 105135. https://www.sciencedirect.com/science/article/pii/S0167494323002133

Choi, H., Choi, E.-K., Yoon, B., & Joung, H.-W. (2020). Understanding food truck customers: Selection attributes and customer segmentation. *International Journal of Hospitality Management*, *90*, 102647. https://doi.org/10.1016/j.ijhm.2020.102647

Della Corte, V., Del Gaudio, G., Sepe, F., & Sciarelli, F. (2019). Sustainable tourism in the open innovation realm: A bibliometric analysis. *Sustainability*, *11*(21), 6114. https://www.mdpi.com/2071-1050/11/21/6114

Dhiraj, A., & Kumar, S. (2023). Impact of E-learning on the higher education sector during the Covid-19 pandemic through pedagogy tools: An observational study. *Revista de Educación y Derecho*, *27*. https://doi.org/10.1344/REYD2023.27.40935

Dubois, L.-E., & Dimanche, F. (2021). The future of entertainment-dependent cities in a post-COVID world. *Journal of Tourism Futures*, *7*(3), 364–376. https://www.emerald.com/insight/content/doi/10.1108/JTF-11-2020-0208/full/html

Fitria, T. N. (2023). Augmented Reality (AR) and Virtual Reality (VR) technology in education: Media of teaching and learning: A review. *International Journal of Computer and Information System (IJCIS)*, *4*(1), 14–25. http://www.ijcis.net/index.php/ijcis/article/view/102

Gannon-Leary, P., Baines, S., & Wilson, R. (2006). Collaboration and partnership: A review and reflections on a national project to join up local services in England. *Journal of Interprofessional Care*, *20*(6), 665–674. https://www.tandfonline.com/doi/abs/10.1080/13561820600890235

Haiduwa, T., Ntinda, M. N., Hasheela-Mufeti, V., & Ngololo, E. N. (2022). Integrating complementary learning tools in Moodle as a response to the COVID-19 pandemic. In *Teaching and learning with digital technologies in higher education institutions in Africa: Case studies from a pandemic context* (p. 93). https://www.google.com/books?hl=en&lr=&id=rjmVEAAAQBAJ&oi=fnd&pg=PT11&dq=Integrating+complementary+learning+tools+in+Moodle+as+a+response+to+the+COVID-19+pandemic.+Teaching+and+Learning+with+Digital+Technologies+in+Higher+Education+Institutions

+in+Africa:+Case+Studies+from+a+Pandemic+Context,&ots=e0PadOBtpG&sig=BABWaqIu5_jGxcwlLZbwxIlIE3Q

Hao, F. (2021). Acceptance of contactless technology in the hospitality industry: Extending the unified theory of acceptance and use of technology 2. *Asia Pacific Journal of Tourism Research, 26*(12), 1386–1401. https://www.tandfonline.com/doi/abs/10.1080/10941665.2021.1984264

Hockings, M., Dudley, N., & Elliott, W. (2020). Editorial essay: Covid-19 and protected and conserved areas. *Parks, 26*(1). https://par.nsf.gov/servlets/purl/10390418

Ivanova, A. (2018). VR & AR technologies: Opportunities and application obstacles. *Strategic Decisions and Risk Management, 3*, 88–107. https://www.jsdrm.ru/jour/article/view/787?locale=en_US

Kazandzhieva, V., & Filipova, H. (2019). Customer attitudes toward robots in travel, tourism, and hospitality: A conceptual framework. In *Robots, artificial intelligence, and service automation in travel, tourism and hospitality* (pp. 79–92). Emerald Publishing Limited. https://www.emerald.com/insight/content/doi/10.1108/978-1-78756-687-320191004/full/html

Khang, A. (2023). *Applications and principles of quantum computing* (1st Ed.). IGI Global Press. ISBN: 9798369311684. https://doi.org/10.4018/979-8-3693-1168-4

Khang, A., & AIoCF. (2024). *AI-oriented competency framework for talent management in the digital economy: Models, technologies, applications, and implementation* (1st Ed.). CRC Press. ISBN: 9781032576053. https://doi.org/10.1201/9781003440901

Khang, A., Muthmainnah, M., Seraj, P. M. I., Al Yakin, A., Obaid, A. J., & Panda, M. R. (2023). AI-aided teaching model for the education 5.0 ecosystem. In *AI-based technologies and applications in the era of the metaverse* (1st Ed., pp. 83–104). IGI Global Press. https://doi.org/10.4018/978-1-6684-8851-5.ch004

Khang, A., Rana, G., Tailor, R. K., & Hajimahmud, V. A. (2023). *Data-centric AI solutions and emerging technologies in the healthcare ecosystem* (1st Ed.). CRC Press. https://doi.org/10.1201/9781003356189

Khang, A., Rani, S., Gujrati, R., Uygun, H., & Gupta, S. K. (2023). *Designing workforce management systems for industry 4.0: Data-centric and AI-enabled approaches* (1st Ed.). CRC Press. https://doi.org/10.1201/9781003357070

Khang, A., Rath, K. C., Satapathy, S. K., Kumar, A., Das, S. R., & Panda, M. R. (2023). Enabling the future of manufacturing: Integration of robotics and IoT to smart factory infrastructure in industry 4.0. In *AI-based technologies and applications in the era of the metaverse* (1st Ed., pp. 25–50). IGI Global Press. https://doi.org/10.4018/978-1-6684-8851-5.ch002

Kim, S., Park, E., Hong, S., Cho, Y., & del Pobil, A. P. (2011). *They are designing digital signage for better wayfinding performance: New visitors' navigating campus of a university* (pp. 35–40). https://ieeexplore.ieee.org/abstract/document/6014528/

Kohnke, L., Moorhouse, B. L., & Zou, D. (2023). ChatGPT for language teaching and learning. *RELC Journal*, 00336882231162868. https://journals.sagepub.com/doi/abs/10.1177/00336882231162868

Kretschmer, T., & Khashabi, P. (2020). Digital transformation and organization design: An integrated approach. *California Management Review, 62*(4), 86–104. https://journals.sagepub.com/doi/abs/10.1177/0008125620940296

Kumar, S., Dhiraj, A., & Hassan, S. C. C. (2023). Metaverse and cultural marketing in hospitality and tourism. In *Cultural marketing and metaverse for consumer engagement* (pp. 224–233). IGI Global. https://www.igi-global.com/chapter/metaverse-and-cultural-marketing-in-hospitality-and-tourism/321743

Lee, Y., Lee, S., & Kim, D.-Y. (2021). Exploring hotel guests' perceptions of using robot assistants. *Tourism Management Perspectives, 37*, 100781. https://www.sciencedirect.com/science/article/pii/S2211973620301483

Lin, C. C., Yu, W. W., Wang, J., & Ho, M.-H. (2015). Faculty's perceived integration of emerging technologies and pedagogical knowledge in the instructional setting. *Procedia-Social and Behavioral Sciences, 176*, 854–860. https://www.sciencedirect.com/science/article/pii/S187704281500587X

Logan, R. M., Johnson, C. E., & Worsham, J. W. (2021). Development of an e-learning module to facilitate student learning and outcomes. *Teaching and Learning in Nursing, 16*(2), 139–142. https://www.sciencedirect.com/science/article/pii/S1557308720301177

Lukanova, G., & Ilieva, G. (2019). Robots, artificial intelligence, and service automation in hotels. In *Robots, artificial intelligence, and service automation in travel, tourism and hospitality* (pp. 157–183).

Emerald Publishing Limited. https://www.emerald.com/insight/content/doi/10.1108/978-1-78756 -687-320191009/full/Hotels.com

Lutfiani, N., Aini, Q., Rahardja, U., Wijayanti, L., Nabila, E. A., & Ali, M. I. (2021). Transformation of blockchain and opportunities for education 4.0. *International Journal of Education and Learning, 3*(3), 222–231. https://doi.org/10.31763/ijele.v3i3.283

Machado, A., Sousa, M., & Rocha, Á. (2020). *Blockchain technology in education* (pp. 130–134). https://www .researchgate.net/profile/Snejana-Dineva/publication/327557908_The_Benefits_of_Combining_ Social_Media_and_e-learning_for_Training_Improving_in_FTT_Yambol/links/5b966f34a6fdccf d543a4e6d/The-Benefits-of-Combining-Social-Media-and-e-learning-for-Training-Improving-in -FTT-Yambol.pdf#page=271

Manser Payne, E., Peltier, J. W., & Barger, V. A. (2017). Omni-channel marketing, integrated marketing communications and consumer engagement: A research agenda. *Journal of Research in Interactive Marketing, 11*(2), 185–197. https://www.emerald.com/insight/content/doi/10.1108/JRIM-08-2016 -0091/full/html

Mbunge, E. (2020). Integrating emerging technologies into COVID-19 contact tracing: Opportunities, challenges and pitfalls. *Diabetes & Metabolic Syndrome: Clinical Research & Reviews, 14*(6), 1631– 1636. https://www.sciencedirect.com/science/article/pii/S1871402120303325

Mukherjee, S., Baral, M. M., Venkataiah, C., Pal, S. K., & Nagariya, R. (2021). Service robots are an option for contactless services due to the COVID-19 hotel pandemic. *Decision, 48*(4), 445–460. https://link .springer.com/article/10.1007/s40622-021-00300-x

Muthmainnah, M., Khang, A., Seraj, P. M. I., Al Yakin, A., Oteir, I., & Alotaibi, A. N. (2023). An innovative teaching model – The potential of metaverse for English learning. In *AI-based technologies and applications in the era of the metaverse* (1st Ed., pp. 105–126). IGI Global Press. https://doi.org/10.4018 /978-1-6684-8851-5.ch005

Nayak, R., & Padhye, R. (2018). Artificial intelligence and its application in the apparel industry. In *Automation in garment manufacturing* (pp. 109–138). Elsevier. https://doi.org/10.1016/B978-0-08 -101211-6.00005-7

Nayyar, A., Mahapatra, B., Le, D., & Suseendran, G. (2018). Virtual Reality (VR) & Augmented Reality (AR) technologies for the tourism and hospitality industry. *International Journal of Engineering & Technology, 7*(2.21), 156–160. https://www.academia.edu/download/61827146/IJET-1185820200119 -129462-1xdqt7y.pdf

Pestek, A., & Sarvan, M. (2021). Virtual reality and modern tourism. *Journal of Tourism Futures, 7*(2), 245–250. https://doi.org/10.1108/JTF-01-2020-0004

Pillai, R., & Sivathanu, B. (2020). Adoption of AI-based chatbots for hospitality and tourism. *International Journal of Contemporary Hospitality Management, 32*(10), 3199–3226. https://www.emerald.com/ insight/content/doi/10.1108/IJCHM-04-2020-0259/full/html

Saarikko, T., Westergren, U. H., & Blomquist, T. (2020). Digital transformation: Five recommendations for the digitally conscious firm. *Business Horizons, 63*(6), 825–839. https://www.sciencedirect.com/ science/article/pii/S0007681320300975

Santamaría, L., Nieto, M. J., & Rodríguez, A. (2021). Failed and successful innovations: The role of geographic proximity and international diversity of partners in technological collaboration. *Technological Forecasting and Social Change, 166*, 120575. https://www.sciencedirect.com/science/article/pii/ S004016252100007X

Short, C. E., & Short, J. C. (2023). The artificially intelligent entrepreneur: ChatGPT, prompt engineering, and entrepreneurial rhetoric creation. *Journal of Business Venturing Insights, 19*, e00388. https://doi .org/10.1016/j.jbvi.2023.e00388

Solberg, E., Traavik, L. E., & Wong, S. I. (2020). Digital mindsets: Recognizing and leveraging individual beliefs for digital transformation. *California Management Review, 62*(4), 105–124. https://journals .sagepub.com/doi/abs/10.1177/0008125620931839

Sterling, S. (2004). Higher education, sustainability, and the role of systemic learning. In *Higher education and the sustainability challenge: Problematics, promise, and practice* (pp. 49–70). Springer. https://link .springer.com/content/pdf/10.1007/0-306-48515-X.pdf#page=59

Torres, A. M. (2018). Using a smartphone application as a digital key for hotel guest rooms and its other app features. *International Journal of Advanced Science and Technology, 113*, 103–112. https://www.researchgate.net/profile/Arnelyn-Torres/publication/324843176_Using_A_Smartphone_Application_as_A_Digital_Key_for_Hotel_Guest_Room_and_Its_Other_App_Features/links/5bf62580a6fdcc3a8de8c2ec/Using-A-Smartphone-Application-as-A-Digital-Key-for-Hotel-Guest-Room-and-Its-Other-App-Features.pdf

Tussyadiah, I. (2020). A review of research into automation in tourism: Launching the annals of tourism research curated collection on artificial intelligence and robotics in tourism. *Annals of Tourism Research, 81*, 102883. https://www.sciencedirect.com/science/article/pii/S016073832030027X

Wei, Z., Zhang, J., Huang, X., & Qiu, H. (2023). Can gamification improve the virtual reality tourism experience? Analyzing the mediating role of tourism fatigue. *Tourism Management, 96*, 104715. https://www.sciencedirect.com/science/article/pii/S026151772200228X

Wirtz, B. W., Weyerer, J. C., & Geyer, C. (2019). Artificial intelligence and the public sector—Applications and challenges. *International Journal of Public Administration, 42*(7), 596–615. https://doi.org/10.1080/01900692.2018.1498103

Xu, F. Z., Zhang, Y., Zhang, T., & Wang, J. (2021). Facial recognition check-in services at hotels. *Journal of Hospitality Marketing & Management, 30*(3), 373–393. https://www.tandfonline.com/doi/abs/10.1080/19368623.2020.1813670

Yang, Y., Wu, L., Yin, G., Li, L., & Zhao, H. (2017). A survey on security and privacy issues in internet-of-things. *IEEE Internet of Things Journal, 4*(5), 1250–1258. https://doi.org/10.1109/JIOT.2017.2694844

Chapter 11

Leveraging Digital Transformation Technologies in the Hospitality Industry

---

Periasamy P. and Dinesh N.

11.1 Introduction

As the world continues to embrace the digital revolution, the hospitality industry in India is no exception. Digital transformation technologies and tools have reshaped various sectors, and the hospitality industry is now poised to leverage these advancements to provide seamless, personalized, and efficient services to guests. In this chapter, we will explore how the next generation of hospitality in India can harness digital transformation technologies to enhance guest experiences, streamline operations, and stay competitive in a rapidly evolving market (Walton, 2020).

11.1.1 Smart Reservations and Booking Systems

One of the critical aspects of the hospitality industry is managing reservations and bookings effectively. Digital transformation technologies offer innovative solutions to streamline this process. Next-gen hotels and resorts in India can leverage advanced reservation systems powered by Artificial Intelligence (AI) and Machine Learning (ML) algorithms to optimize room rates based on demand patterns, guest preferences, and external factors like events and holidays. These systems can also enable guests to book rooms, spa services, restaurants, and other amenities seamlessly through mobile apps, websites, or Chatbots (Bakker, 2019).

11.1.2 Smart Reservations and Booking Systems in the Indian Hospitality Industry

The Indian hospitality industry has witnessed significant advancements in recent years due to the rapid growth of technology. Smart reservation and booking systems have emerged as

DOI: 10.4324/9781032688305-11

crucial tools to enhance guest experiences, streamline operations, and boost revenue for hotels, resorts, and other accommodation providers. This chapter explores the evolution of reservation and booking systems in the Indian context, highlighting the challenges and opportunities they present. It also delves into the various technologies and strategies employed by the industry to optimize these systems, ultimately creating a seamless and personalized guest journey (Baum et al., 2020).

11.2 Literature Review

11.2.1 Overview of the Indian Hospitality Industry

The Indian hospitality industry is a dynamic and vibrant sector that encompasses a wide range of services, including hotels, resorts, restaurants, travel agencies, and more (Walton, 2020). Known for its rich cultural heritage and warm hospitality, India attracts millions of domestic and international tourists every year. The industry caters to diverse traveler preferences, offering luxury accommodations, budget-friendly options, and eco-friendly experiences. India's hospitality landscape showcases a mix of traditional and modern hospitality concepts, with a focus on personalized guest experiences, culinary diversity, and immersive cultural encounters. The industry is continually evolving, embracing innovative technologies and sustainable practices to meet the ever-changing demands of travelers and to create unforgettable memories for guests from all walks of life.

11.2.2 Importance of Reservations and Booking Systems

Reservations and booking systems play a pivotal role in the success and efficiency of businesses in various industries, particularly in the hospitality sector. These systems are of paramount importance as they enable businesses to manage and allocate their resources effectively, ensuring a seamless and organized experience for both customers and service providers. In the context of the hospitality industry, reservations and booking systems facilitate the efficient allocation of rooms, tables, or services, optimizing occupancy rates and revenue streams. They empower guests with the convenience of booking services in advance, allowing them to plan their trips and experiences with ease.

For businesses, these systems provide valuable data insights, enabling better decision-making through demand forecasting and resource planning. The adoption of online and mobile booking systems has further amplified their significance, catering to the growing digital-savvy consumer base and enabling businesses to stay competitive in an ever-evolving marketplace. Ultimately, the importance of reservations and booking systems lies in their ability to streamline operations, enhance customer satisfaction, and boost the overall profitability and growth of businesses in the hospitality industry and beyond (Brouder et al., 2020).

11.2.3 Objectives of the Chapter

The objectives of this chapter is to discuss the evolution of reservation and booking systems in India, challenges in smart reservations and booking systems, advantages of smart reservations and booking systems, technology enablers for smart reservations, case studies, overcoming challenges, and future outlook (Brouder et al., 2020).

11.3 Evolution of Reservations and Booking Systems in India

11.3.1 Traditional Methods of Reservations and their Limitations

Traditional methods of reservations in the hospitality industry have long relied on manual processes, phone calls, and physical paperwork. In the past, guests would typically make reservations by directly contacting the hotel, resort, or restaurant through telephone calls or in-person visits. While these methods were effective to a certain extent, they came with several limitations. Firstly, they were time-consuming and required dedicated staff to handle bookings and record guest information manually. This led to potential errors and miscommunication, resulting in double bookings or missed reservations.

Additionally, the lack of real-time updates made it challenging for both guests and businesses to keep track of availability and changes in reservations. Furthermore, traditional methods limited accessibility, as guests had to be in proximity to the business or had to navigate time zone differences for international bookings. As the industry evolved and embraced digitalization, these limitations prompted the need for more efficient and convenient online reservation systems to overcome the drawbacks of traditional methods.

11.3.2 Emergence of Online Booking Platforms

The emergence of online booking platforms has revolutionized the hospitality industry, transforming the way guests make reservations and businesses manage bookings. These platforms have emerged as game-changers, offering a convenient and user-friendly interface that allows guests to book accommodations, dining experiences, and other services from the comfort of their own homes or on-the-go using their smartphones or computers. The rise of online booking platforms has significantly streamlined the reservation process, reducing the dependency on manual methods and paperwork.

Businesses can now manage their inventory and availability in real-time, ensuring accurate updates and minimizing the risk of double bookings. Moreover, online booking platforms have enhanced accessibility for both domestic and international travelers, breaking geographical barriers and enabling businesses to reach a global audience. With secure payment gateways and instant confirmation, these platforms have instilled a sense of trust and confidence among guests, making them an indispensable tool in the modern hospitality landscape.

11.3.3 Impact of Mobile Technology on Reservations

The impact of mobile technology on reservations in the hospitality industry has been nothing short of revolutionary. With the widespread adoption of smartphones and the ever-increasing use of mobile applications, guests can now make reservations with unprecedented ease and convenience. Mobile booking platforms have enabled travelers to browse through a wide array of options, from hotels and flights to restaurants and tours, all from the palm of their hands. The integration of location-based services and real-time updates allows guests to find available options nearby or at their intended destinations instantly.

Mobile technology has also facilitated last-minute bookings and spontaneous travel decisions, empowering guests with greater flexibility. For businesses, mobile reservations have opened up new avenues for engagement and personalized marketing, as they can target specific customer segments and offer tailored promotions. The seamless integration of mobile payment options has further expedited the booking process, reducing friction and enhancing guest satisfaction. Overall, the impact of mobile technology on reservations has redefined the guest experience, revolutionizing how travelers plan and book their trips in the fast-paced digital age.

11.4 Challenges in Smart Reservations and Booking Systems

11.4.1 Internet Penetration and Digital Divide in India

Internet penetration and the digital divide in India have been significant areas of concern. While India has made significant progress in increasing internet accessibility in recent years, there still exists a considerable gap between urban and rural areas, as well as between different socioeconomic groups. Urban centers generally enjoy better internet connectivity and access to advanced digital services, whereas remote rural regions face challenges in infrastructure and connectivity. Additionally, disparities in education and income levels have contributed to the digital divide, with certain segments of the population having limited access to technology and the internet. Bridging this divide is crucial for ensuring that all citizens can benefit from the vast opportunities that the digital world offers, including improved access to information, education, healthcare, and economic opportunities (Khang & Muthmainnah et al., 2023). Efforts are being made by the government and various organizations to expand internet connectivity and digital literacy initiatives, striving to create a more inclusive and digitally empowered society in India (Khang & Medicine, 2023).

11.4.2 Data Security and Privacy Concerns

Data security and privacy concerns have become increasingly prominent in the digital age. With the vast amount of personal information being collected and stored online, there is a growing need to safeguard this data from unauthorized access, breaches, and misuse. Individuals are rightly concerned about the protection of their sensitive information, such as financial data, personal details, and browsing habits. Additionally, organizations are also faced with the responsibility of ensuring the security of their customers' data and complying with relevant data-protection regulations. Data breaches can lead to severe consequences, including financial losses, reputational damage, and loss of trust from customers. Addressing data security and privacy concerns requires robust security measures, encryption protocols, and ongoing monitoring to detect and respond to potential threats. It is essential for individuals and organizations alike to prioritize data protection and stay vigilant in safeguarding sensitive information in an increasingly digital world.

11.4.3 Integrating Legacy Systems with Smart Technologies

Integrating legacy systems with smart technologies is a critical step towards modernizing and optimizing existing processes. Legacy systems, though reliable, often lack the flexibility and advanced features of newer technologies. By seamlessly connecting these older systems with smart technologies, businesses can enhance their efficiency, data accessibility, and overall performance. This integration enables the legacy systems to work in harmony with modern solutions, providing a more comprehensive and innovative approach to various tasks. Upgrading without replacing the entire infrastructure also helps companies save costs and minimize disruptions. Whether it's in manufacturing, healthcare, or hospitality, integrating legacy systems with smart technologies paves the way for a more streamlined and technologically advanced future (Khang & Abuzarova et al., 2023).

11.5 Advantages of Smart Reservations and Booking Systems

11.5.1 Streamlining the Booking Process

Streamlining the booking process is crucial for enhancing customer satisfaction and operational efficiency. By simplifying and optimizing the steps required to make a reservation, businesses can attract more customers and secure bookings promptly. Implementing user-friendly online booking platforms and mobile applications allows guests to browse through options, check availability, and make reservations with ease. Offering real-time updates on room or service availability ensures that customers have accurate information at their fingertips. Moreover, integrating secure and efficient payment gateways expedites the booking process, reducing any potential friction. A streamlined booking process not only improves the customer experience but also allows businesses to manage their resources effectively, leading to increased revenue and a competitive edge in the market.

11.5.2 Real-time Availability and Pricing

Real-time availability and pricing are essential aspects of the booking process in the hospitality industry. By providing up-to-date information on room or service availability, businesses can offer customers a seamless and transparent booking experience. Real-time availability ensures that customers can view the current options and make informed decisions based on actual availability. This reduces the likelihood of double bookings or the frustration of not securing the desired services. Moreover, real-time pricing enables businesses to adjust their rates dynamically based on demand and other factors, optimizing revenue and occupancy rates. By implementing dynamic pricing strategies, businesses can offer competitive rates during periods of low demand and maximize profits during peak seasons. Real-time availability and pricing not only improve customer satisfaction but also enable businesses to respond quickly to market changes, ensuring a more efficient and profitable operation.

11.5.3 Personalization and Guest Preferences

Personalization and guest preferences are at the heart of providing exceptional customer experiences in the hospitality industry. Understanding and catering to individual guest preferences can create a sense of exclusivity and make guests feel valued and appreciated. Personalization starts from the moment of booking, where businesses can offer tailored recommendations based on previous preferences, past stays, or special occasions. This attention to detail extends to the guest's arrival, where personalized greetings, room preferences, and amenities can be provided based on their profiles. By collecting and analyzing guest data, hotels and resorts can anticipate needs and offer bespoke experiences that align with each guest's unique tastes and preferences. Whether it's customizing in-room amenities, recommending local experiences, or curating personalized dining options, hospitality businesses can forge a deeper emotional connection with their guests, fostering loyalty and ensuring memorable stays. The implementation of personalized experiences fosters a positive word-of-mouth reputation, encouraging guests to return and share their exceptional experiences with others, making personalization a powerful tool for building long-term relationships with customers.

11.5.4 Upselling Opportunities and Revenue Management

Upselling opportunities and revenue management are integral strategies in the hospitality industry that boost profitability and enhance guest experiences. Upselling involves offering guests additional services, amenities, or room upgrades to enhance their stay and generate additional revenue for the business. By identifying and understanding guest preferences, hotels and resorts can tailor upselling offers that resonate with each guest's interests and needs. This can range from offering spa packages, late check-outs, or room upgrades to personalized dining experiences. Effective upselling not only increases revenue but also improves guest satisfaction as guests feel valued and cared for with these tailored offerings.

Revenue management is a strategic approach to optimizing pricing and inventory to maximize revenue and profitability. Through data analysis and demand forecasting, businesses can adjust pricing dynamically based on factors such as seasonality, demand trends, and competitor rates. By implementing revenue management techniques, hotels can ensure that they are capturing the right market segments at the right time, optimizing revenue potential. This approach allows businesses to avoid overbooking during peak periods and minimize empty rooms during low-demand periods. Combined, upselling opportunities and revenue management contribute to the overall financial health of the hospitality business while creating personalized and memorable experiences for guests. These strategies align business objectives with guest preferences, ensuring a win–win situation for both the hotel and its valued guests.

11.6 Technology Enablers for Smart Reservations

11.6.1 Cloud-based Reservation Systems

Cloud-based reservation systems are digital platforms that enable businesses in the hospitality industry to manage and streamline their booking processes efficiently. Unlike traditional on-premise systems, cloud-based solutions store data and run applications on remote servers accessible through the internet. This cloud-based approach offers several advantages, including enhanced accessibility, real-time updates, and scalability. Businesses can access the reservation system from anywhere with an internet connection, allowing for flexibility and remote management. Real-time updates ensure that inventory and availability information is always current, reducing the risk of overbooking or underutilization.

Additionally, cloud-based reservation systems can easily scale to accommodate changing business needs and handle increased demand during peak seasons. With their cost-effectiveness, ease of use, and adaptability, cloud-based reservation systems have become a valuable asset for the hospitality industry, empowering businesses to provide seamless and efficient booking experiences for their customers.

11.6.2 AI and ML in Bookings

Artificial Intelligence (AI) and Machine Learning (ML) have revolutionized the booking process in the hospitality industry. These advanced technologies enable businesses to provide personalized and efficient booking experiences for their customers. AI-powered Chatbots and virtual assistants can interact with guests in realtime, answering inquiries and guiding them through the booking process, enhancing customer service and engagement. ML algorithms analyze vast amounts of data to predict customer preferences and behavior, enabling businesses to offer tailored recommendations and promotions. Additionally, AI-driven revenue management systems optimize pricing and inventory, ensuring that rates are competitive and inventory is effectively utilized. With AI and ML in bookings, hotels and resorts can deliver seamless, data-driven, and personalized experiences that foster customer loyalty and satisfaction.11.6.3 Big Data Analytics for Demand Forecasting

Big data analytics have transformed demand forecasting in the hospitality industry. By harnessing the power of vast amounts of data, businesses can gain valuable insights into customer behavior, market trends, and historical booking patterns. Big data analytics allow hotels and resorts to predict demand fluctuations with greater accuracy, helping them optimize room rates and inventory management. By understanding peak seasons and periods of low demand, businesses can align their resources and staffing accordingly, maximizing revenue during high-demand periods and reducing costs during low-demand periods. Additionally, big data analytics enable businesses to identify emerging trends and preferences, allowing for the creation of targeted marketing campaigns and personalized experiences. With big data analytics for demand forecasting, the hospitality industry can make data-driven decisions that enhance operational efficiency, improve customer experiences, and drive overall business success.

11.6.4 Blockchain for Secure and Transparent Transactions

Blockchain technology has emerged as a revolutionary solution for secure and transparent transactions in various industries, including finance and supply chain management. In the context of the hospitality industry, blockchain offers immense potential to enhance the security and transparency of transactions. By employing a decentralized and immutable ledger, blockchain ensures that all transaction records are securely stored and cannot be altered or tampered with. This feature enhances trust between parties, such as hotels, customers, and payment processors, as they can rely on the accuracy and integrity of the transaction data. Additionally, blockchain enables realtime updates and visibility of transaction status, promoting transparency throughout the process. With blockchain's robust security measures and transparency, the hospitality industry can create a more efficient and trustworthy ecosystem for financial transactions, fostering greater customer confidence and streamlining business operations.

11.7 Case Studies: Best Practices in Indian Hospitality

11.7.1 OYO Rooms: Leveraging Technology for Efficient Reservations

- **Introduction**: OYO Rooms, India's largest hospitality company, has been at the forefront of leveraging technology to revolutionize the reservations process in the hotel industry. Founded in 2013 by Ritesh Agarwal, OYO Rooms started as a budget hotel aggregator but quickly expanded its offerings to encompass a wide range of hotels and properties. The company's relentless focus on technology has enabled it to provide a seamless and efficient booking experience for its customers, cementing its position as a leading player in the Indian hospitality market (Moro & Rita, 2018).

■ **Streamlining the Booking Process**: OYO Rooms has adopted a mobile-first approach, recognizing the increasing preference of customers to use smartphones for travel planning and bookings. The company has developed a user-friendly mobile app and website that allow customers to browse through a diverse selection of hotels, view real-time availability, and make instant bookings. The intuitive interface ensures that the entire reservation process can be completed in just a few taps, providing customers with a hassle-free experience.

■ **Dynamic Pricing and Inventory Management**: One of OYO Rooms' key strengths lies in its data-driven approach to pricing and inventory management. The company uses advanced analytics and ML algorithms to analyze vast amounts of data, including historical booking patterns, customer behavior, and market trends. This data-driven approach enables OYO Rooms to implement dynamic pricing strategies, adjusting room rates in real-time based on demand and supply dynamics. As a result, the company can optimize revenue and occupancy rates, ensuring that rooms are priced competitively and efficiently utilized.

■ **Personalized Recommendations and Loyalty Programs**: OYO Rooms utilize customer data to offer personalized recommendations and incentives through its loyalty program. The platform tracks customer preferences, previous bookings, and feedback to curate tailored suggestions for each guest. These personalized recommendations enhance customer satisfaction and increase the likelihood of repeat bookings. Additionally, OYO's loyalty program rewards frequent customers with exclusive discounts and benefits, fostering customer loyalty and retention.

■ **Real-time Updates and Instant Confirmation**: OYO Rooms' technology ensures that all reservation data are updated in real time across its platform. Customers can instantly check the availability of rooms, view updated rates, and receive immediate confirmation upon completing their booking. This real-time update feature minimizes the risk of over-booking and keeps customers informed about their reservation status, enhancing trust and reliability.

■ **Conclusion**: OYO Rooms' commitment to leveraging technology for efficient reservations has redefined the hotel booking experience in India. By adopting a mobile-first approach, implementing dynamic pricing, and offering personalized recommendations, the company has set new standards for customer convenience and satisfaction. Through continuous technological advancements, OYO Rooms continues to optimize its reservation process, providing travelers with a seamless and delightful booking experience in the dynamic and competitive hospitality industry.

11.7.2 MakeMyTrip: Transforming the Online Booking Landscape

■ **Introduction**: MakeMyTrip, founded in 2000 by Deep Kalra, is India's leading online travel platform. The company's vision was to empower travelers with a one-stop solution for all their travel needs. Over the years, MakeMyTrip has played a significant role in transforming the online booking landscape in India, revolutionizing how people plan and book their trips.

■ **Comprehensive Platform and User-Friendly Interface**: MakeMyTrip offers a comprehensive platform that caters to various travel services, including flights, hotels, holiday packages, bus bookings, and more. The user-friendly website and mobile app provides a seamless experience for customers to search, compare, and book their desired travel options. With an extensive range of choices and filters, customers can tailor their travel plans based on preferences and budget.

■ **Real-time Pricing and Offers**: MakeMyTrip leverages technology to provide real-time updates on pricing and availability, ensuring customers have access to the latest offers and deals. The platform's dynamic pricing system enables customers to book flights and hotels at the best available rates, with instant confirmation. Additionally, the website showcases exclusive deals and discounts, encouraging customers to book through MakeMyTrip to avail themselves of special offers.

■ **Personalization and Customer Engagement**: MakeMyTrip employs data analytics to understand customer preferences and behavior, enabling personalized recommendations and targeted marketing. The platform uses AI-driven algorithms to curate customized travel packages, offering customers tailored suggestions based on their past bookings and interests. By engaging customers through targeted promotions, personalized deals, and loyalty programs, MakeMyTrip fosters long-term relationships with its users.

■ **Seamless Integration and Travel Planning**: MakeMyTrip's integration of various travel services streamlines the entire travel planning process for customers. Users can effortlessly book flights, reserve hotels, and schedule activities all in one place, creating a cohesive and convenient experience. Additionally, the platform provides in-depth information about destinations, travel itineraries, and reviews, empowering customers to make informed decisions.

■ **Expansion and Global Reach**: What started as an online travel agency catering to domestic travel has expanded its reach globally. MakeMyTrip now serves not only the Indian market but also international travelers, offering bookings for flights and hotels worldwide. This expansion has broadened its customer base and strengthened its position as a leading player in the online travel industry.

■ **Conclusion**: MakeMyTrip's relentless focus on technology, innovation, and customer-centricity has transformed the online booking landscape in India. With its user-friendly platform, real-time pricing, personalization, and seamless integration, MakeMyTrip has revolutionized the way people plan and book their travel. Its commitment to providing a holistic travel experience, along with its global expansion, has made MakeMyTrip a trusted and preferred platform for millions of travelers, reshaping the travel industry in India and beyond (Moro & Rita, 2018).

11.7.3 Marriott Hotels: Personalized Experiences through Loyalty Programs

■ **Introduction**: Marriott International, a global hospitality giant founded in 1927, has become synonymous with luxury, innovation, and exceptional guest experiences. To enhance customer loyalty and foster long-term relationships, Marriott Hotels has invested heavily in personalized experiences through its renowned loyalty program – Marriott Bonvoy.

■ **Integration of Multiple Brands**: Marriott Hotels boasts an extensive portfolio of hotel brands, ranging from luxury to budget-friendly options. The Marriott Bonvoy loyalty program seamlessly integrates all these brands, offering members a unified rewards system regardless of where they stay. This integration allows guests to earn and redeem loyalty points across a vast network of hotels and resorts, creating a seamless and consistent experience.

■ **Data-Driven Personalization**: Marriott Bonvoy utilizes data analytics to gain valuable insights into guest preferences, behaviors, and travel patterns. By analyzing this data, Marriott can personalize the guest experience, providing tailored recommendations and offers based on individual preferences. From room preferences to local activities and dining options, guests receive customized suggestions that resonate with their tastes, creating a sense of exclusivity and making them feel valued.

■ **Tiered Membership Benefits**: The Marriott Bonvoy program offers tiered membership levels based on a member's frequency of stays and spending. Each tier – Silver, Gold, Platinum, Titanium, and Ambassador – comes with a unique set of benefits, such as room upgrades, late check-outs, and access to exclusive lounges. The tiered structure motivates guests to achieve higher membership levels, enticing them with increasingly luxurious perks and enhancing their overall loyalty to Marriott.

■ **Mobile App Convenience**: Marriott's mobile app plays a crucial role in delivering personalized experiences to members. The app allows members to book stays, manage reservations, and check-in digitally, providing a seamless and contactless experience. The app's personalized dashboard showcases upcoming stays, relevant promotions, and offers tailored to each member's preferences, ensuring that guests stay engaged with the program and its benefits.

■ **Innovative Partnerships and Experiences**: Marriott Bonvoy goes beyond traditional hotel loyalty programs by forming innovative partnerships with various brands and experiences. Members can redeem points for unique experiences like VIP access to concerts, sports events, and cultural activities, further enriching their travel journeys and creating lasting memories.

■ **Conclusion**: Marriott Hotels' commitment to personalized experiences through the Marriott Bonvoy loyalty program has solidified its position as a leader in the hospitality industry. By leveraging data-driven insights, integrating multiple brands, and offering innovative rewards, Marriott has successfully built strong customer loyalty. The program's ability to provide guests with tailored experiences, matched with its global presence and luxury offerings, has made Marriott Hotels the preferred choice for travelers seeking exceptional hospitality and personalized service.

11.8 Overcoming Challenges and Future Outlook

11.8.1 Bridging the Digital Gap in India

Bridging the digital gap in India is a crucial mission to ensure inclusive growth and equal access to opportunities for all citizens. The digital gap refers to the disparity in access to technology and digital services between urban and rural areas, as well as among different socioeconomic groups. To address this challenge, the Indian government and various organizations are implementing initiatives to enhance digital literacy, expand internet connectivity, and provide affordable access to digital devices. By empowering people with digital skills and knowledge, and making technology accessible to even the most remote areas, India can unlock the full potential of its population, driving socioeconomic development and creating a more equitable society (Khang & Shah et al., 2023).

11.8.2 Enhancing Cybersecurity Measures

Enhancing cybersecurity measures is of paramount importance in today's interconnected digital world. With the increasing reliance on technology and the internet, cyber threats pose significant risks to individuals, businesses, and governments. Strengthening cybersecurity involves implementing robust protocols, utilizing advanced encryption techniques, and regularly updating security systems to protect against cyberattacks. It also entails educating users about cybersecurity best practices and fostering a culture of vigilance and awareness. By prioritizing cybersecurity, organizations and individuals can safeguard sensitive data, prevent data breaches, and ensure a safe and secure digital environment for everyone (Khang & Kali et al., 2023).

11.8.3 Training and Upskilling the Hospitality Workforce

Training and upskilling the hospitality workforce is essential to ensure exceptional guest experiences and elevate the overall quality of service in the industry. By investing in training programs, employees can develop new skills, enhance their existing abilities, and stay updated with the latest trends and best practices. These initiatives can cover a wide range of areas, from customer service and communication skills to technical expertise in using modern technology and systems.

Upskilling the workforce not only boosts employee confidence and job satisfaction but also fosters loyalty and retention. Ultimately, a well-trained and skilled hospitality workforce plays a vital role in creating unforgettable moments for guests, leading to increased customer satisfaction and loyalty, and ultimately driving the success of hotels and resorts in a competitive market.

11.8.4 Embracing Emerging Technologies

Embracing emerging technologies is vital for businesses to stay competitive and thrive in the rapidly evolving world. Technologies like AI, blockchain, the Internet of Things (IoT), and virtual reality offer unprecedented opportunities to enhance efficiency, customer experiences, and decision-making. By adopting these innovations, companies can streamline processes, automate tasks, and offer personalized solutions to customers.

Embracing emerging technologies not only boosts productivity and profitability but also demonstrates a commitment to innovation and staying ahead in the market. As technology continues to shape industries, businesses that embrace and leverage these cutting-edge tools will be better equipped to meet the ever-changing needs and expectations of their customers and secure a successful future (Traskevich & Fontanari, 2021).

11.9 Results and Discussion

8.1 Recapitulation of key points: Hitherto we have discussed the evolution of reservation and booking systems in India, challenges in smart reservations and booking systems, advantages of smart reservations and booking systems, technology enablers for smart reservations, technology enablers for smart reservations and case studies except on overcoming challenges and future outlook which will be discussed subsequently.

11.9.1 The Future of Smart Reservations in the Indian Hospitality Industry

According to Traskevich, A., & Fontanari, M. (2021), the future of smart reservations in the Indian hospitality industry looks incredibly promising. As technology continues to advance, smart reservation systems will become even more sophisticated and intuitive, offering seamless and personalized booking experiences for travelers. AI-powered Chatbots and virtual assistants will become even smarter, providing instant and accurate responses to customer inquiries and assisting with bookings round the clock. Additionally, real-time data analytics will enable businesses to optimize pricing and inventory management, ensuring that room rates are dynamically adjusted based on demand and supply.

Integration with emerging technologies like blockchain will enhance the security and transparency of transactions, instilling greater trust in the booking process. With the continued emphasis on mobile technology, booking platforms will become more accessible and user-friendly, catering to the growing digital-savvy customer base. The future of smart reservations in the Indian hospitality industry holds the promise of elevating guest experiences, boosting operational efficiency, and staying ahead in the competitive landscape, shaping a more innovative and customer-centric hospitality sector (Brouder et al., 2020).

11.9.2 Personalized Guest Experience

The future of hospitality lies in providing personalized experiences to guests. Digital technologies such as data analytics, Internet of Things (IoT) devices, and facial recognition can be integrated into the guest experience. Hotels can collect and analyze guest data to understand preferences, behavior, and previous interactions, enabling them to tailor services and offers accordingly. IoT devices can be used to adjust room settings automatically, based on the guest's preferences, while facial recognition can expedite check-ins and enhance security.

The Indian hospitality industry has long been recognized for its warm hospitality and cultural richness. With the rapid integration of technology and a growing focus on customer-centricity, the industry has shifted towards providing personalized guest experiences. This chapter explores the significance of personalized guest experiences in the Indian context, examining the factors driving this trend and its impact on guest satisfaction and loyalty. We will delve into the strategies employed by the industry to deliver tailored services and create lasting impressions on guests, ensuring a competitive edge in an increasingly global market (Traskevich & Fontanari, 2021).

11.9.3 Immersive Virtual and Augmented Reality

Virtual Reality (VR) and Augmented Reality (AR) have the potential to revolutionize the way guests interact with hotels and destinations. Through VR, potential guests can take virtual tours of hotel rooms and facilities, giving them a realistic feel of the accommodation. AR can be used to enhance on-site experiences, offering guests interactive guides to explore local attractions, restaurants, and cultural events. By integrating VR and AR into their marketing strategies, hotels can create a more engaging and captivating experience for potential guests (Wagler & Hanus, 2018).

The Indian hospitality industry is embracing cutting-edge technologies to enhance guest experiences and stay competitive in the global market. Immersive Virtual Reality (VR) and Augmented Reality (AR) have emerged as powerful tools, transforming the way guests interact with hotels, resorts, and tourist destinations (Wagler & Hanus, 2018). This chapter explores the applications of VR and AR in the Indian hospitality industry, examining how these technologies are revolutionizing marketing, guest engagement, training, and more. We will also delve into the challenges and opportunities associated with implementing immersive technologies and their potential to redefine the future of hospitality in India (Perles-Ribes et al., 2021).

11.9.4 Contactless Technology and Mobile Integration

The recent global events have accelerated the adoption of contactless technologies in the hospitality industry. Mobile integration allows guests to check-in, access their rooms, and make payments through their smartphones, reducing the need for physical contact. Hotels can equip rooms with IoT devices, enabling guests to control lighting, temperature, and entertainment systems using their mobile devices. Moreover, mobile apps can also provide real-time communication with hotel staff, enhancing guest satisfaction and improving service efficiency.

In response to the global pandemic and changing guest preferences, the Indian hospitality industry has accelerated its adoption of contactless technology and mobile integration. This chapter explores the significant role of these innovations in redefining guest experiences and operational efficiency. We will delve into the various contactless solutions implemented by hotels, restaurants, and travel agencies, examining their impact on safety, convenience, and personalization. Additionally, the chapter will address challenges, opportunities, and the future potential of contactless technology and mobile integration in the context of the vibrant Indian hospitality landscape (Perles-Ribes et al., 2021).

11.9.5 *AI and Chatbots*

AI-powered Chatbots are transforming customer service in the hospitality industry. These virtual assistants can handle guest inquiries, provide information about hotel amenities, and assist with reservations and bookings. By using Natural Language Processing (NLP), Chatbots can engage with guests in a human-like manner, offering a seamless and efficient experience. They are available 24/7, reducing the need for additional customer support staff and ensuring guests receive immediate responses to their queries (Salet, 2021).

The Indian hospitality industry is undergoing a technological revolution, and AI and Chatbots have emerged as game-changers in enhancing guest experiences, streamlining operations, and optimizing customer service. This chapter explores the diverse applications of AI and Chatbots in the Indian hospitality landscape, from personalized guest interactions and efficient booking systems to data-driven decision-making and revenue management. We will delve into the challenges, benefits, and future potential of AI and Chatbots, illustrating how these intelligent technologies are shaping the future of hospitality in India (Samarathunga & Gamage, 2020).

11.9.6 *Blockchain for Security and Trust*

Blockchain technology can significantly enhance security and trust within the hospitality industry. Smart contracts powered by blockchain can facilitate secure and transparent transactions between hotels, customers, and other service providers. Guests can have confidence in the authenticity of reviews and ratings, while hotels can efficiently manage loyalty programs through decentralized systems. Furthermore, blockchain can secure guest data and protect it from potential breaches, strengthening the overall cybersecurity framework (Sharma, Thomas, & Paul, 2021).

In an era where data security and trust are paramount, the Indian hospitality industry is exploring innovative solutions to safeguard sensitive information and enhance guest confidence. Blockchain technology has emerged as a promising tool to address these concerns (Sharma, Thomas, & Paul, 2021). This chapter explores the applications of blockchain in the Indian hospitality sector, highlighting its role in securing guest data, improving transparency, and streamlining various processes. We will delve into real-world use cases, challenges, and the potential for blockchain to revolutionize security and trust in the dynamic and diverse landscape of Indian hospitality (Samarathunga & Gamage, 2020).

11.10 Conclusion

The next generation of the hospitality industry in India stands at the precipice of a digital transformation revolution. Embracing the various digital technologies and tools available can offer substantial benefits, including improved guest experiences, increased operational efficiency, and enhanced competitiveness. By investing in smart reservations and booking systems, personalization, virtual and augmented reality, contactless technology, AI-powered Chatbots, and blockchain for security, hotels can redefine the guest experience and position themselves as leaders in the industry. With a strategic approach and a commitment to innovation, the hospitality sector in India can unlock the full potential of digital transformation and pave the way for a brighter and more dynamic future (Sharma, Thomas, & Paul, 2021; Salet, 2021).

References

Bakker, M. (2019). A conceptual framework for identifying the binding constraints to tourism-driven inclusive growth. *Tourism Planning & Development*, 16(5), 575–590. https://www.tandfonline.com/doi/abs/10.1080/21568316.2018.1541817

Baum, T., & Hai, N. T. T. (2020). Hospitality, tourism, human rights and the impact of COVID-19. *International Journal of Contemporary Hospitality Management*. https://www.emerald.com/insight/content/doi/10.1108/IJCHM-03-2020-0242/full/

Brouder, P., Teoh, S., Salazar, N. B., Mostafanezhad, M., Pung, J. M., Lapointe, D., Higgins Desbiolles, F., Haywood, M., Hall, C. M., & Clausen, H. B. (2020). Reflections and discussions: Tourism matters in the new normal post COVID-19. *Tourism Geographies*, 22(3), 735–746. https://doi.org/10.1080/14616688.20.1770325

Buhalis, D., & O'Connor, P. (2005). Information communication technology revolutionizing tourism. *Tourism Recreation Research*, 30(3), 7–16. https://doi.org/10.1080/02508281.2005.11081482

Khang, A. (2023). *AI and IoT-Based Technologies for Precision Medicine* (1st Ed.). IGI Global Press. ISBN: 9798369308769. https://doi.org/10.4018/979-8-3693-0876-9

Khang, A., Abdullayev, V. A., Alyar, A. V., Khalilov, M., & Murad, B. (2023). AI-aided data analytics tools and applications for the healthcare sector. *AI and IoT-Based Technologies for Precision Medicine* (1st Ed.). IGI Global Press. ISBN: 9798369308769. https://doi.org/10.4018/979-8-3693-0876-9.ch018

Khang, A., Muthmainnah, M., Seraj, P. M. I., Al Yakin, A., Obaid, A. J., & Panda, M. R. (2023). AI-aided teaching model for the education 5.0 ecosystem. *AI-Based Technologies and Applications in the Era of the Metaverse* (1st Ed., pp. 83–104). IGI Global Press. https://doi.org/10.4018/978-1-6684-8851-5.ch004

Khang, A., Rath, K. C., Satapathy, S. K., Kumar, A., Das, S. R., & Panda, M. R. (2023). Enabling the future of manufacturing: Integration of robotics and IoT to smart factory infrastructure in industry 4.0. *AI-Based Technologies and Applications in the Era of the Metaverse* (1st Ed., pp. 25–50). IGI Global Press. https://doi.org/10.4018/978-1-6684-8851-5.ch002

Khang, A., Shah, V., & Rani, S. (2023). *AI-Based Technologies and Applications in the Era of the Metaverse* (1st Ed.). IGI Global Press. https://doi.org/10.4018/978-1-6684-8851-5

Moro, S., & Rita, P. (2018). Brand strategies in social media in hospitality and tourism. *International Journal of Contemporary Hospitality Management*. https://www.emerald.com/insight/content/doi/10.1108/IJCHM-07-2016-0340/full/html?fullSc=1&fullSc=1&mbSc=1&utm_source=TrendMD&utm_medium=cpc&utm_campaign=International_Journal_of_Contemporary_Hospitality_Management_TrendMD_1&WT.mc_id=Emerald_TrendMD_1

Perles-Ribes, J. F., Ramón-Rodríguez, A. B., Jesús-Such-Devesa, M., & Aranda-Cuéllar, P. (2021). The immediate impact of Covid19 on tourism employment in Spain: Debunking the myth of job precariousness? *Tourism Planning and Development*. Routledge. https://doi.org/10.1080/21568316.2021.1886163.

Rogerson, C. M., & Rogerson, J. M. (2020). Camping tourism: A review of recent international scholarship. *GeoJournal of Tourism & Geosites*, 28(1). http://gtg.webhost.uoradea.ro/PDF/GTG-1-2020/gtg.28127 -474.pdf

Salet, X. (2021). The search for the truest of authenticities: Online travel stories and their depiction of the authentic in the platform economy. *Annals of Tourism Research*, 88, 103175. https://www.sciencedirect .com/science/article/pii/S0160738321000372

Samarathunga, W., & Gamage, D. (2020). Alternative tourism as an alternate to mass tourism during the Post-COVID-19 recovery phase: The case of Sri Lanka. Academic Press. https://www.researchgate .net/profile/Whms-Samarathunga/publication/341809478_Alternative_Tourism_as_an_Alternate _to_Mass_Tourism_during_the_Post-COVID-19_Recovery_Phase_the_Case_of_Sri_Lanka/links /5f053c5ea6fdcc4ca455cb86/Alternative-Tourism-as-an-Alternate-to-Mass-Tourism-during-the-Post -COVID-19-Recovery-Phase-the-Case-of-Sri-Lanka.pdf

Sharma, G. D., Thomas, A., & Paul, J. (2021). Reviving tourism industry post-COVID-19: A resilience-based framework. *Tourism Management Perspectives*, 37, 100786. https://www.sciencedirect.com/sci ence/article/pii/S2211973620301537

Traskevich, A., & Fontanari, M. (2021). Tourism potentials in Post-COVID19: The concept of destination resilience for advanced sustainable management in tourism. *Tourism Planning & Development*, 1–25. https://doi.org/10.1080/21568316.2021.1894599

Wagler, A., & Hanus, M. D. (2018). Comparing virtual reality tourism to real-life experience: Effects of presence and engagement on attitude and enjoyment. *Communication Research Reports*, 35(5), 456–464. https://www.tandfonline.com/doi/abs/10.1080/08824096.2018.1525350

Walton, J. K. (2020). Tourism | Definition, history, types, importance, & industry | Britannica. https:// www.britannica.com/topic/tourism

Zhang, H., & Xu, H. (2019). Impact of destination psychological ownership on residents' "place citizenship behavior." *Journal of Destination Marketing & Management*, 14, 100391. https://www.sciencedirect .com/science/article/pii/S2212571X19301398

Zhuang, X., Yao, Y., & Li, J. J. (2019). Sociocultural impacts of tourism on residents of world cultural heritage sites in China. *Sustainability*, 11(3), 840. https://www.mdpi.com/2071-1050/11/3/840

Chapter 12

Emerging Technology for Sustainable Development: A Revolution in the Hospitality Industry

Asha Sharma, Aditya Mishra, and Renu Sharma

12.1 Introduction

Tourism and Information and Communication Technologies (ICT) are long interconnected; thus AI for the majority of the market remains undiscovered. In the rapidly changing economic era of globalization and industrialization, the tourism sector has emerged as one of the world's largest industries. The concern on Tourism and development has assumed phenomenal significance at the global, national, and local levels. Consequently, the globalized economic order, there is now a free exchange of trade and culture among the countries of the world.

In fact, tourism is an emerging pertinent industry and it is considered a major engine of economic growth in various parts of the globe, especially in the Asia-Pacific region, including certain countries of Europe and South-East Asia. Several countries of the world have transformed their economies, particularly certain small countries of Europe like Switzerland, followed by some of the South-East Asian countries, mainly Singapore, Malaysia, Thailand, Mauritius, South Korea, Japan, and Sri Lanka using their tourism potential to the fullest. Its output is very fruitful because tourism possesses vast employment opportunities of diverse kinds, from the most specialized to the unskilled lion share population of human society.

Technological innovations support increased efficiency in every industrial sector. Artificial intelligence (AI) is among the most important innovative solutions. Intelligence is measurable and clearly defined. The meaning of AI is not clearly defined; however, the term is most often associated with practical advantages and development (Khanh & Khang et al., 2021).

In the term AI, mainly two factors or technologies are taken here, i.e., big data (cloud compound) and Robotics. Big data is the data-processing application software to adequately deal with.

DOI: 10.4324/9781032688305-12

With cross-sell and up-sell now being challenging tasks in the well-informed clients' market, big data analysis has come into the notice of almost all the businesses to understand the individualistic needs of clients based on their past preferences. Many hotels have undergone a sea-change in their services, like the old-traditional rooms revamped into a smart room with voice-activated control of room temperature, television, curtains, etc.

Not to stop at this but the intelligent face-recognition front-desk receptions to relax the guest from carrying physical ID-proofs everywhere; Chatbots to guide the guest about the services at the hotel, and also the smart mattresses that remember a guest's sleeping patterns. The hotels are making an effort to keep a record of all this data to achieve return-clients and loyalty. This voluminous big data has become a crucial part of the hotel space for the past couple of years. Even at an early stage, diverse big data have been applied to tourism research and made an amazing improvement. Robotics is the technology dreamed up for those blockbuster productions is the same as what we see entering our reality today (Khang & Kali et al., 2023).

12.2 Review of Literature

Review of research on the tourism sector is necessary for the purpose of understanding the facts about the tourism industry. Research papers related to the tourism sector have been reviewed. These goals (SDGs) were established to advance the transition to a more just and sustainable society. According to the findings of a 2017 World Economic Forum (WEF) study on AI and robotics, the global economy is not prepared for "Automation and Robotization," which could result in high unemployment rates. This study explores the pros and cons of AI, as well as contemporary beliefs, its pervasiveness in society, and the various ways it has been used (Aslam et al., 2023).

A review of AI's impact on the realization of the Sustainable Development Goals is necessary given its emergence and steadily expanding impact across numerous sectors. We discover that AI can facilitate the accomplishment of 134 targets across all the goals via a consensus-based expert elicitation procedure, but it may also block 59 targets (Vinuesa et al., 2020).

AI is quickly opening up a new frontier. This article examines the effects of AI in three case studies in an effort to answer these questions. The analysis of the effects of AI on sustainable development in this chapter combines the viewpoints of business strategy and public policy, with an emphasis on the advancement of the SDGs. It also includes some managerial learning and leadership development lessons for a sustainable world (Goralski & Tan, 2020) (Khang & Muthmainnah et al., 2023).

It has only just become clear how the industrial and digital revolutions have altered the social and economic structures of the world. The objective of these guidelines is to benefit people. Too complicated a concept could leave the viewers perplexed. These advancements offer the opportunity to improve tools, solutions, and services in an effort to address some of the most serious issues in the world and promote progress towards the United Fragile healthcare systems in low- and middle-income nations are in danger due to rising NCD rates (Aerts & Bogdan-Martin, 2021) (Khang & Medicine, 2023).

It is stated that the major issues that are restraining the industry from achieving high economic value are shortage of qualified personnel, shortage of tourism training institutes, shortage of well-qualified trainers, and working conditions for the employees (Banerjee, 2018).

Management challenges with the maintenance of tourism experience concept innovations: Towards a new research agenda described a new research agenda within the debates about tourism, the experience economy, and innovation. Knowledge about innovation and value co-creation within experience-based sectors has increased, but most studies focus on the initial steps of the innovation process (Eide et al., 2017).

It is explored in the article "Dawning of the age of robots in hospitality and tourism: Challenges for teaching and research" that it is evident that robotics will challenge businesses to unify robots into an already composite system of employees, customers, suppliers, and information technologies. This chapter expressed a wide range of utilization of robotics in tourism, from industrial robots in the back of the house to service robots in the front of the house, and underlines the importance of human–robot interaction (Murphy et al., 2017).

Robotic technologies promote service augmentation; particularly, chatbots and virtual receptionists appear supportive to humans' skills and knowledge by infiltrating online communication between customers and intermediaries. In the tourism field, those technologies enable users to interact with digital assistants, using natural language to answer travel-related inquiries and process bookings and reservations (Pan et al., 2013).

12.3 Application of AI-Digital Landscape In the Hospitality Industry

Tourism industry is no exception to the many sectors affected by AI: Different smart systems are used in travel agencies and air transport companies. Predictions about the near future foresee the development of personalized solutions, which will lead to further re-arrangement in the technological revolution that has been going on for decades in the tourism industry as shown in Figure 12.1 (a, b).

12.3.1 Big Data

The hotel industry is a data-rich industry that gathers and uses the data for understanding segment behavior, needs, and expectations; identifying profitable customer segments and their buying preferences; and identifying opportunities to attract new guests. But all of that starts with having a clear customer-driven vision before embarking on integrating and standardizing guest data from multiple channels, systems, and properties into a unified, accurate view of all interactions.

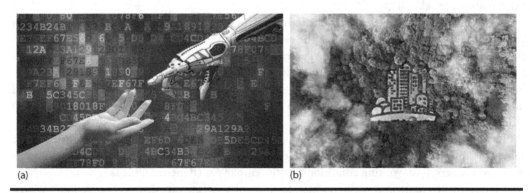

Figure 12.1   Hotel tech in the tourism industry. *Source*: **https://www.hotelierindia.com/operations/allure-of-artificial-intelligence.**

It is vitally important for hoteliers to be able to understand guest preferences (locations, activities, and room types), purchase behavior (frequency, length of stay, and time of year), and profit potential in order to increase the brand loyalty and wallet share of their most valuable guests.

To maximize profits, hotels need to increase the loyalty and wallet share of their most valuable guests by marketing their preferences and encouraging repeat visits. Focusing on the wrong guests reduces profitability across the enterprise. For example, if a hotel targeted guests who would likely take advantage of spa services, golf, and restaurants, rather than guests who only generate room nights, they could significantly increase revenues and profitability. Unfortunately, money often gets spent on blanket campaigns that don't target individual guests or segments with offers they're most likely to respond to. As a result, guests may feel that the hotel doesn't care about them, or simply doesn't offer services designed to meet their needs.

Hoteliers are starting to use more and more predictive analytics to move from reactive to proactive decision-making, which would enable them to stay one step ahead of trends, set strategy, and achieve goals. The segmentation approach might look as follows: initial learning from this type of segmentation could be used in developing a marketing strategy that is data-driven (Khang & Abuzarova et al., 2023). We would certainly expect that local events held by the oil and gas industry might be more appropriate in one city, while financial services-type events may be more prevalent somewhere else.

12.3.2 Robotics

This technology is applicable to almost every industry, thanks to customer interaction – a prime area for smart tech to be implemented. The current status and potential adoption of service automation and robots by tourist, travel, and hospitality companies have increased in a fantastic way. Hospitality robots are clearly at a tipping point. They're now cost-effective to build, are attaining cultural acceptance, and use sophisticated technology to safely live and work among us. But what's next in this fast-moving field? In this article, the five key robot trends set to emerge in the hospitality sector are shown in Figure 12.2 (a, b).

12.3.3 Five Key Robot Trends

- The number of people helped by hospitality robots will double by the end of 2017.
- Robots will create a large number of jobs in hospitality and other sectors.
- Hospitality will be a pioneering industry for human--robot interaction.

(a) (b)

Figure 12.2 AI and robotics in the tourism industry. *Source*: **https://www.hotelierindia.com/ operations/allure-of-artificial-intelligence.**

■ Robots will be a critical data source.
■ Anxiety about robots will be replaced with feelings of comfort and delight.

12.3.4 Technology Trends Transforming the Hotel Industry

With the use of smart room technology, visitors can adapt their accommodations to their specific needs. IoT applications create the ideal hotel room with voice-activated customer care, digital key cards, and other features. Big data is revolutionizing the hotel technology industry as shown in Figure 12.3.

Hotels are able to gather a lot of consumer data that can be used to analyze consumer behavior and provide more individualized services to visitors. Mobile check-in options limit interactions between customers and staff. One of the most notable advancements in hospitality technology during the epidemic is contactless payments. For international visitors who speak different languages, translation tools are crucial hospitality technology trends. Robotic services are used in hotels for housekeeping and room service. To protect visitor data, robust cybersecurity procedures are also required (Khang & Vladimir, 2022).

12.4 Research Methodology

12.4.1 Data Collection

Primary data will be collected from tourists via questionnaires. The tourists will be approached in order to acquire their response through questionnaire. Questionnaires from 384 tourists, tourist guides, and local artisans were filled but 250 were found suitable.

12.4.2 Objective

The study focuses on two important objectives. The aim of the study is to focus on the application of AI in the hospitality sector. The purpose of the study is to find the impact of leveraging AI-digital landscape on sustainable development.

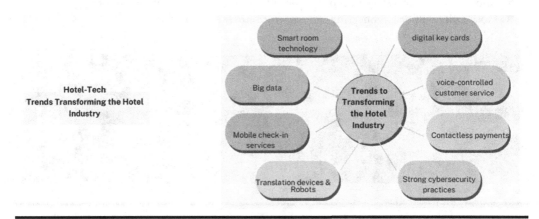

Figure 12.3   Components of transforming the hotel industry. *Source*: Own compilation.

12.4.3 Hypothesis

■ H_{01}: There is no significant impact of the application of AI-digital landscape on sustainable overall development.
■ H_{02}: There is no significant social impact of AI-digital landscape on social development.
■ H_{03}: There is no significant economic impact of AI-digital landscape on economic development.

12.5 Result and Discussion

Hypotheses have been tested at various levels of potential at social, economic, cultural, and overall development levels of tourism industry. For study and analysis purposes, it is divided further into four sub parts:

■ Impact of AI-digital landscape on sustainable overall development.
■ Impact of AI-digital landscape on social development.
■ Impact of AI-digital landscape on economic development

For all the questions that have been asked to the respondents about their satisfaction level towards different parameters of the social cost and benefit measured on a five-point Likert scale, with the options are a total of 12 questions, as shown in Table 12.1.

12.5.1 SPSS Output – Case 1

It had been found that there was no significant difference in the tourism demand and adaptation of AI. The p-value is found to be less than .05, so the null hypothesis is rejected and the alternative hypothesis is accepted. The hypothesis is rejected on the basis of all the criteria of social benefit, whether it is application, adaptation, or awareness. This means a positive impact of the adaptation of AI on sustainable overall development. as shown in Table 12.2.

12.5.2 SPSS Output – Case 2

It had been found that there was no significant difference in the tourism demand and social benefit. The p-value is found to be less than .05, so the null hypothesis is rejected and the alternative hypothesis is accepted, as shown in Table 12.3.

Table 12.1   A Total of 12 Questions Were Framed and Segregated into Various Dimensions Based on the Nature of Questions

Sl no.	Dimensions	Questions
1	Overall sustainable benefit	1,2,3
2	Social benefit	4,5,6,7
3	Economic benefit	8,9,11,12

Table 12.2 ANOVA

		Sum of squares	df	Mean square	F	Sig.
Awareness	Between groups	51.269	4	12.817	15.290	.000
	Within groups	207.060	247	.838		
	Total	258.329	251			
Adoption	Between groups	55.688	4	13.922	16.107	.000
	Within groups	213.498	247	.864		
	Total	269.187	251			
Application	Between groups	70.051	4	17.513	21.408	.000
	Within groups	202.056	247	.818		
	Total	272.107	251			

Table 12.3 ANOVA

		Sum of squares	df	Mean square	F	Sig.
Job generate	Between groups	48.010	4	12.002	15.616	.000
	Within groups	189.843	247	.769		
	Total	237.853	251			
Crowd worker job	Between groups	68.634	4	17.158	20.065	.000
	Within groups	211.219	247	.855		
	Total	279.853	251			
Community	Between groups	106.657	4	26.664	31.940	.000
	Within goups	206.200	247	.835		
	Total	312.857	251			
Socio-eco	Between groups	104.198	4	26.050	34.138	.000
	Within groups	188.480	247	.763		
	Total	292.679	251			

The hypothesis is rejected based on the basis of all the criteria of social benefit, whether it is job generation; new types of jobs, i.e., crowd worker and data handling, good for community, social benefits. It means a positive impact of the AI on social development.

12.5.3 SPSS Output – Case 3

It had been found that there was no significant difference in the tourism demand and economic benefit. The p-value is found to be less than .05, so the null hypothesis is rejected and the alternative hypothesis is accepted, as shown in Table 12.4.

Table 12.4 ANOVA

		Sum of squares	df	Mean square	F	Sig.
Revenue	Between groups	99.495	4	24.874	27.949	.000
	Within groups	219.822	247	.890		
	Total	319.317	251			
Price Mgt	Between groups	90.813	4	22.703	24.866	.000
	Within groups	225.516	247	.913		
	Total	316.329	251			
Earning	Between groups	96.029	4	24.007	28.775	.000
	Within groups	206.078	247	.834		
	Total	302.107	251			

Table 12.5 Model Summary

Training	Cross eEntropy error	.036
	Percent incorrect predictions	0%
	Stopping rule used	Training error ratio criterion (.001) achieved
	Training time	0:00:00.03
Testing	Cross entropy error	.173
	Percent incorrect predictions	0%

Dependent variable: sustainable development

The hypothesis is rejected based on the riteria of economic benefit, whether it is revenue, earnings, or price management. It means a positive economic impact of AI on economic development.

12.6 Testing Model Fitness with Neural Network

12.6.1 SPSS Output of Neural Network Model

In the training samples, the sum of squared error is equal to .03, and the relative error is .173 for training. Errors are therefore relatively rare and information about the outcomes of the neural network training in summary is shown in Table 12.5.

12.6.2 SPSS Output of Classification

Table 12.6 depicts the model fitness. Results analyzed and model suggested for overall lead time reduction is correct with a very high percentage of 100%, as shown in Table 12.6

Table 12.6   Classification

Sample	Observed	Predicted		
		0	1	Percent correct
Training	0	60	0	100.0%
	1	0	111	100.0%
	Overall percent	35.1%	64.9%	100.0%
Testing	0	25	0	100.0%
	1	0	56	100.0%
	Overall percent	30.9%	69.1%	100.0%

There are three connected graphs: an input, a hidden layer, and an output. Additionally, it classifies synaptic weights into two categories: less than 0 and more than 0. The grey-colored layers have had a greater influence than 0. These layers describe which factors' individual components are more weighted or significant.

The chart highlights how the network categorizes potential applicants. Therefore, statistical models will be useful in this case. Close collaboration with suppliers (100%), improved ability to manage supply chain inventories (69.4%), and just-in-time (JIT) supply (67.1%) are of the utmost significance as shown in Figure 12.4.

12.7 Conclusion

Glancing through the amendments that AI can bring to the hospitality industry, industry experts have deduced that its application in the Indian hotel spaces and other hospitality-providing institutions is in its nascent stage. AI is a new form of intelligence, which is able to synthesize several different ideas simultaneously. Today's technological revolution requires effectiveness, sustainability, and productivity at the same time. The use of AI – which can be utilized in numerous different fields – is expanding in every industrial sector. For the users of the online world, it is natural to share data or send back information to big companies, and because of that, entrepreneurs are able to analyze big data and create a profile for each of their customers.

AI-digital landscape is widely adopting within the hospitality sectors; it is predicted to be used more often in the future in order to increase the quality of the tourism demand, and socio-eco and overall sustainable benefit of the tourism industry. Every aspect of life is being significantly impacted by the ongoing technical revolution in the field of AI. It is essential to utilize AI's capacity for our economic, environmental, and social well-being while minimizing its unfavorable ethical ramifications (Khang & Shah et al., 2023).

Figure 12.4 Depicts the impact of the AI-digital landscape on sustainable development information on the network.

References

Aerts, A., & Bogdan-Martin, D. (2021). Leveraging data and AI to deliver on the promise of digital health. *International Journal of Medical Informatics, 150*. https://doi.org/10.1016/j.ijmedinf.2021.104456

Aslam, A., Khan, F. A., & Aslam, A. (2023). Socio-economic shocks due to advancement in artificial intelligence techniques. *Recent Trends in Artificial Intelligence & It's Applications, 2*(1). https://doi.org/10.46610/rtaia.2023.v02i01.002

Eide, D., Fuglsang, L., & Sundbo, J. (2017). Management challenges with the maintenance of tourism experience concept innovations: Toward a new research agenda. In *Tourism management* (Vol. 63). https://doi.org/10.1016/j.tourman.2017.06.029

Goralski, M. A., & Tan, T. K. (2020). Artificial intelligence and sustainable development. *International Journal of Management Education, 18*(1). https://doi.org/10.1016/j.ijme.2019.100330

Khang, A. (2023). *AI and IoT-based technologies for precision medicine* (1st Ed.). IGI Global Press. ISBN: 9798369308769. https://doi.org/10.4018/979-8-3693-0876-9

Khang, A., Abdullayev, V. A., Alyar, A. V., Khalilov, M., & Murad, B. (2023). AI-aided data analytics tools and applications for the healthcare sector. In *AI and IoT-based technologies for precision medicine* (1st Ed.). IGI Global Press. ISBN: 9798369308769. https://doi.org/10.4018/979-8-3693-0876-9.ch018

Khang, A., Hahanov, V., Abbas, G. L., & Hajimahmud, V. A. (2022). Cyber-physical-social system and incident management. In *AI-centric smart city ecosystems: Technologies, design and implementation* (1st Ed.), 7 (12), CRC Press. https://doi.org/10.1201/9781003252542-2

Khang, A., Muthmainnah, M., Seraj, P. M. I., Al Yakin, A., Obaid, A. J., & Panda, M. R. (2023). AI-aided teaching model for the education 5.0 ecosystem. In *AI-Based Technologies and Applications in the Era of the Metaverse* (1st Ed., pp. 83–104). IGI Global Press. https://doi.org/10.4018/978-1-6684-8851-5.ch004

Khang, A., Rath, K. C., Satapathy, S. K., Kumar, A., Das, S. R., & Panda, M. R. (2023). Enabling the future of manufacturing: Integration of robotics and IoT to smart factory infrastructure in industry 4.0. *AI-based technologies and applications in the era of the metaverse* (1st Ed., pp. 25–50). IGI Global Press. https://doi.org/10.4018/978-1-6684-8851-5.ch002

Khang, A., Shah, V., & Rani, S. (2023). *AI-based technologies and applications in the era of the metaverse* (1st Ed.). IGI Global Press. https://doi.org/10.4018/978-1-6684-8851-5

Khanh, H. H., & Khang, A. (2021). The role of artificial intelligence in blockchain applications. *Reinventing Manufacturing and Business Processes through Artificial Intelligence, 2*(20–40). CRC Press. https://doi.org/10.1201/9781003145011-2

Murphy, J., Hofacker, C., & Gretzel, U. (2017). Dawning of the age of robots in hospitality and tourism: Challenges for teaching and research. In *European Journal of Tourism Research* (Vol. 15). https://doi.org/10.54055/ejtr.v15i.265

Pan, Y., Okada, H., Uchiyama, T., & Suzuki, K. (2013). Listening to vs overhearing robots in a hotel public space. In *ACM/IEEE international conference on human-robot interaction*. https://doi.org/10.1109/HRI.2013.6483573

Vinuesa, R., Azizpour, H., Leite, I., Balaam, M., Dignum, V., Domisch, S., Felländer, A., Langhans, S. D., Tegmark, M., & Fuso Nerini, F. (2020). The role of artificial intelligence in achieving the Sustainable Development Goals. In *Nature Communications* (Vol. 11, Issue 1). https://doi.org/10.1038/s41467-019-14108-y

Visvizi, A. (2022). Artificial Intelligence (AI) and Sustainable Development Goals (SDGs): Exploring the impact of AI on politics and society. In *Sustainability (Switzerland)* (Vol. 14, Issue 3). https://doi.org/10.3390/su14031730

Chapter 13

Application of the Bayesian Algorithm for Mall Attractiveness

Le Thi Kim Hoa and Bui Huy Khoi

13.1 Introduction

The year 2020 differs from the years before, as COVID-19 has had a major impact. It has brought deep changes to the nature of the lives of humans (Chen et al., 2020). As today's world finds itself embroiled in one of the biggest health and humanitarian crises ever seen in the last century, the global implications of COVID-19 remain difficult to gauge (Sánchez-Cañizares et al., 2020). The collateral effects of the war against the virus include paralysis of productive activity, with significant global economic and social consequences (Bapuji et al., 2020). Retail is one of the industry's most vulnerable to health and safety challenges, political transitions, economic crises, and natural catastrophes (Çakar et al., 2020). The COVID-19 pandemic is a contagious pandemic with the agent of the virus, SARS-CoV-2, spreading on a global scale. From the beginning of December 2019 to the beginning of September 2020, the COVID-19 pandemic spread in 210 countries/ regions, with nearly 33.5 million cases and over 1 million deaths (News, 2020).

Currently, the pandemic is still spreading in many countries, alarming complications in Europe, countries in Asia, and America, negatively affecting all socioeconomic activities in the world, including Vietnam. Almost all economic sectors and fields are affected negatively. Talking about the retail model of shopping malls, a recent report said that "When the Covid-19 pandemic passes, a healthy lifestyle and eating will become more important to consumers than before" (Vincom, 2020). In recent years, there have been many studies in the world on the retail model of shopping centers; for example, the study of the factors influencing the intentions of Generation Y in shopping malls (people born in the 1980s and early 1990s) in Malaysia, by Ping and Hwa (Ping et al., 2020). The results have shown four accepted theories, namely convenience and accessibility; the atmosphere in the shopping mall; entertainment; and diverse goods and services.

Çengel and Çakıroğlu (2020) also conducted a study on the attractiveness of shopping centers in Turkey during the period of when shopping centers were flourishing. The authors concluded

DOI: 10.4324/9781032688305-13

that department store management should consider the specific features that customers look for when they evaluate the personality of the shopping mall. If the characteristics exhibited by the shopping center align with the characteristics perceived by the customers, the shopping mall can maintain a long-term relationship with the customer. In Vietnam, the synthesis of previous studies reveals that there have been several research studies on the model of shopping centers, but the focus of the author's has been on the supermarket model. The chapter indicates that Facilities (FA), Product (PR), Promotion Price (PRP), Staff (ST), Customer Service (CS), and Convenience (CO) have had an important and positive impact on Mall Attractiveness (MA) during the COVID-19 pandemic.

This chapter is the application of the Bayesian Algorithm (BIC) for mall attractiveness presented as follows: Section 13.1 presents an overview of this research, Section 13.2 presents a review of the literature on the variables used in this research, and Section 13.3 presents the methodology. Results and analysis with some discussion and implications are presented in Section 13.4. Lastly, Section 5 concludes this chapter.

13.2 Literature Review

13.2.1 Mall Attractiveness (MA)

Çengel and Çakıroğlu (2020) argue that customers aim for an environment that offers a wide variety of goods, experience of a good atmospheree, a high level of social interaction, and no security concerns. Attraction is awareness, achieved through an individual's needs, requirements, and preferences (Dębek et al., 2015). Customers are attracted to shopping malls because they are large shopping areas and have many types of products in a single location. Shopping malls have expanded over the years, offering additional service shops and entertainment opportunities. Today, even small shopping malls have food courts, restaurants, hair salons, and movie theaters. Shopping centers are places that provide consumers comfort away from traffic and noise. Interesting experiences such as effectively managed retail spaces and environments are also because of shopping centers (Dalmoro et al., 2019).

13.2.2 Facilities (FA)

Drezner et al. (2020) have analyzed that shopping centers with unique features are more attractive than other shopping centers. These unique features are facilities such as seats inside the shopping mall, which are not only intended for customers to rest but also as a public place for them to perform various relaxing activities. Shopping centers can create comfort with facilities such as convenient parking, suitable operating hours, clean toilets, and entertainment places for children, teenagers, and the elderly.

13.2.3 Product (PR)

Commodity is an important visual attribute because it represents the "core product" of the mall (Evans et al., 2001). According to Jasmani and Sunarsi (2020), a product is anything that can be brought to the market to satisfy the needs and desires of its customers. Similarly, Kotler (2015) also argues that many people think a product is tangible, but in reality, a product is anything that is offered to the market to satisfy a need or desire, including goods, materials, services, experiences, and events. The basic purpose of customers when coming to the shopping mall is to purchase necessary products and enjoy services such as dining, entertainment, or meeting groups and friends. However, the department store should have interesting experiences to create positive emotions for customers, such as the design and display of the store in the shopping mall, the products, and the layout of the products sold (Cachero et al., 2017).

13.2.4 Promotion Price (PRP)

In a study conducted in Malaysia by Wong and Nair (2018), it is said that the attractiveness of shopping centers, including marketing promotion activities, is considered an important factor in attracting customers to shopping malls. Also, according to Raghubir et al. (2001), businesses with good advertising and promotion activities will attract consumers and promote their shopping behavior. Besides, in the marketing strategy, promotional policies, discounts, and bonuses are always placed in a very important position. Kotler (2015) considers promotions as "short-term incentives to encourage the purchase or sale of a product or service". Belch and Belch (2003) also conclude that promotions include consumer-oriented sales promotion and commercial-oriented sales promotion.

13.2.5 Staff (ST)

Staff are always an important channel in the marketing of the business, as well as creating the corporate image in the mind of the customer, being the bridge between the business and the customer. Staff and staff advice and help are extremely necessary, contributing to improving the image and friendliness towards customers (Crawford et al., 2003). Therefore, a holistic approach is needed when creating the consumer experience, especially with the staffing factor (Sachdeva et al., 2015). In a study of customer experience in the retail industry, the author suggested that interaction with a store employee can help create a customer experience. If the staff are considered to be skilled and professionally serviced by offering suggestions and advice when required, it creates a positive experience for the customer (Pantano et al., 2018).

13.2.6 Customer Service (CS)

González-Hernández and Orozco-Gómez (2012) suggested in their research that customer service is one of the most important factors attracting customers to shopping centers. Service quality is also considered an important factor in attracting customers (Nwanekezie et al., 2020).

13.2.7 Convenience (CO)

Çengel and Çakıroğlu (Çengel et al., 2020) concluded that convenience is one of the attractive factors of shopping centers. Similarly, in a study conducted by Anselmsson (Anselmsson et al., 2006), convenience is the third most important factor determining customer satisfaction in shopping centers, including hours of operation, parking, easy transportation, and skills to locate locations in a shopping mall as shown in Figure 13.1.

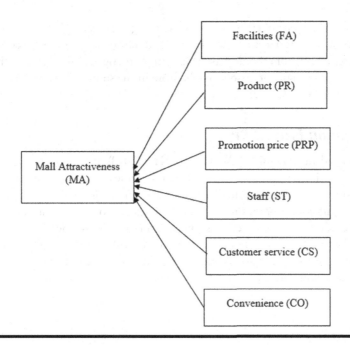

Figure 13.1   The official research model.

13.3 Method

13.3.1 Sample Approach

In this study overall, it is necessary to research the shopping customers of Sense City Shopping Mall in Ho Chi Minh City, Vietnam. They are working people, small businesses, stay-at-home parents, retirees, and students. This population will be at least 15 years old and distributed among several generation groups: Baby Boomers (1944–1961); Generation X (1962–1982); and Generation Y (1983–2000). The author chooses the age of 15 years because this customer group includes high school students who have relative awareness and have conditions to go out to experience for many reasons. However, the two groups – Generations X and Y still make up most of the total.

In this study, information for our quantitative analysis was collected using questionnaires. The respondents' survey responses were the primary method for gathering information. The research was conducted in the year 2023. The research included questions about the status of the determinants that affected the attractiveness of customers. Hair et al. (2006) assume that the minimum sample size is 50, the best is 100, and the observed/variable measurement ratio is 5:1. For the topic using regression analysis, the empirical formula is $n > 50 + 8P$, where n is the minimum sample size and P is the number of independent variables present in the model. The sample size was selected using the conventional method. Respondents were selected from 198 customers living in Ho Chi Minh City, Vietnam. Table 13.1 describes the statistics of sample characteristics.

We use the 5-point Likert scale to evaluate the level of consent for the related factors. Therefore, this chapter also uses the 5-point Likert scale to evaluate the level of consent for all observed variables, with 1: Disagree and 5: Agree as in Table 13.2.

For the duration of the study, all study staff and respondents were blinded. No one from the outside world had any contact with the study participants.

Table 13.1   Statistics of Sample

Characteristics		Amount	Percent (%)
Sex	Male	75	37.9
	Female	123	62.1
Age	Below 18	3	1.5
	18–22	39	19.7
	23–30	91	46.0
	31–40	65	32.8
Qualification	High School	3	1.5
	Vocational College	35	17.7
	College	69	34.8
	University	91	46.0
Job	Student	12	6.1
	Officer	77	38.9
	Business	42	21.2
	Workers and Employees	27	13.6
	Unskilled Labor	16	8.1
	Housewife / Retirement	17	8.6
	Others	7	3.5
Monthly Income (VND to USD at https://vi .coinmill.com on 20 January 2023)	No	20	10.1
	Below 341.29 USD	31	15.7
	341.29–639.93 USD	74	37.4
	682.59–1279.85 USD	55	27.8
	Over 1279.85 USD	18	9.1
Going to the shopping mall	Alone	5	2.5
	Family	89	44.9
	Friends	74	37.4
	Colleagues	24	12.1
	Others	6	3.0

Source: Author calculated based on R software.

Table 13.2 Factor and Item

Factor	Code	Item
Facilities	FA1	The location of the Shopping Mall is convenient for traveling, near my home or work.
	FA2	The Shopping Mall has a large and convenient parking lot for me.
	FA3	The space at the Shopping Mall has been well used to create experiences for customers.
	FA4	Shopping Mall has seating arrangements for visitors during the COVID-19 pandemic.
Product	PR1	Products and services at the Shopping Mall are diversified and plentiful to meet the needs of customers.
	PR2	The design and layout of the store and the goods in the store at the Shopping Mall are beautiful and eye-catching.
	PR3	Shopping Mall has many stores/stalls of famous brands.
	PR4	Shopping Mall has brands I love in the COVID-19 pandemic
Promotion Price	PRP1	The price of goods at the Shopping Mall is in keeping with my income.
	PRP2	There are often promotions that bring real benefits to customers during the COVID-19 pandemic.
	PRP3	Diverse attractive advertising and marketing programs.
Staff	ST1	The staff at Shopping Mall are friendly and enthusiastic, giving me a wonderful experience during the COVID-19 pandemic.
	ST2	The staff at Shopping Mall supported me a lot in searching for goods during the COVID-19 pandemic.
	ST3	The staff at Shopping Mall has excellent skills and provides professional service during the COVID-19 pandemic.
Customer Service	CS1	Shopping Mall has a membership card program for shoppers.
	CS2	There is a customer support information desk during the COVID-19 pandemic.
	CS3	Shopping Mall has an information service desk that quickly responds to customer requests during the COVID-19 pandemic.
Convenience	CO1	Fast sales transactions in the COVID-19 pandemic.
	CO2	Hours of operation of Shopping Malls is convenient for customers in the COVID-19 pandemic.
	CO3	The shops and stalls were streamlined, and goats found.
Mall Attractiveness	MA1	I plan to return to the Shopping Mall.
	MA2	I will recommend to my friends here (Shopping Mall) during the COVID-19 pandemic.
	MA3	I am a loyal customer of the Shopping Mall.
	MA4	When shopping, the Shopping Mall is my first choice during the COVID-19 pandemic.

Source: Author's compilation from research data

13.3.2 Bayes' Theorem

Let H be the hypothesis and D denote the actual data obtained from the collection. Bayes' theorem (Bayes et al., 2006) states that the probability of H given D, denoted as P(H│D), is:

$$P(H / D) = \frac{P(H) * P(D/H)}{P(D)}$$ (13.1)

The probability of the hypothesis before collecting data is called P (H). P (D│H) is the probability that the data happens under the correct hypothesis H; P (D) is the distribution of the data in equation 13.1 (Thang et al., 2021).

13.3.3 Bayes Inference

According to Gelman and Shalizi (2013), based on the Bayes' theorem, we can see that Bayesian inference of Bayes has three types of information: The information we want to know (posterior information), the information we already know (prior information), and practical information (likelihood). Here, "information" can be understood as probability or distribution in equation 13.2. Therefore, Bayesian inference can be generalized.

$$\text{Posterior information} = \text{Prior information} \times \text{Likelihood}$$ (13.2)

13.3.4 Selection of the Model by the Bayesian Model Averaging

Usually, to simply define a model for a research problem, one gives only a single model (the model includes all the collected variables) to estimate and then deduce, as if that model were the model most suitable for the data. Therefore, the method can ignore other models built with some variables from the set of collected variables, and some of those models may be more suitable. Therefore, it is necessary to survey and compare the models of a research problem to find the actual most suitable model for the data (which can also be interpreted as the "best" model) (Raftery et al., 1995). The Bayesian statistical model selection method is the Bayesian Model Averaging (BMA), which uses posterior probabilities and the BIC index to measure the model. The advantage of using the application of the Bayesian (BIC) for workshop attractiveness of the career counseling programs.

13.4 Discussion and Results

13.4.1 BIC Algorithm

There have been many algorithms created and extensively explored for detecting association rules in transaction databases. Other mining algorithms, such as incremental updating, mining of generalized and multilevel rules, mining of quantitative rules, mining of multidimensional rules, constraint-based rule mining, mining with multiple minimum supports, mining associations among correlated or infrequent items, and mining of temporal associations, were also presented to provide more mining capabilities (Gharib et al., 2010).

Big Data Analytics and Deep Learning are two areas of data science that are receiving considerable interest. As many individuals and organizations have been gathering enormous amounts of

Table 13.3   BIC Model Selection

MA	Probability (%)	SD	Model 1	Model 2
Intercept	100.0	0.26207	−0.0090	0.3784
FA	100.0	0.03426	0.1423	0.1582
PR	100.0	0.03043	0.1887	0.1850
CO	100.0	0.03704	0.1659	0.1996
ST	100.0	0.03331	0.1735	0.1791
PRP	92.2	0.06524	0.1619	.
CS	100.0	0.03817	0.1736	0.1802

Source: Author calculated based on R software.

Table 13.4   Model Test

Model	nVar	R2	BIC	Post Prob
Model 1	6	0.594	−1.466	0.922
Model 2	5	0.572	−1.416	0.078
BIC = −2 * LL + log (N) * k				

Source: Author calculated based on R software.

Deep Learning Algorithms for Mall Attractiveness, Big Data has become increasingly important (Najafabadi et al., 2015). Bayesian Information Criteria (BIC) was used to select the best model by R software. In the theoretical environment, BIC has been used to choose models (Khoi et al., 2022). BIC can be used as a regression model to estimate one or more dependent variables from one or more independent variables (Raftery et al., 1997). The BIC is an important and useful metric for determining a full and straightforward model. A model with a lower BIC is chosen based on the BIC information standard (Raftery et al., 1995) (Raftery et al., 1997) (Kaplan et al., 2021). R report shows every step of searching for the optimal model. BIC selects the best two models in Table 13.3.

There are six independent variables and one dependent variable in the models in Table 13.3. Facilities (FA), Product (PR), Staff (ST), Customer Service (CS), and Convenience (CO) have a probability of 100%. Promotion Price (PRP) has a probability of 92.2%.

13.4.2 *Model Evaluation*

According to the results from Table 13.2, BIC shows that Model 1 is the optimal selection because BIC (−1.466) is the minimum. Facilities (FA), Product (PR), Promotion Price (PRP), Staff (ST), Customer Service (CS), and Convenience (CO) impact Mall Attractiveness (MA) during the COVID-19 pandemic in Vietnam with an R2 of 0.594 (59.4%) in Table 13.4. BIC finds that Model 1 is the optimal choice and three variables have a probability of 92.2% (post prob=0.922). The above analysis shows that the regression equation below is statistically significant in equation 3.

$$MA = -0.0090 + 0.1423 \text{ FA} + 0.1887 \text{ PR} + 0.1659 \text{ CO}$$
$$+ 0.1735 \text{ ST} + 0.1619 \text{ PRP} + 0.1736 \text{ CS} \tag{3}$$

Code: Facilities (FA), Product (PR), Promotion Price (PRP), Staff (ST), Customer Service (CS), and Convenience, and Mall Attractiveness (MA).

13.5 Conclusion

This study uses the optimal choice of the application of the Bayesian Algorithm (BIC) for Mall Attractiveness. Results of BIC Algorithm analysis on six factors of Mall Attractiveness (MA) in COVID-19 pandemic have the following results: Facilities (0.1423), Product (0.1887), Promotion Price (0.1619), Staff (0.1735), Customer Service (0.1736), Convenience (0.1659), in which Product (0.1887) has the strongest impact as shown in Figure 13.2.

13.6 Limitations of the Research and Further Research Directions

Some limitations stated below have been mentioned when doing the research. Hopefully, the authors can research more deeply and solve the problems in previous studies to contribute to shopping malls. In terms of research capacity and time, the sample selection and sample size are not as expected, so it is only possible to research on Google. The study subjects are quite complete but still have many shortcomings. The variables running in the model are only some influencing factors, not completely the factors that affect the decision to apply the user's belief. The sample size selected for the study is still small compared to the overall study, which may also adversely affect the reliability of the study results.

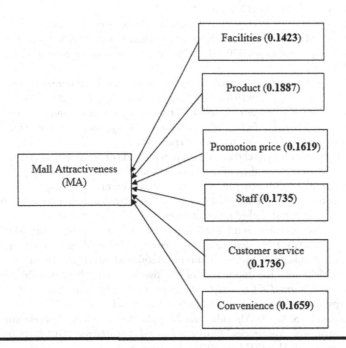

Figure 13.2   Proposed research model.

There are customers who are not very attentive when typing the survey, so there are cases where customers chatter quickly, and as a result, the collected opinions make little sense. After statistical analysis, the test was conducted, but it was not statistically significant. Therefore, it was necessary to re-survey to obtain good data. There are many factors affecting the trust in eWOM of users that have not been mentioned. To explain more clearly about trust in eWOM, these factors should be elaborated on.

Besides the theoretical and practical contributions drawn from the research results, this research topic has many limitations and then suggests the following research: Include factors related to trust impact to increase the reliability of the study. We will increase the number of survey samples compared to the overall population to increase the reliability of the study. It is recommended to expand the survey to many major cities across the country in the next research (Khang & Muthmainnah et al., 2023).

Acknowledgments

This research is funded by the Industrial University of Ho Chi Minh City, Vietnam.

References

Anselmsson J., "Sources of customer satisfaction with shopping malls: A comparative study of different customer segments," *International Review of Retail, Distribution and Consumer Research*, vol. 16, pp. 115–138, 2006. https://www.tandfonline.com/doi/abs/10.1080/09593960500453641

Bapuji H., C. Patel, G. Ertug, and D. G. Allen, "Corona crisis and inequality: Why management research needs a societal turn," *Journal of Management*, vol. 46, pp. 1205–1222, 2020. https://journals.sagepub.com/doi/abs/10.1177/0149206320925881

Bayes T., "LII. An essay towards solving a problem in the doctrine of chances. By the late Rev. Mr. Bayes, FRS communicated by Mr. Price, in a letter to John Canton, AMFR S," *Philosophical Transactions of the Royal Society of London*, pp. 370–418, 1763. https://royalsocietypublishing.org/doi/abs/10.1098/rstl.1763.0053

Belch G. E. and M. A. Belch, *Advertising and promotion: An integrated marketing communications perspective*, The McGraw– Hill, 2003. https://thuvienso.hoasen.edu.vn/handle/123456789/8039

Cachero-Martínez S. and R. Vázquez-Casielles, "Stimulating curiosity and consumer experience in a retailer," *American Journal of Industrial and Business Management*, vol. 7, p. 473, 2017. https://www.scirp.org/journal/paperinformation.aspx?paperid=75723

Çakar K., "Tourophobia: Fear of travel resulting from man-made or natural disasters," *Tourism Review*, vol. 22, 2020. https://www.emerald.com/insight/content/doi/10.1108/TR-06-2019-0231/full/html

Çengel Ö. and I. Çakıroğlu, "The impact of mall attractiveness on mall patronage intention: The mediating effect of mall personality," *International Journal of Commerce and Finance*, vol. 6, pp. 204–226, 2020. http://ijcf.ticaret.edu.tr/index.php/ijcf/article/view/178

Chen C., Y. Zhang, A. Xu, X. Chen, and J. Lin, "Reconstruction of meaning in life: Meaning made during the pandemic of COVID-19," *International Journal of Mental Health Promotion*, 2020. https://cdn.techscience.cn/uploads/attached/file/20200814/20200814024641_16907.pdf

Crawford G. and T. Melewar, "The importance of impulse purchasing behaviour in the international airport environment," *Journal of Consumer Behaviour: An International Research Review*, vol. 3, pp. 85–98, 2003. https://onlinelibrary.wiley.com/doi/abs/10.1002/cb.124

Dalmoro M., G. Isabella, S. O. de Almeida, and J. P. dos Santos Fleck, "Developing a holistic understanding of consumers' experiences," *European Journal of Marketing*, 2019. https://www.emerald.com/insight/content/doi/10.1108/EJM-10-2016-0586/full/html

Dębek M., "What drives shopping mall attractiveness?," *Polish Journal of Applied Psychology*, vol. 13, pp. 67–118, 2015. http://archive.sciendo.com/PJAP/pjap.2015.13.issue-1/pjap-2015-0026/pjap-2015 -0026.pdf

Drezner T., Z. Drezner, and D. Zerom, "Facility dependent distance decay in competitive location," *Networks and Spatial Economics*, vol. 20, pp. 915–934, 2020. https://link.springer.com/article/10.1007 /s11067-020-09507-4

Evans J. R. and B. Berman, "Conceptualizing and operationalizing the business-to-business value chain," *Industrial Marketing Management*, vol. 30, pp. 135–148, 2001. https://www.sciencedirect.com/sci-ence/article/pii/S0019850100001395

Gelman A. and C. R. Shalizi, "Philosophy and the practice of Bayesian statistics," *British Journal of Mathematical and Statistical Psychology*, vol. 66, pp. 8–38, 2013. https://bpspsychub.onlinelibrary .wiley.com/doi/abs/10.1111/j.2044-8317.2011.02037.x

Gharib T. F., H. Nassar, M. Taha, and A. Abraham, "An efficient algorithm for incremental mining of temporal association rules," *Data & Knowledge Engineering*, vol. 69, pp. 800–815, 2010. https://www .sciencedirect.com/science/article/pii/S0169023X10000364

González-Hernández E. M. and M. Orozco-Gómez, "A segmentation study of Mexican consumers based on shopping centre attractiveness," *International Journal of Retail & Distribution Management*, 2012. https://www.emerald.com/insight/content/doi/10.1108/09590551211263173/full/html

Hair J. F., W. C. Black, B. J. Babin, R. E. Anderson, and R. L. Tatham, *Multivariate data analysis* (Vol. 6), ed: Upper Saddle River, NJ: Pearson Prentice Hall, 2006. https://papers.ssrn.com/sol3/papers.cfm ?abstract_id=3498766

Jasmani J. and D. Sunarsi, "The influence of product mix, promotion mix and brand image on consumer purchasing decisions of Sari Roti Products in South Tangerang," *PINISI Discretion Review*, vol. 1, pp. 165–174, 2020. https://www.neliti.com/publications/314454/the-influence-of-product-mix-promo-tion-mix-and-brand-image-on-consumer-purchasin

Kaplan D., "On the quantification of model uncertainty: A Bayesian perspective," *Psychometrika*, vol. 86, pp. 215–238, 2021. https://link.springer.com/article/10.1007/s11336-021-09754-5

Khang A., M. Muthmainnah, P. M. I. Seraj, A. Al Yakin, A. J. Obaid, and M. R. Panda, "AI-aided teaching model for the education 5.0 ecosystem," *AI-based technologies and applications in the era of the meta-verse*, 1st Ed., 83–104, IGI Global Press, 2023. https://doi.org/10.4018/978-1-6684-8851-5.ch004

Khoi B. H., "Bayesian model selection for trust in Ewom," *Innovations in bio-inspired computing and appli-cations: Proceedings of the 13th International Conference on Innovations in Bio-Inspired Computing and Applications (IBICA 2022) held during December 15–17, 2022, 2023*, pp. 610–620. https://www .google.com/books?hl=en&lr=&id=Pxi2EAAAQBAJ&oi=fnd

Kotler P., *Framework for marketing management*, Pearson Education India, 2015. https://doi.org/10.1201 /9781032688305

Najafabadi M. M., F. Villanustre, T. M. Khoshgoftaar, N. Seliya, R. Wald, and E. Muharemagic, "Deep learning applications and challenges in big data analytics," *Journal of Big Data*, vol. 2, pp. 1–21, 2015. https://journalofbigdata.springeropen.com/articles/10.1186/s40537-014-0007-7

News, 2020. https://news.google.com/covid19/map?hl=vi&gl=VN&ceid=VN%3Avi

Nwanekezie O. F. and I. J. Onuoha, "Employers' and customers' perception of the factors influencing shop-ping mall attractiveness in Owerri, Nigeria," https://www.researchgate.net/profile/Iheanyichukwu -Onuoha/publication/337784165_EMPLOYERS'_AND_CUSTOMERS'_PERCEPTION_ OF_THE_FACTORS_INFLUENCING_SHOPPING_MALL_ATTRACTIVENESS_ IN_OWERRI_NIGERIA/links/5dea2649299bf10bc343e4e4/EMPLOYERS-AND -CUSTOMERS-PERCEPTION-OF-THE-FACTORS-INFLUENCING-SHOPPING-MALL -ATTRACTIVENESS-IN-OWERRI-NIGERIA.pdf

Pantano E. and A. Gandini, "Shopping as a 'networked experience': An emerging framework in the retail industry," *International Journal of Retail & Distribution Management*, 2018. https://www.emerald .com/insight/content/doi/10.1108/IJRDM-01-2018-0024/full/html?fullSc=1

Ping A. C. C. and C. K. Hwa, "A study on factors influencing generation y's intention to visit shopping malls in Klang Valley, Malaysia," *BERJAYA Journal of Services & Management*, vol. 14, pp. 37–52, 2020. https://www.researchgate.net/profile/Kin-Choe/publication/343574653_A_Study_On_Factors

_Influencing_Generation_Y's_Intention_To_Visit_Shopping_Malls_In_Klang_Valley_Malaysia/
links/5f325a83a6fdcccc43bf0f47/A-Study-On-Factors-Influencing-Generation-Ys-Intention-To-Visit
-Shopping-Malls-In-Klang-Valley-Malaysia.pdf

Raftery A. E., "Bayesian model selection in social research," *Sociological Methodology*, pp. 111–163, 1995.
https://www.jstor.org/stable/271063

Raftery A. E., D. Madigan, and J. A. Hoeting, "Bayesian model averaging for linear regression models,"
Journal of the American Statistical Association, vol. 92, pp. 179–191, 1997. https://www.tandfonline
.com/doi/abs/10.1080/01621459.1997.10473615

Raghubir P., J. J. Inman, and H. Grande, "The three faces of consumer promotions," *California Management
Review*, vol. 46, pp. 23–42, 2004. https://journals.sagepub.com/doi/abs/10.2307/41166273

Sachdeva I. and S. Goel, "Retail store environment and customer experience: A paradigm," *Journal of
Fashion Marketing and Management*, 2015. https://www.emerald.com/insight/content/doi/10.1108/
JFMM-03-2015-0021/full/html

Sánchez-Cañizares S. M., L. J. Cabeza-Ramírez, G. Muñoz-Fernández, and F. J. Fuentes-García, "Impact
of the perceived risk from Covid-19 on intention to travel," *Current Issues in Tourism*, pp. 1–15, 2020.
https://www.tandfonline.com/doi/abs/10.1080/13683500.2020.1829571

Thang L. D., "The Bayesian statistical application research analyzes the willingness to join in area yield
index coffee insurance of farmers in Dak Lak province," University of Economics Ho Chi Minh City,
2021. https://journals.riverpublishers.com/index.php/JICTS/article/view/13319

Vincom, "Why do consumers tend to stick with the mall more after the epidemic (Vietnamese)?" 2020.
https://vincom.com.vn/vi/su-kien-khuyen-mai/vi-sao-nguoi-tieu-dung-co-xu-huong-gan-bo-voi
-trung-tam-thuong-mai-hon-sau-dich

Wong S. C. and P. B. Nair, "Mall patronage: Dimensions of attractiveness in urban context," *International
Journal of Business & Society*, vol. 19, 2018. http://www.ijbs.unimas.my/images/repository/pdf/Vol19
-no2-paper2.pdf

Chapter 14

Future of Digital Marketing: Hyper-Personalized Customer Dynamic Experience with AI-Based Predictive Models

Bhupinder Singh and Christian Kaunert

14.1 Introduction

The intersection of technology and digital marketing has given rise to a new era of hyper-personalization in the ever-accelerating digital landscape. Digital marketing is being fundamentally altered by this paradigm change, becoming more dynamic, responsive, and customer-focused than ever. Predictive models of Artificial Intelligence (AI) and Machine Learning (ML) are at the core of this transition and are what will power the future of digital marketing. Hyper-personalization is not just a trendy term; it is a method of marketing that goes beyond conventional segmentation and overcomes the drawbacks of one-size-fits-all strategies (Vinaykarthik, 2022). It's a journey that starts with data, lots of data, and ends with a customized, in-the-moment customer experience.

Marketers can now foresee client demands, provide individualized content, and predict preferences even before those preferences are consciously realized thanks to the complex dance between AI and ML. This chapter explores the nuances of hyper-personalization in digital marketing with an emphasis on how it affects marketing plans and brand advocacy. It looks at how AI and ML-powered prediction models are ready to transform the customer experience. The trip is no longer a straight line but a dynamic, responsive experience that customers and businesses have jointly constructed (Kamal & Himel, 2023).

It unravels the dimensions of hyper-personalization, analyzing its profound implications on customer loyalty and brand advocacy. This scrutinizes the strategies that forward-thinking marketers are adopting to harness the potential of AI and ML. Data analytics, real-time interactions, and the delicate balance between automation and the human touch will all be on our radar. This chapter also addresses the ethical considerations that come hand in hand with the power of

DOI: 10.4324/9781032688305-14

hyper-personalization, such as data privacy and transparency. It will also peer into the future of digital marketing, beyond hyper-personalization, contemplating the dynamic customer journey and the role of AI-driven creativity and innovation (Ahmed, 2022). The stage is set for a digital marketing revolution where brands, equipped with predictive models and customer insights, are not just communicating with their audience but co-creating value. The future of digital marketing is dynamic, data-driven, and deeply personalized. It's a future where customers, now brand advocates, become the strongest proponents of the brands they passionately endorse.

14.1.1 Background and Rationale

The landscape of digital marketing has undergone a seismic upheaval, propelled by the inexorable march of technology. The days of one-size-fits-all marketing tactics that catered to various target segments are long gone. At every point of contact with a brand nowadays, people demand a personalized, interesting, and relevant experience. The growing amount of data available and the impressive capabilities of AI and ML have hastened this transition toward hyper-personalization. These forces have come together to usher in a new era of digital marketing where hyper-personalized client journeys are created by predictive models of AI and ML (Vuong & Mai, 2023).

The revolutionary potential of hyper-personalization serves as the foundation for our investigation. Businesses can foster brand loyalty and advocacy like never before by comprehending and accommodating unique customer wants and preferences (Singh, 2024). In an era where client attention is a valuable resource and the capacity to pierce through the digital noise and establish a real connection is a competitive advantage, the stakes are high. This chapter tries to explore the complex effects of hyper-personalization on digital marketing, with an emphasis on marketing tactics and brand advocacy (Auttri et al., 2023). It aims to shed light on the tactics influencing the future of digital marketing by exploring the workings of predictive models driven by AI and ML.

14.1.2 Objectives

The objectives seek to provide a thorough understanding of the function and impact of hyper-personalization in digital marketing as shown in Figure 14.1, as well as insights into the tactics and moral issues involved, and projects the industry's future:

- Give a thorough analysis of the new movements toward hyper-personalization in digital marketing while highlighting the major forces behind AI and ML.
- Examine the deep effects of hyper-personalization on brand advocacy and customer loyalty, and discover how personalized experiences influence the development of brand advocates and devoted followers.
- Explore the tactics and best practices used by forward-thinking marketers to fully utilize the hyper-personalization potential of AI- and ML-driven predictive models. This includes data analytics, real-time interactions, and balancing automation with the human touch.
- Address the ethical considerations that come with the power of hyper-personalization, including data privacy, transparency, and the responsible use of customer data.
- Look ahead and consider the future of digital marketing beyond hyper-personalization, contemplating the dynamic customer journey, the role of AI-driven creativity and innovation, and the challenges and opportunities that lie ahead in the ever-evolving digital marketing landscape.

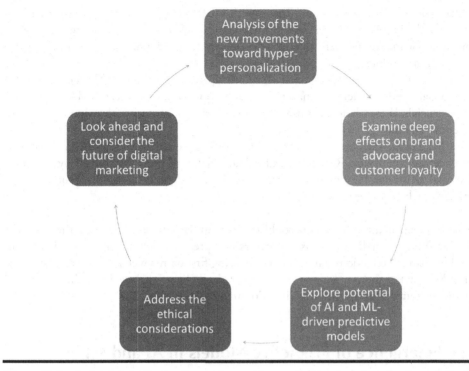

Figure 14.1   Insights into the tactics and moral issues involved, and projection of the industry's future.

14.2 Evolution of Digital Marketing and Personalization

The evolution of digital marketing has been intrinsically linked with the concept of personalization, which has grown from its infancy to become a central pillar of modern marketing strategies (Zaki, 2022). The brief overview of the evolution of digital marketing and personalization is as follows:

1. Early Internet and Static Websites: In the early days of the internet, digital marketing primarily consisted of static websites that provided basic information about a company or product. Only static content that did not alter based on the actions of specific users qualified as personalized.
2. Email Marketing and Segmentation: Email marketing gained popularity as the internet developed. Marketers started to divide their email lists into different groups depending on user information like demographics and purchase history. This was a rudimentary form of personalization, but it was personalization nonetheless.
3. Social Media and Behavioral Targeting: The emergence of social media platforms made it possible to more closely tailor advertising depending on the actions, interests, and social connections of the user. This data were used by marketers to create more pertinent content and advertising.
4. Content Marketing and the User-centered Approach: Content marketing gained popularity by emphasizing the creation of useful and educational content that catered to certain target audience's needs and interests. This change to a user-centric strategy represented a huge advancement in personalization (Khang & Muthmainnah et al., 2023).

5. Big Data and Advanced Analytics: The growth of data collection and sophisticated analytics technologies allowed marketers to understand consumer behavior more thoroughly. Campaigns for marketing were able to be extremely targeted and customized due to this data-driven methodology.

6. Marketing Automation and Customer Relationship Management (CRM): For managing customer data and interactions, marketing automation platforms and CRM systems have become crucial. These platforms support lead nurturing, customer path mapping, and tailored email marketing.

7. AI and ML: Large datasets are analyzed using predictive algorithms to predict customer preferences and behavior. Real-time, individualized interactions are offered by Chatbots and virtual assistants. Personalization has evolved into a dynamic, real-time process that is adapted to each user at every touchpoint.

Digital marketing personalization is more sophisticated and data-driven than ever. The customer experience is highly personalized because of factors like predictive modeling, dynamic content creation, and real-time interactions, rather than only using first names when writing to customers. With AI and ML paving the way for even more customized client journeys in the future, digital marketing and customization are still evolving (Soliman & Al Balushi, 2023).

14.3 The Emergence of Predictive Models in AI and ML

An important turning point in data science and technology has been the appearance of predictive models in AI and ML. These models have completely changed the way we look at data, evaluate it, and decide what to do next, and even predict the future. There are many aspects as to how predictive models in AI and ML emerged and became important (Bhatnagar, 2022).

1. Early Concepts in ML: The inception of AI and ML saw the establishment of the fundamental principles for predictive models. The field began with elementary statistical models like linear regression, which sought to forecast results based on historical data. These initial models, although basic, played a pivotal role in comprehending the fundamentals of predictive modeling.

2. Proliferation of Data: The advent of the internet and digital technologies led to a surge in data creation. With the escalating availability of data, there arose an increasing demand for more advanced models to derive meaningful insights. Predictive modeling became indispensable for businesses and industries striving for a competitive advantage.

3. Evolution of Sophisticated Algorithms: The advancement of more complex algorithms, including decision trees, support vector machines, and neural networks, furnished the necessary tools for constructing predictive models. These algorithms could handle intricate data patterns and make precise predictions across a wide spectrum of applications.

4. Big Data and Cloud Computing: The ascent of big data and cloud computing supplied the infrastructure needed to process and scrutinize colossal datasets. Predictive models could now manage vast volumes of data, unlocking fresh possibilities for businesses concerning customer insights, operational efficiency, and more.

5. Diverse Industry Applications: Predictive models discovered utility in various sectors. In finance, they served for risk assessment and detecting fraud. In healthcare, predictive models aided in patient diagnosis and recommendations required for the treatment. Retailers

employed them for anticipating demand and managing inventory. The versatility of predictive models across different domains highlighted their potential for resolving intricate issues (Khang & Smart Healthcare, 2024).

6. Emergence of Reinforcement Learning and Deep Learning: The rise of reinforcement learning and deep learning has extended the frontiers of predictive modeling. These subdomains of ML allow for the creation of models capable of making sequential decisions and handling unstructured data, such as images and natural language.

7. Real-time Predictive Analytics: As data processing speeds improved, real-time predictive analytics became achievable. Predictive models could furnish instantaneous suggestions and responses, rendering them invaluable in applications like recommendation systems, Chatbots, and autonomous vehicles.

8. Integration of AI and ML into Daily Life: Today, predictive models have become an integral part of our everyday lives. The power of virtual assistants, recommendation systems on streaming platforms, and personalized advertising. They are utilized to forecast weather, optimize transportation routes, and even predict disease outbreaks.

The emergence of predictive models in AI and ML has made data-driven decision-making accessible to a broad spectrum of industries and applications. As these models continue to develop, their influence on various sectors and their capacity to stimulate innovation and efficiency are set to expand (Singh, 2023).

14.4 Hyper-Personalization and Customer Experience

Hyper-personalization has become a potent force that holds out the prospect of a time when interactions with businesses are personalized to specific preferences, wants, and behaviors. By utilizing cutting-edge technology like AI and ML to generate highly tailored experiences, hyper-personalization elevates personalization to a new level (Henke & Jacques Bughin, 2016). Customers are no longer to be addressed by their first names; rather, it is now necessary to anticipate their needs before they express them, provide materials and solutions in real-time, and create engaging experiences at each touchpoint.

A dedication to treating each consumer as a part of one is at the core of hyper-personalization. Delivering what clients need, often before they even realize they need it, while establishing a sense of connection and comprehension, are key components of this strategy. This strategy fosters brand loyalty and advocacy while also improving customer happiness. The future of customer experience is highly personalized, dynamic, and intensely focused on the demands of the customer, where businesses anticipate needs and clients feel truly understood and not just seen (Kaushal & Yadav, 2023).

14.4.1 Hyper-Personalization in Digital Marketing

The world of digital marketing is changing as a result of hyper-personalization. This paradigm change emphasizes content and experiences at the personal level rather than just using standard segmentation. Hyper-personalization, which is made possible by AI and ML, is dependent on data-driven insights to foresee client demands and deliver customized messages, offers, and experiences in real-time (Singh, 2023). With this strategy, marketing transitions from a static, one-size-fits-all paradigm to a dynamic, customer-centric strategy where each interaction is carefully crafted to resonate with the unique needs of each person.

With the help of hyper-personalization, businesses may communicate with consumers directly and cater to their particular tastes and habits. It entails making product suggestions based on prior purchases, sending communications at the most effective times, and even changing content to take into account the customer's present situation. Hyper-personalization distinguishes brands at a time when consumers are swamped with digital content by providing not only relevance but a highly tailored and interesting experience (King, 2022). Hyper-personalization has become essential as the landscape of digital marketing continues to change. Customers are demanding this level of customization, and businesses that can meet their needs will see an increase in customer loyalty, better conversion rates, and stronger brand advocacy. While hyper-personalization has enormous promise, it also raises crucial questions regarding data privacy and the moral use of client information. As this marketing strategy continues to catch on, these questions must be carefully addressed (Babet, 2020).

14.4.2 AI and ML Predictive Models: Strategic Overview

A new era of data-driven decision-making and predictive modeling has arrived because of AI and ML. These cutting-edge technologies are revolutionizing sectors, increasing productivity, and influencing tactical choices. This change is being led by AI and ML prediction models, which give businesses priceless insights and the capacity to foresee outcomes with astounding accuracy.

Predictive models are algorithms created that use historical data to forecast upcoming actions or events. They have found use in a wide range of industries, including marketing, manufacturing, healthcare, and finance. In-depth discussion of the importance and function of AI and ML predictive models in directing organizational strategy is provided in this strategic review. By analyzing huge amounts of information, these predictive models find patterns, correlations, and trends that could otherwise go undetected, enabling data-driven decision-making. Strategic planning is influenced by this information, which enables businesses to make wise decisions about how to allocate resources, manage risks, and communicate with customers (Sadowski, 2023).

The predictive models are essential for businesses looking to boost operational effectiveness. For instance, these models can estimate demand, improve inventory levels, and streamline logistics in supply chain management, which ultimately lowers costs and boosts customer satisfaction. Predictive models in healthcare help in patient diagnosis, enabling early intervention and raising the standard of treatment (Khang & Rana et al., 2023). Predictive models using AI and ML are also strategically important in marketing since they promote customer interaction and customization. These models can recommend items, customize content, and foresee user preferences by studying customer data. Customer loyalty and brand advocacy have both been shown to increase significantly with this tailored strategy. The deployment of AI and ML predictive models does, however, present some difficulties (Sharma & Singh, 2022). The protection of personal information and ethical considerations are crucial. The data that businesses acquire and use must be handled with care. Predictive models also require a strong infrastructure, qualified personnel, and constant maintenance as they become more complicated.

It is impossible to exaggerate the strategic significance of AI- and ML-predictive models. These models equip businesses with the tools they need to make data-driven choices, increase productivity, and enhance customer experiences. Predictive models will become more and more important as technology develops in determining strategic priorities and promoting innovation. Organizations must adopt these models carefully, morally, and with a clear strategic vision if they are to realize their full potential.

14.4.3 Customer Insights and Data Analytics

The customer insights and data analytics are now the cornerstones of strategic planning and well-informed decision-making in the digital age. A wealth of information can be found in the enormous data sets produced by client contacts, online activities, and transactions. However, it goes beyond only gathering data; it involves drawing out takeable insights that direct companies in their pursuit of excellence. Customer insights cover a wide range of knowledge about consumer preferences, actions, and problems. Businesses can use data analytics to find patterns and trends in this data, giving important details about what influences consumer satisfaction and loyalty. These insights serve as the cornerstone for personalized marketing strategies, enabling companies to cater their messages and product offerings to specific client requirements.

Data analytics goes beyond simple trend analysis thanks to ML and AI. For instance, using predictive analytics, organizations can foresee future customer behavior and make preemptive decisions. This could entail making real-time product recommendations, anticipating customer attrition, or forecasting sales patterns (Gao & Liu, 2022). Since data analytics is real-time, organizations can react quickly to shifting consumer preferences and market dynamics. Businesses can improve client experiences, hone their product or service offerings, and boost overall operational effectiveness by incorporating customer insights into their strategy.

14.4.4 Crafting Dynamic and Personalized Content

In the world of digital marketing, personalized content is king and reigns supreme. The art of creating dynamic and tailored content transcends simple messaging. It involves giving people customized experiences that resonate with them and help them feel seen, heard, and valued. Each interaction is relevant and interesting thanks to dynamic content's real-time adaptation to user behavior and preferences. Advanced technologies, like AI and ML, which analyze massive databases to predict what customers want often before they are fully aware of it, power this personalization. Dynamic content can range from tailored news feeds on social media to product recommendations on e-commerce platforms (Rajamannar, 2021).

In marketing, dynamic and tailored content is a strategic asset that increases client loyalty and engagement. Businesses may improve conversion rates, increase customer retention, and build brand advocacy by creating content that is specific to each client's needs. Additionally, it lessens the noise of unimportant information, ensuring that clients only get the information that actually matters to them. The personalization doesn't end with the content itself but it extends to the timing, format, and channel of delivery. In a world where customers are inundated with digital content, crafting dynamic and personalized content is the key to standing out and making a meaningful connection. It transforms marketing from a one-size-fits-all approach to a dynamic, customer-centric strategy, elevating the customer experience and driving brand success in the digital age.

14.4.5 Real-time Customer Interactions

In today's frantic and connected world, real-time customer contacts have emerged as a pillar of customer-centric enterprises. These interactions include more than just quick responses; they also involve instantly identifying and satisfying client demands, which results in a dynamic, highly engaging experience. Modern tools like Chatbots, virtual assistants, and AI enable real-time customer engagements. With the aid of these solutions, organizations can offer 24/7 customer service and information that is immediate and tailored. For instance, Chatbots can instantly respond to inquiries, address problems, and even make product or service recommendations (Ancillai et al., 2019).

Real-time interactions are important for many different sectors. In e-commerce, this entails providing prompt answers to client inquiries, facilitating smooth transactions, and even making product recommendations in real-time. It allows for quick access to medical advice and appointment booking in the healthcare industry (Khang & Medicine, 2023). Real-time interactions are essential in the financial sector for fraud detection and prompt client support. Because customers feel valued and understood when they receive prompt and accurate responses, real-time interactions promote trust and client loyalty. This increases both customer happiness and brand advocacy because happy customers are more inclined to tell others about a brand. In the digital age, these in-the-moment consumer contacts are at the heart of a customer-centric strategy.

14.4.6 The Role of Chatbots and Virtual Assistants

The digital transformation is leading with Chatbots and virtual assistants, which are altering how companies engage with customers. These AI-powered products have a variety of functions, acting as both brand ambassadors and problem solvers. Chatbots in customer care provide round-the-clock assistance by responding to inquiries right away. They free up human agents to deal with more complicated problems by handling mundane activities like tracking orders or responding to frequently asked questions. This improves efficiency while also cutting down on response times, which increases customer happiness (Singh, 2022).

By accessing client information and interests, virtual assistants go beyond basic personalization and provide individualized recommendations for everything from trip itineraries to product recommendations. This degree of customization promotes brand loyalty and enhances customer interaction. Chatbots and virtual assistants excel in data analytics, in addition to providing excellent customer care and customization. They can collect and analyze data from client interactions, giving organizations useful insights (Analytics, 2016). These insights serve as a decision-making tool, assisting businesses in honing their tactics, streamlining their operations, and better comprehending the wants of their clients. Chatbots and virtual assistants play a crucial role in defining a whole client experience, going beyond simple job completion. As they continue to advance and become more sophisticated, their contribution to businesses will only increase, making them indispensable in the ever-evolving digital landscape.

14.5 Impact on Brand Advocacy: Brand Advocacy and Its Significance

The significance of brand advocacy lies in the power of genuine recommendations. In today's world, customers are bombarded with marketing messages from all directions. In this cacophony, a recommendation from a friend, family member, or colleague carries unparalleled weight. Such recommendations are not perceived as advertising but as trusted guidance. Brand advocacy represents one of the most coveted accomplishments for businesses in the digital age. It refers to customers becoming enthusiastic promoters of a brand, willingly and authentically endorsing it to their networks. The impact of brand advocacy is profound, as it translates into organic growth, heightened trust, and invaluable word-of-mouth marketing (George, 2023).

Hyper-personalization plays a pivotal role in nurturing brand advocacy. When brands offer experiences, products, and services tailored precisely to individual customer preferences, they elevate customer satisfaction. Satisfied customers, in turn, are more likely to become advocates, eagerly sharing their positive experiences with others. In this context, Chatbots and virtual assistants, powered by AI and ML, contribute significantly to the equation. They enable real-time, personalized interactions with customers, addressing their needs promptly and effectively. These technologies enhance the customer experience, making it memorable and delightful. Consequently, customers are more inclined to become vocal advocates, spreading the word about the brand's excellence (Wind & Hays, 2016).

Ultimately, the impact on brand advocacy is a testament to the brand's ability to connect with its audience on a personal level. As advocates share their experiences, they become an extension of the brand's marketing team, contributing to its growth and long-term success. This organic, authentic advocacy is the ultimate goal for businesses, and it's a reflection of their commitment to hyper-personalized customer experiences and customer-centric strategies (Kuusinen, 2019).

14.5.1 Customer Loyalty and Advocacy in the Digital Age

The customer loyalty and advocacy have taken on new dimensions during the digital age. With an ever-expanding array of choices at their fingertips, consumers are more discerning and demanding than ever. Building loyalty is no longer just about offering quality products or services; it's about crafting exceptional experiences and personal connections (Singh, 2022). Customer loyalty is now intricately linked with brand advocacy. The satisfied and engaged customers not only return but become enthusiastic advocates, sharing their positive experiences and influencing others (Wheeler, 2023). Brands that prioritize personalized interactions, real-time engagement, and exceptional customer service are the ones poised to thrive in this digital landscape, where customer loyalty and advocacy are the true currency of success.

14.5.2 Building Trust and Emotional Connections

Building trust and emotional connections with customers are fundamental to the success of businesses. Every successful client connection is built on trust, which is acquired via openness, dependability, and consistency. Businesses must conduct honorably and remain committed to keeping their word regarding anything from product quality to data privacy. On the other hand, emotional ties are fostered through unique experiences that connect with each consumer on a deeper level. Brands can identify client preferences and wants with cutting-edge technology like AI and ML, then customize their interactions and products to produce sincere, emotionally charged experiences. Through these ties, clients become brand evangelists who not only trust the company but also fervently recommend it to others (Sedkaoui, 2018).

14.6 Marketing Strategies in the Age of Hyper-Personalization: Data-Driven Decision-making

In the age of hyper-personalization, data-driven decision-making has emerged as the keystone of effective marketing campaigns. Businesses now have unparalleled access to massive data reservoirs thanks to cutting-edge technologies like AI and ML, which provide insights into customer behavior, preferences, and demands. They can develop highly focused and tailored marketing strategies that appeal to certain clients by utilizing this data. In order to make data-driven decisions, it is important to extract relevant insights from the data that inform strategic decisions. To predict trends and customer preferences, marketers might examine consumer interactions, purchase histories, and online habits (Neuwirth, 2023). AI- and ML-powered predictive models can predict future behaviors and proactively inform strategies.

With the use of this information, firms are able to optimize every aspect of their marketing plans, from timing and channel selection to content and product recommendations. They may act quickly using real-time data analysis to ensure that clients receive pertinent and interesting information. Data-driven decision-making, however, entails a need to protect consumer privacy and follow ethical data usage principles. It involves finding the right balance between individualized attention and observance of private boundaries. In the era of hyper-personalization, many marketing tactics rely heavily on data-driven judgment. Understanding the value of data, applying AI and ML to gain useful insights, and customizing approaches to produce engaging, tailored experiences are all important. Businesses that adopt data-driven decision-making are better positioned to satisfy client expectations in this dynamic environment.

14.6.1 Ethical Considerations and Transparency: Addressing Privacy Concerns and Regulatory Compliance

Transparency and ethical issues now dominate marketing efforts. Personalization improves the user experience, but it brings up serious privacy and regulatory problems. For businesses, addressing these issues is not only required by law, but also morally right. The first pillar of ethical concerns is transparency, which is being open and truthful with clients about how their data are gathered, utilized, and safeguarded. It is crucial to educate clients on data practices, secure their informed consent, and provide them with unambiguous opt-in and opt-out choices. Privacy concerns loom large in this context. Customer data are a valuable asset, but its collection and usage must be done by respecting privacy regulations and customer expectations. This includes compliance with data protection laws like GDPR or CCPA, as well as ensuring robust security measures to safeguard sensitive information. These ethical considerations extend to data sharing and third-party partnerships. Brands should be transparent about any data sharing and provide customers with control over their data even when it's shared with affiliates or partners (Schaeffer, 2017).

Navigating the ethical landscape of hyper-personalization also requires a commitment to responsible data usage. It's about using data not just to increase profits but to enhance the customer experience. Data-driven insights should be used for the benefit of customers, whether that's in the form of personalized recommendations or improved services. The ethical considerations and transparency are non-negotiable in the age of hyper-personalization. Businesses that prioritize privacy, data security, and responsible data usage not only comply with regulations but also foster trust and long-term customer relationships. In this digital era, ethical marketing isn't just a legal requirement; it's a pathway to ethical and sustainable business practices.

14.6.2 Balancing Automation and the Human Touch

So, striking the right balance between automation and the human touch is the defining challenge for businesses. Automation, powered by AI and ML, offers unmatched efficiency and personalization. However, it must coexist harmoniously with the warmth and empathy that only humans can provide. Automation brings speed and precision to customer interactions. Chatbots and virtual assistants can address routine inquiries instantly, and predictive models can recommend products or services based on individual preferences. This is a crucial aspect of delivering personalized experiences, as it ensures real-time responses and convenience. Yet, the human touch remains indispensable. In more complex or emotionally charged situations, customers often seek human interactions (Singh, 2019). The human touch encompasses empathy, understanding, and the ability to handle nuanced situations. It's about resolving issues, providing reassurance, and making customers feel heard and valued.

As balancing these two elements requires a strategic approach, automation should be employed where it enhances efficiency and personalization, leaving the human touch to shine in areas that demand emotional intelligence and personalized problem-solving. It's about knowing when to automate and when to bring in the human touch. Moreover, transparency is crucial. Customers should be aware when they are interacting with automation versus a human agent. This transparency fosters trust and allows customers to manage their expectations. The finding of equilibrium between automation and the human touch is an art in the era of hyper-personalization. When executed effectively, it ensures efficiency, personalization, and empathy, creating an unparalleled customer experience that builds loyalty and advocacy (Venkatesh, 2021).

14.6.3 Future of Digital Marketing: Beyond Hyper-Personalization – The Dynamic Customer Journey

As we gazes into the future of digital marketing, it envisions a landscape that goes beyond hyper-personalization and delves into the concept of the dynamic customer journey. While hyper-personalization has been a game-changer, the dynamic customer journey takes personalization to the next level, embracing the fluidity and unpredictability of individual customer pathways. In this future, marketing strategies will be adaptive and responsive. AI and ML will continuously analyze real-time customer data to anticipate shifts in preferences, behaviors, and context. Marketers will not merely respond to customer actions; they will proactively shape the customer journey based on predictive insights.

The dynamic customer journey acknowledges that customers' needs and desires are not static. They evolve, often in response to external factors, life events, or changing interests. In this context, digital marketing strategies will provide content and experiences that reflect these changes, offering the right message at the right time. This future envisions a seamless integration of marketing touchpoints, from social media and websites to email and in-app interactions. These touchpoints will not exist in isolation but will form part of a cohesive, fluid customer journey. Every interaction will contribute to a personalized narrative that guides the customer toward a deeper relationship with the brand.

While the dynamic customer journey holds incredible potential, it also raises ethical considerations. Businesses must navigate the fine line between personalization and intrusion, respecting privacy and obtaining informed consent for data usage. The future of digital marketing is not just about hyper-personalization but embracing the dynamic nature of customer journeys. It's about how customer needs evolve, and effective marketing strategies must evolve with them. The dynamic customer journey promises not just personalization but proactive, fluid, and relevant customer experiences that pave the way for long-term loyalty and brand advocacy (Reviglio della Venaria, 2020).

14.6.4 The Role of AI-Driven Creativity and Innovation

AI has emerged as a powerful catalyst for creativity and innovation, transforming the way we conceive, design, and implement ideas. Its role in these realms extends beyond automation; AI-driven creativity and innovation empowers individuals and organizations to envision and realize groundbreaking solutions. AI's capacity to process vast datasets and recognize complex patterns equips it to unearth novel insights. It can analyze customer behaviors, market trends, and even creative works, offering inspiration and fresh perspectives. This data-driven creativity often results in more targeted and effective innovations.

AI can generate creative content itself, such as art, music, or even written text. These AI-generated works challenge traditional boundaries and introduce new dimensions to human creativity. They serve as tools for artists, writers, and musicians, sparking innovation by merging human ingenuity with AI's computational power. AI-driven innovation goes beyond creativity, facilitating the development of disruptive technologies. In fields like healthcare, AI assists in drug discovery and disease diagnosis (Khang & Abuzarova et al., 2023). In autonomous vehicles, it is revolutionizing transportation. In finance, it is optimizing investment strategies. These innovations improve efficiency, solve complex problems, and create entirely new opportunities.

The responsible use of AI in creativity and innovation involves transparency, accountability, and consideration for potential biases so ethical considerations are paramount. Striking a balance between AI-driven and human-driven creativity is an ongoing challenge. AI-driven creativity and innovation are reshaping industries and pushing the boundaries of what's possible. They offer unprecedented opportunities to generate fresh ideas, optimize processes, and solve complex problems. While ethical considerations remain, the collaborative potential of AI and human creativity promises an exciting future of innovation and exploration (Maes, 2018).

14.7 Conclusion and Vision for the Future of Digital Marketing

Hyper-personalization and real-time customer experiences are the driving forces behind the future of digital marketing. With advanced technologies, businesses can engage customers on a deeply personal level, delivering tailored content and interactions in the blink of an eye. This flexible method anticipates needs, encourages trust, and creates enduring connections. The key to successful marketing in the current digital era is the marriage of hyper-personalization and real-time dynamics, which provide customers with more than just content but also meaningful experiences. The dynamic environment of digital marketing in the future will be characterized by hyper-personalization, moral considerations, and the seamless fusion of automation and human interaction. It's a field where making decisions based on data, being transparent, and using data sensibly are essential. It involves developing experiences that connect with specific customers and encourage loyalty and trust.

The vision is based on ethics and accountability; nevertheless, it places a high priority on consumer permission, data security, and privacy in our quest for personalization. This makes a commitment to developing emotional bonds and trust because it understands that these are the foundations of brand advocacy. The future of digital marketing involves people as much as technology. It's about how cutting-edge technology and the human touch can come together to create experiences that are not just unique but also highly engaging and meaningful. In the future, marketing plans will be based on people rather than just data, acknowledging that each consumer is an individual with their own requirements and wants (Khang & Kali et al., 2023).

Businesses will succeed in this era not merely by meeting but by exceeding customer expectations. By anticipating their clients' requirements in addition to just meeting them, they will build long-lasting relationships with them. It's a future where brands collaborate with consumers along their journey, act as their guides through a changing environment, and travel alongside them as the digital world develops. Digital marketing has a bright future ahead of it, and this vision that emphasizes innovation, accountability, and client centricity. In this future, trust, loyalty, and advocacy are not just results but also the pillars of success where businesses and consumers collaborate to create meaningful experiences.

References

Ahmed, A. (2022). Marketing 4.0: The unseen potential of AI in consumer relations. *International Journal of New Media Studies: International Peer Reviewed Scholarly Indexed Journal*, 9(1), 5–12. https://ijnms.com/index.php/ijnms/article/view/163/135

Analytics, M. (2016). *The Age of Analytics: Competing in a Data-Driven World*. McKinsey Global Institute Research. https://www.cosmeticinnovation.com.br/wp-content/uploads/2017/01/MGI-The-Age-of-Analytics-Full-report.pdf

Ancillai, C., Terho, H., Cardinali, S., & Pascucci, F. (2019). Advancing social media driven sales research: Establishing conceptual foundations for B-to-B social selling. *Industrial Marketing Management*, 82, 293–308. https://www.sciencedirect.com/science/article/abs/pii/S0019850118300099

Auttri, B., Chaitanya, K., Daida, S., & Jain, S. K. (2023). Digital transformation in customer relationship management: Enhancing engagement and loyalty. *European Economic Letters (EEL)*, 13(3), 1140–1149. https://eelet.org.uk/index.php/journal/article/view/410

Babet, A. (2020). Utilization of personalization in marketing automation and email marketing. https://lutpub.lut.fi/handle/10024/161404

Bhatnagar, S. (2022). Digital disruptions and transformation of bank marketing. https://nibmindia.org/static/working_paper/NIBM_WP13_SB.pdf

Gao, Y., & Liu, H. (2022). Artificial intelligence-enabled personalization in interactive marketing: A customer journey perspective. *Journal of Research in Interactive Marketing*, (ahead-of-print), 1–18. https://www.emerald.com/insight/content/doi/10.1108/JRIM-01-2022-0023/full/html

George, A. S. (2023). Future economic implications of artificial intelligence. *Partners Universal International Research Journal*, 2(3), 20–39. https://www.puirj.com/index.php/research/article/view/129

Henke, N., & Jacques Bughin, L. (2016). The age of analytics: Competing in a data-driven world. https://www.cosmeticinnovation.com.br/wp-content/uploads/2017/01/MGI-The-Age-of-Analytics-Full-report.pdf

Kamal, M., & Himel, A. S. (2023). Redefining modern marketing: An analysis of AI and NLP's influence on consumer engagement, strategy, and beyond. *Eigenpub Review of Science and Technology*, 7(1), 203–223. https://studies.eigenpub.com/index.php/erst/article/view/22

Kaushal, V., & Yadav, R. (2023). Learning successful implementation of Chatbots in businesses from B2B customer experience perspective. *Concurrency and Computation: Practice and Experience*, 35(1), e7450. https://onlinelibrary.wiley.com/doi/abs/10.1002/cpe.7450

Khang, A. (2023). *AI and IoT-Based Technologies for Precision Medicine* (1st Ed.). IGI Global Press. ISBN: 9798369308769. https://doi.org/10.4018/979-8-3693-0876-9

Khang, A. (2024). *AI and IoT Technology and Applications for Smart Healthcare Systems*. Taylor and Francis Group – CRC Press. HBK: 9781032684901 PBK: 9781032679648 EBK: 9781032686745. https://doi.org/10.1201/9781032686745

Khang, A., Abdullayev, V. A., Alyar, A. V., Khalilov, M., & Murad, B. (2023). AI-aided data analytics tools and applications for the healthcare sector. *AI and IoT-Based Technologies for Precision Medicine* (1st Ed.). IGI Global Press. ISBN: 9798369308769. https://doi.org/10.4018/979-8-3693-0876-9.ch018

Khang, A., Muthmainnah, M., Seraj, P. M. I., Al Yakin, A., Obaid, A. J., & Panda, M. R. (2023). AI-aided teaching model for the education 5.0 ecosystem. *AI-Based Technologies and Applications in the Era of the Metaverse* (1st Ed.). IGI Global Press, 83–104. https://doi.org/10.4018/978-1-6684-8851-5.ch004

Khang, A., Rana, G., Tailor, R. K., & Hajimahmud, V. A. (2023). *Data-Centric AI Solutions and Emerging Technologies in the Healthcare Ecosystem* (1st Ed.). CRC Press. https://doi.org/10.1201/9781003356189

Khang, A., Rath, K. C., Satapathy, S. K., Kumar, A., Das, S. R., & Panda, M. R. (2023). Enabling the future of manufacturing: Integration of robotics and IoT to smart factory infrastructure in industry

4.0. *AI-Based Technologies and Applications in the Era of the Metaverse* (1st Ed.). IGI Global Press, 25–50. https://doi.org/10.4018/978-1-6684-8851-5.ch002

Khang, A., Shah, V., & Rani, S. (2023). *AI-Based Technologies and Applications in the Era of the Metaverse* (1st Ed.). IGI Global Press. https://doi.org/10.4018/978-1-6684-8851-5

King, K. (2022). *AI Strategy for Sales and Marketing: Connecting Marketing, Sales and Customer Experience.* Kogan Page Publishers.

Kuusinen, M. (2019). Scenarios for digital marketing: A Delphi-based analysis for 2028. https://lutpub.lut .fi/handle/10024/159341

Maes, P. (2018). *Disruptive Selling: A New Strategic Approach to Sales, Marketing and Customer Service.* Kogan Page Publishers. https://www.google.com/books?hl=en&lr=&id=8PoItiB7bicC&oi=fnd&pg =PR5

Neuwirth, R. J. (2023). Prohibited artificial intelligence practices in the proposed EU artificial intelligence act (AIA). *Computer Law & Security Review*, 48, 105798. https://www.sciencedirect.com/science/ article/abs/pii/S0267364923000092

Rajamannar, R. (2021). *Quantum Marketing: Mastering the New Marketing Mindset for Tomorrow's Consumers.* HarperCollins Leadership. https://www.google.com/books?hl=en&lr=&id=19TtDwAAQBAJ&oi =fnd&pg=PP1&dq=Quantum+marketing:+mastering+the+new+marketing+mindset+for+tomor- row%27s+consumers.+HarperCollins+Leadership&ots=SBihNowQtY&sig=HI-1lMbNApz0xD 6lhscHWpV_THs

Reviglio della Venaria, U. (2020). Personalization in social media: Challenges and opportunities for demo- cratic societies. http://amsdottorato.unibo.it/id/eprint/9529

Sadowski, J. (2023). Total life insurance: Logics of anticipatory control and actuarial governance in insur- ance technology. *Social Studies of Science*, 03063127231186437. https://journals.sagepub.com/doi/full /10.1177/03063127231186437

Schaeffer, E. (2017). *Industry X.0: Realizing Digital Value in Industrial Sectors.* Kogan Page Publishers. https://www.google.com/books?hl=en&lr=&id=PNy_DgAAQBAJ&oi=fnd&pg=PA1

Sedkaoui, S. (Ed.). (2018). *Big Data Analytics for Entrepreneurial Success.* IGI Global. https://www .google.com/books?hl=en&lr=&id=LSFzDwAAQBAJ&oi=fnd&pg=PR1&dq=Big+data+analyt- ics+for+entrepreneurial+success.+IGI+Global&ots=Omm2Z2WGs9&sig=BSH1HV0MVBsGVCl ZPyf3Qb-cUuY

Sharma, A., & Singh, B. (2022). Measuring impact of E-commerce on small scale business: A systematic review. *Journal of Corporate Governance and International Business Law*, 5(1). https://lawjournals.cel- net.in/index.php/jcgibl/article/view/1087

Singh, B. (2019). Profiling public healthcare: A comparative analysis based on the multidimensional health- care management and legal approach. *Indian Journal of Health and Medical Law*, 2(2), 1–5. https:// lawjournals.celnet.in/index.php/ijhml/article/view/399

Singh, B. (2022a). COVID-19 pandemic and public healthcare: Endless downward spiral or solution via rapid legal and health services implementation with patient monitoring program. *Justice and Law Bulletin*, 1(1), 1–7. https://apricusjournals.com/index.php/jus-l-bulletin/article/view/1

Singh, B. (2022b). Relevance of agriculture-nutrition linkage for human healthcare: A conceptual legal framework of implication and pathways. *Justice and Law Bulletin*, 1(1), 44–49. https://apricusjournals .com/index.php/jus-l-bulletin/article/view/4

Singh, B. (2023a). Blockchain technology in renovating healthcare: Legal and future perspectives. *Revolutionizing Healthcare Through Artificial Intelligence and Internet of Things Applications*. IGI Global, 177–186. https://www.igi-global.com/chapter/blockchain-technology-in-renovating-health- care/324943

Singh, B. (2023b). Federated learning for envision future trajectory smart transport system for climate pres- ervation and smart green planet: Insights into global governance and SDG-9 (Industry, innovation and infrastructure). *National Journal of Environmental Law*, 6(2), 6–17. https://lawjournals.celnet.in /index.php/jel/article/view/1369

Singh, B. (2024). Legal dynamics lensing metaverse crafted for videogame industry and e-sports: Phenomenological exploration catalyst complexity and future. *Journal of Intellectual Property Rights Law*, 7(1), 8–14. https://lawjournals.celnet.in/index.php/jiprl/article/view/1372

Soliman, M., & Al Balushi, M. K. (2023). Unveiling destination evangelism through generative AI tools. *ROBONOMICS: The Journal of the Automated Economy*, 4(54), 1. https://www.researchgate.net/profile/Maha-Al-Balushi-2/publication/372477564_Unveiling_destination_evangelism_through_generative_AI_tools/links/64b90af3b9ed6874a530637e/Unveiling-destination-evangelism-through-generative-AI-tools.pdf

Venkatesh, D. N. (2021). *Winning with Employees: Leveraging Employee Experience for a Competitive Edge.* SAGE Publishing India. https://journals.sagepub.com/doi/abs/10.1177/097215090500600204

Vinaykarthik, B. C. (2022, October). Design of Artificial Intelligence (AI) based user experience websites for E-commerce application and future of digital marketing. *2022 3rd International Conference on Smart Electronics and Communication (ICOSEC)*. IEEE, 1023–1029. https://doi.org/10.1109/ICOSEC54921.2022.9952005

Vuong, N. A., & Mai, T. T. (2023). Unveiling the synergy: Exploring the intersection of AI and NLP in redefining modern marketing for enhanced consumer engagement and strategy optimization. *Quarterly Journal of Emerging Technologies and Innovations*, 8(3), 103–118. https://injole.joln.org/index.php/ijle/article/view/2

Wheeler, J. (2023). *The Digital-First Customer Experience: Seven Design Strategies from the World's Leading Brands*. Kogan Page Publishers. https://www.google.com/books?hl=en&lr=&id=KAHGEAAAQBAJ&oi=fnd&pg=PP1&dq=The+Digital-First+Customer+Experience:+Seven+Design+Strategies+from+the+World%E2%80%99s+Leading+Brands.+Kogan+Page+Publishers&ots=mArZszdnzn&sig=5STNzIDhLJCIhhUbk5SMQGG230k

Wind, Y. J., & Hays, C. F. (2016). *Beyond Advertising: Creating Value through all Customer Touchpoints.* John Wiley & Sons. https://www.google.com/books?hl=en&lr=&id=PSmsBwAAQBAJ&oi=fnd&pg=PA15

Zaki, H. O. (2022). The impact of artificial intelligence on content marketing. *Journal of Strategic Digital Transformation in Society*, 2(3). https://www.emerald.com/insight/content/doi/10.1108/MIP-12-2022-0568/full/html

Chapter 15

Information Sharing Model and Electronic Data Exchange in Supply Chain Management

Rashmi Gujrat, Cemalettin Hatipoğlu, and Hayri Uygun

15.1 Introduction

Supply Chain Management (SCM) is the organization, planning, control, and realization of the product flow, which includes everything from designing and purchasing to manufacturing and distribution to the final consumer, all in accordance with market requirements for cost-effectiveness and efficiency. The SCM system enables the firm to greatly improve its ability to meet the demand for its goods while also drastically reducing the expenses of transportation and buying. The term "SCM" refers to the process of procuring raw materials, manufacturing, and distributing finished goods. In general terms, Supply Chain Management is divided into six primary sectors, according to researchers: production, suppliers, location, warehouse inventory, transportation, and information technology.

The following responsibilities are performed: Service-level improvement; optimization of profitability; and control of the manufacturing process benefits (Dubey et al., 2017). The enormous possibilities provided by the Internet have characterized the current trends in the development of SCM technology in recent years. Manufacturers, suppliers, contractors, transportation, and trade firms are all connected in the most intimate manner, and they have already developed into real-world Internet networks. Companies blend into the business community, and the lines that formerly divided them are no longer visible. As a result of the openness of collaborative actions, performers are able to swiftly adjust to client expectations and bring new items to market in a timely manner, thanks to sophisticated techniques of prediction and planning.

The Internet is the most straightforward, least expensive, and most efficient technical way of managing and controlling partner networks. Companies often begin by combining the most basic tasks by utilizing email and workflow automation technologies, progressing to the virtual docking of the most critical business processes, and finally merging into a single virtual company within which the whole network is synchronized. This is already the beginning of the transition to global

DOI: 10.4324/9781032688305-15

e-commerce, in which all commercial transactions and payments are conducted exclusively over the Internet. It follows as a consequence of this that not only does productivity grow greatly, but also that all processes accelerate significantly, resulting in qualitatively new results.

15.2 The Supply Chain as a Concept

Houlihan (1985) is credited as being the first person to use the term "supply chain." Figure 15.2 presents a basic supply chain (adapted from Hutchinson, 1987). It is made up of three modules: The supplier, the company, and the consumer (or client). Material flows may be bidirectional, with one direction being forward and the other being backward. The movement of material (goods) from the supplier to the client is shown in Figure 15.2.

Actually, a supply chain may be made up of many different enterprises that give raw materials or services to other businesses in the form of input. Vollman, Berry, and Whybark (1997) defined the supply chain as a spider web of business units (nodes) that are both supplied by and supply a large number of other business units (suppliers and distributors). It has been pointed out by Lambert et al. (2001) that the rivalry is between supply networks rather than between enterprises (Lambert et al., 2001). When discussing supply chains, Harland (1996) identified the following sorts of arrangements: Internal supply chains, two-party connections, a chain of linked enterprises, and a network of interconnected businesses. However, the majority of the prior research concentrated on dyadic interactions (i.e., buyer–supplier relationships) in the context of material and information flows within supply chains, rather than on supply networks as a whole (Harland, 1996; Huang et al., 2003).

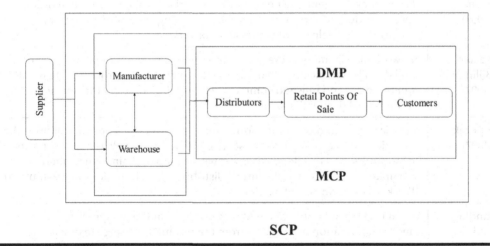

Figure 15.1   Processes of Supply Chain Management. *Source*: Boiko et al., 2017

Figure 15.2   A Simple Supply Chain

15.3 Supply Chain Management's Evolution

Japanese automobile manufacturers were the first to adopt "Supply Chain Management" practices (Mentzer et al., 2000). The early attempts to implement Supply Chain Management were quite restricted in scope. The majority of businesses concentrated their efforts on lowering logistical costs (Anderson and Lee, 1999; Copacino, 1997). Several years after corporations began to experience worldwide competitive challenges and an increase in demand for customized short life cycle goods, they began to recognize that Supply Chain Management may be a source of improved performance and started implementing it (Narasimhan and Jayaram, 1998).

In recent years, with advancements in information technology and the widespread adoption of logistical alliances, Supply Chain Management has emerged as a viable strategy for competing effectively (Stock and Lambert, 1990). Supply chain literature has a variety of alternative definitions of Supply Chain Management as indicated in Table 15.1.

Table 15.1 Supply Chain Management Definitions

Authors	Definition
Berry et al. (1994)	One of the goals of Supply Chain Management is to reduce the number of suppliers to a specific Original Equipment Manufacturer (OEM). This allows management resources to be devoted to building meaningful, long-term relationships with customers, suppliers, and manufacturers, rather than on administrative tasks.
Ellram (1991)	It is the management of a network of enterprises that collaborate in order to give a product or service to a final client, linking processes from raw material supply to final delivery of the product or service.
Lee and Billington (1992)	Network management is the administration of a network of manufacturing and distribution facilities that purchases raw materials, processes them into intermediate and finished commodities, and then delivers the finished goods to their final destinations.
Kopczak (1997)	Materials, commodities, and information are moved via a network of firms that includes suppliers and logistics service providers, as well as manufacturers, distributors, and resellers; this is known as Supply Chain Management. Companies such as manufacturers, distributors, and resellers are examples of this kind of business entity.
Handfield and Nichols (1998)	When looking at Supply Chain Management from the perspective of the flow and transformation of products from the raw material stage (extraction) through to the end user, all activities involved in the flow and transformation of products as well as the information flows that are associated with these activities are included. Materials and information pertaining to the supply chain are exchanged both up and down the supply chain. To achieve a prolonged competitive advantage via improved supply chain interactions, the purpose of supply chain management, which is the integration of multiple activities, is to achieve a sustainable competitive edge.

Source: Radhakrishnan A., 2005

Basic Supply Chain Management includes all activities performed inside a network, including ordering, shipping, storing and retrieving goods, producing and processing goods for distribution, and delivering goods to customers. It also includes after-sale services and support. The goal of Supply Chain Management (SCM) is to guarantee that these processes, as well as the information flow associated with them, are correctly managed across a network of organizations in order to provide the best possible service to the end user.

15.4 Supply Chain Types

The supply chain may be classified into several forms (Fisher, 1996; Lee, 2002). In 1996, Fisher postulated two types of supply networks, which differed in terms of the nature of the items which they dealt with. The author divided items into two categories: Those that are utilitarian and those that are innovative. Functional goods include the following characteristics: Consistent demand, a product life cycle of more than two years, a smaller contribution margin, a lesser product diversity, a lower stock out rate, and a longer production lead time. Functional products are also more expensive. Aspects of innovative goods that distinguish them include unexpected demand, a product life cycle of less than 6 months, a larger contribution margin, a greater range of items, a higher stock out rate, and a shorter production lead-time. In the author's opinion, the supply chain could cope with a functional product if it was physically efficient.

The fundamental purpose of a physically efficient supply chain is to lower the overall cost of production in the manufacturing process. The purpose of cost-cutting is to achieve a high average utilization rate while concurrently boosting inventory turns by maintaining inventory levels throughout the supply chain as low as feasible, according to the supply chain. The author said, on the contrary, that a supply chain that is responsive to the market will be able to handle the introduction of new products. One of the key objectives of a market-responsive supply chain is to increase its responsiveness to changes in the market environment.

It is necessary to maintain a buffer stock of completed products and components inventories in order to fulfill any unexpected demand. Fundamentally, the goal of a physically efficient supply chain is to reduce the entire cost of production throughout the manufacturing process. According to the supply chain, the goal of cost-cutting is to achieve a high average utilization rate while simultaneously increasing inventory turns by keeping inventory levels across the supply chain as low as is reasonably possible.

The author argued that a supply chain that is sensitive to the market would be able to manage the introduction of new items, rather than the opposite. One of the most important goals of a market-responsive supply chain is to improve its ability to respond to changes in the market environment as they occur. Specifically, the author said that there should be a perfect connection between the supply chain type and the product being dealt with. Based on the level of demand uncertainty and supply uncertainty associated with the items they are involved with, Lee (2002) established four kinds of supply chains that were further developed from Fisher's work. The demand uncertainty for a functional product is minimal, but the demand uncertainty for an innovative product is considerable. Both functional and innovative items might be subjected to either low or high supply uncertainty depending on their characteristics.

According to the author, supply chains were divided into four categories: Physically efficient supply chains for functional products with low supply uncertainty, risk hedging supply chains for functional products with high supply uncertainty, market responsive supply chains for innovative products with low supply uncertainty, and flexible and agile supply chains for innovative products with high supply uncertainty. Each supply chain has a distinct focus that differs from the others. If the focus is on lowering costs in a efficient supply chain, while the emphasis is on pooling and sharing resources in a risk hedging supply chain, then the risks associated with a supply interruption may be shared as well.

The primary goal of a market responsive supply chain is to respond and be flexible in response to the changing and diverse needs of customers, whereas agile supply chains strive to not only be responsive and flexible in response to customer needs, but also to hedge the risks of supply distortions by employing appropriate strategies such as inventory pooling or other capacity resources. The author also emphasized that there should be a good connection between the type of supply chain and the environment in which it operates.

Finally, multiple kinds of supply chains exist based on the amount to which supply and demand uncertainties exist, and each supply chain type has a distinct emphasis that differs from the others. This analysis makes use of all four kinds of supply chains that are available. Different kinds of supply chains are subjected to varying degrees of supply and demand uncertainty, which necessitate the development of a variety of strategies for dealing with these uncertainties. The two most common strategies used by supply chains to deal with uncertainty are (a) developing buffers that will reduce the impact of uncertainty, and (b) implementing structural mechanisms and information processing capabilities that will increase the flow of information and, as a result, reduce uncertainty. Traditional examples of the first technique include maintaining inventory buffers to minimize the impacts of changes in the market or supply, as well as establishing alternative supplier networks. By using an interorganizational information system to improve information flow across organizations, for example, the second technique may be implemented successfully.

According to Galbraith (1977), an information processing model was established in order to offer a theoretical framework for the function of interorganizational information systems in mitigating the risks that various kinds of supply chains confront in the face of uncertainty. In order to obtain optimum performance, it is critical to understand that this theoretical model incorporates three essential ideas: Information processing needs, information processing capabilities, and the fit between the two concepts in order to achieve optimal performance (Galbraith, 1977). The use of interorganizational information systems in supply chains, according to this concept, may enhance the flow of information and, as a consequence, minimize the level of uncertainty in the supply chain. Information sharing in supply chains has received a great deal of attention recently, and this part examines the literature on the subject as well as the benefits of information sharing.

15.5 Benefits of Information Sharing

The literature on information sharing and its influence on the performance of the supply chain are discussed in detail in this section. The importance of information sharing is also highlighted. Using Internet-based information technology, businesses may be connected together to build a unified and coordinated system in which information flows across the whole supply chain, making information accessible to all parties involved, including suppliers, manufacturers, retailers, and consumers. Table 15.2 summarizes the literature on information sharing and its influence on supply chain performance.

Table 15.2 Research on Information Sharing in Supply Chains: A Summary

Reference	Research Objective	Research Methodology	Key findings
Forrester (1958)	In this article, the main concepts of industrial dynamics are discussed, including information distortion, the causes of this distortion, and potential alternatives.	Serial system that can be managed remotely by a computer. It is made up of many components, including a manufacturer, warehouse, distributor, and retailer.	Bullwhip effect has been identified. Bullwhip impact mitigation techniques have been identified.
Sterman (1989)	It was the purpose of this research to explore the impact of decisions made by decision-makers on the functioning of the supply chain.	MIT's Sloan School of Management made use of a lab research. To illustrate, play a game of Beer Distribution.	When supply chain sections have access to local information rather than global information, evidence for the occurrence of the Bullwhip effect has been produced (i.e., order pattern shows amplification and phase lag).
Lee et al. (1997a)	Demonstrated empirical proof of the existence of the Bullwhip effect as well as its sources.	Consolidation of literature and insights from the industry.	The occurrence of the Bullwhip effect in businesses has been documented.
Lee et al. (1997b)	Bullwhip effect has been investigated in detail, as well as various countermeasures.	The Bullwhip effect may be represented mathematically as an analytic mathematical model (inventory model) of the components that contribute to it.	They discovered that demand signal processing, rationing game, order batching, and price volatility were all contributing elements to the Bullwhip effect. They recommended information sharing and simplified pricing systems, among other things, as a countermeasure to the situation.
Bourland et al. (1996)	The researchers specifically examined the effect of timely demand information exchange on inventories and levels of service at alternative supplier and final production lines that are subject to unpredictable demand patterns.	In this two-stage system, the analytical model assumes that each business has a periodic base stock inventory strategy with the same cycle durations as the other firms. The advantages of the whole system and each layer are listed.	Inventory at the supplier's facility decreases, while inventory at the assembly factory grows when information exchange is not performed and replenishment intervals are not coordinated, according to the study. They saw an improvement in the supplier's service standards as a consequence of the information exchange.

(Continued)

Table 15.2 (Continued) Research on Information Sharing in Supply Chains: A Summary

Reference	Research Objective	Research Methodology	Key findings
Fisher and Raman (1996)	There have been methods designed to improve planning and production scheduling in a single-capable supplier, multiple retailer, and seasonal multiple-product demand situation.	The development of a capacity-constrained newsvendor model for use in production planning is underway. An example of the Quick Response approach being used by a sports clothing company is provided.	Stock outs and markdown expenses are reduced at Sport Obermeyer (a sports clothing company) as a consequence of the use of the Quick Response approach.
Mason-Jones and Towill (1998)	In a supply chain environment, the researchers looked at the influence of reducing information flow time and material flow time on inventory levels and capacity utilization levels.	They demonstrate a computer simulation of an integrated serial supply chain, which comprises a supplier, manufacturer, and retailer.	It has been discovered that reducing the time it takes for information to flow and materials to move decreases inventory levels while simultaneously improving capacity utilization levels across the supply chain. Results indicate that the efficient use of information systems, such as Electronic Data Interchange (EDI) will aid in the decrease of information flow time.
Chen (1998)	It was discovered that the relevance of information communication and coordination among the participants in an n-stage serial supply chain was explored. Determine if there is a relationship between environmental conditions and the functioning of the supply chain management system.	The inquiry into developing (R, nQ) inventory models for a serial inventory system with N stages and random client demand at the final phase has started. In this paper, two models are contrasted: One with local installation stocks and the other with central echelon stocks.	Cost savings are achieved by centralized information exchange.

(Continued)

Table 15.2 (Continued)   Research on Information Sharing in Supply Chains: A Summary

Reference	Research Objective	Research Methodology	Key findings
Chen et al. (1999)	Bullwhip effect and the role of aggregated consumer demand information were explored in connection to the Bullwhip effect.	In this paper, they provide an analytical model of a two-stage supply chain in which each firm operates under an order-up-to-inventory strategy.	Customers' demand information aggregated in a consolidated place enhances the forecasting accuracy of upstream players and decreases the Bullwhip effect.
Gilbert and Ballou (1999)	When working in a two-stage make – to-order setting, the potential advantages of sharing advanced order commitments were investigated.	Design and implementation of (s,S) inventory models for the purpose of estimating inventory and excess capacity expenses. The influence of advanced orders (as a result of information sharing) on overtime production costs was investigated using a queuing model.	The bigger the number of advanced order commitments and the sooner the commitment, the greater the potential cost savings are.
Gavimeni, Kapuscinski, and Tayur (1999)	While examining at a supplier–retailer supply chain from the perspective of information exchange, capacity, and inventory, a study was conducted.	To determine the entire cost effect of each technique while examining alternative information exchange strategies, inventory models such as order-up-to (s, S) and modified order-up-to are often examined.	Cost savings are realized in both partial information sharing and total information exchange situations. Furthermore, cost reductions are inversely related to production rates.
Lee et al. (2000)	Scientists were able to estimate the value of information sharing by looking at data from a single-product, multiple supply chain with dynamica demand.	There is currently work being done on the construction of optimum order-up-to-inventory models. A computer simulation was performed in order to determine the cost savings that may be realized as a result of information sharing.	When demand is highly correlated over time, demand varies widely within time periods, or lead times are long, suppliers may benefit from information sharing by decreasing demand correlation over time.

(Continued)

Table 15.2 (Continued) Research on Information Sharing in Supply Chains: A Summary

Reference	Research Objective	Research Methodology	Key findings
Cachon and Fisher (2000)	In all circumstances, a research was done to ascertain the value of information sharing, lead cycle time, and production reduced size in situations involving a supplier and N matched retailers.	They constructed (R, nQ) inventory models to investigate issues such as information exchange, delivery schedules, and lot size problems.	When comparing the scenario of complete information-sharing scenario to the partial and no-information-sharing situations, the greatest cost reductions are realized in the full information-sharing scenario. The cost savings achieved via batch size reduction outweigh the cost savings achieved through information sharing.
Chen et al. (2000)	An extensive study has examined the effects of centralized information on a Multi-Stage Serial Supply Chain (MSSS).	It was necessary to employ a simulation study from the authors' earlier work in order to confirm the conclusions of analytical models that were constructed using order-up to inventory models.	Despite the fact that retailer demand data are exchanged in real time, all levels of the supply chain use the same forecasting and inventory management strategies, resulting in increasing inventory at every point of the supply chain. Demand variability increases less in the centralized information scenario than it does in the no-centralized information scenario when comparing the two scenarios.
Croson and Donohue (2003)	There has been research on the implications of point-of-sale data sharing in stable businesses that deal with functional items.	A beer distribution game with a serial supply chain setup that is susceptible to information delays and stochastic demand to demonstrate this.	The findings imply that sharing POS information with upstream members minimizes the order oscillation of those members.

(Continued)

Table 15.2 (Continued)   Research on Information Sharing in Supply Chains: A Summary

Reference	Research Objective	Research Methodology	Key findings
Fu and Piplani (2004)	By taking choices in a two-tiered supply chain into consideration, we were able to evaluate supply side cooperation (via information exchange).	The performance of distributors (i.e., service levels and stabilizing impact at the distributor) was evaluated using a computer simulation before and after the implementation of supply side cooperation.	Supply-side cooperation (facilitated by information sharing) increases the performance of distributors (i.e., both service levels and the stabilizing impact at the supplier improve as a result).
Sahin and Robinson (2004)	Concerning the performance of a make-to-order supply network, the researchers examined the effect of information sharing and material flow management on the overall system's performance.	Formalized two-stage mixed-integer programming issue and via simulation, produced a rolling timetable based on simulation results.	Improvements in cost performance are achieved by complete information exchange and comprehensive system coordination.
Chatfield et al. (2004)	The effects of unpredictable lead times, the amount of information sharing, and the quality of information sharing on a supply chain environment in which members use a periodic order-up-to-level inventory system were researched in order to determine what effect they had on the supply chain.	It was decided to create a simulation model known as "SISCO."	A supply chain's variance amplification is exacerbated by lead-time unpredictability, which has been established.unpredictability. It has also been shown that information sharing and information quality may both help to reduce the amount of variance amplification in a supply chain.

Source: Radhakrishnan A., 2005

15.6 Flow of Information in the Supply Chain

Manufacturers have the challenge of cutting product development time, enhancing quality, and lowering the cost and lead-time associated with manufacturing in a highly competitive market environment. Their capacity to integrate facilities into a closely integrated supply chain will be critical in determining whether or not they will be successful in addressing these hurdles. Organizing and managing material flow across several locations within the same firm presents additional problems for both companies and managers in their day-to-day work.

The complexity of this task is exacerbated by the disparate interests of the many parties involved in the supply chain. According to empirical research (Helper and Sako, 1995; Udo, 1993), many manufacturers are exchanging information with their suppliers using interorganizational information systems (IOIS) in order to enhance the overall performance of the supply chain in terms of cost and customer service delivery. According to Mayo (1986), J.C. Penny implemented a large-scale computerized inventory system that automatically reordered items from 281 vendors, which accounted for more than half of their total business. The extent to which information sharing helps distinct organizational units is not properly measured nor well understood.

Other empirical research has shown that sharing information with suppliers has resulted in considerable improvements in the performance of Chrysler and Toyota, among other companies (Srinivasan et al., 1994; Cole and Konsyski, 1985).

According to Cash and Konsynski (1985), interorganizational information systems, under the premise of quicker information flow, in many instances resulted in suppliers shouldering the cost of inventory keeping and other expenditures on their shoulders. According to a prior research conducted by Swaminathan (1996), the supply chain performs better in terms of cost and quality of services when information exchange is encouraged and implemented. The purpose of the study was to establish whether or not information sharing between suppliers had an influence on the performance of the supply chain in terms of expenditures, profits, and the pace at which demand was met. It is based on a simulation model of two suppliers running for a large number of periods with no backordering that these conclusions are derived. According to their findings, information exchange enhances the performance of both the manufacturer and the low-cost suppliers.

Swaminathan (1996) discovered that when a more costly supplier is obliged to provide information, the supplier does not reap the benefits of the arrangement. Afterwards, they conducted a study to determine the effect of the introduction of supplier adoption fees (costs to set up and maintain the information links). Based on previously conducted research, it seems to be customary for manufacturers to provide a subsidy to suppliers in order to compensate them for the higher costs involved with establishing and maintaining the information connection (Klien, 1992; Kelleher, 1986). Furthermore, they observed that the amount of subsidy received is exactly proportional to the cost of the information connection.

According to Swaminathan (1996), if the cost of implementing an information system is quite expensive, it is preferable for the manufacturer to avoid establishing information ties with any of the suppliers. It is important to highlight that, in order to reduce adoption costs, it is preferable for the manufacturer to establish information ties with one or more of the vendors. Furthermore, the greater the degree of demand uncertainty that exists in the system, the more probable it is that the manufacturer will build and maintain information ties with the system (Khang and Anuradha et al., 2024).

Interorganizational information systems have mostly been examined using economic models, according to the literature (Riggins et al., 1994; Marcus, 1990; Oren and Smith, 1981). These models take into account the utility function of the user in order for him or her to join the information network. Wang and Siedman (1995) utilize an economic model to investigate the impact of Electronic Data Exchange (EDI) and the adoption of EDI by suppliers in the manufacturing industry. They take into account a deterministic demand for the maker that is downward sloping. The authors conclude that when supplier adoption costs are high, it is best for the manufacturer to use EDI with a smaller number of suppliers, which is critical to the study's goal.

15.7 Information Systems for Interorganizational Communication

Interorganizational information systems have reduced the length of time it takes to complete a commercial transaction in practically every sector. Because of these challenges, as well as severe worldwide rivalry, information exchange among product designers, producers, and distributors has become more important in the industry (Wang and Seidman, 1995). As a result, a robust information system for sharing data and information is required at all stages of the supply chain, including the manufacturing floor. It is especially important for businesses today to link information flow throughout the entire supply chain, from raw materials procurement and research and development to production and distribution as well as after-sale product support (Cash and Konsynski, 1985; Clemons and McFarlan, 1988; Gurbaxani and Whang, 1991). Texas Instruments claims that it's Intelligent Ordering and Inventory System (IOIS) enables them to satisfy 60,000 orders per month for 45,000 distinct models with a 95% delivery dependability (Business W eek, 1998).

The majority of manufacturers and suppliers in the United States, on the other hand, do not employ any kind of interorganizational information system to share data between their respective organizations. In an unreported study conducted by the North American Purchasing Managers (NAPM) group, fewer than 3% of the enterprises asked said that they were using Electronic Data Interchange (EDI) (1999). An additional 17% of manufacturing and service businesses said that they used some type of e-commerce to exchange data, although the vast majority of them stated that they believed e-commerce was the same as Electronic Data Interchange (EDI).

The NAPM poll also revealed that consumers are still uninformed of the potential of Electronic Data Interchange (EDI) and the Internet as a data-transfer medium. There is little doubt that industry practitioners are skeptical about the efficacy of electronic data exchange systems, as shown by the fact that fewer than 20% of total survey respondents indicated that they were employing some type of electronic data exchange (Khanh and Khang, 2021).

Organizations have failed to implement IOIS for a variety of reasons, according to research. The most common is the expenses of installation and maintenance, as well as the security of private information. In the past, IOIS has been too costly to adopt, install, and maintain, preventing it from being widely used. A further barrier to broad adoption is the unwillingness of many businesses to disclose information with their vendors and suppliers, such as inventory status and purchase information, which has severely hindered its general adoption (Wang and Seidman, 1994).

With the introduction of the personal computer, fiber optic networks, the proliferation of the Internet, and the creation of the World Wide Web, the low cost of information resources has made it possible to link supply chain networks more easily and to eliminate information-related delays in the process (Handfield and Nichols, 1999). Increasingly, organizations are evolving toward an electronic commerce environment, in which transactions are done using a variety of electronic media, rather than paper.

Electronic commerce takes several forms, including Electronic Data Interchange (EDI), Point of Sale (POS) data transmission, encrypted Internets, and bar-coding, amongst many more. In order to minimize the need for paper records and increase the efficiency of other operational aspects, various information technologies are being used (Khang and Shah et al., 2023).

15.8 Transmission of Information through Electronic Data Interchange (EDI)

When there is a shortfall of a particular product in the warehouse or on the shelf, organizations that utilize EDI make orders with distributors and suppliers to fill the gap. Most of the time, in this procedure, a buyer is responsible for buying hundreds of items each week, with the orders being placed once or twice a week. In most cases, while employing this electronic media, the EDI process makes use of the already existing buying infrastructure.

EDI does provide several benefits over conventional buying systems, including the elimination of the paper trail, the reduction of ordering lead times, and the establishment of direct contacts with suppliers, among other things. Some writers contend that the adoption of Electronic Data Interchange (EDI) may be leveraged to gain a competitive edge (Galliers et al., 1995). Table 15.3 lists some of the possible advantages associated with the usage of Electronic Data Interchange (EDI) systems rather than conventional procurement processes (Handfield and Nichols, 1999; Bowersox and Closs, 1996; Murphy and Daley, 1996).

The outcomes of using EDI technology have been inconsistent. Many of the firms that have implemented EDI systems have reported that these systems have had little or no influence on their overall performance. Carter (1990), for example, found that the majority of businesses that used EDI did not reach the degree of cost reductions anticipated. According to Erickson (1990), only a small number of businesses have gained considerable cost reductions or other advantages through electronic data interchange.

Wallace (1988) discovered that 95% of survey respondents were unable to identify any benefits from the adoption of Electronic Data Interchange (EDI). When Hollis (1991) concluded that EDI systems in most companies were underutilized, he was joined by Riggins and Mukhopadhyah (1994) in asserting that the cost of developing EDI systems is often greater than expected and the benefits are less than expected for many firms that implement Electronic Data Interchange (EDI).

Despite widespread publicity about the advantages of EDI for ordering, only a few enterprises in the retail sector have realized considerable savings as a result of automating the ordering process

Table 15.3 Advantages of the Electronic Data Interchange

Sr. No	Advantages of the Electronic Data Interchange
1	Reduced Paperwork
2	Improved Communication
3	Increased Productivity
4	Improved Tracing and Expediting
5	Cost Efficiency
6	Competitive Advantage
7	Improved Billing
8	Reduced Labor and Materials Costs
9	Reduced IT Telecommunications Costs
10	Reduced clerical costs are just a few of the benefits of digitization.

using EDI. Firms that did achieve savings also reported that their business processes had been altered to accommodate the new information technology.

15.9 Data Exchange via the Internet

The majority of the literature on Extranet/Internet implementation has been anecdotal in character or case-oriented in nature, which is unfortunate. Some of those situations, as well as the usefulness of the Internet and Extranets in practice, will be highlighted in this portion of the literature study. Businesses would trade an estimated $17 billion dollars' worth of products and services in the year 1999, according to industry estimates. By 2002, it is predicted to reach 327 billion dollars (Business Week, 1996).

The rise in pace and unpredictability in the supply chain was not triggered by the Internet in the first place. Several decades have passed since major merchants and manufacturers began using interorganizational information systems to place orders for items and communicate information with vendors and suppliers. Data interchange formats are restricted and data transfer rates are sluggish with older systems such as EDI, rendering the technology unsuitable for use in build-to-order manufacturing methods (Business Week, 1996). The Internet is less expensive than traditional methods of data sharing, and it enables almost everyone in the supply chain to do so at a reasonable cost. The Internet is more versatile than conventional EDI systems, enabling firms to share a bigger volume of information and with a higher level of detail than they could before.

Security concerns around the sharing of sensitive information are the key issue with Internet/Extranet systems, and here is where the majority of the problems arise. Some types of private information, such as email and banking information, may be sent over the Internet; nevertheless, the Internet does not have sufficient security to safeguard all of the transactions that a company may need to do. Because the capacity to safeguard transactions is restricted, less than one in every seven firms is willing to use the Internet to share data because of the security concerns (Business Week, 1996). It may be very expensive for businesses to implement and maintain a security system for Internet transactions, and the costs and manpower involved with doing so might be prohibitively expensive.

The unreliability of the Internet and the difficulty of system management are two further issues that companies which utilize the Internet to communicate information must contend with. By making data available in a variety of formats and kinds, data are transmitted in a non-standardized manner, which might cause challenges for those who are attempting to analyze the information. Because data are sent in non-standardized formats, businesses must have on-site workers to update web pages for data exchange on a regular basis, in addition to having the conventional personnel for the buying function.

15.10 Conclusion

Interorganizational information systems are being considered by many businesses as a means of mitigating the effects of demand amplification. The most significant advantage of exchanging information is that it helps to lessen the bullwhip effect, which may distort demand information and raise relevant supply chain costs when it occurs. The exchange of information between suppliers and customers might result in a source of competitive advantage for both. Since the implementation of Just-in-Time (JIT) manufacturing by US companies, Electronic Data Interchange (EDI) has been used to send critical bits of information across businesses. Manufacturing and service industries typically use this data exchange mechanism to communicate inventory reordering and purchase information (Khang and Kali et al., 2023).

Most of the time, the purpose of these EDI type systems is to decrease or eliminate the amount of unpredictability in a system, which may be accomplished by lowering lead-time and paperwork in the system, as well as by offering real-time monitoring of logistical and warehousing operations. Despite the fact that EDI has shown to be beneficial for many firms, the high cost of implementing EDI systems has prevented its general adoption. Companies are increasingly resorting to e-commerce and Internet-based applications as a method of establishing informational ties with consumers, suppliers, vendors, and distributors in the recent past. The Internet enables businesses to create data communication linkages in different departments and with numerous organizations at the same time, saving time and money. Almost half of all significant firms in the United States are actively rethinking their information network infrastructures in order to take advantage of the Internet's capabilities.

There are many important benefits to using Internet technology over conventional modes of data transmission, the most notable of which is the huge decrease in cost of the application and the ability to transfer a variety of different types of information, including graphical data. Despite the widespread use of information-sharing technologies such as the Internet and Electronic Data Interchange (EDI) to communicate information across businesses, most enterprises and supply chains believe that they have had no meaningful influence on their performance or costs.

EDI systems have had little success in the past due to a variety of concerns, the most significant of which is the cost prohibitive nature of the product and the inability to adjust existing processes to accommodate the new technology. However, although the Internet helps to alleviate some of the costs associated with the adoption of new technology, it does not compel an organization to reengineer its processes in order to take advantage of the new technology. Only via the re-engineering of business process channels will an organization be able to reach the full potential for increasing the performance of the organization.

While the automation of operations in the supply chain will have little influence on performance, the process's overall structure will have a significant impact on performance. Numerous writers now contend that firms must alter their business operations in order to enjoy the cost reductions made possible by new technologies. According to recent research, just adhering to a philosophy or technology will have little influence on the performance of a business unless the infrastructural practices of the firm are taken into consideration (Khang and Muthmainnah et al., 2023).

References

Anderson, D. and Lee, H. (1999). Synchronized Supply Chains: The New Frontier. *Montgomery Research (online), Ascet*, 1, 01/04/99. http://www.ascet.com/documents.asp?d_ID=l 98

Berry, D., Towill, D.R. and Wadsley, N. (1994). Supply Chain Management in The Electronics Product Industry. *International Journal of Physical Distribution & Logistics Management*, 24, No. 10, pp. 20–32. https://www.emerald.com/insight/content/doi/10.1108/09600039410074773/full/html

Boiko, A., Shendryk, V. and Boiko, O. (2018). Information Systems for Supply Chain Management: Uncertainties, Risks and Cyber Security. In *ICTE in Transportation and Logistics 2018*. ICTE 2018, Procedia Com. https://www.sciencedirect.com/science/article/pii/S1877050919301152

Bourland, K.E., Powell, S.G. and Pyke, D.F. (1996). Exploiting Timely Demand Information To Reduce Inventories. *European Journal of Operational Research*, 92, pp. 239–253. https://www.sciencedirect.com/science/article/pii/0377221795001360

Cachon, G. and Fisher, M. (2000). Supply Chain Inventory Management and Value of Shared Information. *Management Science*, 46, No. 8, pp. 1032–1048. https://pubsonline.informs.org/doi/abs/10.1287/mnsc.46.8.1032.12029

Chatfield, D.C., Kim, J.G., Harrison, T.P. and Hayya, J.C. (2004). The Bullwhip Effect – Impact of Stochastic Lead Time, Information Quality, and Information Sharing: A Simulation Study. *Production and Operations Management*, 13, No. 4, pp. 340–354. https://onlinelibrary.wiley.com/doi/abs/10.1111/j.1937-5956.2004.tb00222.x

Chen, F. (1998). Echelon Reorder Points, Installation Reorder Points, and the Value of Centralized Demand Information. *Management Science*, 44, No. 12, pp. 221–234. https://pubsonline.informs.org/doi/abs/10.1287/mnsc.44.12.s221

Chen, F. and Samroengraja, R. (2000). The Stationary Beer Game. *Production and Operations Management*, 9, No. 1, pp. 19–30. https://onlinelibrary.wiley.com/doi/abs/10.1111/j.1937-5956.2000.tb00320.x

Chen, F., Drezner, D., Ryan, J.K. and Simchi-Levi, D. (1999). The Bullwhip Effect: Managerial Insights on the Impact of Forecasting and Information on Variability in a Supply Chain. In *Quantitative Models for Supply Chain Management*. Editors: Tayur, S., Ganeshan, R. and Magazine, M. Boston, MA: Kluwer Publishing, 418–439. https://link.springer.com/chapter/10.1007/978-1-4615-4949-9_14

Copacino, W.A. (1997). *Supply Chain Management*. Boca Raton, FL: The St. Lucie Press. https://www.taylorfrancis.com/books/mono/10.4324/9780203737859/supply-chain-management-william-copacino

Croson, R. and Donohue, K. (2003). Impact of POS Data Sharing on Supply Chain Management: An Experimental Study. *Production and Operations Management*, 12, No. 1, pp. 1–11. https://onlinelibrary.wiley.com/doi/abs/10.1111/j.1937-5956.2003.tb00194.x

Dubey, R., Gunasekaran, A., Papadopoulos, T., Childe, S.J., Shibin, K.T. and Wamba, S.F. (2017). Sustainable Supply Chain Management: Framework and Further Research Directions. *Journal of Cleaner Production*, 142, pp. 1119–1130. https://www.sciencedirect.com/science/article/pii/S0959652616301883

Ellram, L.M. (1991). Supply Chain Management: The Industrial Organization Perspective. *International Journal of Physical Distribution and Logistics Management*, 21, No. 1, pp. 13–22. https://www.emerald.com/insight/content/doi/10.1108/09600039110137082/full/html

Fisher, M.L. (1996). What Is the Right Supply Chain for Your Product? *Harvard Business Review*, 75, No. 2, pp. 105–117. https://www.academia.edu/download/63444236/2011_WhatIsTheRightSupplyC_HarvardBusinessReview20200527-45370-13dt4w.pdf

Forrester, J.W. (1958). Industrial Dynamics. *Harvard Business Review*, July–Aug, pp. 37–66. https://pubsonline.informs.org/doi/abs/10.1287/mnsc.14.7.398

Fu, Y. and Piplani, R. (2004). Supply-Side Collaboration and Its Value in Supply-Chains. *European Journal of Operational Research*, 152, No. 1, pp. 281–288. https://www.sciencedirect.com/science/article/pii/S0377221702006707

Galbraith, J.R. (1977). *Organizational Design*. Boston, MA: Addison-Wesley. https://www.google.com/books?hl=en&lr=&id=VTOi1wmzQM4C&oi=fnd&pg=PA325&dq=Organizational+Design.+Boston,+MA:+Addison-+Wesley&ots=TcN7RokX3O&sig=GhkbRSrAab99-p16KfhrY-44jw8

Gavimeni, S., Kapuscinski, R. and Tayur, S. (1999). Value of Information in Capacitated Supply Chains. *Management Science*. 45, No. 1, pp. 16–24. https://pubsonline.informs.org/doi/abs/10.1287/mnsc.45.1.16

Gilbert, S.M. and Ballou, R.H. (1999). Supply Chain Benefits From Advanced Customer Commitments. *Journal of Operations Management*, 18, pp. 61–73. https://www.sciencedirect.com/science/article/pii/S0272696399000121

Handheld, R.B. and Nichols, E.L. (1998). *An Introduction to Supply Chain Management*. Upper Saddle River, NJ: Prentice Hall, p. 11. http://ndl.ethernet.edu.et/bitstream/123456789/23257/1/2%202013.pdf

Harland, C.M. (1996). Supply Chain Management: Relationships, Chains, and Networks. *British Journal of Management*, 7, pp. S63–S80. https://onlinelibrary.wiley.com/doi/abs/10.1111/j.1467-8551.1996.tb00148.x

Houlihan, J.B. (1985). International Supply Chain Management. *International Journal of Physical Distribution and Materials Management*, 15, pp. 22–38. https://www.emerald.com/insight/content/doi/10.1108/eb014601/full/html

Huang, G.Q., Lau, J.S.K. and Mak, K.L. (2003). The Impacts of Sharing Production Information on Supply Chain Dynamics: A Review of the Literature. *International Journal of Production Research*, 41, No. 7, pp. 1483–1517. https://www.tandfonline.com/doi/abs/10.1080/0020754031000069625

Hutchinson, N.E. (1987). *An Integrated Approach to Logistics Management*. New Jersey: Prentice Hall Press. https://www.inderscienceonline.com/doi/abs/10.1504/IJTM.2008.018105

Khang, A., Misra, A., Hajimahmud, V.A. and Litvinova, E. (2024). *Machine Vision and Industrial Robotics in Manufacturing: Approaches, Technologies, and Applications* (1st Ed.). CRC Press. ISBN: 9781032565972. https://doi.org/10.1201/9781003438137

Khang, A., Muthmainnah, M., Seraj, P.M.I., Al Yakin, A., Obaid, A.J. and Panda, M.R. (2023). AI-aided teaching model for the education 5.0 ecosystem. In *AI-Based Technologies and Applications in the Era of the Metaverse* (1st Ed.). IGI Global Press, 83–104. https://doi.org/10.4018/978-1-6684-8851-5.ch004

Khang, A., Rath, K.C., Satapathy, S.K., Kumar, A., Das, S.R. and Panda, M.R. (2023). Enabling the future of manufacturing: Integration of robotics and IoT to smart factory infrastructure in industry 4.0. In *AI-Based Technologies and Applications in the Era of the Metaverse* (1st Ed.). IGI Global Press, 25–50. https://doi.org/10.4018/978-1-6684-8851-5.ch002

Khang, A., Shah, V. and Rani, S. (2023). *AI-Based Technologies and Applications in the Era of the Metaverse* (1st Ed.). IGI Global Press. https://doi.org/10.4018/978-1-6684-8851-5

Khanh, H.H. and Khang, A. (2021). The Role of Artificial Intelligence in Blockchain Applications. *Reinventing Manufacturing and Business Processes through Artificial Intelligence*, 2. CRC Press, 20–40. https://doi.org/10.1201/9781003145011-2

Kopczak, L.R. (1997). Logistics Partnerships and Supply Chain Restructuring: Survey Results From The US Computer Industry. *Production and Operations Management*, 6, No. 3, pp. 226–247. https://onlinelibrary.wiley.com/doi/abs/10.1111/j.1937-5956.1997.tb00428.x

Lambert, D.M. and Pohlen, T.L. (2001). Supply Chain Metrics. *The International Journal of Logistics Management*, 12, No. 1, pp. 1–19. https://www.emerald.com/insight/content/doi/10.1108/IJLM-03-2020-0121/full/

Lee, H.L. (2002). Aligning Supply Chain Strategies with Product Uncertainties. *California Management Review*, 44, No. 3, pp. 105–119. https://journals.sagepub.com/doi/abs/10.2307/41166135

Lee, H.L. and Billington, C. (1992). Managing Supply Chain Inventory: Pitfalls and Opportunities. *Sloan Management Review*, 33, No. 3, pp. 65–73. http://allman.rhon.itam.mx/~gigola/Curso_pron_inv/Pitfulls.pdf

Lee, H.L., Padmanabhan, P. and Whang, S. (1997a). Information Distortion in a Supply Chain: The Bullwhip Effect. *Management Science*, 43, No. 4, pp. 546–558. https://pubsonline.informs.org/doi/abs/10.1287/mnsc.43.4.546

Lee, H.L., Padmanabhan, P. and Whang, S. (1997b). The Bullwhip Effect in Supply Chains. *Sloan Management Review*, 38, No. 3, pp. 93–102. https://www.google.com/books?hl=en&lr=&id=LrdF0Pito8MC&oi=fnd&pg=PA37&dq=The+Bullwhip+Effect+in+Supply+Chains.&ots=GI8691USaK&sig=E31hkUtbem4KcbCNBG4xLV2hAYk

Lee, H.L., So, K.C. and Tang, C.S. (2000). The Value of Information Sharing in a Two- Level Supply Chain. *Management Science*, 46, No. 5, pp. 626–643. https://pubsonline.informs.org/doi/abs/10.1287/mnsc.46.5.626.12047

Mason-Jones, R. and Towill, D.R. (1998). Time Compression in the Supply Chain: Information Management is the Vital Ingredient. *Logistics Information Management*, 11, No. 2, pp. 93–104. https://www.emerald.com/insight/content/doi/10.1108/09576059810209964/full/html

Mentzer, J.T., Foggin, J.H. and Golicic, S.L. (2000). Collaboration: The Enablers, Impediments, and Benefits. *Supply Chain Management Review*, Sept/Oct, pp. 52–58. https://www.emerald.com/insight/content/doi/10.1108/13598540810850300/full/html

Narasimhan, R. and Jayaram, J. (1998). Causal Linkages in Supply Chain Management: An Exploratory Study of North American Manufacturing Firms. *Decision Sciences*, 29, No. 3, pp. 579–605. https://onlinelibrary.wiley.com/doi/abs/10.1111/j.1540-5915.1998.tb01355.x

Sahin, F. and Robinson, E.P. (2002). Flow Coordination and Information Sharing In Supply Chains: Review, Implications, and Directions for Future Research. *Decision Sciences*, 33, No. 4, pp. 505–536. https://onlinelibrary.wiley.com/doi/abs/10.1111/j.1540-5915.2002.tb01654.x

Sterman, J.D. (1989). Modelling Managerial Behavior: Misperceptions of Feedback in a Dynamic Decision Making Experiment. *Management Science*, 35, No. 3, pp. 321–339. https://pubsonline.informs.org/doi/abs/10.1287/mnsc.35.3.321

Stock, J.R. and Lambert, D.M. (1990). *Strategic Logistics Management* (4th Ed.). New York: McGraw-Hill Irwin. http://sutlib2.sut.ac.th/sut_contents/H74607.pdf

Vollman, T.E., Berry, W.L. and Whybark, D.C. (1997). *Manufacturing Planning and Control* (4th Ed.). Prentice-Hall Press. http://www.ime.unicamp.br/~moretti/ms715/1S_2007/ProdPlanCh.pdf

Chapter 16

The Dependence of the Stability of Social Systems and Application of Technology on the Food Price Indices

Mariia Orel and Alex Khang

16.1 Introduction

The initial characteristic of the current stage of development of technology and civilization is a fundamental change in the geopolitical, geo-economics, and geocultural spaces in the life and interaction of peoples, civilizations, and states (Kulinich et al., 2022). Managers must make decisions regarding migration issues; innovation (Sytnyk et al., 2022) and development (Sytnyk et al., 2022); the impact of migration of highly skilled workers on the country's competitiveness and economic growth (Oliinyk et al., 2021); principles of natural capital preservation in the context of the strategy of state environmental safety (Radchenko et al., 2021); analysis of production and sales of organic products in agricultural enterprises (Ostapenko et al., 2020) (Khang & Santosh et al., 2023); the carriage of goods for indefinite, fuzzy, and stochastic parameters (Kotenko et al., 2020); conflicts (Allansson, 2020; "Conflict Trends: A Global Overview, 1946–2019", 2020); and others. This year the Global Risks Report also draws on the views of over 12,000 country-level leaders who identified critical short-term risks to their 124 countries (Global Risks Report, 2022).

National risk assessments and resilience strategy reviews should be used to reveal where momentum is insufficient and greater government intervention is needed. It is not desirable or feasible for governments to seek to fill all gaps themselves: instead, they should look to harness the capabilities and energies of other sectors to complement enhanced competencies that ought to lie in the public realm. Strategies should set out what is needed and examine all available levers with fresh eyes (Global Risks Report, 2022). While food security research is the subject of many organizations worldwide, this effort is distinct for a number of reasons. This index is the

DOI: 10.4324/9781032688305-16

first to examine food security comprehensively across the three internationally established dimensions. Moreover, the study looks beyond hunger to the underlying factors affecting food insecurity (Khang & Gadirova et al., 2023).

The EIU has created a number of unique qualitative indicators, many of which relate to government policy, to capture drivers of food security which are not currently measured in any international dataset (Global Food Security Index, 2022). The Global Food Security Index (GFSI) considers the issues of food affordability, availability, quality and safety, and sustainability and adaptation across a set of 113 countries. The index is a dynamic quantitative and qualitative benchmarking model constructed from 68 unique indicators that measure the drivers of food security across both developing and developed countries (Global Food Security Index, 2022)

The 2022 edition of the GFSI incorporated 14 new indicators to reflect the global nature and interconnectedness of the food system and to highlight the importance of the first mile or farm-level metrics in determining food security for populations. The focus on the first mile (the segment of agriculture (Khang & Agriculture et al., 2023) that includes production and links farmers to the nearest market, allowing them to operate efficiently and profitably to sell the goods they produce), is critical as the path to enhancing food security requires concerted efforts across the value chain. Some of the new measures reflect the support available to farmers including their access to extension services as well as community organizations like cooperatives, and whether they are female (Global Food Security Index, 2022).

Food security trends down. The GFSI release highlights that the global food environment has been deteriorating, making it vulnerable to shocks. The world has made great gains in food security from 2012 to 2015, with overall GFSI scores jumping 6 percent. However, structural problems in the global food system led to subsequent slowing down of growth, and over the past three years, the trend in the overall food security environment has reversed. Researchers analyzed the dynamics of the food price index over the years and the factors that shape it (Ruben et al., 2021). This study needs to identify the relationship between the food price index, the migration crisis – social upheavals in the world's leading countries.

16.2 Methods

In the article, general scientific and special research methods were used for the study. The analytical method was used to analyze and summarize the most pressing problems and areas of research. The work used statistical data from the food price index and analyzed and identified the presence of dependencies. A comparative method was also used to identify relationships between changes in the food price index and points of socio-political destabilization.

16.3 Results and Discussion

Over a time period of 20 years, a number of social unrest were considered (on the example of some countries), types of destabilization, and their consequences. Food price data are routinely collected by governments but have not been utilized to their full potential for tracking the cost of nutritious diets. Food prices typically are used to monitor only the cost of a basket of goods purchased by consumers (Herforth et al., 2019). Food security is defined as the state in which people at all times have physical, social, and economic access to sufficient and nutritious food that meets their dietary needs for a healthy (Khang & Medicine, 2023) and active life (United Nations Convention to Combat Desertification).

The Global Food Security Index considers the core issues of affordability, availability, and quality across a set of 113 countries. The index is a dynamic quantitative and qualitative scoring model, constructed from 68 unique indicators, that measures these drivers of food security across both developing and developed countries. The overall goal of the study is to assess which countries are most and least vulnerable to food insecurity through the categories of Affordability, Availability, and Quality and Safety (United Nations Convention to Combat Desertification) as shown in Figure 16.1.

In 2022, the GFSI was dragged down by falls in two of its strongest pillars – accessibility, and food quality and safety – and saw continued weakness in the other two pillars – availability, and sustainability and adaptation. In particular, affordability, the top-scoring pillar, was dragged down by sharp rises in food costs, declining trade freedom, and decreased funding for food safety nets (Economist Impact GFSI, 2022; Global Report, 2022).

Concurrently, the index's remaining two pillars – availability and sustainability and adaptation – remain weak. To boost availability, there is a need for inputs like finance, but also community support, extension services, and strong infrastructure.

In 2022, the score for the availability pillar is only 57.8, while long-term systemic issues and weakness in the global food security environment continue as sustainability and adaptation trail behind at 54.1. Farmers need political and social support to access markets and infrastructure, but the 2022 index shows that armed conflicts and political instability are being accompanied by a growing dependency on chronic food aid. Moreover, political upheaval and worsening climate change threaten to pull these pillars down further (Economist_Impact_GFSI_2022_Global_Report, 2022) as shown in Table 16.1.

The data in Table 16.1 analyzes the dynamics of the food price index over the past 23 years.

Research has shown that the difference between the top performer and the country at the bottom of the ranking has continued to widen since 2019, reflecting the inequality in the global food system as shown in Figure 16.2.

The FAO Food Price Index (FFPI) is a measure of the monthly change in international prices of a basket of food commodities. It consists of the average of five commodity group price indices

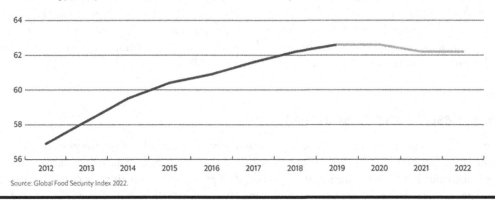

GFSI average overall score, global 2012-22

After climbing year on year between 2012 to 2018, the overall food security score has not improved since 2019.

Source: Global Food Security Index 2022.

Figure 16.1   GFSI average overall score, global 2012–-22. *Source:* Global Food Security Index 2022.

Table 16.1   Monthly World Food Price Index

Month	Nominal	Real
2000	53.3	67.1
2001	55.0	71.8
2002	53.1	70.2
2003	57.8	72.6
2004	65.6	77.1
2005	67.4	76.9
2006	72.6	80.7
2007	94.3	98.8
2008	117.5	114.3
2009	91.7	95.1
2010	106.7	106.8
2011	131.9	118.8
2012	122.8	111.5
2013	120.1	109.5
2014	115.0	106.3
2015	93.0	95.1
2016	91.9	97.8
2017	98.0	100.8
2018	95.9	94.2
2019	95.1	95.6
2020	98.1	99.2
2021	125.7	125.1
2022	143.7	140.6
2023	131.2	126.1

Source: Food and Agriculture Organization of the United Nations https://www.fao.org/world-foodsituation/foodpricesindex/en/

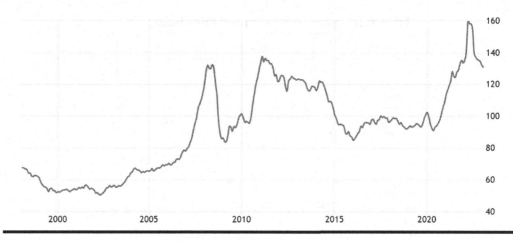

Figure 16.2   World Food Price Index. Source: Author and World Food Price Index

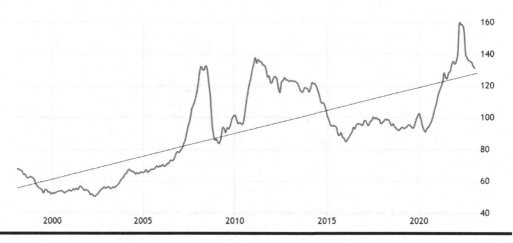

Figure 16.3   Variance of World Food Price Index and trend. *Source: Author and World Food Price Index*

weighted by the average export shares of each of the groups (Food and Agriculture Organization of the United Nations) as shown in Figure 16.3.

In Figure 16.4, the black line shows battle-related deaths. The figure shows the following categories: colonial wars, interstate wars, civil wars, and internationalized civil wars, global state-based conflict trends between 1946 and 2019.

The number of civil conflicts was increasing in recent years, particularly since the 1970s. On the other hand, conflict between states has become rare. The year 2019 saw two interstate conflicts between India and Pakistan over Kashmir, and between Iran and Israel, both of which were relatively low-intensity conflicts (Júlia Palik et al., 2020). However, in 2022, the Ukrainian crisis began as shown in Figure 16.5.

1: "Global Word Economic Crisis."
2: "Arabian Spring."
3: "Beginning of the Migration Crisis in Europe."

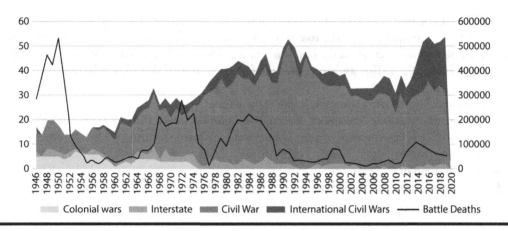

Figure 16.4 Major conflict trends.

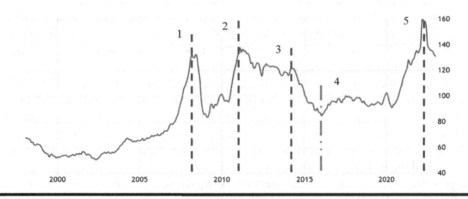

Figure 16.5 The correlation between the dynamic of the world food price index and crisis points. *Source:* **Author.**

4: "The End of the Acute Phase of the Migration Crisis in the EU."
5: "Ukrainian Crisis."

The presence of this dependence shows that a sharp change in the food price index (increase) may indicate the danger of increased destabilization in society. This indicates a direct relationship between the stability of social systems and the food price index. As a result, this chapter can conclude that the monitoring of the food price index should become one of the key indicators in the process of making managerial decisions by management entities in modern conditions.

The relationship between the food price index, the crisis of migration, and social upheavals in the world's leading countries was found. Food price data are routinely collected by governments but have not been utilized to their full potential for tracking the cost of nutritious diets, technology for assessing the socio-political destabilization of society as a social system, and approaches to classifying and assessing security hazards in the process of preparing management decisions to respond to them.

The implementation of anti-crisis measures should take into account all possible consequences, even those that may arise as a result of their implementation. Effective coordination of activities and interaction between central and regional authorities, between state authorities and local governments is of great importance. The role of a comprehensive multi-level system for assessing risks and threats to national security as the basis for strategic planning in the state is also being updated (Reznikova et al., 2020). This study proposes the following general algorithm of actions:

- Analysis of the security situation (input information).
- Opportunity analysis. The ability of state institutions, systems, and institutions to effectively respond to the development of a crisis situation is assessed (ensuring readiness for response; response; recovery).
- Identification of vulnerabilities.
- Definition of strategic guidelines for development in the post-crisis period.

16.4 Conclusion

What makes us different is the combination of policy research and insights, creative innovation, and our global influence. It's a formula that drives business and public administration value and creates change. In modern conditions, in the stage of development of civilization, it is necessary to take into account the cardinal changes in geopolitical, geo-economic, and geocultural spaces in the life and interaction of peoples, civilizations, and states.

The dynamics of changes in the food price index for food have an impact on the stability of social systems. An analysis of the dynamics of the food price index over the past 20 years has revealed the factors that form it. Also, during this period of time, a number of social upheavals (on the examples of individual countries), types of destabilization, and their consequences were considered. The chapter shows that there is a relationship between the food price index, the migration crisis, and social unrest in the leading countries of the world.

The presence of this dependence indicates that a sharp change in the food price index (increase) may indicate the danger of increased destabilization in society. This chapter presents the relationship between the stability of social systems and the food price index. Food systems are the backbone of society. Monitoring the food price index should become one of the key indicators in the process of making managerial decisions by management entities in modern conditions.

By influencing the food price index, it will be possible to start and extinguish crisis processes (migration crises, which, in turn, can cause tension and destabilization in the target regions). This chapter proposes the following general algorithm of actions: analysis of the security situation (input information); opportunity analysis (ensuring readiness for response; response; recovery); identification of vulnerabilities; definition of strategic guidelines for development in the post-crisis period. Therefore, further research should be devoted to monitoring the food price index and including it as one of the key indicators in the process of making managerial decisions by management entities in modern conditions. Considerable attention is paid to: approaches to the classification and assessment of the dangers of security threats in the process of preparing managerial decisions on responding to them.

It is necessary to develop clear technologies for assessing the socio-political destabilization of society as a social system. Also, this chapter needs to assess the complex impact of geopolitical, geo-economic, and cultural processes on national development and develop a new paradigm approach. This examination of food price index trends reveals notable differences between core and non-core foods. Future studies need to investigate the extent to which such changes in the food environment have actually contributed to individual behavior (Khang & Quantum, 2023).

References

Allansson, M. (2020). FAQ. Department of Peace and Conflict Research, Uppsala University, Sweden. www.pcr.uu.se/research/ucdp/faq/#The_Mexican_Drug_Wars_.

Conflict Trends: A Global Overview, 1946–2019. Prio. (2020). https://www.prio.org/publications/12442.

Economist Impact GFSI 2022 Global_Report. (2022). https://impact.economist.com/sustainability/project/food-security-index/reports/Economist_Impact_GFSI_2022_Global_Report_Sep_2022.pdf.

Food and Agriculture Organization of the United Nations. https://www.fao.org/worldfoodsituation/foodpricesindex/en/.

Global Food Security Index. (2022). https://impact.economist.com/sustainability/project/food-security-index#introduction.

Herforth, A., Masters, W., Bai, Y., & Sarpong, D. (2019). The Cost of Recommended Diets: Development and Application a Food Price Index Based on Food-Based Dietary Guidelines (P10-033-19). *Current Developments in Nutrition*, 3(1), 10–033–19. https://doi.org/10.1093/cdn/nzz034.P10-033-19. https://academic.oup.com/cdn/article/3/Supplement_1/nzz034.P10-033-19/5517155.

Khang, A. (2023a). *AI and IoT-Based Technologies for Precision Medicine* (1st Ed.). IGI Global Press. ISBN: 9798369308769. https://doi.org/10.4018/979-8-3693-0876-9.

Khang, A. (2023b). *Advanced Technologies and AI-Equipped IoT Applications in High-Tech Agriculture* (1st Ed.). IGI Global Press. https://doi.org/10.4018/978-1-6684-9231-4.

Khang, A. (2023b). *Applications and Principles of Quantum Computing* (1st Ed.). IGI Global Press. ISBN: 9798369311684. https://doi.org/10.4018/979-8-3693-1168-4.

Khang, A., Elmina, G., & Abdullayev, V. A. (2023). Role of Photochemical Reactions in the Treatment of Water used in the High-Tech Agriculture. *Advanced Technologies and AI-Equipped IoT Applications in High-Tech Agriculture* (1st Ed., pp. 326–325). IGI Global Press. https://doi.org/10.4018/978-1-6684-9231-4.ch018.

Khang, A., Rath, K. C., Panda, S., Sree, P. K., & Panda, S. K. (2023). Revolutionizing Agriculture: Exploring Advanced Technologies for Plant Protection in the Agriculture Sector. *Handbook of Research on AI-Equipped IoT Applications in High-Tech Agriculture*. Copyright: © 2023. pp. 1–22. https://doi.org/10.4018/978-1-6684-9231-4.ch001.

Kotenko, S., Nitsenko, V., Hanzhurenko, I., & Havrysh, V. (2020). The Mathematical Modeling Stages of Combining the Carriage of Goods for Indefinite, Fuzzy and Stochastic Parameters. *International Journal of Integrated Engineering*, 12(7), 173–180. https://doi.org/10.30880/ijie.2020.12.07.019.

Kulinich, T., Pikus, R., Kuzmenko, O., Vasilieva, S., Melnik, V., & Orel, M. (2022). Cognitive Aspects of the Strategic Management System under Uncertainty. *Postmodern Openings*, 13(3), 166–179. https://doi.org/10.18662/po/13.3/483; https://lumenpublishing.com/journals/index.php/po/article/view/5057/3826.

Oliinyk, O., Bilan, Y., Mishchuk, H., Akimov, O., & Vasa, L. (2021). The Impact of Migration of Highly Skilled Workers on the Country's Competitiveness and Economic Growth. *Montenegrin Journal of Economics*, 17(3), 7–19. https://doi.org/10.14254/1800-5845/2021.17-3.1

Ostapenko, R., Herasymenko, Y., Nitsenko, V., Koliadenko, S., Balezentis, T., & Streimikiene, D. (2020). Analysis of Production and Sales of Organic Products in Ukrainian Agricultural Enterprises. *Sustainability*, 12(8). https://doi.org/10.3390/SU12083416.

Radchenko, O., Kovach, V., Radchenko, O., Sharov, P., & Semenets-Orlova, I. (2021). Principles of Natural Capital Preservation in the Context of Strategy of State Environmental Safety. *E3S Web of Conferences, 2021*, 280, 09024. https://doi.org/10.1051/e3sconf/202128009024; https://www.e3s-conferences.org/articles/e3sconf/pdf/2021/56/e3sconf_icsf2021_09024.pdf.

Reznikova, O. O., Vojtovs'kyj, K. Ye., & Lepikhov, A. V. (2020). *Natsional'ni systemy otsiniuvannia ryzykiv i zahroz: kraschi svitovi praktyky, novi mozhlyvosti dlia Ukrainy: analit. dop. [National Systems for Assessing Risk and Threat: World Best Practices, New Opportunities for Ukraine: Analytical Report]; za zah. red. O. O. Reznikovoi*. Kyiv: NISD. 84 p. https://niss.gov.ua/sites/default/files/2020-07/dopovid.pdf.

Ruben, R., Cavatassi, R., Lipper, L., Smaling, E., & Winters, P. (2021). Towards Food Systems Transformation-Five Paradigm Shifts for Healthy, Inclusive and Sustainable Food Systems. *Food*

Security, 13(6), 1423–1430. https://doi.org/10.1007/s12571-021-01221-4. Epub 2021 Oct 15. PMID: 34667484; PMCID: PMC8517317.

Semenets-Orlova, I., Kushnir, V., Rodchenko, L., Chernenko, I., Druz, O., & Rudenko, M. (2023). Organizational Development and Educational Changes Management in Public Sector (Case of Public Administration During War Time. https://doi.org/10.26668/businessreview/2023.v8i4.1699.

Sytnyk, H., Orel, M., Ivanova, V., & Taran, Y. (2022). Conceptual Understanding of the Relationship between Political and Administrative Processes in the Context of Social Systems Security. *Cuestiones Políticas*, 40(74), 631–647. https://doi.org/10.46398/cuestpol.4074.34. https://produccioncientificaluz.org/index.php/cuestiones/article/view/38936/43525.

Sytnyk, H. P., Zubchyk, O. A., & Orel, M. H. (2022). Conceptual Understanding of the Peculiarities of Managing Innovation-Driven Development of the State in the Current Conditions. *Science and Innovation*, 18(2), 3–15. https://doi.org/10.15407/scine18.02.003. https://scinn-eng.org.ua/ojs/index.php/ni/article/view/234/99.

The Global Risks Report. (2022). 17th Edition, is published by the World Economic Forum. https://www3.weforum.org/docs/WEF_The_Global_Risks_Report_2022.pdf.

UCDP/PRIO Armed Conflict Database, UCDP Battle Death Database Pettersson, Öberg. (2020). Organized Violence, 1989–2019. *Journal of Peace Research*, 57(4). Lacina and Gleditsch Battle Death Database and Júlia Palic, Siri Aas Rustad and Fredrik Methi (2020) Conflict Trends: A Global Overview, 1946–2019: https://ucdp.uu.se/downloads/index.html#nonstate.

United Nations Convention to Combat Desertification. https://impact.economist.com/sustainability/project/food-security-index/.

Chapter 17

Application of AI-Enabled Digitization Tools for Intellectual Business Development during the Recovery Period of the Economy

Kryshtal Halyna, Kalina Iryna, and Alex Khang

17.1 Introduction

Global world upheavals, such as COVID-19, and the financial crisis forced many enterprises to enter the online space and start their path to digital transformation. For example, through online sales channels, investments in digital marketing, or reorganization of internal processes to reduce disruptions to a minimum. Some of these changes will become irreversible and will determine the direction of recovery in terms of investments, relationships in chains, value creation, skills, and the need for digital transformation.

However, despite the obvious benefits of digitization, some businesses are lagging behind in the technology adoption process, which could widen the existing productivity gap. The digital development of each individual enterprise, in aggregate, can have a significant impact on the intellectual development of the state's economy. Therefore, the hypothesis of the study is to identify the possible influence of digitalization tools on the development of the economy in the intellectual part. The use of digitization tools in the intellectual development of the economy fundamentally changes all traditional principles, approaches, and models of the development of a competitive state.

Digitalization tools should be noted as the subject of research. Since the economic policy of the state is aimed at supporting the digital transformation of enterprises, it should cover both the process of introducing technologies and the need to form a digital culture within each individual enterprise. The economy of the state as a whole depends on the stability of work and profitability of enterprises, as it also includes tax revenues, circulation of funds, and jobs. Therefore, this study proposes to highlight three main areas that are responsible for the development and implementation of the intellectual development of the economy.

■ Improvement of the framework conditions for the digital transformation of the state's economy.
■ Raising the level of skills of the population to achieve successful digital transformation of enterprises and society.
■ Implementation of specific digitalization tools to ensure the intellectual development of the economy.

The issue of using digitalization tools is relevant today because currently all developed countries are trying to move more and more actively towards digitalization. From the perspective of the framework conditions, ensuring that consumers are connected to the Internet is one of the first steps on the way to a successful digital transformation. However, the level of broadband penetration varies significantly between countries and shows differences between urban and rural areas, as well as between small and large enterprises. Countries should accelerate the deployment of affordable high-speed Internet access and close connectivity gaps by encouraging competition and private investment.

You can observe a similar situation in the field of e-commerce: It is characterized by rapid growth, but the stage of development can still be characterized as early. There are serious gaps in the legal framework for the regulation of e-commerce platforms, parcel delivery, consumer protection, and integration with wider European e-commerce markets is limited. Moreover, the current legal framework for the use of electronic signatures does not meet international standards, which hinders cross-border trade operations. Finally, digital security threats can lead to significant economic and social costs and undermine consumer confidence.

In order to make the most of the growth potential that e-commerce can offer to small- and medium-sized enterprises in the region, the authorities responsible for the development and implementation of economic policies in countries should strengthen the legal framework in the field of consumer protection and digital security, as well as set standards for the use of electronic signature, provision of trust services, digital security (Khang & Vladimir, 2022), and data protection in accordance with European Union standards.

Encouraging the development of digital skills plays a key role in digital transformation. However, it is difficult for small- and medium-sized enterprises to fully realize the potential of digital tools and the advantages associated with their implementation. They face challenges in attracting and retaining qualified employees, and they lack opportunities and networking to identify and access talent. The foundations of digital literacy are laid in schools, but school curricula tend not to be flexible enough to adapt to rapidly evolving technologies and often quickly become outdated.

A comprehensive digital literacy policy is still in its infancy, and a greater focus on developing skills among adults will be essential to facilitate job transitions and create a digital economy-ready workforce. In general, governments should consider measures to train managers and employees of small- and medium-sized enterprises in the skills necessary for digital transformation. Such measures include raising the awareness of business leaders about the different types of training available and opportunities to use local ecosystems and communities to access relevant skills and share best practices.

17.2 Study Objectives

The chapter demonstrates that (1) the use of digitization tools is important for the intellectual development of the country's economy; (2) taking into account the expectation of the introduction of the "6th Generation" of the mobile communication generation in the years 2026–2030, attention should be paid to the coverage of households with broadband Internet access, the level of penetration of computer equipment, and other statistics regarding the "hard" digital infrastructure, which is definitely basic; (3) noting the "security" situation in Ukraine, the possibilities of implementation and development of digitization tools were considered, and the importance of finding effective models, mechanisms, and tools for intellectual support of the innovative development of the country and its market subjects, including the economy, was noted; (4) the use of digitization tools in the intellectual development of the economy fundamentally changes all traditional principles, approaches, and models of the development of a competitive state. The intellectual development of the economy is increasingly focused on the growth of the market value of individual companies, in which intangible assets (technological, marketing, customer, etc.) are the main specific weight, which are the result of the effective use and development of the intellectual capital of each individual company.

The chapter also considers the growing role of effective management of the intellectual development of the economy in the conditions of digitalization. The intellectualization of the economy creates conditions for the growth of the role of digitalization as the basis for the formation and development of intellectual resources, the creation and transfer of new knowledge into the economy.

17.3 Literature Review

National digital strategies seem to be the most suitable tools for shaping effective digitalization policies; moreover, they are gaining popularity. However, they rarely include concrete actions to support the digitalization of small- and medium-sized enterprises. At the same time, initiatives to support the digital transformation of enterprises may go beyond comprehensive strategic documents.

In particular, the study of the digital transformation of business allowed us to identify three main stages that reflect the degree of influence of digital tools on the business model of a particular enterprise.

■ Digitization is the process of converting analog information (for example, text or film) into a digital format that can be processed on a computer (for example, PDF or MP4). More broadly, the term can be used to describe the process of integrating digital tools to accomplish existing tasks. At the enterprise level, digitization is usually limited to internal and external documentation without making fundamental changes to value-creating activities (for example, the use of digital forms in orders or digital applications for working with internal financial documents);

■ The term "digitalization" has a broader meaning and refers to "the use of digital technologies, data and relationships that lead to the creation of new types of activities or changes to existing ones." Rapid growth in computing power, data storage capacity, and communication speed has created the conditions for the emergence of a large and diverse ecosystem of technologies. Some of them have been in use for at least a decade (e.g. front- and back-office software, social networks), while others are still in the early stages of adoption (e.g. artificial intelligence, blockchain, Internet of Things).

In the business sector, digitalization is understood as the implementation of digital technologies with the aim of changing existing business processes, for example, creating new communication channels, allowing customers to contact enterprises (for example, customer reviews).

- The term "digital transformation" is even larger and is used to describe the economic and social consequences. Digital technologies can change the way citizens communicate, work, and organize their lives, how businesses produce and sell goods and services, and how governments design and deliver public services.
- The widespread use of digital technologies makes it possible to rethink almost all aspects of life in society, from health care to education, from finance to trade, and from competition to innovation, leading to the digital transformation of public and private life as a result of digitization and digitization.

Digital tools have a wide range of applications in various areas of life, including business, education, healthcare, entertainment, and many others. Here are some digital tools and their advantages and disadvantages.

Social Media:

- Advantages: Community engagement, advertising and marketing, information exchange.
- Disadvantages: Privacy and data security concerns, time-consuming.

Email:

- Advantages: Effective communication, document flow, message archiving.
- Disadvantages: Email overload, spam.

Virtual Conferences:

- Advantages: Remote communication, reduced travel costs.
- Disadvantages: Potential technical issues, limitations in interaction.

Online Media Channels:

- Advantages: Quick access to news, numerous information sources.
- Disadvantages: Risk of spreading fake news; information overload.

E-Books and E-Reading:

- Advantages: Access to a large number of books, convenience for travel.
- Disadvantages: Lack of physical book feel.

Smartphones and Mobile Apps:

- Advantages: Diverse capabilities, convenience, integration of many tools in one device.
- Disadvantages: Potential for dependency, privacy breaches.

Electronic Finance and Online Banking:

- Advantages: Convenience for bill payments, money transfers.
- Disadvantages: Risk of cyber-attacks and fraud.

Online Shopping:

- Advantages: Convenient shopping from home, wider range of products.
- Disadvantages: Deceptive websites, loss of ability to physically inspect products.

Cloud Computing and Storage:

- Advantages: Storage and processing of large volumes of data, accessibility from various devices.
- Disadvantages: Data security concerns, dependence on Internet access.

Enterprise Resource Planning (ERP) Systems:

- Advantages: Process integration, efficient resource management, data analytics.
- Disadvantages: Implementation complexity, high costs.

A large number of scientific works of both domestic and foreign researchersin their works considered "digitalization" as a social process that reflects the pace of changes in society caused by digital technological development (Andrew et al., 2017). This technological development includes many technologies at different stages of maturity.

Digitization can be observed at the following levels: Activity, organizational process, or organizational and ecosystem level (Kane, 2015: 1–25). Digitization is taking the industry beyond its traditional boundaries and providing many new opportunities to improve the productivity, efficiency, and sustainability of logistics. Strong facilitators of digitization are investments in technology and cooperation to promote information sharing and better coordination and cooperation, which is often seen as a stumbling block in a highly competitive environment (Heilig, 2017: 2–3).

In addition to many new opportunities, important economic questions and problems arise. Focusing on the important and complex aspects of coordination and cooperation, a conceptual game-theoretic framework should be presented that allows for the distribution of benefits and costs taking into account organizational perspectives (Heilig, 2017: 2–3). In addition, how this structure can be used to develop tools and methods to support strategic decision-making, stimulate digital transformation, and solve new economic issues and problems should be presented (Heilig, 2017: 2–3).

The current "digital turn" begins with the concept of the information society and questions the emergence of "big data" in the current development of the knowledge-based economy. At the second stage, the authors position the current wave of digitization in the perspective of long waves of economic evolution and changes in techno-economic paradigms (Valenduc & Vendramin, 2017: 121–134).

The digital economy is an economy based on digital computer technologies and Information and Communication Technologies (ICT). Unlike informatization, digital transformation is not limited to the introduction of information technologies but fundamentally transforms spheres and business processes based on the Internet and new digital technologies (Pyshchulina, 2018). Also, the scientist claims in his work that the digital economy is not individual industries or IT companies that are digital.

17.4 Materials and Methods

The following methods were used to solve the set of tasks: Systemic (to adapt institutional theories to the analysis of digitalization); scientific abstraction, analysis and synthesis, functional and systemic analysis, induction and deduction – to reveal theoretical provisions and digitalization tools; historical–logical method – for the study of theoretical views on the role and functions of digitalization for the intellectual development of the economy in Ukraine during the recovery period; analogies, quantitative and qualitative comparisons – regarding the assessment of enterprise activity; extrapolations – when projecting foreign experience onto domestic practice; graphic, economic and statistical methods of collecting and processing information, statistical comparisons of absolute and relative values.

The research design employed in this study is a cross-sectional survey design that supports the use of a primary instrument such as a questionnaire to collect research information from respondents once at a particular geographical location or organization (Ghauri et al., 2020). The study also deployed a deductive research approach which relies more on the positivism philosophy and affirms the use of quantitative data that must be analyzed and interpreted for policymaking in the industry wherein the research was conducted (Sekaran & Bougie, 2016).

The conducted research (survey) gave clear data that the 50+ age group has problems using the digital market opportunities, and the 60+ age group practically does not know how to use the digital products provided by the state. Because they do not have sufficient digital literacy (inability to use the latest gadgets, lack of financial ability to use the latest gadgets, inability to use government programs such as Divine India Youth Association (DIYA), which provides the opportunity to "have all the documents" in one tool). Target audience: Population aged 16–70 years (1,000 respondents surveyed) by questionnaire.

Regarding ethical consent, the participants were assured that the data provided would be used specifically for research purposes only. Secondly, the participants also advised the researchers not to mention their names and organization in the research (Khang & Hajimahmud et al., 2023).

17.5 Related Work

Respondents from Georgia, Azerbaijan, Armenia, Moldova, Ukraine, and the countries of the European Union took part in the experiment (Latvia, Lithuania, Poland, Slovenia, Slovakia, Estonia, the Czech Republic, and Hungary were included in the sample). In general, the level of skills in the use of digital technologies in Ukraine turned out to be much lower than in the countries of the European Union. No more than 25% of the population of Azerbaijan and Georgia has at least "standard" skills, which is about half of the level of more developed countries. Fifty-three percent of the population of Ukraine has below basic digital skills, and 15% has no digital skills at all. About 34% of Armenians do not even have even basic digital skills (Khang & Rani et al., 2023).

This is evidenced by the lower level of Internet use compared to the countries of the European Union as shown in Figure 17.1 and a particularly small percentage of people who use the Internet to buy goods or pay bills. This, in turn, is a serious problem for businesses in Ukraine that are in the process of digital transformation and are trying to use digital technologies to sell their goods through websites and e-commerce platforms, because they need buyers who know how to use these technologies (Khang & Quantum, 2023).

Making payments to sellers via the Internet is another skill that is not very common, as shown in Figure 17.2.

This research will conduct a study of the age group that uses digital services in Ukraine. Table 17.1 presents the survey results.

The results of the study showed that the 50+ age group has problems using the digital market opportunities, and the 60+ age group practically does not know how to use the digital products provided by the government. Because they do not have sufficient digital literacy (inability to use the latest gadgets, lack of financial ability to use the latest gadgets, inability to use government programs such as DIYA, which provides the opportunity to "have all the documents" in one tool). Target audience: Population aged 16–70 (1,000 respondents surveyed) by questionnaire.

As part of the reforms carried out in 2020, Ukraine created a national online platform "Action. Digital education," which contains more than 50 educational programs for the development of digital literacy and the test for the level of digital literacy "Tsifrogram." In addition, a network of 2,000 physical digital education centers have been deployed throughout the country, and work is currently underway to create another 4,000. Their goal is to make 6 million Ukrainians digitally literate by 2024.

At the beginning of 2021, the Cabinet of Ministers approved the Concept of the Development of Digital Competencies until 2025 and the Action Plan for its implementation in order to lay

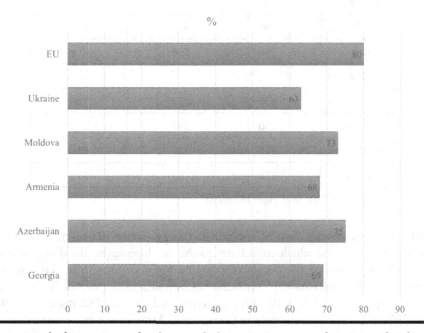

Figure 17.1 **Level of Internet use by the population (%).** *Source*: authors' own development.

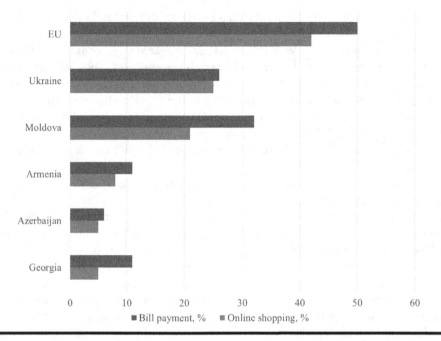

Figure 17.2 Making payments by surveyed respondents. *Source*: authors' own development.

Table 17.1 The Use of Digital Technologies by the Population of Ukraine

Variable	Frequency	Use Digital Services	Percentage (%)
Gender			
Female	500	423	84.6
Male	500	308	61.6
Age Bracket			
17–35 years	250	250	100
36–49 years	250	243	97.2
50–59 years	250	175	70.0
60 + years	250	63	25.2

Source: Authors' own development.

the foundation for the development of a national strategy for the development of digital skills and competencies in society, which contributes to the development of the digital economy and electronic democracy. Ukraine also became the first European country to launch a free computer skills training module "International Certificate of Computer Literacy," which allows citizens to demonstrate compliance of their skills with an international standard (Khang & Kali, 2023).

Almost 70% of the urban workforce in Georgia and Armenia are employed in other service sectors, which shows the least exposure to the risk of automation. In addition, countries with a higher share of manufacturing jobs will show a higher average susceptibility to automation. The results show that all the countries studied measure the digital skills of their population very differently. Most often, the assessment includes indicators of the use of digital technologies in education and indicators of the use of Internet services, and rarely such an indicator as the integration of digital technologies (Khang & Muthmainnah et al., 2023). Ukraine and Georgia measure more than 50% of the basic indicators, while Armenia and Moldova measure less than 30%. At the same time, most measurement methodologies do not correspond to EU practice.

In the business sector, digital transformation has serious organizational implications and requires changes in core business models and value creation processes. Businesses can use technology to access new business opportunities, for example by entering new markets, creating value through improved customer service, or increasing production efficiency through digital tools (such as robotics or data analysis to optimize inventory management).

Digital data, unlike analog data, can be used (stored, processed, monitored, duplicated) without quality degradation, at a very high speed and with little marginal cost. Such features of digital data are one of the factors contributing to the development of digital technologies and a by-product of their use. As a result of the ubiquity of mobile consumer technologies and the increase in time spent online, the world has seen unprecedented growth in the amount of data created, copied, and consumed over the past decade.

Digital technologies can change the way humans produce goods and services, innovate, and interact with other businesses, employees, consumers, and government. This brings a wide range of benefits to the company's activities and, ultimately, a huge potential to improve the company's productivity.

Digital tools and techniques allow companies to improve product design, optimize production processes, attract new customers, and develop relationships with suppliers throughout the value chain. They also help create more flexible business models through lower capital costs (for example, cloud computing offers access to storage and data processing as needed) and labor (artificial intelligence allows businesses to automate increasingly complex tasks).

In the case of online platforms such as Google, Amazon, or Kickstarter, digital technologies enable businesses to perform key business functions (e.g. marketing, sales, financing) while generating significant positive network effects and access to global markets. The ecosystem of digital technologies is developing rapidly. Some can be seen as "established" tools with proven applications and known business value, while others are considered "emerging technologies" that underpin the current wave of digital transformation and the fourth industrial revolution.

- Enterprise Resource Planning (ERP) systems are software tools for integrating and managing internal and external information flows, from material and human resources to finance, accounting, and sales. Such a tool automates planning, inventory, procurement, and other business functions, thereby increasing the efficiency of back-office tasks and strategic planning.
- Radio frequency identification technologies provide short-range communications and are used for product identification, industrial production monitoring and control, supply chain and inventory tracking, or in payment applications (for example, tolls or transport tolls). The use of such tools helps to increase the efficiency of production and logistics.
- Customer relationship management and supply chain management software are used to manage a business' interactions with customers, employees, and suppliers.

- Social networks are Internet applications for connecting, creating, and sharing content online with customers, suppliers, or partners or within an enterprise. The use of social networks by companies develops external interaction, including the image and marketing of enterprises, responding to the opinions, feedback, and questions of customers and hiring employees.
- Electronic commerce is the sale or purchase of goods or services carried out over computer networks using methods specifically designed to receive or place orders (for example, web pages, extranets, or electronic data exchange). E-commerce allows businesses to dramatically expand their customer and supplier base and reach markets beyond traditional physical boundaries.
- Electronic invoicing is a form of invoicing in which transactional documents, such as supply orders and payment terms, are transmitted digitally and in a standardized format to relevant parties.
- Electronic invoicing enables compliance with tax regulations by default and helps strengthen the integration of accounting systems, which ultimately reduces the administrative burden on businesses.

Understanding the importance of the "security issue" for Ukraine, it is worth noting new technologies, the introduction of which on a national scale (from each individual enterprise to the economy of the state as a whole) will ensure the search for effective models, mechanisms, and tools of intellectual support for the innovative development of the country and its market entities.

- 5G networks are the next generation of wireless technology, providing up to 200 times faster connectivity than the currently widely used 4G networks, and are expected to trigger a wave of software and hardware innovation across all sectors. 5G networks will increase bandwidth for more reliable and faster machine-to-machine communication and connect tens of billions of communication devices, machines, and objects to the Internet.
- The Internet of Things covers devices whose state can be changed via the Internet with or without the active participation of individuals. It includes objects and sensors that collect data and exchange it with each other and with people, from devices in the smart home system to wearable devices and control devices.
- Big data analytics refers to the use of various methods and tools to analyze large volumes of data generated as a result of the growing digitization of content, larger-scale monitoring of human activity, and the spread of the Internet of Things. This technology can be used to establish relationships and dependencies and predict outcomes and behavior. For example, retailers use big data analytics on a regular basis to make personalized offers to customers based on their interests, as determined by web browsing and purchasing behavior.
- Cloud computing, accessed via the Internet. Cloud computing offers flexible access to additional computing power, storage capacity, databases, and online software in the amount that meets short-term business needs. Cloud computing minimizes the cost of technology upgrades, freeing businesses from upfront investments in hardware and software and recurring costs for maintenance, IT professionals, and certification.
- The application of artificial intelligence means the ability of machines and systems to acquire and apply knowledge, as well as to implement intelligent behavior. It involves performing a wide range of cognitive tasks, such as perception, processing speech, making logical inferences, learning, making decisions, and demonstrating the ability to move and manipulate objects appropriately. Advances in the application of artificial intelligence are driven by machine learning (when machines make decisions based on probability functions derived

from experience), which allows the creation of new types of software and robots that are widely used in industry, for example, to automate routine tasks.

■ Blockchain is a distributed ledger maintained and stored on a network of computers. The network regularly updates the registry in all areas where it exists, so all copies of it are always identical. This means that records are visible and available for inspection by all network users, eliminating the need for authentication intermediaries. In this way, the technology provides "trust by default" and allows for lower transaction costs by eliminating the need for intermediaries to securely transfer value or sign legal agreements (Khang & Chowdhury et al., 2022).

As a result of the action of all the factors described above, digitalization disrupts the order that has developed in one industry or another industry and allows more flexible enterprises to experiment with new business models, master new niches, and challenge the old-timers of the market. Although digitalization can be of great importance for increasing the productivity of "traditional" enterprises, it also creates the conditions for the emergence of "born digital" enterprises. Businesses decide to invest in digital tools and methods for a variety of reasons: To innovate, to respond to competitive pressure, or to enter new markets. After all, the process of implementing technologies should bring tangible benefits to an enterprise embarking on the path of digital transformation (Khang & Kali et al., 2023).

17.6 Results and Discussion

The chapter examines the application and impact of digitization tools on the intellectual development of the economy. It is noted that digitalization tools are perceived in a rather narrow sense: Means of communication, which should have included, in general, the possibility of telephone communication and SMS messages. The authors conducted a study of the possibilities of using the "5G" toolkit by age group of the population and obtained data that the 50+ age group has problems using the digital opportunities of the market, and the 60+ age group practically does not know how to use them, because they do not have enough digital literacy.

The importance of using digitization tools for intellectual development of the country's economy is noted. Given the expected introduction of the "6G" generation of mobile communication between 2026 and 2030, the focus is on household broadband coverage, computer hardware penetration, and other "hard" digital infrastructure statistics, which are certainly fundamental.

The "security" situation in Ukraine was noted. The possibilities of implementation and development of digitization tools and the importance of finding effective models, mechanisms, and tools of intellectual support for the innovative development of the country and its market entities were considered. The intellectual development of the economy is increasingly focused on the growth of the market value of individual companies, in which the main specific weight is made up of intangible assets (technological, marketing, customer, etc.), which is the result of the effective use and development of the intellectual capital of each individual company.

17.7 Conclusion

The growing role of the effective management of the intellectual development of the economy in the scenario of digitalization creates conditions for the growing role of digitalization and the creation and transfer of new knowledge into the economy. And as a conclusion, this chapter shares the hypothesis of research with readers, which consists in identifying the possible influence of digitalization tools on the development of the economy in the intellectual part (Khang & Shah et al., 2023).

References

Bondarenko, S., Bratko, A., Antonov, V., Kolisnichenko, R., Hubanov, O., & Mysyk, A. (2022). Improving the state system of strategic planning of national security in the context of informatization of society. *Journal of Information Technology Management*, 14, 1–24. https://doi.org/10.22059/jitm.2022.88861

Bondarenko, S., Makeieva, O., Usachenko, O., Veklych, V., Arifkhodzhaieva, T., & Lernyk, S. (2022). The legal mechanisms for information security in the context of digitalization. *Journal of Information Technology Management*, 14, 25–58. https://doi.org/10.22059/jitm.2022.88868

Desai, R., Chauhan, A., & Kudtarkar, D. (2019). Digital marketing – New age consumer behavior (Mumbai Region). *IJRAR*, 6(1), 38–43. http://www.ijrar.org/IJRAR1ABP007.pdf

Dudnik, A., Kuzmych, L., Trush, O., Domkiv, T., Leshchenko, O., & Vyshnivskyi, V. (2020). Smart home technology network construction method and device interaction organization concept. Paper presented at the 2020 IEEE 2nd International Conference on System Analysis and Intelligent Computing, SAIC 2020. https://doi.org/10.1109/SAIC51296.2020.9239220

Ghauri, P., Grønhaug, K., & Strange, R. (2020). *Research Methods in Business Studies*. London: Cambridge University Press.

Half, R. (2022). How to upskill and reskill staff to stay competitive. https://doi.org/10.1017/9781108762427

Heilig, L., Lalla-Ruiz, E., & Voß, S. (2017). Digital transformation in maritime ports: Analysis and a game theoretic framework. *NETNOMICS: Economic Research & Electronic Networking*, 18, 227–254. https://doi.org/10.1007/s11066-017-9122-x

Kane, G. C., Palmer, D., Phillips, A. N., Kiron, D., & Buckley, N. (2015). Strategy, not technology, drives digital transformation. *MIT Sloan Management Review & Deloitte University Press*, 14, 1–25. https://www2.deloitte.com/content/dam/Deloitte/fr/Documents/strategy/dup_strategy-not-technology-drives-digital-transformation.pdf

Khang, A. (2023). *Applications and Principles of Quantum Computing* (1st Ed.). IGI Global Press. ISBN: 9798369311684. https://doi.org/10.4018/979-8-3693-1168-4

Khang, A., & Rath, K. C. (2023). Quantum mechanics primer – Fundamentals and quantum computing. In *Applications and Principles of Quantum Computing* (1st Ed.). IGI Global Press. ISBN: 9798369311684. https://doi.org/10.4018/979-8-3693-1168-4-ch001

Khang, A., Chowdhury, S., & Sharma S. (2022). *The Data-Driven Blockchain Ecosystem: Fundamentals, Applications, and Emerging Technologies* (1st Ed.). CRC Press. https://doi.org/10.1201/9781003269281

Khang, A., Hahanov, V., Abbas, G. L., & Hajimahmud, V. A. (2022). Cyber-physical-social system and incident management. *AI-Centric Smart City Ecosystems: Technologies, Design and Implementation* (1st Ed.), 7(12). CRC Press. https://doi.org/10.1201/9781003252542-2

Khang, A., Hajimahmud, V. A., Gupta, S. K., Babasaheb, J., & Morris, G. (2023). *AI-Centric Modelling and Analytics: Concepts, Designs, Technologies, and Applications* (1st Ed.). CRC Press. https://doi.org/10.1201/9781003400110

Khang, A., Muthmainnah, M., Seraj, P. M. I., Al Yakin, A., Obaid, A. J., & Panda, M. R. (2023). AI-aided teaching model for the education 5.0 ecosystem. In *AI-Based Technologies and Applications in the Era of the Metaverse* (1st Ed., pp. 83–104). IGI Global Press. https://doi.org/10.4018/978-1-6684-8851-5.ch004

Khang, A., Rani, S., Gujrati, R., Uygun, H., & Gupta, S. K. (2023). *Designing Workforce Management Systems for Industry 4.0: Data-Centric and AI-Enabled Approaches* (1st Ed.). CRC Press. https://doi.org/10.1201/9781003357070

Khang, A., Rath, K. C., Satapathy, S. K., Kumar, A., Das, S. R., & Panda, M. R. (2023). Enabling the future of manufacturing: Integration of robotics and IoT to smart factory infrastructure in industry 4.0. In *AI-Based Technologies and Applications in the Era of the Metaverse* (1st Ed., pp. 25–50). IGI Global Press. https://doi.org/10.4018/978-1-6684-8851-5.ch002

Khang, A., Shah, V., & Rani, S. (2023). *AI-Based Technologies and Applications in the Era of the Metaverse* (1st Ed.). IGI Global Press. https://doi.org/10.4018/978-1-6684-8851-5

Legner, C., Eymann, T., Hess, T., Matt, C., Böhmann, T., Drews, P., Mädche, A., Urbach, N., & Ahlemann, F. (2017). Digitalization: Opportunity and challenge for the business and information systems engineering community. *Business & Information Systems Engineering*, 59(4), 301–308. https://doi.org/10.1007/s12599-017-0484-2

Nikonenko, U., Shtets, T., Kalinin, A., Dorosh, I., & Sokolik, L. (2022). Assessing the policy of attracting investments in the main sectors of the economy in the context of introducing aspects of industry 4.0. *International Journal of Sustainable Development and Planning*, 17(2), 497–505. https://doi.org/10.18280/ijsdp.170214

Nitsenko, V., Kotenko, S., Hanzhurenko, I., Mardani, A., Stashkevych, I., & Karakai, M. (2020). Mathematical modeling of multimodal transportation risks. https://doi.org/10.1007/978-3-030-36056-6_41

Novak, A., Pravdyvets, O., Chornyi, O., Sumbaieva, L., Akimova, L., & Akimov, O. (2022). Financial and economic security in the field of financial markets at the stage of European integration. *International Journal of Professional Business Review*, 7(5). https://doi.org/10.26668/businessreview/2022.v7i5.e835

Oliinyk, O., Bilan, Y., Mishchuk, H., Akimov, O., & Vasa, L. (2021). The impact of migration of highly skilled workers on the country's competitiveness and economic growth. *Montenegrin Journal of Economics*, 17(3), 7–19. http://ep3.nuwm.edu.ua/id/eprint/20736

Pyshchulina, O. (2018). Digital economy: Trends, risks and social determinants. https://razumkov.org.ua/uploads/article/2020_digitalization.pdf

Rohm, A. J., Stefl, M., & Saint Clair, J. (2018). Time for a marketing curriculum overhaul: Developing a digital-first approach. https://doi.org/10.1177/0273475318798086

Sekaran, U., & Bougie, R. (2016). *Research Methods for Business: A Skill-Building Approach* (7th Ed.). London: John Wiley & Sons Ltd.

Semenets-Orlova, I., Kushnir, V., Rodchenko, L., Chernenko, I., Druz, O., & Rudenko, M. (2023). Organizational development and educational changes management in public sector (Case of public administration during war time). *International Journal of Professional Business Review*, 8(4), e01699. https://doi.org/10.26668/businessreview/2023.v8i4.1699

27Smith, M. (2021). Stay relevant in the new different. https://www.wiley.com/en-sg/Research+Methods+For+Business%3A+A+Skill+Building+Approach%2C+7th+Edition-p-9781119266846

Valenduc, G., & Vendramin, P. (2017). Digitalisation, between disruption and evolution. *European Review of Labour and Research*, 23(2), 121–134. https://doi.org/10.1177/10242589177013

Data-Driven Customer Relationship Management (CRM) Modeling: Humanistic Connection in Predictive Analytics

Kyle Allison

18.1 Introduction

In the contemporary landscape of data-driven decision-making, the utilization of Customer Relationship Management (CRM) data has emerged as a central pillar in the development and execution of human-centric strategies driven by predictive analytics. This dynamic interplay between technology and human interaction underscores a fundamental shift in the way organizations approach their customer relationships. It's no longer merely about understanding customers; it's about forging genuine, meaningful connections with them. At the core of this transformation is the pivotal role of CRM data.

CRM data represents a treasure trove of information that encapsulates the intricacies of each customer's journey and interactions with a business. This data encompasses everything from purchase history and communication preferences to feedback and complaints. Harnessing this wealth of information empowers organizations to gain profound insights into their customers' needs, preferences, and behaviors. It forms the foundation upon which predictive analytics can be applied to anticipate customer actions, preferences, and potential pain points.

One of the most compelling aspects of utilizing CRM data to fuel human connection in human-centric strategies is its ability to enable businesses to approach customers with a level of personalization and relevance that was once unimaginable. By analyzing historical data and patterns, predictive analytics can forecast future customer behaviors, allowing organizations to proactively tailor their interactions and offerings. This level of personalization not only enhances

DOI: 10.4324/9781032688305-18

customer satisfaction but also fosters a sense of genuine connection, as customers feel valued and understood by the business.

Moreover, CRM data empowers organizations to optimize resource allocation and marketing efforts. By identifying high-value customer segments and predicting their needs, businesses can allocate their resources more efficiently, ensuring that they invest where it matters most. This not only leads to cost savings but also strengthens customer relationships by delivering timely, meaningful interactions that cater to individual preferences and needs.

In conclusion, the strategic integration of CRM data and predictive analytics is reshaping the business landscape, emphasizing the importance of human connection in customer-centric strategies. This data-driven approach enables organizations to move beyond mere customer understanding to engage customers on a personal level. By leveraging CRM data and predictive analytics, businesses can anticipate customer needs, allocate resources wisely, and ultimately create a customer experience that fosters genuine human connections in a data-powered world.

In the current context of data-driven decision-making, the use of CRM data has become fundamental to the formulation and implementation of individual-centric strategies guided by predictive analytics. The dynamic interaction between technology and human interaction exemplifies the fundamental shift in organizations' approach to customer relationships. The emphasis has shifted from merely understanding customers to establishing genuine and meaningful relationships with them. The importance of CRM data is central to this transformation.

CRM data are a valuable source of information that encompasses the complexities of a customer's journey and interactions with a company. The dataset contains a vast array of data, such as purchase history, communication preferences, feedback, and complaints. Utilizing this vast trove of data enables businesses to gain significant insights into the needs, preferences, and behaviors of their customers. It lays the groundwork for the application of predictive analytics to anticipate customer behaviors, preferences, and potential obstacles.

One of the most compelling facets of leveraging CRM data to enhance human connection in strategies centered on humans is its capacity to empower businesses to engage customers with an unprecedented degree of personalization and pertinence, surpassing previous conceptions. Through the examination of historical data and patterns, predictive analytics have the capability to anticipate and predict future customer behaviors. This enables organizations to take proactive measures in customizing their interactions and offerings accordingly. The implementation of this degree of customization not only amplifies customer contentment but also cultivates an authentic bond, as customers perceive themselves as esteemed and comprehended by the enterprise.

Furthermore, the utilization of CRM data enables organizations to enhance the allocation of resources and optimize marketing endeavors. By conducting a thorough analysis of customer segments with high value and accurately forecasting their requirements, organizations can optimize the allocation of their resources, thereby guaranteeing that investments are directed toward areas of utmost significance. This not only results in financial benefits but also enhances customer engagement through the provision of timely and personalized interactions that align with individual preferences and requirements.

In summary, the incorporation of CRM data and predictive analytics in a strategic manner is fundamentally transforming the business environment, underscoring the significance of establishing personal relationships in customer-centric approaches. The utilization of a data-driven approach empowers organizations to transcend basic comprehension of customers and effectively engage with them on an individualized basis. By utilizing CRM data and employing predictive analytics, businesses have the ability to forecast customer requirements, allocate resources efficiently, and ultimately establish a customer experience that cultivates authentic human connections within a data-driven environment.

This research aims to investigate and evaluate the existing literature on CRM Data Modeling in Human Connection within the field of Predictive Analytics. Through a comprehensive examination of the existing body of knowledge, the primary objective is to identify and clarify any gaps or deficiencies in the current research landscape. This endeavor will assist in identifying areas in need of additional research by shedding light on untapped opportunities and pressing research questions. By addressing these gaps, this study aims to contribute to the advancement of our understanding of how CRM data modeling can be utilized to facilitate and deepen human connections in predictive analytics, thereby fostering more customer-centric business strategies in an ever-changing business environment.

18.2 CRM Data Models in Context

In modern society, information disperses throughout the consumer database. After gathering and storing customer information, useful information is found hidden in the database, and the Industry is unable to convert these facts into knowledge, preventing it from achieving its ultimate aim of offering the right services at the right time to the right customers. Retaining clients is the organization's most important objective. The introduction of Information Technology and the widespread use of computers in many spheres of activity have given rise to a new idea in marketing: CRM. Santos and Castelo Almeida (2021) expressed that:

> Companies of various sizes and structures have progressively adopted specialized CRM software that aims to capture customer data and prospects, streamline business processes, and provide greater visibility for the business. The result of these initiatives has been very heterogeneous and strongly dependent of several factors, such as the experience, partnerships, and qualification of the human resources that these companies possess.

This study exposes the need for companies to understand the need not only now, but also understand that CRM modeling is a practice of ongoing management, maintenance of strategic planning. Appreciating the data modeling efforts doesn't stop just at the helm of inception. The optimization and ability to further the ability to use the data with ongoing decision-making, and refinement to the modeling process is the cornerstone to best practices derived from this study and other existing literature.

CRM is a comprehensive business strategy that aims to cultivate and enhance the connection between an entity and its clientele. The concept encompasses a variety of methodologies, technologies, and procedures that facilitate enterprises in efficiently managing, analyzing, and leveraging customer data. The principal aim of CRM is to augment customer satisfaction and loyalty, thereby fostering profitability and long-term viability. Chatterjee, Chaudhuri, and Vrontis (2022) stated, "An organization can also improve its SSP by developing CRM capability, which principally includes the ability to interact with and retain customers." SSP stands for Strategic Sales Performance, and the statement provides the direct viewpoint on the importance of a CRM capability that can deliver an impact on the sales of the organization. The researchers focused on how a focus on CRM modeling around customer data and sales data can provide an impact on the sales strategies being conducted. Foundationally, sales are a core element of CRM strategy, albeit at times financially focused and less on the connection with clients or customers in a qualitative sense.

At its core, CRM focuses on gaining a deeper understanding of customers, tailoring interactions and offerings to their preferences, and delivering exceptional experiences. This involves not only acquiring new customers, but also retaining and cultivating existing ones. CRM systems and strategies permit the consolidation of customer data, the automation of specific tasks, and the provision of analytical tools for the use and exploitation of customer data.

18.2.1 CRM Datasets

The success of CRM hinges on the collection and analysis of a wide array of data types that offer insights into customer behavior, interactions, and preferences. These data types can be categorized into several key categories:

- **Demographic Data**: This includes basic information about customers, such as age, gender, location, and marital status. Demographic data provide a foundational understanding of the customer base and helps in segmenting customers for targeted marketing efforts.
- **Behavioral Data**: Behavioral data track customer actions, such as website visits, product purchases, email interactions, and social media engagement. It provides insights into how customers interact with a brand and its offerings, helping to identify trends and patterns.
- **Transactional Data**: Transactional data records the details of customer purchases, including what was bought, when it was bought, and how much was spent. These data are crucial for assessing customer buying habits and preferences.
- **Communication Data**: This category covers customer interactions with the organization, such as customer service inquiries, complaints, and feedback. Analyzing communication data helps improve customer support and service quality.
- **Psychographic Data**: Psychographic data delves into the psychological aspects of customer behavior, including their values, beliefs, interests, and lifestyles. It provides a deeper understanding of what motivates customers' choices.
- **Social Media and Online Data**: With the proliferation of social media, CRM also involves monitoring and analyzing customer interactions on platforms like Facebook, Twitter, and Instagram. Social data offer real-time insights into customer sentiment and trends.
- **Survey and Feedback Data**: Organizations often collect customer feedback through surveys and feedback forms. This qualitative data help in gauging customer satisfaction and identifying areas for improvement.
- **Predictive Data**: Predictive data encompasses information used to build predictive models, such as historical sales data, customer churn rates, and customer lifetime value calculations. These models are central to CRM's predictive analytics component.

18.2.2 Challenges in CRM Data

Effectively managing and leveraging CRM data come with its fair share of challenges. These challenges can hinder an organization's ability to harness the full potential of its CRM system. Here are some common challenges in CRM data management:

- **Data Quality**: Poor data quality, including inaccurate, incomplete, or outdated information, can significantly impact CRM effectiveness. Inaccurate customer details, duplicate records, and missing data can lead to misguided decisions and ineffective marketing efforts.

- **Data Integration**: Numerous firms utilize numerous systems and platforms for diverse facets of client data, including sales, marketing, and customer care. Integrating data from various disparate sources into a centralized CRM system can be difficult and time-consuming.
- **Data Security and Privacy**: With the rising emphasis on data privacy legislation such as GDPR and CCPA, the protection of sensitive consumer data is a major responsibility. It can be difficult to ensure data security and compliance while allowing authorized individuals to access data.
- **Data Volume and Scalability**: As businesses grow, the volume of CRM data also increases. Handling large datasets efficiently and ensuring scalability can be challenging, particularly for smaller organizations with limited resources.
- **Data Consistency**: Maintaining consistency in data across various touchpoints and departments is crucial for providing a seamless customer experience. Inconsistencies can lead to customer frustration and confusion.
- **User Adoption**: CRM systems are only effective if employees actively utilize them. Especially in resistant-to-change firms, encouraging user adoption and assuring staff members' comfort with the CRM system can be tough.
- **Data Governance**: Establishing clear data governance policies, including data ownership, access controls, and data stewardship, is essential for maintaining data quality and compliance. Developing and enforcing these policies can be challenging.
- **Customization and Configuration**: Tailoring the CRM system to meet the specific needs of the organization can be complex. Finding the right balance between customization and maintaining the system's core functionality is a challenge.
- **Data Analytics and Insights**: Extracting actionable insights from CRM data requires advanced analytics capabilities. Many organizations struggle to effectively analyze their data to derive meaningful insights (Khang & Gujrati et al., 2024).
- **Cost**: Implementing and maintaining a CRM system, along with the necessary infrastructure, can be costly. Smaller businesses may face budget constraints when it comes to CRM technology adoption.
- **Change Management**: Implementing a CRM system often involves organizational changes, including new processes and workflows. Managing these changes and ensuring they are embraced by the workforce can be challenging.
- **Data Migration**: When transitioning to a new CRM system or upgrading an existing one, migrating data from legacy systems can be complex and error-prone. Ensuring data accuracy and integrity during migration is critical.
- **Data Retention and Archiving**: Compliance and data management require the establishment of proper archiving methods and the determination of how long to store client data. It might be challenging to balance data retention obligations with storage expenses.
- **Real-time Data Updates**: In industries where real-time data updates are crucial, ensuring that the CRM system is capable of capturing and processing data changes in real-time can be challenging.

Despite these issues, firms that address them successfully and engage in CRM data management solutions can harness the potential of CRM systems to increase customer connections, enhance marketing activities, and fuel corporate growth. Frequently, overcoming these obstacles takes a combination of technological solutions, process enhancements, and a dedication to data-driven decision-making.

18.2.3 CRM Analysis Methods

Predictive analytics is a critical component of CRM that leverages data and statistical modeling to forecast future customer behavior and trends. There are several modeling frameworks used in predictive analytics within the CRM context.

- **Regression Analysis**: CRM frequently employs regression models to examine the relationship between independent variables (such as customer demographics, purchase history, and communication preferences) and a dependent variable (such as customer lifetime value or likelihood to churn). Regression analysis assists in determining which variables influence customer behavior.
- **Classification Models**: Classification models, including decision trees, random forests, and logistic regression, are used to categorize customers into different segments or predict their likelihood to take a specific action (e.g., make a purchase or respond to a marketing campaign). These models are valuable for targeted marketing efforts.
- **Segmentation Analysis**: CRM relies heavily on segmentation, and clustering techniques like k-means clustering and hierarchical clustering are used to group customers with similar characteristics or behaviors. These segments allow marketers to tailor their strategies and communications.
- **Time Series Analysis**: Time series models, like Auto Regressive Integrated Moving Average (ARIMA), are used to forecast future trends based on historical data. In CRM, time series analysis can be applied to predict future sales, customer demand, or seasonal patterns.
- **Machine Learning Algorithms**: In CRM predictive analytics, techniques such as neural networks, support vector machines, and ensemble methods are increasingly utilized. These algorithms excel at processing complex datasets and can identify intricate customer behavior patterns.
- **Churn Prediction Models**: Churn prediction models are a specialized category of predictive analytics in CRM. They identify customers at risk of churning (i.e., discontinuing their relationship with the company) by analyzing factors like usage patterns, customer service interactions, and historical churn data.
- **Customer Lifetime Value (CLV) Models**: CLV models estimate the long-term value of a customer to a business. They consider factors like purchase history, frequency, and customer acquisition costs to determine the profitability of retaining a specific customer.

In the contemporary business environment that heavily relies on data, CRM emerges as a crucial strategy for organizations aiming to cultivate and improve their interactions with customers. The core focus of CRM lies in the acquisition and examination of a wide range of data categories, encompassing demographic, behavioral, transactional, and psychographic data. The abundance of information serves as the basis for predictive analytics, wherein diverse modeling frameworks are utilized to forecast customer behavior, classify customers into segments, and facilitate focused marketing endeavors.

The enduring appeal of CRM stems from its capacity to utilize data-driven insights in order to customize interactions and offerings based on the specific preferences of individual customers. Through the ongoing improvement of predictive models and the adjustment of strategies informed by customer insights, businesses have the ability to establish more robust and significant relationships with their customer base. This, in turn, can lead to enhanced growth, profitability, and customer loyalty. In an ever-changing business environment, the fundamental principles of

CRM data and predictive analytics offer a distinct advantage to organizations by allowing them to anticipate and fulfill customer requirements in a customer-centric approach.

18.3 Human Connection in CRM

A wave of modern marketing best practices indicates the need to connect with customers on a humanistic level (Song & Kim, 2018). Focusing on human connection involves the ability to advertise, communicate, and deliver service that is on the side of what humans think and feel, and their attitudes and beliefs. Focusing on the ethos of a customer allows us to better find a way to build a connection deeper than just a sales tactic of offering a product or service to solve a need or desire. The affinity and loyalty factor from customer to brand is paramount to be competitive and successful. A study from Song Kim (2018) focusing on one key societal emerging topic of the environment and sustainability demonstrated the need to connect with consumers on a humanistic level on the market's desire for environmentally friendly products.

The authenticity of green marketing was paramount to this research. The researchers focused on a sample of 829 US consumers from the period January 2015 to December 2017, testing various green marketing advertisements to generate an awareness of the connection they can build with these customers. The results of this study showed that four factors, namely, perception of the apparel's quality, its uniqueness, caring, and nature connectedness, predict consumers' intention to purchase green apparel. This case example demonstrates that appealing to consumers on a carefully curated marketing campaign based on connecting their cares, concerns, and belief system generates an ability to bridge affinity to the brand and also shows predictors of future purchases.

Tworek Salamacha (2019) stated:

> There is no doubt that properly implemented CRM might bring a lot of benefits both from the point of view of the client and the organization, such as customer acquisition, customer retention, financial benefits, customer loyalty, cross-selling, customer profitability, value creation for the customer, customization of products and services.

The focal point of this statement is that CRM should bring about the point of view of the customer to generate influence on how firms connect with them on a level that appeals to them directly via various metric building and strategies.

According to Alam and Noor (2020), loyal customers are regarded as the key to success for many service firms. One of the principal aims of CRM is to make their customers loyal since CRM not only confirms an enhanced relationship with customers but also nurtures the loyalty between them, which is essential for the service industry. The researchers conducted a framework for assessing 325 Gen Y shoppers in surveying their viewpoints on the service quality across four department superstores in Bangladesh. The findings from this study indicate that the target audience's responsiveness towards being loyal depends on service and corporate image.

This study accounts for various research conducted where in today's environment the human connection on a service level is one major impact on the performance of a firm's brand image and ultimately financial impacts. Gontur, Gadi Bagobiri (2022) mention that customer satisfaction levels and the global service environment directed to convincing mutually beneficial link for both service quality and customer loyalty. This literature exposes the perspective that with high service level standards, generally derived from humanistic connection of communication, actions, and activities, customers tend to build stronger relationships and loyalties to organizations.

According to Agafonva, Yahkneeva, Mukhametshina (2022), the researchers developed a study focusing on how human-centric marketing in the digital era on customer perception impacts the social environment. The conclusion of this study is that the success of human-centric marketing in the digital era is contingent upon an understanding of the strategic value and threats of digital transformation to business and society, the systematization of CSR programs, and a revision and reinterpretation of the marketing mix.

These studies generate the understanding that CRM best practices involve a sense of human connection and high levels of service to generate value for the organization. Fundamentally, a great volume of the body of knowledge is understanding the need for human connection and centric marketing in today's modern marketing environment in order to generate customer loyalty, acquisition, and ultimately retention in existing and emerging markets.

18.4 Consumer Behavior Application in Predictive Analytics

The modern marketer generally embraces analytics and data to drive decisions. However, from an analytics perspective, the gap may still exist in some firms in how they train data scientists and business analysts to embrace consumer behavior theory and qualitative insight into the mix of predictive and advanced analytics. An example is the study conducted by Necula (2023) that assessed how time spent reading product information influences consumer behavior in e-commerce. Their research focused on acquiring a greater knowledge of customer navigation on e-commerce websites and its effects on purchasing decisions. The study found that using behavioral data and the consumer behavior framework of decision-making is at the forefront of predictability of future e-commerce purchases.

Chaudhary, Al-Rakhami, and Gumaei (2021) conducted a study where they collected data across various social media platforms to predict consumer behavior by conducting a pre- and post-data processing process. They cleaned the data and divided it into two parts. We have taken 80% of the data for training our model and 20% for testing the model. The machine learning algorithms were applied to the data for the prediction of social media consumer behavior. For prediction, supervised learning techniques were utilized. The employment of supervised learning techniques is due to the measurement level provided in the dataset (Chaudhary, Al-Rakhami, & Gumaei, 2021).

The researchers concluded that these models predict consumer behavior on various platforms based on consumer's likes, followers, downloads, etc. The limitation of this model is that it will not work with daily basis consumer data. If this model is used with daily basis data, the results will be very poor. Therefore, the research did find that patterns and trends of consumer behavior can be viewed on social media, with the decision tree capability deriving some statistical significance.

These case research examples demonstrate the importance of using predictive analytics in understanding consumer behavior. However, many studies focus on the numerical nature of trends and statistical output. While the validity is there in the predictive modeling and use of it to generate quantitative views, strategically, the elevated step of introducing the training and skills of data scientists and analysts in thinking through the consumer behavior lens and focusing on varied model approaches, or even mixed methods, may allow for deeper insights gathering. In simple terms, an organization can develop a culture of their data science and analytics team members to think both qualitatively and quantitatively when conducting their predictive marketing analytics.

It starts with the framework of understanding the consumer behavior theories and humanistic connection framework being built from an ethos and qualitative perspective. Knowing those traits and triggers of consumer behavior can bridge the impact of analytics, where a viewpoint that an analyst brings to the model can be thought of beyond its numerical value, but from a foundational marketer perception. The skill sets today for some data scientists are to be the quantitative insights generator, but those insights may just gather higher levels of impact to decision-making if in the same predictive modeling, variations, considerations, and a mindset of humanistic connection to the CRM data is also brought into the framework.

18.5 Gaps in Human Connection in CRM Modeling

In the field of data science predictive analytics, there is a significant gap when considering human-centric factors, particularly in marketing modeling. Although predictive analytics has made significant strides in comprehending customer behavior and forecasting trends, it frequently ignores the emotional and psychological factors that influence consumer decision-making and the formation of meaningful human connections. This gap encompasses a number of crucial aspects that merit closer examination.

18.5.1 Emotional Intelligence in Predictive Models

In predictive analytics models, the absence of emotional intelligence is a crucial omission. Predictions based on these models rely heavily on historical data and quantitative metrics, but they frequently lack the ability to measure emotional factors that influence consumer decisions. Understanding customer emotions, sentiments, and mood is crucial for developing marketing strategies with a deeper, more personal resonance. EI predictive modeling is commonly done in the fields of psychology, sociology, and other social sciences, but the gap that can be considered is further understanding of how EI can be considered in the ethos of consumer decision-making for predictive modeling. Having conducted some fundamental exploration before, researchers Khan and Asim Manzoor (2021) developed a study to understand that predicting consumer decision-making is very crucial for organizations. The consumer's decision-making toward a product is based upon their emotional intelligence, in light of the past studies and research done in the required as well as the related fields.

The authors stated:

> While the dependent variable is the consumer's decision predicting because that is what our main focus is and hence has been divided into 2 factors as well: The emotionality of the consumer. As it is one of the major factors which influences prompt decisions and impulse buying. The rationality, or in other words the whole process of perceiving, understanding, and processing the emotions for the decision making, can also be termed as the EI of the consumer. The basic idea behind this study is to understand the emotional intelligence of the consumer as well their behaviors and then by trying to understand it, predict their decision making.

The authors concluded that consumer's decision-making is primarily related to the understanding of the emotional intelligence of a consumer (seller to be emotionally intelligent) and the understanding of the rationale of a consumer (seller to be rational). Studies such as this propose the need for deeper research in understanding the importance of knowing the EI of customers in their behavior aspects but elevating that viewpoint with how to include that into the framework for predictive modeling in this context.

Example: Consider a retail establishment that uses predictive analytics to suggest products to customers. The purchase history of a customer may indicate a preference for eco-friendly products, but it does not reveal the emotional component of why the customer values sustainability. To better comprehend the emotional connection customers have with eco-friendly products, predictive models could profit from incorporating sentiment analysis of customer reviews and social media interactions.

18.5.2 Beyond Demographics: Incorporating Psychographics

Numerous predictive models segregate customers based solely on demographic information, which, while valuable, provide an incomplete picture of customer identities. These models frequently disregard the significance of psychographic variables, such as values, beliefs, and way of life, which significantly influence customer preferences. Incorporating psychographics is essential for fostering more genuine relationships. The utilization of extensive consumer data holds significant potential to revolutionize the field of applied and empirical marketing research. However, there has been limited research conducted on the impact of big data on consumers' psychological aspects. The utility of psychographics as a market segmentation approach in comprehending consumer preferences has been demonstrated. In the realm of e-commerce, personality is recognized as a significant factor within psychographic segmentation for predicting user preferences. Li (2019) conducted a study focusing on psychographics, specifically on the ability to understand these factors in the purchase decision process of consumers on e-commerce.

The researchers focused on using a methodology of using the Big Five (BFF) personality traits and Shwartz Value Survey (SVS) methods to understand the measurement of behaviors from a psychographic context of consumers. After deep analysis, the authors found that it is relative in context that studying the psychographic dimensions of consumer behavior warrants insights into understanding the predictability of their purchase intent. This draws upon the notion that on a humanistic level of analysis, the community of analytics can think through the lens of human beliefs, attitudes, and thought processes from a psychographic lens when conducting predictive analysis on consumers.

Example: Suppose a car manufacturer wishes to comprehend why certain customers consistently opt for electric vehicles over conventional gasoline-powered vehicles. Psychographic data, such as environmental consciousness and a desire for cutting-edge technology, can provide a more in-depth understanding of what motivates these purchasing decisions than demographic data.

18.5.3 Contextual Understanding in Marketing Strategies

Predictive analytics models often fail to consider the broader context in which customer interactions occur. They may not sufficiently account for situational context or immediate customer needs, overlooking essential elements for crafting marketing strategies that are both relevant and empathetic. Contextual understanding in marketing strategies is greatly enhanced by the integration of predictive analytics. Predictive analytics, as a powerful data-driven tool, allows marketers to leverage historical data and patterns to anticipate future customer behaviors and trends within a given context. By utilizing predictive models, marketers can proactively tailor their strategies to the anticipated context, ensuring that their messaging and offers align with customer needs, preferences, and the evolving landscape (Khang & Shah et al., 2023).

For instance, predictive analytics can be employed to forecast seasonal trends and buying patterns. By analyzing historical data, such as the surge in demand for certain products during specific times of the year, businesses can anticipate the context of changing seasons and adjust their marketing strategies accordingly. This might involve launching targeted campaigns for seasonal products or services as the relevant time approaches, ensuring that customers receive relevant offers in real-time.

Moreover, predictive analytics can aid in understanding the contextual significance of customer data points. For example, when analyzing customer data related to location and weather conditions, predictive models can identify patterns in geographic preferences. By recognizing these patterns, businesses can adapt their marketing strategies to cater to regional variations in customer preferences and needs. This ensures that marketing efforts are not only relevant but also contextually sensitive, acknowledging the diverse contexts within their customer base. In this way, predictive analytics serve as a valuable ally in contextual understanding, empowering marketers to connect with customers in a more meaningful and context-aware manner.

Example: Imagine an e-commerce company using predictive models to recommend products to online shoppers. If the model only considers past purchase history and not the current context, it might recommend winter clothing to a customer who is currently shopping for swimwear because they're planning a vacation. Understanding the customer's immediate context is vital for delivering relevant recommendations.

18.5.4 The Ethical Dimension of Predictive Marketing

In the field of predictive analytics in marketing, addressing ethical concerns is crucial. The potential for abuse or harm is substantial, and models must adhere to ethical standards and guidelines. In order to successfully navigate this aspect of human-centered marketing, it is crucial to place a premium on customer satisfaction and confidence.

The ethical dimension of predictive marketing is a critical consideration in the ever-evolving landscape of data-driven strategies. Predictive analytics, with its capacity to delve deep into customer data, holds immense power and potential. However, with great power comes the responsibility to ensure that these predictive models are deployed ethically, placing customer satisfaction, trust, and well-being at the forefront.

One primary ethical concern in predictive marketing is the issue of privacy. As predictive models analyze vast amounts of customer data to make informed predictions, it is essential to safeguard sensitive information. Striking the right balance between personalization and privacy is a constant challenge. Marketers must be transparent about the data they collect and how it is used, allowing customers to make informed choices about their data. For instance, an e-commerce platform should clearly communicate its data usage policies and provide opt-in/opt-out options for data-driven recommendations, respecting individual privacy preferences.

Additionally, predictive analytics can inadvertently perpetuate bias and discrimination if not carefully managed. Models trained on historical data may inherit biases present in that data, leading to unfair or discriminatory outcomes. Ethical marketing strategies require ongoing monitoring and auditing of predictive models to identify and rectify biased patterns. Moreover, efforts should be made to diversify datasets to ensure that predictions do not disproportionately impact certain groups. For example, a mortgage lending institution must actively work to prevent predictive models from perpetuating biases that may discriminate against marginalized communities.

Furthermore, the responsible use of predictive analytics also extends to the ethical treatment of customer data. Businesses must prioritize data security and protect customer information from breaches or misuse. Implementing robust cybersecurity measures, encryption protocols, and access controls are vital. In the event of a data breach, transparent communication with affected customers is essential to maintain trust and demonstrate commitment to their well-being.

In summary, the ethical dimension of predictive marketing is a cornerstone of customer-centric strategies. Marketers must uphold ethical standards that prioritize privacy, transparency, and fairness. By taking these ethical considerations to heart, businesses can not only harness the power of predictive analytics effectively but also build enduring trust with their customers, fostering more meaningful and empathetic connections in the process.

Example: Suppose an online retailer uses predictive models to determine pricing for products based on individual customer profiles. While personalization can enhance the customer experience, it is essential to ensure that this practice remains transparent and does not lead to price discrimination. Ethical considerations should guide decisions about how personalization is implemented.

In conclusion, addressing these gaps in predictive analytics requires a holistic approach that incorporates qualitative data, embraces empathy, and recognizes the multifaceted nature of human decision-making. Furthermore, it requires a shift from a purely data-driven perspective to one that places equal emphasis on the humanistic aspects of marketing, emphasizing genuine connections, trust, and customer well-being in a data-driven landscape that is constantly evolving.

18.6 Application in Practice

Focusing this application on practice, we focus on a data set of customer shopping behavior on a series of product categories, sales, customer behavior, and demographic information on a sales history of 600 individual customers during an annual time period. (Source of dataset from Kaggle .com.) The following are the variables used in the dataset:

1. Customer ID.
2. Purchase Date.
3. Product Category.
4. Product Price.
5. Quantity.
6. Total Purchase Amount.
7. Payment Method.
8. Customer Age.
9. Returns.
10. Gender.
11. Churn.
12. Customer Shopping Intent.
13. Customer Attitudes.
14. Customer Shopping Behavior.

The goal of this exercise is to practice seeing if there is a predictive set of Clusters through K-means analysis we can use to represent the shopping intent of humanistic behaviors on variables 12-Customers Shopping Intent, 13-Customer Attitudes, and 14-Customer Shopping Behavior on the levels of comparing the attributes of other demographics and product affinity. For the target variables 12, 13, and 14, the values were coded and mapped as such:

1. Customer Shopping Intent
   - 1: Environmental.
   - 2: Money Savings.
   - 3: Neutral.
2. Customer Attitudes
   - 1: Loyal.
   - 2: Non-Loyal.
   - 3: Neutral.
3. Customer Shopping Behavior
   - 1: High Frequency
   - 2: Medium Frequency
   - 3: Low Frequency.

These humanistic traits of variables are standard in the analysis of customer behavior, but predicting product and sales affinity is needed when it comes to the analysis objective.

Which customer humanistic traits matched with demographics and product affinity represent the best targeted segments for future CRM marketing?
For clustering analysis, it is crucial to determine which columns to include. Since the focus is on "Customer Shopping Intent," "Customer Attitudes," and "Customer Shopping Behavior," I will select these columns for clustering. Additionally, it's important to scale the data for clustering, especially when using algorithms like K-means, which are sensitive to the scale of the data.

Next, I'll determine the optimal number of clusters. One common method to determine this is the "Elbow method." In this method, we run the K-means clustering algorithm for a range of values of k (number of clusters) and then for each value of k, compute the sum of squared distances from each point to its assigned center. When these overall dispersions are plotted against k values, the "elbow" of the curve represents an optimal value for k (a balance between precision and computational cost).

The "Elbow" method involves identifying the point where the inertia (or the within-cluster sum of squares) starts to level off. In the plot as shown in Figure 18.1, there's a noticeable change in the slope around $=3k=3$, which suggests that three clusters might be a good choice for this dataset. Given the nature of the data and its coding (three distinct levels for each of the three variables), three clusters also align with our expectations. Here are the centroid values for each of the three clusters as shown in Table 18.1.

18.6.1 Analysis Report Approach

- We aimed to segment the dataset into meaningful clusters based on three key variables: Customer Shopping Intent, Customer Attitudes, and Customer Shopping Behavior.
- We utilized the K-means clustering algorithm, a widely recognized method for partitioning a dataset into groups or clusters where entities in the same group are more similar to each other than those in other groups.
- To decide on the number of clusters, we employed the Elbow method, which pointed toward three clusters as optimal.

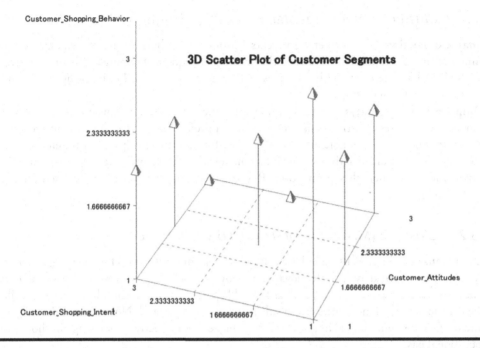

Figure 18.1   **3D Scatter Plot of customer segments for humanistic variables on clustering set.**

Table 18.1   Three Distinct Levels for each of the Three Variables

Cluster	Customer Shopping Intent	Customer Attitudes	Customer Shopping Behavior
0	2.61	2.51	2.47
1	1.04	1.04	1.04
2	1.94	1.01	2.99

18.6.2 Deep Dive into Segments

18.6.2.1 Cluster 0 (Money Savings, Non-Loyal, Low Frequency)

Human Connection: The primary motivating factor for customers within this particular segment is value. The consumers' affiliation with a brand exhibits a predominantly transactional nature, with a diminished emotional component. Consumers exhibit a preference for seeking optimal bargains and may not display significant loyalty toward any specific brand. The infrequent nature of their shopping habits suggests a tendency to only engage in purchases when deemed essential or when a notable value proposition is perceived.

Implication for Analytics: Given their price sensitivity, these customers can be targeted with promotional offers or discounts. Analytics can help identify specific products or categories they are interested in and tailor promotional campaigns accordingly. There's also an opportunity to convert these customers into more loyal ones by understanding their needs better and offering them personalized value.

18.6.2.2 Cluster 1 (Environmental, Loyal, High Frequency)

Human Connection: This segment represents customers who have strong values, especially concerning the environment. Their loyalty to the brand and frequent shopping behavior indicate they trust the brand and resonate with its values. This emotional connection is strong, transcending mere transactional interactions.

Implication for Analytics: Analytics can facilitate the comprehension of the particular products or categories that these customers exhibit a preference for, specifically those that align with eco-friendly or sustainable attributes. Tailored marketing campaigns that emphasize the brand's environmental initiatives or introduce novel sustainable products have the potential to enhance and strengthen this connection. Reward programs can additionally strengthen customer loyalty.

18.6.2.3 Cluster 2 (Mixed Intent, Loyal, Low Frequency)

Human Connection: The customer base exhibits a range of motivations for engaging in shopping activities, despite their demonstrated loyalty. The loyalty exhibited by individuals toward a brand can be attributed to various factors, such as favorable past encounters, confidence in the excellence of the product, or resonance with certain values upheld by the brand. Nevertheless, the infrequent nature of their shopping habits implies that they may exhibit selectivity or engage in shopping on an occasional basis.

Implication for Analytics: It is imperative to comprehend the precise stimuli that prompt individuals to make their purchases. The utilization of analytics can facilitate the segmentation of this particular group into more distinct sub-groups, which can be delineated based on various factors such as purchase patterns, product categories, or the response exhibited toward previous marketing campaigns. Tailored engagement strategies, taking into account individuals' diverse shopping intentions, have the potential to enhance their shopping frequency.

18.6.3 Importance of Considering Shopping Intent, Attitudes, and Behavior

Understanding the shopping intent, attitudes, and behavior is paramount for several reasons:

1. **Personalization**: In today's competitive market, personalization is key. Brands can no longer afford a one-size-fits-all approach. By understanding these three dimensions, brands can tailor their offerings, marketing campaigns, and even customer service experiences.
2. **Building Loyalty**: Loyalty cannot be bought; it has to be earned. By understanding and respecting the customer's intent and attitudes, brands can foster a deeper emotional connection, leading to increased loyalty.
3. **Predictive Analytics**: These dimensions can feed predictive models, helping brands anticipate customer needs, forecast demand, and even identify potential churners.

18.6.4 CRM Strategy Insights and Recommendations

The clustering results provide a granular view of customer segments, enabling the business to make informed decisions. By understanding these segments, businesses can tailor their strategies, enhance customer experience, and ultimately drive sales and growth, as shown in Figure 18.1.

18.6.5 Cluster Characterization

1. Cluster 0 – Environmentally Conscious and Loyal Shoppers:
   - Customers in this group display a high inclination toward environmentally friendly products, showcasing their concern for sustainability.
   - They exhibit high loyalty, indicating satisfaction with the brand or its products.
   - Their shopping frequency varies, suggesting that while they are loyal, their purchases are likely driven by need rather than impulse.
2. Cluster 1 – Budget-Conscious, Neutral Attitude Shoppers:
   - This segment primarily consists of customers looking for money-saving opportunities, possibly attracted by discounts and sales.
   - Their neutral attitude suggests they might switch brands based on price or availability.
   - Their shopping frequency is moderate, indicating regular but not frequent purchases.
3. Cluster 2 – Neutral Intent with Varied Attitudes:
   - Customers here don't exhibit a strong intent toward environmental or budgetary considerations.
   - Their attitudes range from loyal to non-loyal, making this a diverse group.
   - They tend to shop less frequently, suggesting they are not regular customers.

18.6.6 Demographic Overlay

Adding layers of demographic data like age and gender further refines these clusters.

- **Younger Generation**: Might display a stronger inclination toward environmentally friendly products, aligning with global sustainability trends.
- **Older Demographics**: They might lean toward budget-conscious shopping, valuing savings and discounts.
- **Gender Dynamics**: Female customers might shop more frequently, especially in specific product categories, whereas male customers might exhibit bulk or less frequent shopping patterns.

18.6.7 Strategic Insights and Recommendations

1. **Targeted Marketing**: Each cluster represents a distinct customer persona. Tailored marketing campaigns can be designed for each group. For instance, Cluster 0 might appreciate eco-friendly product campaigns, while Cluster 1 could be targeted with discount offers.
2. **Loyalty Programs**: Given the neutral attitudes in Clusters 1 and 2, introducing or enhancing loyalty programs might help in retaining these customers and increasing their shopping frequency.
3. **Product Recommendations**: Using the shopping intent data, personalized product recommendations can be made. For instance, suggesting eco-friendly products to Cluster 0 or budget-friendly options to Cluster 1.
4. **Feedback Mechanisms**: The neutral attitudes and intents observed suggest there's room for improvement in customer satisfaction. Implementing feedback mechanisms can provide insights into areas of enhancement.

Fundamentally, CRM revolves around the comprehension and establishment of connections with individual entities. The process of predictive clustering analysis involves the segmentation of a heterogeneous customer base into discrete groups, characterized by their individual behaviors, attitudes, and intentions. These clusters offer a more comprehensive comprehension of customer personas. In the dataset under consideration, various segments were identified, encompassing environmentally conscious shoppers as well as individuals driven by the desire for savings. By acknowledging these personas, organizations have the ability to customize their communication strategies, guaranteeing that they connect profoundly with the unique values and motivations of each individual. The inclusion of a personal element facilitates a more profound bond, thereby converting detached exchanges into significant engagements.

In the contemporary era of digital interactions, consumers are frequently exposed to a plethora of standardized advertisements and promotional materials. Predictive clustering techniques aid businesses in effectively navigating and surpassing the challenges posed by extraneous data and information. By comprehending the unique attributes of each cluster, organizations can develop customized marketing campaigns. For example, a specific consumer segment that demonstrates a pronounced preference for environmentally conscious shopping practices can be effectively reached through the implementation of green initiatives or the introduction of sustainable product lines. The act of personalization extends beyond conventional marketing practices, as it serves as an indication to the customer that the business possesses an understanding and appreciation for their distinct preferences. Consequently, this fosters a feeling of inclusion and commitment, thereby cultivating a sense of loyalty.

Predictive clustering not only serves to emphasize customer preferences but also possesses the capability to detect potential pain points or areas of dissatisfaction. An instance of a cluster exhibiting a neutral or non-loyal disposition toward a brand could potentially highlight deficiencies in the brand's service or product offerings. By taking proactive measures to address these concerns, businesses have the potential to convert customers who are initially passive or dissatisfied into enthusiastic advocates for their brand. The implementation of a proactive strategy, which is rooted in empathy and comprehension, serves to strengthen the humanistic bond between enterprises and their clientele.

Feedback serves as the fundamental basis for fostering ongoing improvement. The utilization of predictive clustering has the potential to identify and highlight particular segments that could potentially derive advantages from the implementation of focused feedback mechanisms. By initiating dialogues with these clusters, such as through the use of surveys, focus groups, or interactive sessions, businesses are able to acquire more profound insights into the needs and aspirations of their customers. Furthermore, it serves as a significant indication to the customer that their opinion holds significance, thereby strengthening the interpersonal connection (Khang & Kali et al., 2023).

In the contemporary era characterized by advanced digital technologies, there exists a potential peril wherein interpersonal exchanges may devolve into mere transactions, thereby diminishing the inherent human element. Predictive clustering employs sophisticated data analytics techniques to effectively address the digital divide (Khang & Semenets et al., 2024). By converting extensive datasets into practical insights, it enables businesses to develop strategies and engagements that prioritize the needs and experiences of individuals.

The clusters derived from our dataset, encompassing both environmentally conscious shoppers and budget-driven consumers, should not be regarded merely as data points. Rather, they should be recognized as representations of actual individuals who possess aspirations, preferences, and values. Predictive clustering offers a framework through which one can analyze and appreciate these unique narratives, thereby establishing the basis for authentic interpersonal bonds.

Predictive clustering, at its core, is grounded in the field of data analytics. However, its primary strength lies in its capacity to augment the humanistic aspect, transforming CRM into more than just a sales tool, but rather a platform for cultivating significant connections (Khang & Muthmainnah et al., 2023).

18.7 Conclusion and Further Research

In summary, it is imperative to address the existing gaps in predictive analytics in a manner that surpasses mere recognition. This necessitates adopting a comprehensive and proactive approach that fundamentally transforms our approach to data modeling and decision-making. The implementation of a comprehensive strategy necessitates an understanding of the intricate aspects of human decision-making. It is crucial to acknowledge that consumers are not solely data points, but rather intricate individuals with a wide range of needs, motivations, and emotions.

The incorporation of qualitative data is an essential element of this methodology. Although quantitative data are valuable for gaining insights, qualitative data, including customer feedback, surveys, and open-ended responses, enables organizations to explore the underlying reasons behind customer behavior in greater depth. Qualitative data provides insights into the emotional and psychological determinants of decision-making, offering a deeper understanding of the intricacies that cannot be fully captured by quantitative data alone. Therefore, it is imperative for organizations to allocate resources toward the implementation of strategies aimed at gathering, examining, and incorporating qualitative data within their predictive analytics frameworks.

Furthermore, it is of utmost importance to cultivate empathy within the realm of data modeling practices. This entails adopting the perspective of customers, comprehending their sources of dissatisfaction, desires, and cultural contexts. By demonstrating empathy towards customers, data scientists and analysts have the ability to construct models that not only forecast behavior but also correspond with the values and requirements of customers. The current trend toward empathy requires a cultural transformation within organizations, highlighting the significance of customer-centricity across all levels.

In order to bolster the argument for the incorporation of human-centric training in the education of data scientists and analysts, it is imperative to conduct further research and examine real-world test cases. Research endeavors can explore the influence of human-centric methodologies on customer satisfaction, loyalty, and sustained business prosperity. The utilization of test cases and pilot programs can effectively illustrate the concrete advantages of adopting empathy and qualitative data within the realm of predictive analytics. These initiatives serve to showcase notable enhancements in marketing outcomes, a decrease in customer churn, and an overall improvement in brand reputation.

In the dynamic and ever-changing realm of data-driven environments, the transition from a solely data-centric approach to one that equally recognizes the humanistic dimensions of marketing is not merely an option, but rather an imperative. The aforementioned approach facilitates the establishment of authentic relationships, the cultivation of trust, and the prioritization of customer welfare. By engaging in continuous research and prioritizing training that focuses on human needs, organizations can guarantee that their practices of data modeling and decision-making are in accordance with these principles. Consequently, this will lead to a transformation of the marketing landscape, wherein a more empathetic and customer-centric approach is adopted, thereby reshaping the future of CRM strategy.

References

Agafonova, A. N., Yakhneeva, I. V., & Mukhametshina, G. R. (2020). Human-centric marketing in the digital era. Lecture Notes in Networks and Systems, 10–17. https://doi.org/10.1007/978-3-030-60929-0_2

Alam, M. M. D., & Noor, N. A. M. (2020). The relationship between service quality, corporate image, and customer loyalty of generation Y: An application of s-o-r paradigm in the context of superstores in Bangladesh. *SAGE Open*, 10(2), 215824402092440. https://doi.org/10.1177/2158244020924405

Chatterjee, S., Chaudhuri, R., & Vrontis, D. (2022). Big data analytics in strategic sales performance: Mediating role of CRM capability and moderating role of leadership support. *Euromed Journal of Business*, 17(3), 295–311. https://doi.org/10.1108/emjb-07-2021-0105

Chaudhary, K., Alam, M., Al-Rakhami, M. S., & Gumaei, A. (2021, May 25). Machine learning-based mathematical modelling for prediction of social media consumer behavior using big data analytics. *Journal of Big Data*. Springer Science+Business Media. https://doi.org/10.1186/s40537-021-00466-2

Khan, O. A., Asim, M., & Manzoor, S. (2021, June 30). Emotional intelligence: Conceptualisation and prediction of consumer decision making. *NICE Research Journal*. https://doi.org/10.51239/nrjss.vi.198

Khang, A., Gujrati, R., Uygun, H., Tailor, R. K., & Gaur, S. S. (2024). *Data-Driven Modelling and Predictive Analytics in Business and Finance* (1st Ed.). CRC Press. ISBN: 9781032600628. https://doi.org/10.1201/9781032600628

Khang, A., Inna, S.-O., Alla, K., Rostyslav, S., Rudenko, M., Lidia, R., & Kristina, B. (2024). Management model 6.0 and business recovery strategy of enterprises in the era of digital economy. In *Data-Driven Modelling and Predictive Analytics in Business and Finance* (1st Ed.). CRC Press. https://doi.org/10.1201/9781032600628-16

Khang, A., Muthmainnah, M., Seraj, P. M. I., Al Yakin, A., Obaid, A. J., & Panda, M. R. (2023). AI-aided teaching model for the education 5.0 ecosystem. In *AI-Based Technologies and Applications in the Era of the Metaverse* (1st Ed., pp. 83–104). IGI Global Press. https://doi.org/10.4018/978-1-6684-8851-5.ch004

Khang, A., Rath, K. C., Satapathy, S. K., Kumar, A., Das, S. R., & Panda, M. R. (2023). Enabling the future of manufacturing: Integration of robotics and IoT to smart factory infrastructure in industry 4.0. In *AI-Based Technologies and Applications in the Era of the Metaverse* (1st Ed., pp. 25–50). IGI Global Press. https://doi.org/10.4018/978-1-6684-8851-5.ch002

Khang, A., Shah, V., & Rani, S. (2023). *AI-Based Technologies and Applications in the Era of the Metaverse* (1st Ed.). IGI Global Press. https://doi.org/10.4018/978-1-6684-8851-5

Liu, H., Huang, Y., Wang, Z., Li, K., Hu, X., & Wang, W. (2019, May 15). Personality or value: A comparative study of psychographic segmentation based on an online review enhanced recommender system. *Applied Sciences*. Multidisciplinary Digital Publishing Institute. https://doi.org/10.3390/app9101992

Necula, S. C. (2023, May 23). Exploring the impact of time spent reading product information on E-Commerce websites: A machine learning approach to analyze consumer behavior. *Behavioral Sciences*. Multidisciplinary Digital Publishing Institute. https://doi.org/10.3390/bs13060439

Rai, P. (2018). A comprehensive study of CRM through data mining techniques. *International Journal for Research in Applied Science and Engineering Technology*, 6(4), 472–479. https://doi.org/10.22214/ijraset.2018.4082

Chapter 19

The Role of Enterprise Resource Planning (ERP) in Improving the Accounting Information System for Organizations

Md. Halimuzzaman and Jaideep Sharma

19.1 Introduction

Enterprise Resource Planning (ERP) systems are comprehensive and integrated information systems that can manage and integrate all the resources, information, and business activities in shared data stores. Since ERP systems can integrate business-based information into a single central database and allow that information to be retrieved from different organizational structures, they can improve accountants' ability to fulfill roles by giving managers access to relevant performance and real-time data in support of decision-making and administrative control (Samiei & Habibi, 2020).

ERP systems have many functions and features for data integration (internal and external data integration, easy retrieval, conversion, and uploading of data, unwanted and unrelated data removal, personal data of any level of management), prediction, and modeling (supports analytics used for predictable and decisive analysis using historical and real-time data, whether it is focused on quality or quantity) (Appelbaum et al., 2017).

ERP systems are generally divided into modules or sub-programs, such as sales, purchasing, financial, accounting, and human resource management (Al-Harthi & Saudagar, 2020). Financial

DOI: 10.4324/9781032688305-19

information systems are specialized modules in ERP accounting systems and embedding accounting systems that obtains financial information in the purchasing system, trading system, payment system, payment systems, etc. Although the information generated in the accounting information system can work well in the decision-making process, the purchase, installation, and use of such a system is beneficial if the benefits outweigh its costs (Chofreh et al., 2020).

With social and economic prosperity, advanced scientific and technological advancements, business competition under market pressure is also growing. ERP, as an advanced information management system, has been used in many businesses for real production management. The ERP system is built on information technology, based on strategic management thinking, through business processes, flow, financial flow, and information flow, to integrate overall balance and management efficiency and coordinate various management departments, focusing on market-focused business activities, thus developing the core business competition. This enables to achieve the best economic management system that incorporates the most advanced business management theory in the world, but also business knowledge which provides an important basis for decision-making. Therefore, instead of ERP, making full use of the internal accounting information to manage a business point, giving full play to ERP system activities, in business development, plays an important role. Thus accounting aims, as an information system, to provide various users with a variety of useful information to meet their different needs.

Therefore, accounting aims to take advantage of the environment in order to improve the quality and quantity of information and the delivery system to users. The relationship between accounting and computers began 60 years ago. This relationship continued to emerge and expanded in the 1980s and has continued to develop over the last eight decades due to the development of networks and decision-making systems, where it takes place in a broad and flexible process known as computerization of accounting. Recently, as a result, some accounting software has been developed to make it popular on the shelves (outside of stores) in order to reach more people who are interested in it at a reasonable cost.

On the other hand, although there are some organizations that prefer to improve their systems, either individually or professionally, many business organizations have recently embraced the use of comprehensive business plans consisting of a few sub-systems including an accounting system. These programs are known as the ERP program, which are characterized by providing integrated non-departmental outcomes and assisting them in improving the quality of their decisions and preparing comprehensive integrated plans (Brehm & Marx Gomez, 2010). This study focused on the main contributions of ERP in developing the different financial and non-financial activities of AIS.

19.2 Significance of the Study

The high costs associated with the transformation of business entities into the implementation of the Enterprise Resource Planning (ERP) program are studied. Staff and employee rehabilitation requirements, and their impact on working hours and performance of work and management systems and programs are also examined. The research focuses on the effectiveness of the accounting system in view of these changes. We recognize that such a system has significant implications for decision-making processes, whether internal or external, and its role in a competitive environment, asset protection, and confidentiality of functions and information security. This study is very important to way out the development of the accounting information system through the implementation of enterprise resource planning.

19.3 Objectives of the Study

In fact, there are many objectives to the Accounting Information System (AIS) through Enterprise Resource Planning (ERP). A few objectives of this study are the following:

(i) To obtain the results of the Accounting Information System using ERP.
(ii) To clarify the role of ERP in improving internal control of the accounting information systems.
(iii) To find out the organizational use of ERP in accounting information systems.

19.4 Limitations of the Study

The main limitations of this study by the researcher are as follows:

(i) Accounting information and financial data are highly confidential, so that the researcher cannot collect sufficient data.
(ii) The implementation of ERP is a costly affair, and that is why many organizations can incorporate it as a barrier to this study.
(iii) There may be a few errors due to lack of knowledge and research of the researcher.

19.5 Related Literature Review

There are many researchers such as Scapens and Jazayeri (2003); Spathis and Constantinides (2004); Nicolaou and Bhattacharya (2006), and Galani et al. (2010) who studied the relationship between (ERP) and the quality of accounting information. For example,Scapens and Jazayeri (2003) who aimed to identify the system as a result of the implementation of the ERP system in management accounting, especially after the widespread use of these systems, particularly in large companies. They indicated that there is a need to address the issue of ERP in the accounting literature. They explored the experience of the American system (SAP) and concluded that the implementation of the Enterprise Resources Planning (ERP) system decreases routine administrative functions, provides managers directly with useful information, and increases of the role of managerial accountants. They recommended further studies to be carried out on the application of the ERP system and managerial accounting.

Spathis and Constantinides (2004) studied the improvements offered by the ERP system for the process of accounting information in business and to identify the ways to develop ERP system therein in the future. They surveyed a sample of (26) Greek companies applying ERP system using a questionnaire. They used the mean and standard deviation to describe the collected data. They found that the ERP system improves the effectiveness of internal control in business organizations as well as improves the quality of accounting information and increases its reliability. It also encourages the managements towards improving their performance. The study recommended other companies to implement the ERP system because of its positive effects on the financial and administrative performance of companies.

Correspondingly, Nicolaou and Bhattacharya (2006) suggested that the successful adoption of information technology parameters would be beneficial to organizations, and the widespread ERP system would affect the various stages and steps of organizations' work process. They aimed to examine the impact of the adoption of the ERP system on the financial performance of companies. They used data for (247) US companies that applied the ERP system. They found that there is an improvement in companies' financial performance after two years of adopting ERP. He recommended that further research should be conducted in this area.

Wadi et al. (2021) found that Information technology (IT) has significantly impacted the accounting function in businesses, enabling them to access accounting and finance services from off-site locations, which is equally effective and accurate. IT has helped overcome barriers and limitations, allowing users to quickly access information in a more satisfactory way. The use of IT has transformed traditional paper-based accounting methods into electronic methods, improving the efficiency and effectiveness of the task.

Nicolaou and Bhattacharya (2006) aimed to examine the long-term financial performance as a result of changes in the ERP system. The results revealed that companies that implement ERP system showed early improvements in the financial performance more than others.

Jean-Baptiste (2009) focused on identifying the contributions of accountants in the process of implementing an ERP system in the post-implementation phase. A questionnaire was sent to a sample of 219 graduates of the Institute of Chartered Accountant Administrative Accounting of America. The study used frequencies and *t*-tests to test hypotheses besides linear regression analysis. He found that there is a positive relationship between the contribution of accountants, especially those with technical skills, and successful implementation of ERP.

Galani et al. (2010) also aimed to explain the effect of the ERP system on the Accounting Information System and the practices of administrative accounting through a field study carried out on a sample of Greek companies, from the perspective of users of the system. The results showed that the ERP system improves the quality of information and increases satisfaction with the management and users on the performance of their organization. The study also found that the ERP system improves the function of administrative accounting and thus the performance of management, increases their ability to take appropriate decisions, facilitates the proper application of new accounting practices, assists in reducing costs, establishes linkages with suppliers and reduces response time to customer needs.

AlBar et al. (2014) discussed the opportunities, challenges, emergence, implementation, and importance of using ERP inside the organization. Rahad et al. (2014) proposed a new method for accessing the ERP system regarding foreign network. Kabir (2020) evaluated the impact of ERP implementation on the productivity and profitability of BSRM Steels Limited. The study reveals that both the productivity and profitability of BSRM have significantly improved after ERP implementation.

Bagranoff and Brewer (2003) conducted a case study to conclude that implementation of the ERP could save an estimated $30 million annually for the company by reducing unnecessary inventory. Olhager and Selldin (2003) surveyed the use of ERP systems by Swedish manufacturing firms. They concluded that ERP maturity is high in those firms. Even though the ERP system does not reduce information technology costs, the system rapidly improved the availability and quality of information and integration and interactions throughout the firm.

Rao and Rao (2009) have reported that information technology, corporate processes, and information exchange significantly affect product turnover efficiency. Kallunki et al. (2011) said that the application of the ERP system leads to improved financial returns and management control system helps the firm achieve future performance goals than informal types.

Alzoubi (2012) found that integration of the Accounting Information System within ERP systems improves the quality of accounting results and internal controls in organizations. Firms adopting ERP systems are the result of their high performance as well. Samiei and Habibi (2020) found that ERP improves the information management process, internal and external business communications, and financial efficiency.

Nur D.P. and Irfan (2020) found that the use of high-quality accounting systems produces useful information. In addition, the implementation of Accounting Information Systems under ERP is related to user competence, satisfaction, and information sharing, which enhance personal skills that contribute to the higher performance of the organization.

Mardi et al. (2020) found that accounting systems and team performance positively and significantly affect the timely delivery of the financial reporting component, which is part of useful information. Agbani and Nadi (2020) found that the accounting system had a significant impact on profitability. It can help the organization plan and make far-reaching decisions that will help the organization gain a competitive advantage.

19.6 Research Method

The study focused on understanding the impact of ERP on the organization's accounting data processes and development. Based on the scope of the research to be evaluated, this type of research is a field of study to investigate whether there is no basis for evaluation of the impact of ERP implementation against a business. The type of data source in the survey is the basic data in the form data field obtained from surveys and direct reference to the data source. The data collection method was developed using open and in-depth interviews of experienced entrepreneurs before and after using the ERP.

19.7 Discussion

19.7.1 Enterprise Resource Planning (ERP)

ERP systems typically handle production processes, inventory, distribution, and accounting. This program helps to manage business activities such as sales, delivery, production, asset management, quality management, and human resources. Not only large companies can use ERP, SMEs can now use ERP-based systems (Romney et al., 2012). Small- and medium-sized businesses often have different ERP software requirements that require a complete yet competent and easy-to-use system. The need for great technology is inevitable. This is required for a data collection system, data analysis, and forecasting performance based on existing IT-based data (Khanh & Khang et al., 2021).

With the use of ERP, it will be possible to provide complete and detailed reports (sales, purchases, inventories), and so no manual report leads to the report being invalid and unreliable. For companies using ERP, it has been possible to change the flexible general system paradigm integrated into the use of information technology that integrates information that flows most smoothly at the departmental or organizational level. Typically, the ERP system provides a positive impact on user performance such as the number of tasks and the level of work in accordance with certain standards, job information and materials, regardless of his or her responsibility for company by creating solutions to problems arising from work, and fainting when completing his or her work.

Benefits of the use of ERP, inter alia: (1) the availability of financial data integration –; in ERP, all data are stored in one place, so that company executives can get the data up-to-date and better manage the financial company; (2) the presence of a standardization process – the ERP system uses standards, in which all sections use the system in the same way and in doing so, the company's operations will operate more efficiently and effectively; (3) the existence of a one-time data suspension information – the central website creates a data setup, so that information can be retrieved easily and flexibly at all stages within the company.

19.7.2 Accounting Information System (AIS)

The volatile impacts of using accounting systems by removing manual information systems in the private and public sectors cannot be overstated. The benefits of this change of set of procedures include increased mathematical accuracy, pre-defined fields and coding tasks, and emphasis on manual labor by harnessing staff expertise in data processing. Reporting can be done automatically, facilitating the ability to manage and remotely control and the growth of global businesses.

Potential damages are rarely addressed in an accurate, complete, and timely manner as information system vendors, management coordinators, and procurement companies run toward the most popular state of the art. The systems are fully integrated as continuous improvements in processing speed, performance, and power. Users of these automated systems may not consider the effects of large images and may not wisely consider the ethical risks to their businesses by focusing on that global reach and impact on senior management levels without providing adequate resources to ensure the accuracy, completeness, and timeliness of information systems.

19.7.3 Developments of Accounting Information Systems under ERP

Development of Accounting Information Systems under Enterprise Resource Planning (ERP) is defined as a computer-based system responsible for collecting transactions, files, records, and processing both financial and non-financial information from various ERP sub-systems, while sharing and communicating financial information that is collected from all users of the organization. Major firms have adopted ERP systems for linking and storing information, business processes, and resources. The integration of AIS and ERP leads to collaboration in the organization, which also increases the quality of decisions. The effectiveness of the use of accounting systems under ERP depends on the quality of the release of useful information that can meet the needs of users.

Typically, AIS under ERP provides daily and weekly financial reports and provides useful information for monitoring user decision-making processes. It helps a senior manager to see an operational vision across all segments, including managing production processes, products, and services to respond. But ERP systems have their disadvantages, which are their high costs. The implementation of accounting systems under the ERP provides the necessary accounting and financial information, both internal and external to users.

In particular, in the decision-making process, a well-designed accounting system provides useful information to managers in a timely manner. It helps management decision-making to be effective, timely, and accurate, plays a key role in fulfilling management accountability, and provides information on how to use resources and operations. Therefore, it can be concluded that there is a positive correlation between accounting information systems, performance, information quality, information usage, and decision-making quality.

19.7.4 Integration between AIS and ERP Systems

Connecting AIS to ERP systems is a calculated step for companies looking to improve the overall productivity and optimize workflows. While ERP systems cover a wider variety of organizational operations like HR, supply chain, and customer relationship management, AIS normally concentrates on financial transactions and reporting.

Whereas, ERP offers a comprehensive software package and is intended for internal users, ERP integrates financial and nonfinancial data, going beyond financial data like AIS does. It functions as a comprehensive platform that offers an all-encompassing method of managing organizational resources and operations by streamlining diverse business processes. AIS is essentially a focused instrument for financial data, whereas ERP is a more comprehensive solution that covers a range of business requirements. In fact, ERP is the integration of many assets into a business or company into an organization.

This encompassing integration not only streamlines operations but also unifies disparate aspects of an organization, fostering a seamless flow of information and augmenting overall efficiency. The Accounting/AIS component assumes the role of the conductor, organizing a unified financial narrative. AIS and ERP systems have merged, bringing financial data management into line with more general organizational procedures. This is a critical convergence. This smooth connection bridges the gap between specific accounting functions and the broader ERP architecture, enabling the real-time transmission of critical financial information.

Businesses may guarantee consistency and accuracy in financial reporting, expedite transactional procedures, and enable a comprehensive view of organizational resources by integrating AIS into the ERP environment. In addition to improving financial operations' efficiency, this integration helps the ERP system function more cohesively and effectively as a whole as a cohesive business solution.

19.7.5 Communication Obstacles

ERP eliminates the common barriers that exist between departments within a company. ERP is a common term used by this company to describe how each component of the organization works as a whole. Service fees are the end result of ERP for many organizations, is a complete reduction in operating costs, in addition, the price of information management used to generate business activity. With a single management plan, there is no need for special management systems to be maintained, so computer technology can have the ability to store all organizational requests

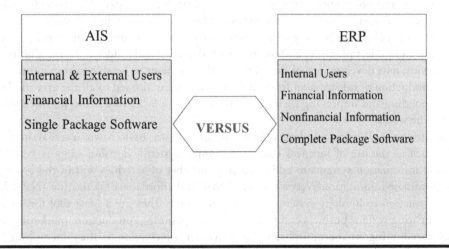

Figure 19.1   AIS versus ERP software.

Figure 19.2   Integration between AIS and ERP Systems

without having to learn about eight different software bundles. Additionally, power consumption is reduced because ERP systems may be server-based or perhaps preserved off the road by another party.

Information technology programs have made great strides. They can change the way information is collected, stored, processed, and distributed between internal and external organizations. Information technology plays a role in a variety of activities for communication purposes, problem solving, and project planning and management decisions (Adamides & Karacapilidis, 2020). There is continuous development of machinery and equipment to be able to respond to the support and production of information from such systems. It has also led to all the arts and business sectors responding and improving their operating systems in order to develop knowledge to keep pace with the world.

In addition, the business industry has developed many of its own internal information systems, such as the use of business resource planning systems, decision support systems, and accounting information systems to address a large number of activities within the organization and to coordinate information everywhere in a broad and affordable organization (Nabeeh et al., 2019), information technology systems are very important. They are a great tool for integrating and coordinating various business components, such as planning, production, marketing, human resources, accounting, finance, purchasing, etc., to share information on the same website. This is to support the efficient operation of the organization's business processes

19.8 Findings

The major findings of this research are as follows:

1. ERP systems are widely used by both large companies and small- and medium-sized businesses (SMEs) to manage various business activities such as production, inventory, distribution, accounting, sales, and human resources.
2. ERP systems provide several benefits, including financial data integration, standardization of processes, and centralized information access, which leads to improved efficiency and effectiveness in company operations.
3. AIS plays a crucial role in organizations by automating manual processes, increasing accuracy, facilitating reporting, and enabling remote control and management.
4. ERP encompasses a wider range of organizational processes, whereas AIS is primarily concerned with financial transactions. The integration ensures a smooth flow of information and harmonizes diverse corporate operations, much like a symphony. This connection improves financial reporting accuracy and efficiency and offers a complete picture of company resources. This crucial convergence turns AIS into a conductor directing a cohesive financial story within the larger ERP framework.
5. The effectiveness of accounting systems under ERP depends on the quality of information released and their ability to meet the needs of users. Well-designed accounting systems contribute to effective and accurate decision-making, resource utilization, and operational management.
6. ERP implementation involves integrating various assets and departments within an organization, leading to improved communication, simplified processes, and reduced operating costs.
7. Communication obstacles between departments can be overcome through the use of ERP systems, as they provide a unified platform for all organizational functions, eliminating the need for multiple software packages and enabling efficient information sharing.
8. Information technology plays a vital role in supporting and enhancing organizational processes, communication, problem-solving, and decision-making. Continuous developments in technology enable organizations to improve their information systems and keep pace with the changing business landscape.

19.9 Recommendations

Among the different recommendations, the exclusive recommendations are given as under: It would be helpful to include specific examples of widely used ERP systems and their adoption by both large companies and SMEs. This can add credibility to the statements and provide more context for the readers. While the statement mentions improved efficiency and effectiveness, it would be beneficial to elaborate on specific benefits such as streamlined operations, reduced costs, improved customer satisfaction, and better decision-making. When discussing ERP systems, it is essential to highlight the importance of data security and the measures taken to protect sensitive information. This can address concerns about potential risks associated with centralizing data within an ERP system and include limitations or challenges (Khang & Shah et al., 2023).

Acknowledge that ERP implementation can be complex and challenging, requiring careful planning, significant investments, and organizational change management. Discussing potential challenges, such as resistance from employees or the need for extensive training, provides a more comprehensive understanding of ERP system implementation. Mentioning the flexibility and scalability of ERP systems, highlighting their ability to adapt to specific business requirements and grow alongside the organization, can demonstrate that ERP systems are not a one-size-fits-all solution and can be tailored to meet unique business needs (Khang & Kali et al., 2023).

Expanding on the integration capabilities of ERP systems, not only with AIS but also with other software and systems used within an organization, can emphasize the potential for seamless data flow and collaboration across various departments and processes. It can provide insights into effective strategies for successful ERP implementation, such as conducting thorough needs analysis, involving key stakeholders throughout the process, setting realistic timelines, and ensuring adequate training and support for end-users.

Mentioning the importance of ongoing system maintenance, upgrades, and support services to ensure the long-term effectiveness of ERP systems can highlight the need for dedicated resources and partnerships with vendors or consultants to optimize system performance. Make sure that the ERP and AIS integrate seamlessly to create a well-balanced organizational process symphony that improves financial reporting accuracy and offers a comprehensive perspective of corporate resources. Imagine your AIS as the conductor, guiding the larger ERP structure while crafting a cogent financial story.

19.10 Conclusion

The information technology used in information systems is rapidly evolving; ERP (business resource planning) is a business-based information systems application that allows the integration of data contained across all existing units within the organization, thus enabling business organizations to make decisions more accurately and quickly. From the discussion that took place, it can be concluded that the ERP system and the business world cannot be separated because the ERP system will support and assist operations to improve accounting information systems, which provides benefits to the company end.

Based on the discussions, the conclusion of this study is that the execution of ERP in organizations has a very positive impact on the quality of accounting information. Emphasizing the flexibility and scalability of ERP systems, as well as their integration capabilities with other software and systems, showcases their adaptability and ability to meet unique business requirements. This helps readers understand that ERP systems can be tailored and integrated seamlessly within an organization. Insights into effective strategies for successful ERP implementation, such as needs analysis, involving key stakeholders, setting realistic timelines, and providing adequate training and support, offer valuable guidance to organizations considering or undergoing an ERP implementation.

Finally, highlighting the importance of ongoing system maintenance, upgrades, and support services emphasizes the need for dedicated resources and partnerships with vendors or consultants to ensure the long-term effectiveness of ERP systems (Khang & Muthmainnah et al., 2023).

References

Adamides, E., & Karacapilidis, N. (2020). Information technology for supporting the development and maintenance of open innovation capabilities. *Journal of Innovation & Knowledge*, 5(1), 29–38. https://doi.org/10.1016/j.jik.2018.07.001

Agbani, E., & Nnadi, C. S. O. (2020). *The Role of Accounting Information Systems on Organizational Performance (A Study of Nigerian Bottling Company, 9th Mile Corner, Enugu).* http://www.sgojahds .com/index.php/SGOJAHDS/article/view/62

AlBar, A. M., Hddas, M. A., & Hoque, M. R. (2014). Enterprise resource planning (ERP) systems: Emergence, importance and challenges. *The International Technology Management Review, 4*(4), 170–175. https://doi.org/10.2991/itmr.2014.4.4.1

Al-Harthi, N. J., & Saudagar, A. K. J. (2020). Drivers for successful implementation of ERP in Saudi Arabia public sector: A case study. *Journal of Information and Optimization Sciences, 41*(3), 779–798. https:// doi.org/10.1080/02522667.2019.1616909

Alzoubi, A. (2012). The effectiveness of the accounting information system under the Enterprise Resources Planning (ERP). *Research Journal of Finance and Accounting, 2*(11), 10–19. https://www.iiste.org/ Journals/index.php/RJFA/article/view/1289

Appelbaum, D., Kogan, A., Vasarhelyi, M., & Yan, Z. (2017). Impact of business analytics and enterprise systems on managerial accounting. *International Journal of Accounting Information Systems, 25*, 29–44. https://doi.org/10.1016/j.accinf.2017.03.003

Bagranoff, N. A., & Brewer, P. C. (2003). PMB investments: An enterprise system implementation. *Journal of Information Systems, 17*(1), 85. https://doi.org/10.2308/jis.2003.17.1.85

Brehm, N., & Marx Gomez, J. (2010). Federated ERP-systems on the basis of web services and P2P networks. *International Journal of Information Technology and Management, 9*(1), 75–89. https://doi.org /10.1504/IJITM.2010.029435

Chofreh, A. G., Goni, F. A., Klemeš, J. J., Malik, M. N., & Khan, H. H. (2020). Development of guidelines for the implementation of sustainable enterprise resource planning systems. *Journal of Cleaner Production, 244*, 118655. https://doi.org/10.1016/j.jclepro.2019.118655

Galani, D., Gravas, E., & Stavropoulos, A. (2010). The impact of ERP systems on accounting processes. *International Journal of Economics and Management Engineering, 4*(6), 774–779. chrome-extension:// efaidnbmnnnibpcajpcglclefindmkaj/https://publications.waset.org/14239/pdf

Jean-Baptiste, R. (2009). Can accountants bring a positive contribution to ERP implementation? *International Management Review, 5*(2), 81. https://www.proquest.com/openview/b582587a4cffa75 8f690b9468f81f653/1?pq-origsite=gscholar&cbl=28202

Kabir, M. R. (2020). Impact of ERP implementation on productivity and profitability: An empirical study on the largest Bangladeshi steels manufacturer. *International Journal of Entrepreneurial Research, 3*(4), Article 4. https://doi.org/10.31580/ijer.v3i4.1535

Kallunki, J.-P., Laitinen, E. K., & Silvola, H. (2011). Impact of enterprise resource planning systems on management control systems and firm performance. *International Journal of Accounting Information Systems, 12*(1), 20–39. https://doi.org/10.1016/j.accinf.2010.02.001

Khanh, H. H., & Khang, A. (2021). The role of artificial intelligence in blockchain applications. *Reinventing Manufacturing and Business Processes through Artificial Intelligence, 2*, 20–40. CRC Press. https://doi .org/10.1201/9781003145011-2

Khang, A., Shah, V., & Rani, S. (2023). *AI-Based Technologies and Applications in the Era of the Metaverse* (1st Ed.). IGI Global Press. https://doi.org/10.4018/978-1-6684-8851-5

Khang, A., Rath, K. C., Satapathy, S. K., Kumar, A., Das, S. R., & Panda, M. R. (2023). Enabling the future of manufacturing: Integration of robotics and IoT to smart factory infrastructure in industry 4.0. In *AI-Based Technologies and Applications in the Era of the Metaverse* (1st Ed., pp. 25–50). IGI Global Press. https://doi.org/10.4018/978-1-6684-8851-5.ch002

Khang, A., Muthmainnah, M., Seraj, P. M. I., Al Yakin, A., Obaid, A. J., & Panda, M. R. (2023). AI-aided teaching model for the education 5.0 ecosystem. In *AI-Based Technologies and Applications in the Era of the Metaverse* (1st Ed., pp. 83–104). IGI Global Press. https://doi.org/10.4018/978-1-6684-8851-5 .ch004

Mardi, M., Perdana, P. N., Suparno, S., & Munandar, I. A. (2020). Effect of accounting information systems, teamwork, and internal control on financial reporting timeliness. *The Journal of Asian Finance, Economics and Business, 7*(12), 809–818. https://www.dbpia.co.kr/Journal/articleDetail?nodeId =NODE10629577

Nabeeh, N. A., Abdel-Basset, M., El-Ghareeb, H. A., & Aboelfetouh, A. (2019). Neutrosophic multi-criteria decision making approach for IOT-based enterprises. *IEEE Access, 7*, 59559–59574. https://doi.org/10.1109/ACCESS.2019.2908919

Nicolaou, A. I., & Bhattacharya, S. (2006). Organizational performance effects of ERP systems usage: The impact of post-implementation changes. *International Journal of Accounting Information Systems, 7*(1), 18–35. https://doi.org/10.1016/j.accinf.2005.12.002

Nur, D. P. E., & Irfan, M. (2020). ERP-based accounting information system implementation in organization: A study in Riau, Indonesia. *The Journal of Asian Finance, Economics and Business, 7*(12), 147–157. https://doi.org/10.13106/JAFEB.2020.VOL7.NO12.147

Olhager, J., & Selldin, E. (2003). Enterprise resource planning survey of Swedish manufacturing firms. *European Journal of Operational Research, 146*(2), 365–373. https://doi.org/10.1016/S0377-2217(02)00555-6

Rahad, K. A., Ahmed, F., & Al Mamun, S. (2014). *A New Initiative for ERP System Architecture with Mobile Cloud Aspects of Bangladesh*, 1–4. https://doi.org/10.1109/ICEEICT.2014.6919146

Rao, C. M., & Rao, K. P. (2009). Inventory turnover ratio as a supply chain performance measure. *Serbian Journal of Management, 4*(1), 41–50. chrome-extension://efaidnbmnnnibpcajpcglclefindmkaj/https://www.sjm06.com/SJM%20ISSN1452-4864/4_1_2009_May_1-136/4_1_41-50.pdf

Romney, M., Steinbart, P., Mula, J., McNamara, R., & Tonkin, T. (2012). *Accounting Information Systems Australasian Edition.* Pearson Higher Education AU. https://books.google.com.bd/books?id=FhTiBAAAQBAJ&printsec=frontcover#v=onepage&q&f=false

Samiei, E., & Habibi, J. (2020). The mutual relation between enterprise resource planning and knowledge management: A review. *Global Journal of Flexible Systems Management, 21*, 53–66. https://link.springer.com/article/10.1007/s40171-019-00229-2

Scapens, R. W., & Jazayeri, M. (2003). ERP systems and management accounting change: Opportunities or impacts? A research note. *European Accounting Review, 12*(1), 201–233. https://doi.org/10.1080/0963818031000087907

Spathis, C., & Constantinides, S. (2004). Enterprise resource planning systems' impact on accounting processes. *Business Process Management Journal, 10*(2), 234–247. https://doi.org/10.1108/14637150410530280

Wadi, R. M. A., Kukreja, G., & Jaber, R. J. (2021b). The role of information technology in accounting: Literature review. In B. Alareeni, A. Hamdan, & I. Elgedawy (Eds.), *The Importance of New Technologies and Entrepreneurship in Business Development: In the Context of Economic Diversity in Developing Countries* (pp. 822–829). Springer International Publishing. https://doi.org/10.1007/978-3-030-69221-6_63

Chapter 20

Opportunities, Issues, and Challenges of Cloud Computing: A Business Perspective

Adnan Raza and Sathish P.

20.1 Introduction

An array of interconnected, virtualized computers that are dynamically provisioned and presented as one or more unified computing resources according to Service-Level Agreements (SLAs) negotiated between the service provider and customers makes up the parallel, distributed computing system known as cloud computing (Leimeister et al., 2020). The corporation has made a significantly larger investment in genuine physical infrastructure than it has in the cloud. The statist's portal estimates that close to 75% population will be cloud users worldwide in 2025. These statistical findings unequivocally demonstrate the exponential growth of cloud computing technology and its impending dominance of the information technology industry. Due to this technology's explosive growth, every sort of organization should be aware of the wave that is fundamentally shaking the entire sector (Bo, 2018). The company is constantly strongly impacted by cloud computing. Its internal organization, particularly the IT sector, is affected by this technology in addition to its overall performance. The standard techniques for data backup are being improved by this technology. For the business adopting it, cloud computing is introducing fresh approaches and resources (Baciu, 2015).

Although Google Cloud, Microsoft Azure, and Amazon Web Services are all significant public cloud providers and are thus reachable via web browsers, using them is not a requirement for adopting cloud computing. Additionally, "Hybrid clouds" combine the management and security of a private cloud with the bigger scale of a public cloud, as well as "private clouds" that only one organization may access. Cloud computing software can improve the efficiency of your company's

DOI: 10.4324/9781032688305-20

or organization's internal data center if it already has one. Consumer Packaged Goods (CPG) corporations and Small and Medium-Sized businesses (SMEs) both use the cloud to a similar extent – 47% and 46%, respectively.

The purpose of this study is to emphasize the beneficial effects of cloud computing on companies. Companies are encountering some difficulties and security concerns as they transition to this technology, and it is important to recognize and communicate these difficulties in order to improve the planning and strategy (Mastering Cloud Computing, n.d.), (Ahirwar & Parihar, 2021).

20.2 Opportunities of Cloud Computing in Business Organizations

Cloud computing benefits commercial organizations by boosting their revenue and assisting them in achieving their objectives. Instead of developing their own infrastructure, businesses would rather use the cloud's services. The advantages of cloud computing technologies that encourage commercial organizations to go from local infrastructure to the cloud are depicted in Figure 20.2.

20.2.1 Reduced IT Costs

Because resources are only purchased when necessary and used, and because there is no upfront investment with cloud computing, the costs of the business are reduced. The infrastructure is not

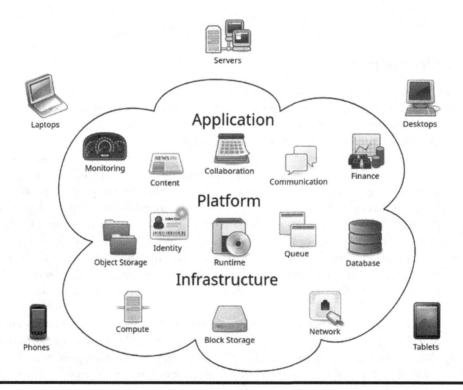

Figure 20.1   Architecture of Cloud Computing (Khan & Nawsher et al., 2012).

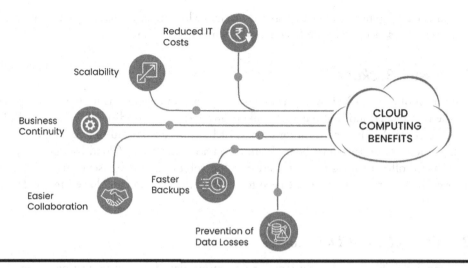

Figure 20.2 Cloud computing benefits (ESDS 2020).

purchased, which lowers the startup costs as well as ongoing maintenance costs. Although they can use cloud services online, they are not the proprietors of the infrastructure (Bhopale, n.d.), (Iwona & Stefana, 2014), (Ankey, 2011), (THBS, 2018).

20.2.2 Unlimited Scalability

The main advantage of cloud computing is that clients can scale up or down according to the demands of the organization. Companies don't have to worry about upcoming demands because they can easily get more services at any moment. Additionally, if a firm expands over time, the cloud can easily scale to meet the rising demand (Lakshmi, 2014), (Huth, 2011), (Cloud Computing Challenges, n.d.), (Opara-Martins et al., 2016).

20.2.3 Essential Business Continuity

Business continuity is a critical component of any modern organization's strategy for ensuring continuous operations, particularly during disruptive occurrences. Cloud computing has numerous advantages that dramatically improve business continuity. One of the most significant advantages is data redundancy and backup. Cloud platforms spread data across numerous geographically diverse data centers, lowering the risk of data loss and allowing for rapid recovery in the event of a disaster.

20.2.4 Easier Collaboration

Cloud computing has transformed how teams interact, providing various advantages that make collaboration easier and more successful. One of the most significant benefits is real-time access to shared documents and data. Cloud-based collaboration solutions allow team members to collaborate on the same document at the same time, removing the need for time-consuming email attachments and difficulties with version control difficulties. Because updates are instantaneously accessible to all team members, regardless of their location, this promotes seamless cooperation.

Furthermore, cloud solutions offer centralized storage, which ensures that everyone has access to the most recent files, decreasing confusion and optimizing operations.

20.2.5 Faster Backups

The utilization of cloud-based storage is one of the principal benefits, as it allows enterprises to offload the cost of maintaining physical backup infrastructure. Traditional backup techniques frequently include the time-consuming process of backing up data to physical tapes or disks, which is prone to error and must be maintained on a regular basis. Cloud backup services, on the other hand, offer a fully automatic and seamless solution. Data are sent directly to remote servers over the Internet, removing the need for manual intervention and lowering the danger of human errors.

20.2.6 Prevention of Data Losses

Cloud technology offers strong solutions for preventing data loss and protecting organizations from the catastrophic consequences of data breaches and disasters. One of the most important advantages is the data redundancy and backup capabilities provided by credible cloud providers. Cloud platforms distribute data across numerous geographically diverse data centers, ensuring that data remains accessible from other locations even if one location experiences an outage or hardware failure. Backups are frequently made automatically and on a regular basis, avoiding the danger of losing crucial information due to inadvertent deletions or system failures (Khang & Abuzarova et al., 2023).

20.3 Security Issues of Cloud Computing in Business Organizations

The use of cloud technology has grown to be an integral part of contemporary business operations due to its flexibility, scalability, and cost-effectiveness. However, because of its extensive adoption, enterprises now face a number of security issues. Additionally, since cloud service providers are in charge of data management, questions concerning data ownership and control have arisen (Khang & Vladimir, 2022).

20.3.1 Web Association Breakdowns

Some of the main cloud security issues that can have a big impact on enterprises and organizations are the failure of web associations. The communication links between users or clients and cloud-based services are disrupted in these breakdowns. Such breakdowns can arise due to various reasons, and they can pose serious risks to data security and business continuity (Pai & Aithal, 2016).

20.3.2 Concerns about the Loss of Control over Sensitive Data

The loss of control over sensitive data is one of the main issues with cloud security. Businesses that use the cloud to store their data are essentially losing control over that data to the cloud service provider. Businesses that handle sensitive data, including financial information or Consumer

Personally Identifiable Information (Consumer PII), may have issues with this (Pai & Aithal, 2016).

20.3.3 Lack of Underlying Cloud Infrastructure Details

The fact that users are unable to acquire information about the underlying cloud architecture is a major worry. Cloud service providers frequently abstract the infrastructure, making it difficult for clients to fully understand and control the underlying architecture of their data and applications. The provider's security procedures and the precise site of data storage may be unknown as a result of this lack of transparency. So, organizations can find it difficult to evaluate their risk exposure and ensure that they are adhering to any industry-specific rules or data sovereignty obligations (Pai & Aithal, 2016).

20.3.4 Lack of Data Replication Mechanisms at Various Geographic Locations

Data are frequently stored in several data centers or geographical locations in a cloud environment. However, there is a higher risk of data loss due to hardware malfunctions, natural catastrophes, or cyberattacks directed at certain data centers if a cloud provider does not put strong data replication procedures in place. A single point of failure can result in the irreversible loss of crucial data if there is insufficient replication, which could disrupt corporate operations and result in losses (Pai & Aithal, 2016).

20.4 Challenges of Cloud Security in Business Organizations

20.4.1 Multi-level Tenancy

Users can access a variety of cloud applications via the Internet, from small Internet-based widgets to large enterprise software applications, each of which has different security requirements depending on the kind of data being stored on the infrastructure of the software vendor. The main factor driving the need for multi-tenancy in these application requests is cost. Multiple users of the same hardware, application servers, and databases may have an impact on other users'

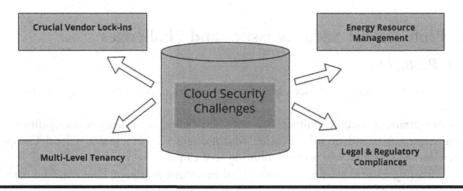

Figure 20.3   Cloud security challenges.

performance and response times. Resources are shared at each infrastructure tier for application-layer multi-tenancy, raising legitimate security and performance issues. The number of connections to an HTTP server has been reached. Therefore, the service must wait for a connection to become available or, in the worst-case scenario, drop the service request. Other examples include multiple service requests accessing resources at once increasing wait times but not necessarily CPU time (Padhy et al., 2011).

20.4.2 Energy Resource Management

It has become a major priority to design energy-efficient data centers in order to cut energy expenses as well as to adhere to regulations and environmental norms. Traditional data centers have struggled with severe energy consumption issues as the demand for data processing and storage grows tremendously. Furthermore, the dynamic workloads and fluctuating demand patterns associated with cloud computing make it difficult to deploy energy resources effectively (Padhy et al., 2011).

20.4.3 Crucial Vendor Lock-ins

In a vendor lock-in, a customer who wishes to switch vendors must pay the cost of doing so. Despite several initiatives like open systems and platform-independent languages, vendor lock-in has been observed in every technology up to this point. When a business is locked into a particular cloud vendor, it may face limited flexibility and bargaining power, as well as potential challenges in adapting to changing business needs or emerging technologies (Dar, 2018).

20.4.4 Legal and Regulatory Compliances

The adherence to legal and regulatory requirements in relation to business continuity is an essential element of the challenges pertaining to cloud security that organizations need to confront when embracing cloud services. As an illustration, healthcare organizations are obligated to adhere to regulations such as the Health Insurance Portability and Accountability Act (HIPAA) in order to ensure the protection of patients' sensitive data (Khang & Rana et al., 2023). Similarly, financial institutions are required to comply with the Gramm-Leach-Bliley Act (GLBA) in order to safeguard financial information. Noncompliance with these regulations may lead to legal obligations, substantial financial penalties, and damage to business organization goals (Dar, 2018).

20.5 Protocols for Security Issues and Challenges

20.5.1 Protocol 1

Determine the Root Cause: Conduct a thorough investigation to determine why web associations are failing.

Misconfigurations, network difficulties, software faults, or security vulnerabilities are all common causes. A Cloud Security Posture Management (CSPM) tool, a Cloud Compliance Management (CCM) tool, and a cloud auditing tool can also help you identify and remediate security misconfigurations, ensure that your cloud environment is compliant with industry regulations, and track and record all activity in your cloud environment.

20.5.2 Protocol 2

Establish reliable monitoring and logging procedures. Cloud settings create massive amounts of log data, which can be used to gain insight into security events and potential threats. Organizations can gain visibility into their cloud infrastructure's activities and discover suspicious behavior quickly by employing advanced monitoring technologies and integrating centralized logging systems.

20.5.3 Protocol 3

Based on business demands and regulatory restrictions, select appropriate geographic sites for data replication. Choose geographically diverse locations to limit the possibility of regional disasters affecting all copies of the data at the same time. Drills and simulated scenarios are used to test the data replication systems and disaster recovery processes on a regular basis. This will aid in identifying potential flaws and holes, allowing firms to fine-tune their strategies and guarantee data recovery objectives are reached in the event of a true disaster (Khang & Medicine, 2023).

20.5.4 Protocol 4

Create detailed Service-Level Agreements (SLAs) with cloud providers. Check that the SLAs cover data ownership, data privacy, security measures, and compliance. If service levels are not met, clear and well-defined SLAs can hold cloud vendors accountable and provide enterprises with legal redress. Negotiate shorter contract terms and avoid tying the company up in long-term contracts with automatic renewals. Contracts with shorter periods permit reevaluation and allow the firm to react to shifting technology trends or business demands.

20.6 Results and Discussion

According to the findings of Vaikunth Pai and Aithal (2016), since the detected opportunities were insufficient from the perspective of the business continuity, the described critical opportunity leads to inappropriate operation of the cloud service. Furthermore, a premature cloud rollout may result in inadequate planning and integration with current systems, which can result in concerns with interoperability, data fragmentation, and operational inefficiencies. In the long run, these issues can stymie company processes, restrict productivity, and result in increased downtime, threatening business continuity.

As in Figure 20.4, the findings were that the key security issue which affected the business growth was loss of control over data. The loss of essential data can cause delays, lost productivity, and missed opportunities in normal corporate operations. Furthermore, in industries with stringent data protection rules, such instances might result in noncompliance, subjecting the firm to fines and legal consequences. Intellectual property theft as a result of a data breach can rob a company of its competitive advantage, stifling innovation and long-term growth. To address this, we developed the essential standards that would improve not only the organization's security but also the detailed business continuity of each and every milestone (Sharma, 2014).

Recently, according to a report titled "Data Protection Trends 2020," many firms are still struggling to complete the digital transformation process due to out-of-date data protection solutions. The economic crisis has made enterprises aware of the need to develop and adopt new

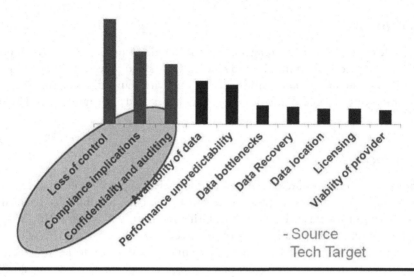

Figure 20.4 Loss of control of data (Sharma et al., 2014).

Table 20.1 Different Aspects which Impacts the Security Issues and Challenges

Aspect	Percentage / Duration	Impact
Companies using legacy systems	40%	Vulnerability to cyber threats
System outages duration	Approximately 2 hours (117 minutes)	Economic losses

paradigms in their working methods. Smart working systems and cloud apps are necessary, but they unavoidably expose organizations to new cyber dangers as the attack surface has expanded, as shown in Table 20.1.

According to the data in Table 20.1, companies face a number of threats when utilizing legacy systems. In order to achieve their business growth objectives, organizations prefer cloud services with good, reliable opportunities that will benefit the overall business milestones and eliminate the mitigation of security issues and challenges over the long term.

The use of those mentioned protocols would significantly reduce the ongoing business issues, which would have a significant impact on cloud markets and would also compel customers to store their confidential, critical, and sensitive data without risk.

20.7 Conclusion

This chapter describes the overall opportunities provided for significant benefits to commercial organizations, leading to increased revenue and successful achievement of their objectives. Businesses can streamline their operations, optimize resource utilization, and deliver enhanced services to their customers. It elucidates different security issues and challenges that trigger the business continuity while emphasizing the need for effective security measures in guaranteeing continued operations. The reality is clear that a one-size-fits-all security approach is insufficient and enterprises must implement a multi-layered, proactive strategy to successfully protect their cloud systems (Khang & Kali et al., 2023).

In this chapter, we have discussed a few security protocols ranging from root cause analysis to negotiating the different Service-Level Agreements (SLAs) that will reduce the overall financial crises and promote business growth. Both cloud security providers and consumers can benefit from a mutually beneficial cooperation by adhering to a set of protocols that prioritize proactive security measures, compliance, and open communication. They can work together to construct a secure and stable cloud-computing environment that allows for smooth company operations, improves data security, and fosters confidence among customers and stakeholders (Khang & Shah et al., 2023).

References

Ankey, J. (2011). Heads in the cloud. *Entrepreneur*, 39, 50–51. https://academic.oup.com/spp/article-abstract/39/2/258/1616224.

Baciu, I. E. (2015). Advantages and disadvantages of cloud computing services, from the employee's point of view. *National Strategies Observer*, 1(2). Available at SSRN: https://ssrn.com/abstract=2787612.

Bhpale, S. D. (n.d.). Cloud migration benefits and its challenges issue – IOSR journals. https://iosrjournals.org/iosr-jce/papers/sicete-volume1/8.pdf.

Bo, K. S. (2018). Cloud computing for business. *International Journal of Advances in Scientific Research and Engineering (IJASRE)*, 4(7), July, 156–160. ISSN: 2454-8006. https://doi.org/10.31695/IJASRE.2018.32816.

Dar, A. (2018). Cloud computing-positive impacts and challenges in business perspective. *Journal of Computer Science & Systems Biology*, 12. https://doi.org/10.4172/jcsb.1000294.

Devasena, L. (2014). Impact study of cloud computing on business development. *Operations Research and Applications: An International Journal (ORAJ)*, 1, 1. https://www.academia.edu/download/38205543/Final_1.pdf.

Huth, A., & Cebula, J. (2011). The basics of cloud computing | semantic scholar. https://www.semantic-scholar.org/paper/The-Basics-of-Cloud-Computing-Huth-Cebula/ccd479e42ec0f007deda15445bc1ccc2e33dedb4.

IRACST. (2011). International Journal of Computer Science and Information Technology & Security (IJCSITS), 1(2), December. https://ijsrcseit.com/CSEIT2282108.

Iwona, M. W., & Stefana, C. I. (2014). Cloud computing drives innovation. https://projekter.aau.dk/projekter/files/207512928/4.4_Cloud_Computing.pdf.

Khang, A. (2023). *AI and IoT-Based Technologies for Precision Medicine* (1st Ed.). IGI Global Press. ISBN: 9798369308769. https://doi.org/10.4018/979-8-3693-0876-9.

Khang, A., Abdullayev, V. A., Alyar, A. V., Khalilov, M., & Murad, B. (2023). AI-aided data analytics tools and applications for the healthcare sector. *AI and IoT-Based Technologies for Precision Medicine* (1st Ed.). IGI Global Press. ISBN: 9798369308769. https://doi.org/10.4018/979-8-3693-0876-9.ch018.

Khang, A., Hahanov, V., Abbas, G. L., & Hajimahmud, V. A. (2022). Cyber-physical-social system and incident management. *AI-Centric Smart City Ecosystems: Technologies, Design and Implementation* (1st Ed.), 7 (12). CRC Press. https://doi.org/10.1201/9781003252542-2.

Khang, A., Rana, G., Tailor, R. K., & Hajimahmud, V. A. (2023). *Data-Centric AI Solutions and Emerging Technologies in the Healthcare Ecosystem* (1st Ed.). CRC Press. https://doi.org/10.1201/9781003356189.

Khang, A., Rath, K. C., Satapathy, S. K., Kumar, A., Das, S. R., & Panda, M. R. (2023). Enabling the future of manufacturing: Integration of robotics and IoT to smart factory infrastructure in industry 4.0. *AI-Based Technologies and Applications in the Era of the Metaverse* (1st Ed.). IGI Global Press, 25–50. https://doi.org/10.4018/978-1-6684-8851-5.ch002.

Khang, A., Shah, V., & Rani, S. (2023). *AI-Based Technologies and Applications in the Era of the Metaverse* (1st Ed.). IGI Global Press. https://doi.org/10.4018/978-1-6684-8851-5.

Leimeister, S., Böhm, M., Riedl, C., & Krcmar, H. (2010). The business perspective of cloud computing: Actors, roles and value networks. European Conference on Information Systems. https://aisel.aisnet.org/ecis2010/56/.

Opara-Martins, J., Sahandi, R., & Tian, F. (2016). Critical analysis of vendor lock-in and its impact on cloud computing migration: a business perspective. *Journal of Cloud Computing*, 5. https://doi.org/10.1186/s13677-016-0054-z.

Sharma, S., Gupta, G., & Laxmi, P. R. (2014). A survey on cloud security issues and techniques. ArXiv, abs/1403.5627.

THBS. (2018). Cloud computing overview. https://www.thbs.com/thbs-insights/cloud-computing-overview.

Tutorials Point. (2018). Cloud computing: Cloud computing challenges. https://www.tutorialspoint.com/cloud_computing/cloud_computing_challenges.htm.

Vaikunth Pai, T., & Aithal, P. S. (2016). Cloud computing security issues – Challenges and opportunities. *International Journal of Management, Technology and Social Sciences (IJMTS)*, 1(1), 33–42. http://dx.doi.org/10.47992/IJMTS.2581.6012.0004.

Yimam, D., & Fernández, E. (2016). A survey of compliance issues in cloud computing. *Journal of Internet Services and Applications*, 7. https://doi.org/10.1186/s13174-016-0046-8.

Chapter 21

Detecting Fake News on Social and Collaboration Networks Using Python and Machine Learning

Sonam Gour and Alex Khang

21.1 Introduction

This project creates programs using Natural Language Processing (NLP) approaches for identifying "Fake information," or false news stories that originate from unreliable sources. This can easily be done by building a model based mostly on a matter vectorizer (the usage of word tallies) or a Term Frequency Inverse Document Frequency (TF-IDF) matrix, which both use phrase tallies relative to how frequently they are used in different articles for your dataset. However, these trends do not ignore important characteristics like sentence arrangement and context. It is highly likely that articles with comparable phrase counts will have entirely different meanings.

The information technology network has responded by combating the issue. Facebook is employing AI to weed out phony news reports from users' feeds, and there may be a Kaggle challenge named the "fake information mission." The traditional textual content categorization mission with a reliable proposition is combating fake news (Trump and Libel, 2017). Is it possible to build a model which could differentiate between "real" news and "Fake" information? So, the proposed work is on assembling a dataset of fake and real information and renting a Naive Bayes classifier to create a model that can classify an article into fake or actual based on its words and phrases (Abdullah et al., 2019).

21.2 Related Work

21.2.1 A Top-level View and Comparative Examination of AI Equipment for Fake Information Detection

This chapter studied Artificial Intelligence (AI) tools for fake information identification using Machine Learning (ML) methods, NLP, and other techniques. Assessments are given based only on keywords: False information, device learning, NLP, datasets. Datasets are subjected to device learning techniques such as Nave Bayes, Bayes networks, neural communities, and several classifiers. Calculations for precision, accuracy, clarity, and various other aspects use results of the kind (realistic or spectacular, truthful, or deceptive, etc.).

21.2.2 Detecting Fake News Using Machine Learning

Supervised Machine Learning classifiers that require labeled records for training are discussed. Labeled records are not always readily available and may be used to train classifiers to detect fake news. In the future, studies can also focus on using unsupervised Machine Learning classifiers to detect fake news (Nation and Snowling et al., 2007).

There is a need to identify fake information; device mastering classifiers are used for numerous functions and can also be used to detect fake news. Classifiers are first trained using a dataset known as the training dataset. These classifiers can automatically detect fake messages, so the education dataset that is passed to these classifiers must include only relevant information.

21.2.3 Data Pre-processing and Data Cleaning

Supervised Machine Learning classifiers that require labeled data for training are mentioned. Labeled data are not quite simply available and may be used to train classifiers to detect fake news. Future studies may also focus on the usage of unsupervised Machine Learning classifiers to detect fake information (Wei and Ye et al., 2020).

There may be a need to etect fake news. System collecting knowledge of classifiers is used for various purposes and can also be used to detect fake news. Classifiers are first trained using a dataset called the education dataset. These classifiers can then automatically detect false positives, so the training dataset that is passed to those classifiers should contain only valuable data.

21.2.4 The State of the Art, Current Trends, and Challenges in Natural Language Processing

Natural Language Processing (NLP) is an interdisciplinary subfield of computer science and linguistics has recently attracted a lot of attention for the computational representation and assessment of human discourse (Abbad and Kumar et al., 2021). Its uses have been broadened to include device translation, email spam detection, statistics extraction, summarization, medical, and question answering, among others. Third, the item separates four stages of discussion on various stages of NLP and additions to the Natural Language Era (NLG), along with a presentation of the development and history of contemporary characteristics and challenging situations (Khang and Abuzarova et al., 2023).

21.2.5 Fake News Detection on Social Media: A Data Mining Process

The subsequent elements make it difficult to resolve the detection of fake news:

- Formal definition and method of the trouble are important and are required prior to reading the fake news detection problem that is a brand new studies hassle which is the subject of this chapter (Sharma and Rai et al., 2022).
- Use of textual information from the social media, a collection of textual statistics about the profiles, descriptions, and contents of the information articles, creators, and subjects may be received. A green function extraction and learning method is required to capture indicators revealing their reliability.
- Fusion of heterogeneous information, the authorship and article–situation relationships among them also function as indicators of the credibility labels of information articles, authors, and subjects that have enormously strong correlations.

21.2.6 Fake Detector: Effective Fake News Detection with Deep Diffusive Neural Network

The call for detection and intervention of fake news has multiplied because of fake information's explosive boom and the damage it does to democracy, justice, and public beliefs. Based on the assessment, the survey also shows some potential study initiatives. To sell interdisciplinary research on fake news, we specially discover and describe associated essential theories throughout diverse disciplines. We hope that this survey will encourage collaboration among experts in journalism, political science, social sciences, and computer and records sciences to study fake information so that inexperienced and, more importantly, understandable fake information detection can be accomplished.

21.2.7 Fake News Detection Using Machine Learning Approaches

Making use of natural language processing is often done to adhere to one or more sets of rules or system specializations. Speech understanding and speech generation can be combined using an algorithmic gadget's Natural Language Processing (NLP) score. There are two main categories for data-mining techniques: Supervised and unsupervised. A class of algorithms called Machine Learning (ML) allows software systems to achieve more correct consequences while not having to directly reprogram them.

21.2.8 Fake News Detection in Social Media

Linguistic cue techniques: In linguistic cue strategies, researchers study various communicative behaviors to discover deception. Consistent with researchers, liars and truth-tellers communicate in numerous ways. In text-based communication, liars often use more words than do reality-tellers. Community analysis tools, on the other hand, are wholly content-based approaches that rely on verbal clues to anticipate deceit. The community analysis strategy differs from the linguistic approach in that it requires "a current body of collective human understanding to evaluate the actuality of newest claims."

21.2.9 A Survey of Fake News: Fundamental Theories, Detection Methods, and Opportunities

The explosive increase in fake news and its erosion of democracy, justice, and public beliefs have accelerated the call for fake news detection and intervention. The survey additionally highlights some research responsibilities based on the evaluation. We discover and detail relevant fundamental theories across various disciplines to encourage interdisciplinary research on fake information. It is our hope that this survey can facilitate collaborative efforts among experts in computer and records sciences, social sciences, political science, and journalism to analyze fake news, where such efforts can result in fake news detection that is not only efficient but, greater importantly, explainable.

21.2.10 Fake News Detection

The accuracy of information on the Internet and on social media is a concern of increasing importance, but web-scale information hampers the capacity to become aware of, examine, and correct such statistics, or so referred to as "fake information," found in these systems. In this chapter, we propose a method for the detection of "Fake information" and methods to use it on Facebook, one of the most popular online social media platforms. This method uses a Naive Bayes class model to predict whether the publication on Facebook could be labeled as actual or fake. The results can be improved by using various strategies that are discussed in the chapter. Acquired results suggest that fake news detection problem can be addressed with Machine Learning methods.

21.2.11 Fake News Detection Using Machine Learning Approaches

Fake news on social media and various other media is widely spreading and is an issue of concern across nations as it causes damage with adverse influences. This chapter analyzes the studies associated with detection of fake news and explores the traditional Machine Learning models to pick out the best which can classify fake news as genuine or fake, by using languages like Python scikit-research. This technique will result in feature extraction and vectorization; we recommend the use of Python scikit-research library to perform tokenization and feature extraction of text data, because this library contains useful gear-like CountVectorizer and TF-IDF Vectorizer

21.2.12 Raising a Model for Fake News Detection Using Machine Learning in Python

Fake news has grown in popularity and has sped up the transmission of false information. The 2016 US presidential election is one of the most glaring examples of this trend. Before the vote, a lot of false reports were shared that enhanced Donald Trump's image over Hillary Clinton (Singh et al. n.d.). Because there is so much false information, it becomes necessary to use computational tools to identify it. As a result, it is suggested to identify false news in public information sets using algorithms of device learning like "CountVectorizer," "TF-IDF Vectorizer," a Naive Bayes model, and Natural Language Processing.

21.2.13 A Predominant Advent into Fake News Detection Using Machine Learning Algorithm

Fake news is written intentionally to force the target market to simply accept deceptive facts. Because of this, we want helping information including usage of social media interactions on social media to resource choice making.

Customers' social experiences with fake information generate copious amounts of unreliable, amorphous, and noisy data, and exploiting this ancillary information is itself motivating. As a result, detecting fake information on social media has become a new studies subject matter. Fake information monitoring on social media has many different signs and characteristics, making vintage identification algorithms unreliable or obsolete.

21.2.14 Fake News Detection on Social Media

Fake articles, misleading news, and lies existed earlier than the net. A widely identified description of an Internet fake or fake news is a misleading article created to mislead the reader. This will be the most moving article in terms of most viewedaside from the typical ones read by people.

21.2.15 Online-based Content Utilizing a Classification Technique to Spot Fake News

This work uses a non-fiction database to illustrate the usage of a device studying model, Scikit-learn, a library in Python. Information has been extracted from the database. This consists of the use of the textual content example mode, in addition to phrase bag, inverse file frequency for term frequency, and bigram frequency. The bigram frequency model becomes a good deal less accurate in topic separation compared to the dictionary and its TF-IDF.

21.2.16 Identification of True and False News

Inside the fake information detection assignment, we built a version which could decide whether news is fake or not. Using this version enhances the accuracy of the facts in society. At the start of the work, the version was created using TensorFlow. Then, I trained a model with a loss function and an optimizer. Ultimately, a plot of accuracy versus lost time was produced to efficiently evaluate the model. Subsequently a newmodel was arrived at that you can use to assess whether your message is fake.

21.3 Machine Learning

Machine Learning (ML) is a branch of Artificial Intelligence (AI) that allows computers to "analyse by themselves" from training data and improve it over the years without being explicitly programmed. Machine Learning algorithms can understand patterns in records and learn to make their own predictions from them. In other words, systems getting to know algorithms and models learn through experience. In traditional programming, computer engineers write a sequence of instructions that teach the computer to transform input data right into a desired output.

Statements are based totally on their IF–THEN shape. If certain situations are met, this system will carry out certain moves. Machine Learning, on the other hand, is an automated process that allows machines to solve problems with little human input and act based on past observations. Artificial Intelligence and Machine Learning are often used interchangeably; however, they are distinct concepts. Artificial Intelligence is a broader concept in which machines make decisions, analyze new skills, and solve problems in an analogous manner to human beings, but Machine Learning is a subset of Artificial Intelligence in which smart structures learn new things from data and can be found out autonomously.

21.4 Natural Language Processing (NLP)

Making computer systems recognize natural language is the core of Natural Language Processing. But that is not always an easy task. It is possible for computers to understand structured data like spreadsheets and database tables, but unstructured data like human languages, texts, and voices are more challenging for computers to understand, necessitating the use of Natural Language Processing (Gupta and Kumar et al., 2021).

There are loads of natural language statistics available in numerous articles, and it would be extremely easy if computers could understand and process that information. We can update on the changing trends according to the predicted output in various approaches available. Human beings have been writing for numerous years and there are quite a few literature available, and it would be remarkable if we could make computer systems understand that the task is in no way going to be smooth. There are various challenges like understanding the ideal, which means of the sentence; accurate Named–Entity Reputation (NER); correct prediction of diverse parts of speech and coreference decision.

21.5 Design and Implementation

Details of Hardware/Software/Platform for Fake News Detection as shown in Figure 21.1 to be used by various researchers.

1.) Machine Learning
2.) Natural Language Processing
3.) Spacy
4.) TensorFlow

Details of analytics of the content as shown in Figure 21.2 to be used by various researchers.

Details of input and output in the research model as shown in Figure 21.3 to be used by various researchers.

Details of input and output requirements, variables, and assumptions related to the system as shown in Figure 21.4 to be used by various researchers.

21.6 Experimental Scenario

Experimental results and analysis as shown in Figure 21.5, Figure 21.6, and Figure 21.7.

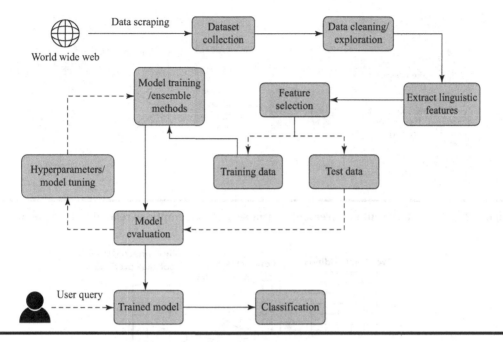

Figure 21.1   Architecture of the design for fake news detection.

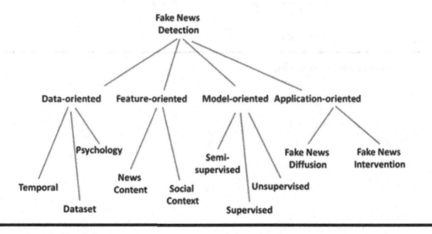

Figure 21.2   Analysis of the content.

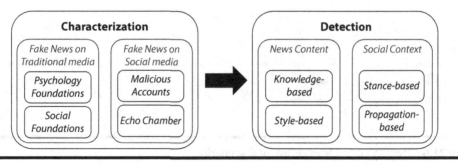

Figure 21.3   Details of input and output used in the research model.

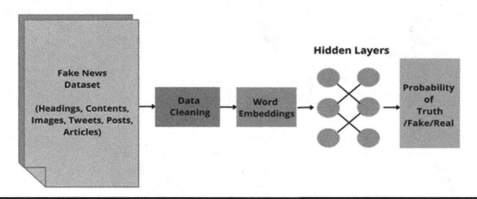

Figure 21.4 Input/Output requirements, variables, and assumptions related to the system.

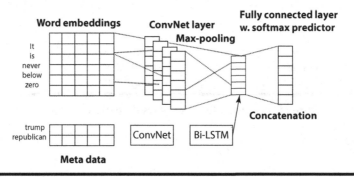

Figure 21.5 Experimental scenario.

```
In [1]: import pandas as pd
        import numpy as np


In [3]:
        fake_df=pd.read_csv(r"C:\Users\sanath\Desktop\FakeNewProjectForSanath\FakeNewProjectForSanath\fake.csv")
        real_df=pd.read_csv(r"C:\Users\sanath\Desktop\FakeNewProjectForSanath\FakeNewProjectForSanath\real_news.csv")



        print(fake_df.shape)
        print(real_df.shape)

        (12999, 20)
        (15712, 11)

In [4]: real_df2 = real_df[['title', 'content', 'publication']]
        real_df2['label'] = 'real'
        real_df2.head()

        c:\users\sanath\appdata\local\programs\python\python37\lib\site-packages\ipykernel_launcher.py:2: SettingWithCopyWarning:
        A value is trying to be set on a copy of a slice from a DataFrame.
        Try using .loc[row_indexer,col_indexer] = value instead

        See the caveats in the documentation: https://pandas.pydata.org/pandas-docs/stable/user_guide/indexing.html#returning-a-view-ve
        rsus-a-copy
```

Figure 21.6 Python code for experimental scenario.

```
In [5]: fake_df2 = fake_df[['title', 'text','site_url']]
        fake_df2['label'] = 'fake'
        fake_df2.head()

        c:\users\sanath\appdata\local\programs\python\python37\lib\site-packages\ipykernel_launcher.py:2: SettingWithCopyWarning:
        A value is trying to be set on a copy of a slice from a DataFrame.
        Try using .loc[row_indexer,col_indexer] = value instead

        See the caveats in the documentation: https://pandas.pydata.org/pandas-docs/stable/user_guide/indexing.html#returning-a-view-ve
        rsus-a-copy
```

Out[5]:

	title	text	site_url	label
0	Muslims BUSTED: They Stole Millions In Gov't B...	Print They should pay all the back all the mon...	100percentfedup.com	fake
1	Re: Why Did Attorney General Loretta Lynch Ple...	Why Did Attorney General Loretta Lynch Plead T...	100percentfedup.com	fake
2	BREAKING: Weiner Cooperating With FBI On Hilla...	Red State : InFox News Sunday reported this mo...	100percentfedup.com	fake
3	PIN DROP SPEECH BY FATHER OF DAUGHTER Kidnappe...	Email Kayla Mueller was a prisoner and torture...	100percentfedup.com	fake
4	FANTASTIC! TRUMP'S 7 POINT PLAN To Reform Heal...	Email HEALTHCARE REFORM TO MAKE AMERICA GREAT ...	100percentfedup.com	fake

Figure 21.7   Run Python code for experimental scenario and the result.

21.6 Results and Discussion

As previously stated, the idea of detection of fake news on social media is very novel, and studies are now being conducted with the hopes that specialists may additionally discover specific strategies to identify fake-information-infested subjects. These studies may therefore be used to assist other researchers in figuring out the great strategy to become aware of bogus news in social media.

The method offered in this study is an offer for a fake news detection algorithm. I would like to test the Naive Bayes classifier, Support Vector Machine (SVM), and semantic analysis techniques in the future, but due to my limited knowledge and time, this will have to wait. It is important that we have a system in place for identifying fake information, or at the very least, that we are aware that not all that we read on social media are necessarily true and that we need to always exercise a critical outlook. By doing this, we may help human beings in making better judgments and prevent them from being duped into believing what other people wish to persuade them into think (Khang and Quantum, 2023).

21.7 Conclusion

The work involved takes a political dataset, applying a TF-IDF Vectorizer, initializing a Passive Aggressive Classifier, and shaping our model. Eventually, we obtained an accuracy of 82% of the dimensions. In this work, LIAR datataset is used as a brand-new database to search for fake information. In comparison to the preceding data, LIAR is a massive order that allows for the development of statistical and automatic strategies for acquiring false statistics. In the future work, we plan to take a closer look at the precis of feature extraction techniques and classifiers, as we were able to choose a text instance model that performs exceptionally with the classifier (Khang, 2023).

References

Abbad M., Kumar G., Samiullah M., and Kumar N. S., "A Predominant Advent to Fake News Detection using Machine Learning Algorithm," 2021 International Conference on Intelligent Technologies (CONIT), 2021, pp. 1–4. https://doi.org/10.1109/CONIT51480.2021.9498436.

Abdullah-All-Tanvir, Mahir E. M., Akhter S., and Huq M. R., "Detecting Fake News using Machine Learning and Deep Learning Algorithms," 7th International Conference on Smart Computing & Communications (ICSCC), Sarawak, Malaysia, Malaysia, 2019, pp. 1–5. https://doi.org/10.1109/ICSCC.2019.8843612.

Gupta M., Kumar R., Pradhan G., and Kumawat D., "Content Based Offline Fake News Detection using Classification Technique," 2021 International Conference on Innovative Computing, Intelligent Communication and Smart Electrical Systems (ICSES), 2021, pp. 1–6. https://doi.org/10.1109/ICSES52305.2021.9633857.

Khang A., *Advanced Technologies and AI-Equipped IoT Applications in High-Tech Agriculture* (1st Ed.). IGI Global Press, 2023a. https://doi.org/10.4018/978-1-6684-9231-4.

Khang A., *Applications and Principles of Quantum Computing* (1st Ed.). IGI Global Press, 2023b. ISBN: 9798369311684. https://doi.org/10.4018/979-8-3693-1168-4.

Khang A., Abdullayev V. A., Alyar A. V., Khalilov M., and Murad B., "AI-Aided Data Analytics Tools and Applications for the Healthcare Sector," *AI and IoT-Based Technologies for Precision Medicine* (1st Ed.). IGI Global Press, 2023. ISBN: 9798369308769. https://doi.org/10.4018/979-8-3693-0876-9.ch018.

Khang A., Muthmainnah M., Seraj P. M. I., Al Yakin A., Obaid A. J., and Panda M. R., "AI-Aided Teaching Model for the Education 5.0 Ecosystem," *AI-Based Technologies and Applications in the Era of the Metaverse* (1st Ed., pp. 83–104). IGI Global Press, 2023. https://doi.org/10.4018/978-1-6684-8851-5.ch004.

Khang A., Rath K. C., Satapathy S. K., Kumar A., Das S. R., and Panda M. R., "Enabling the Future of Manufacturing: Integration of Robotics and IoT to Smart Factory Infrastructure in Industry 4.0," *AI-Based Technologies and Applications in the Era of the Metaverse* (1st Ed., pp. 25–50). IGI Global Press, 2023. https://doi.org/10.4018/978-1-6684-8851-5.ch002.

Nation K., Snowling M. J., and Clarke, P., "Dissecting the Relationship between Language Skills and Learning to Read: Semantic and Phonological Contributions to New Vocabulary Learning in Children with Poor Reading Comprehension," *Advances in Speech Language Pathology*, 9(2), 131–139, 2007. https://www.tandfonline.com/doi/abs/10.1080/14417040601145166.

Shah V., and Khang A., "Metaverse-Enabling IoT Technology for a Futuristic Healthcare System," *AI-Based Technologies and Applications in the Era of the Metaverse* (1st Ed., pp. 165–173). IGI Global Press, 2023. https://doi.org/10.4018/978-1-6684-8851-5.ch008.

Sharma A., Singh I., and Rai V., "Fake News Detection on Social Media," 2022 2nd International Conference on Advance Computing and Innovative Technologies in Engineering (ICACITE), 2022, pp. 803–807. https://doi.org/10.1109/ICACITE53722.2022.9823660.

Trump C., Libel C., New T., and Times Y., "Can Trump Change Libel Laws?," 2017, pp. 2–5. https://www-media.floridabar.org/uploads/2017/10/Libel-NYT-Can-Trump-Change-Libel-Laws.pdf.

Wei T., Ye J., Yan Y., and Duan L., "Identification of True and False News," 2020 2nd International Conference on Information Technology and Computer Application (ITCA), 2020, pp. 564–569. https://doi.org/10.1109/ITCA52113.2020.00124.

Chapter 22

The Impact of the Cyber–Physical Environment and Digital Environment on the Socialization Environment

Alex Khang, Vladimir Hahanov,
Vugar Abdullayev Hajimahmud, Eugenia Litvinova,
Ragimova Nazila Ali, and Abuzarova Vusala Alyar

22.1 Introduction

Man is a living being, integrated with nature from the moment of his existence. In terms of religion, humans are descended from Adam and Eve. On the other hand, the existing human community has gone through various evolutionary processes until it took the human form that man is today. Both in terms of religion and science, today's human communities have originated from a common point and diversified in different forms. Since its inception, the human race has existed in various forms according to different periods of evolution. So, the last evolutionary process of man with different sexes is now called "Homo sapiens," which literally means "man" and "sapiens" is a combination of words. However, this term known as the wise man, the wisest man, represents the present people.

Homo sapiens is the subclass of the last representatives of their category (Homo type) that did not die out. From the time of their existence as beings, humans began to live as a part of a certain group. On the other hand, at least they have been in bilateral relations. The period of socialization of humans began with their unity and thus their numbers increased. So, in the beginning, humans united in groups (which these groups evolved in different forms) and then started their development from these groups, adapted to nature, and evolved over time.

The main issue to be considered here is the role of other people in human development. So, if a person is not exposed to social influences from the time of his birth, his development will take a different turn than normal, mainly in a negative way. Therefore, for the wholistic development

DOI: 10.4324/9781032688305-22

of a person, he needs socialization. "Man is a social being" – this and similar ideas have been put forward for man and an understanding of his nature by philosophers who want to understand man and human nature.

In the social environment, the human community – consisting of groups and individuals – has group–group, intra-group, and individual–individual relations. These relationships represent social processes in the environment of human society, involving the formation of friendship, respect, hatred, love, jealousy, etc. In short, social processes refer to the ways of establishing mutual relations between groups and individuals. The directions considered in the chapter are as follows:

- Social Processes: Man as a Social Being.
- Influence of the Human Gene on the Socialization Process.
- Social Processes Theory.
- Digitization and Socialization.
- Cyber–Physical System (CPS) Environment as a Space of Social Processes.
- Cyber–Physical Social Environment.
- The Impact of the Digital Environment on the Socialization Environment.

22.2 Social Processes: Man as a Social Being

When we look at the life cycle of a person, it becomes clear that he is a social being. From the moment of his birth, he is in contact with others every day, every hour. The process of socialization is an important factor in learning life, developing, and maintaining a normal life.

Human existence is constantly interconnected and constantly affects one another. There is never a moment in which there is no interaction between two individuals. The presence of two people in the same environment – even if they do not speak – causes them to affect each other with a certain natural energy. During socialization, at least two individuals have not only verbal effects on each other, but also any other physical and mental effects.

Socialization is the main process through which a person learns for both himself (self) and the surrounding world. During this period, a person learns all the laws of the social group to which he belongs. Small groups such as a social group, a family, a group of friends, a work team, as well as a certain army, urban population, etc. there are large social groups. In this regard, social groups are divided into two parts: Small and large.

The process of socialization itself takes place in certain stages. The first social group for a person is the family. During this period, a person constantly communicates with family members, and thus begins their first socialization process. Later, as time passes, a person has groups of friends and enters the second stage of socialization by stepping into society; at the same time, this includes and begins the next stage of formation of human character and nature.

As an individual, a person begins the process of character formation in the family, and the moment he steps into society, he moves to the next process of formation. School life, friendships are some of the main factors in the formation and settlement of a person's character. Although the human character is constantly developing, the main influences on a person's real self are fully formed in his childhood stages. Although minor effects occur in later age periods, the human character is formed earlier and a person enters society with the former model as an individual.

It is at this point that a person's real, ideal, and social selves are created. At the moment when the human character is formed, these three models complete their formation process in the human soul. Social processes (in general, social processes) that affect a person's real self, ideal, and social self are divided into certain types as shown in Figure 22.1.

They are described as follows.

- ***Competition***: Human nature – as a developmental mechanism – encourages individuals to be in constant competition with others.
  - Within competition, people are in an ongoing relationship with other people. Thus, competition is a process that occurs between individuals, groups, organizations, and even countries to improve their quality of life.
  - Competition also has positive and negative aspects. Competition in a positive form is aimed at a person's personal development and is mainly based on "friendly" competition. On the other hand, negative competition can cause a person to harm another person. It is mainly based on "hostile" competition. Competition is the most visible among social processes.
- ***Conflict***: The struggle for leadership eventually leads to conflict. On the other hand, various differences of opinion create conflicts, which later lead to stratification and social class divisions.
  - Conflicts, in turn, can be small – between individuals, groups, and large – between countries and nations.
  - Conflicts can occur in general, between family members, various collectives, organizations, socio-ethnic groups, religious groups, countries, and nations in a wider environment.
- ***Cooperation***: A type of cooperation, which is one of the social processes affecting the personal development of a person, represents the development of people who have common goals by working together. Cooperation, the opposite of competition, helps to achieve greater success and helps a person to have clearer thoughts and become a "better" person.

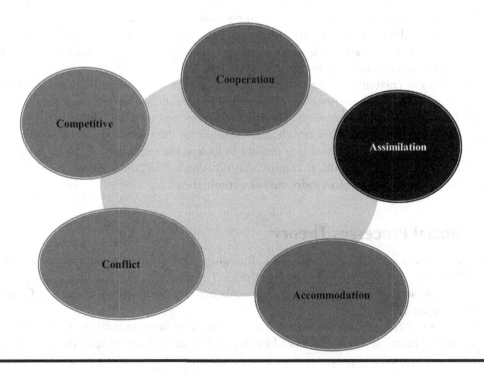

Figure 22.1 Five components in social process.

- ***Accommodation***: When a person joins a new social group, they have to adapt to the laws and ideas of that group. By accepting the laws of a social group, a person becomes a part of it and completely adapts to that social group over time. On the other hand, if one does not accept the views of the social group to which one belongs, if the social group does not comply with the internal law, then there is an opposite relationship between the group and the individual, which causes the person to leave that group. Another case is the general disagreements that arise within the group, which in the worst case leads to the complete destruction of the group.
- **Assimilation**: This process is mainly a case of a small group (nation, etc.) mixing with them by accepting the laws and ideas of another large group. This is more common when small nationalities align with the official nationality of the country they live in. These cases are more common in countries like Canada and the United States. Assimilation can be voluntary or forced.

22.3 Influence of the Human Gene on the Socialization Process

Two factors influence a person's personal development: Human genetics and the influence of society. Both factors influence the development of a person and also their formation for later life. Sometimes a perfectly good family can have a criminal individual – which is greatly influenced by society. However, genetics also play an important role here. So, if you look at the person's family tree, any person who is related to them by blood may have had such an event many years ago.

However, it is wrong to place all the blame entirely on genetics or societal influences. Genes influence each individual's behavioral and psychological characteristics, including intellectual ability, personality, and risk of mental illness – all of which affect both parents and children within the family. Parents' genes influence their own behavior (including the way they raise their children), and children's genes influence their own behavior (including the way they respond to their parents). The transmission of genes from parent to child is an important link that will lead to similarity in behavior between parent and child (Baker, 2007).

However, the environment also affects a person. Within society, people find it interesting because they encounter an environment different from their family, and over time, they are influenced and adapt to this environment. The effects from society are also divided into two parts: Positive and negative. Society has the greatest influence on the transformation of a person as a social being into a negative person. It is possible to look at the social process theory in terms of the effects of social processes. This is a theory that exists mainly in criminology and considers the influences on the formation of an individual as a criminal.

22.4 Social Processes Theory

Psychology, Sociology, Anthropology, and Criminology deal with the study of social processes. Social Processes Theory exists as a theory studied in Criminology. This is a theory based on the influence of society on people. The main keywords here are Society → Criminal → Crime as shown in Figure 22.2.

In other words, society is perceived as the main source that turns an individual into a criminal. Social process theory considers crime as a function of the interaction of people with various organizations, institutions, and processes in society; people from all walks of life have the potential to become criminals if they perpetuate destructive social relationships (Larry, 2000).

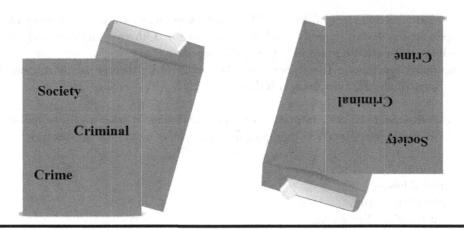

Figure 22.2 Society breeds the criminal, and the criminal commits the crime.

One of the sociological theories of crime, "social process theories," suggests that criminal behavior can be passed down from generation to generation. There are also theories that suggest that it is transmitted from one generation or group to another through learning and cultural means. The most commonly used concept in these theories is the concept of "interaction" (Bingöl, 2022).

Social Process Theory is divided into three parts:

1. Social Learning Theory: This theory describes the process by which an individual learns to commit a crime.
2. Social Control Theory: This theory reflects the inability to control an individual's propensity for crime – the propensity to commit a crime.
3. Social Reaction Theory (also known as label theory): This theory reflects the theory that negative reactions lead people to crime.

As an example of this theory, we can mention the following:

Social Learning Theory: A person can imitate another person by watching them. Or he can learn new things from another person. Children are the most open to innovation in terms of learning. For example, a child can learn any new action from its parent. On the other hand, it also happens while the individual is part of the social group. An individual who begins to adapt to that social group gets used to the laws of the social group over time and begins to apply these laws. A criminal candidate can also learn about the criminal process from individuals of the social group to which he belongs. For example, a person who is going to steal does it either with a person who has been engaged in this work before and gains experience in this direction, or again in the same form, he acquires knowledge about it by receiving advice from a person who is a professional in this work. Basically, when a person learns anything, he needs theoretical and practical knowledge and learns it from more professional people, crime is no exception here.

Social Learning theory is divided into several types.

1. Differential Association Theory: This theory was proposed by Edwin Sutherland. According to the author, a person (or in this case a criminal) can learn by interacting with others as well as by observing them.

2. Differential Reinforcement Theory: This theory supports that a person is more likely to repeat actions that are reinforced and rewarded in return. Otherwise, it is extremely unlikely that the actions that resulted in failure will be repeated.

3. Neutralization Theory: This theory is also known as "Drift Theory," and Matza and Sykes put forward several principles of this theory.

The basis of this theory is "the criminal avoids his responsibility, in other words, he refuses what he has done." Sykes and Matza (1957) propose five principles of neutralization theory:

1. Disclaimer.
2. Denial of injury.
3. Denial of the victim.
4. Condemnation of prisoners.
5. Appeal to higher loyalty.

Social Control Theory: It is based on simple daily routine – lifestyle and activities. For example, a person goes to work every days, after a while it becomes a routine. Or it is based on such daily activities, which characterize the function of internal social control or self-management (control). This characterizes the self-control tendency of the criminal. The theory is widely used in criminology and aims to examine why a person chooses not to engage in criminal activity (Hirschi, 1967).

The main factors here are people's attitudes, obligations, values, norms, and beliefs. Hirschi and Travis (2005) can make them inclined to criminality – to break the law, to commit a crime. On the other hand, internal control can keep a person away from crime and deviance by making him bound by beliefs and so on. The main responsibility here is on internal control – self-management and different beliefs, values, and attitudes can push a person away from committing a crime and keep him away from such situations.

One of the main ideas related to Social Control Theory belongs to Emile Durkheim (1951). According to him, "The more weakened the groups to which [the individual] belongs, the less he depends on them, the more he consequently depends only on himself and recognizes no other rules of conduct than what are founded on his private interests" (Durkheim, 1951, p. 209; originally published in 1897).

Social Reaction Theory: Negative reactions, in other words, society's imposition of certain characteristics (mainly negative ones) on a person can lead a person to crime. And these negative reactions will create negative characteristics such as hatred, anger, etc., which will eventually lead to deviance in a person.

To understand this expression in a more convenient form, a simple example can be shown. A person is judged negatively when in fact he is innocent, or in other words, a child is judged for a mistake made by his parents in the past. Other people keep him away from them and treat him badly, which briefly force the child to withdraw from society, and the child becomes more and more isolated. At this point, including the internal control mechanism, certain feelings and thoughts begin to arise in the child in response to the behavior of other people toward him.

The emergence of such negative emotions such as hatred, anger, and malice toward those people who treat him badly can result in this individual turning into a bad person – in other words, turning into a criminal. It should also be noted that this may not always be the case; that is, a person may choose the right path. On the other hand, this is also related to the previous theory. In fact, all three theories are related to each other.

Furthermore, according to Krohn, Lizotte, and Howell (1993), "The main weakness of social process theories is that they are based only on social factors and thus ignore the role of biological and psychodynamic factors that may also contribute to crime." Although it is impossible to say exactly which one – society or genetics – is the attack, both of them have a great role in the later life and development of a person.

22.5 Digitalization and Socialization

With the onset of the digital era, various changes have taken place in thedaily lives of people. One of them is in the socialization process. The process of socialization can be divided into two time periods, before and after digitization as shown in Figure 22.3.

Along with digital socialization, people's attitudes toward it have also changed. Thus, while adult people prefer real relationships, the younger generation, especially those born in the age of digital socialization, prefer relationships on social networks. They are more exposed to such relationships and are also forced into it. Currently, those who are kids still socialize in the previous form, but teenagers and young people who have access to the Internet are becoming a part of digital socialization. There are advantages and disadvantages to socializing using social networks.

The main disadvantage is that people stay away from real communication, which has a negative effect on the real behavior of the individual. A large part of human life is spent in the virtual environment, which has negative effects on both human health and psychology. Being away from real relationships creates different thoughts in a person toward real life, which affects the individual's later life (Khang & Medicine, 2023).

A person's lack of social skills is one of the main obstacles in their formation as a normal person. People who create a "life" in a virtual environment no longer enjoy real life and isolate themselves from physical society. On the other hand, this process has some advantages. It is possible to connect with more people through social networks. More information can be accessed in a convenient form. It is possible to discover more people, places, but each of these only takes place in a virtual environment (Khang & Rani et al., 2023).

In addition, as an exception, acquaintances in the virtual environment can eventually move to the physical world, which is one of the advantages. Moreover, by using social networks correctly, people can advance their personal development in a positive direction. They can also develop and expand their careers. The process of socialization, along with the era of digitization, has had to adapt to this era, even if this process has positive and negative effects on people. Although socialization in real life is an important process, one should not stay away from the process of digital socialization (Khang & Abuzarova et al., 2023).

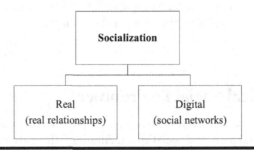

Figure 22.3   Two time periods, before and after digitization.

22.6 Cyber–Physical System Environment as a Space of Social Processes

Along with the integration of socialization into the virtual environment, society also began to be integrated with the virtual environment. Socialization has started to happen not only between humans but also between human–machine and machine–machine pairs.

Connections between machine–machine and machine–human take place within a certain network. The most well known of these networks is the Internet of Things (IoT) network. On the other hand, one of the main concepts that includes the Internet of Things network is Cyber–Physical Systems.

CPS is a system that connect the physical world with the virtual processing world. CPS has different ingredients. These components include modern preventive information technologies. In a cyber–physical system, various data from the real world (physical space) are collected by IoT devices and processed and analyzed in the virtual world (cyber space).

Cyber–Physical Systems continue to be an integral part of socialization as a network of relational "relationships." A new model of socialization is emerging along with machine–machine relations that go beyond human–human relations. Nevertheless, man remains the main factor of social relations. During socialization, there must be at least a two-way relationship. Today, while one side of these relations is organized by a person, the other side can already be organized by a robot, bot – artificial intelligence.

In terms of the implementation of socialization processes, Artificial Intelligence-based technologies can replace parties such as competitors and friends as well as real people. However, social processes in the Cyber–Physical System environment reflect human–machine and machine–machine relationships. For socialization, each individual must become a component (piece) of this social environment. But in today's era, asocialism is starting to increase more. The main reason for this is that people avoid or even fear real relationships. In relationships where the trust factor plays a key role, there is a different presence today, in other words, a lack of trust.

Lack of trust is more common, especially among the new generation. This, of course, depends on relationships and experiences in this direction. The fact that a large part of people's main relationships take place over social networks leads to this result. The main step to be taken to prevent this is to "bring back to life" the real relations. On the other hand, the friendships created in the Cyber–Physical environment also simulate the relationships of the future. In other words, human–machine friendship is created. Although one of the main goals is that the human being is the central part of a social environment and process, there is also an idea that other relationships are with machines.

Another similar idea that emerges is to try to implement this in the real world, as the Cyber–Physical System environment involves machine–machine and human–machine relationships, that is, Cyber–Physical "Social" systems. By creating a social environment, these systems envisage the implementation of human–machine relations in a real environment in all processes – living, working, entertainment, etc.

22.7 Cyber–Physical Social Environment

Cyber–Physical Social System environment is an integrated environment that seamlessly integrates cyberspace, physical space, and social space. Although there are many concepts of the system, some of them are as follows:

- Cyberspace (CS): This can be considered as an invisible party where calculations are made. Here, processes such as calculations, management, monitoring and control, etc. are carried out.
- Physical-Space (PS): This is the side with traditional physical systems.
- Socio-Space (SS): This is the side of human–social society. Factors such as human habits, thinking, interpersonal relationships, etc. belong here.
- Relations: Between KM and FM, the process of exchanging information obtained from the environment is carried out. This is characteristic of KFS. SM also enters into these relationships.
- A Cyber–Physical Social System is a perfect business model and a system environment that are important to be integrated into everyday life.
- From the human point of view, Cyber–Physical Social Systems have the feature of "Cognitive Analysis."
- Cognitive Analysis: One of the basic needs of any social environment is the presence of cognitive ability. The development of social behavior placed man at the center of the basic system. That is, he accepted the person as a part of the system and not separate from the system. This created the concept of "Human in the Loop" with another concept.

These systems, in which the concept of "Human in the Loop" is integrated, can be called Cyber–Physical–Human Systems (CPHS), which can be considered as a subsystem of Cyber–Physical Social Systems. Personal traditional Cyber–Physical components involved in CPHS (Sulayman et al., 2016) are shown in Figure 22.4.

Cognition, Predictiveness, and Motivation are described as follows:

- *Cognition*: Humans have brains, eyes, and ears, while computer systems use CPUs, RAM/ROM, sensors, and actuators.
- **Predictiveness**: People do not perform the same task in the same way every time, they may choose not to follow instructions, or they may lose focus in the middle of a task.
- **Motivation**: Without proper motivation, a person may not perform such a task even after agreeing to it.

One of the main factors in the socialization environment is motivation. The right motivation encourages people to have the right attitude. The "trust" factor plays one of the main roles in relationships in socialization. The trust here will be against both humans and machines. Humans

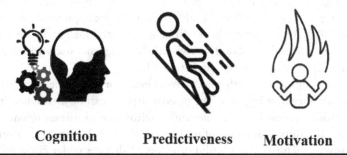

Cognition   **Predictiveness**   **Motivation**

Figure 22.4   The components of cognition, predictiveness, and motivation personal traditional cyberphysical components.

must also have a certain level of trust in the machines they interact with, especially for future human-model machines. One of the main goals of Artificial Intelligence is the creation of human-like machines. So, in the near future, it will no longer be "fantastic" to have such mutual relations. Already, Artificial Intelligence-based technologies will become a member of the family in the true sense.

Representing the impact of Cyber–Physical Social Systems in real life will also result in the creation of a society of man and machine – Smart Society. The trust factor in socialization – the concept of social trust – is one of the most difficult processes. There are different types of trust: general trust, in-group trust, and out-group trust.

- General Trust: This is a person's trust toward strangers. Trust between people and government can be an example of common trust. This also includes another category known as political trust.
- In-group Trust: This characterizes the trust between the members of the group – family, friends, work team – to which the individual belongs.
- Out-group Trust: This characterizes trust toward individuals outside the group to which the individual belongs. This is mainly related to in-group trust.

On the other hand, in addition to people's trust in humans, it is also aimed at people's trust in machines. Unfortunately, people's confidence is not so high both in their own race and in machines. Their distrust of machines is also related to their distrust of humans. It must be recognized that it is quite difficult to overcome. The change in people's trust has also evolved and waned over the years.

It is possible to improve people's trust in Artificial Intelligence-based systems and smart devices by eliminating the security problems of these types of devices and systems. Security has become a global problem like the problems of nature. Eliminating this problem is possible by preparing and applying the right security policy (Khang & Vladimir, 2022).

22.8 Impact of Digital Environment on Socialization Environment

A person develops social skills by interacting with other people. This process has always remained the same and should be the same today. Face-to-face communication has a positive effect on a person, both in terms of psychology and in terms of socialization. When a person communicates with another person face to face, they feel more comfortable and can understand and analyze the other party's feelings, emotions, and gestures more easily. But this process was forced to change along with technological development – digitalization. There are approximately 8 billion people in the world, and by 2023, 4.9 billion of them will be using social media. This is a very large number. These figures also mean that more than two-thirds of Internet users and one in three people worldwide are on social media platforms (Rohit, 2023).

Technological development directly affects social behavior and causes changes. These changes have both positive and negative impacts. The positive aspects can be mentioned in a simple form: Obtaining information, a more comfortable work environment, business orientation, convenient access, accessibility, the implementation of mutual relations in "a virtual environment" from far distances in a convenient form, the possibility of establishing a wider circle of "friends," communicating with more people in "a virtual environment", etc.. However, the main negative effect of these is the reduction of socialization in the real environment, disruption of social behaviors, "abnormal" development of real development, avoidance of real communication, and many similar processes. People are encouraged to move to an environment of "asocialization" instead of more "socialization."

This has a direct negative effect on human psychology. It causes loneliness, lack of self-confidence, and depression. "Friendships" created through social networks should be reduced, both for the adult generation and for children. In other words, television, computer, especially telephone time should be reduced. This can be reduced among kids, young people, and adults as follows.

- **Kids:** People who are closest to kids are especially their parents and some friends. The main role here is that of parents. Parents should not keep their children away from the social environment and force them to spend time only with them at home. In the process of development, kids must have a relationship with their peers, and should be more in touch with the environment. Devices such as phones and tablets should not be given to kids for long-term use. However, it can be given with a tiem limit. In addition, parental control programs should be used.
- **Parents**: Parents should constantly communicate with kids (this is also more important for people in adolescence) and talk to them about all topics. A person's best friend should be their parents. Parents should spend more time with their children and do it mainly in a real environment, through hobbies, playing games, in short, doing many different activities. It is more appropriate to keep kids away from smart devices unless necessary.
- **Teenagers and Young People**: The main group on which virtual socialization has an adverse effect are teenagers and young people. In particular, individuals of this age face problems such as asociality, loneliness, and depression more often and are more affected. The social circle of this group of people are becoming wider, which in recent times have been mainly in the virtual environment – social networks. Teenagers and young people need more socialization. This group of people is more concerned about the future, which over time makes them introverts and they begin to "fake" their outward selves. The fact that they also have trust issues makes them more likely to be negatively affected. They start rebuilding their lives on social networks and again withdraw from social life. The relationship between teenagers and their families should be especially strong during this period. This is also true for young people. If parents can be ideal friends for their children from childhood, if they can instill this in their children, it will have a positive effect on the future life of those people. On the other hand, creating a life in the virtual world will cut them off from the real world, and will lead to the development of all their social skills in a negative direction.

Unfortunately, although the era of digitalization promises many innovations to people, it also has a negative feature, such as the robotization of people. Of course, this is a process that depends on the human factor and is related to the development of social skills in a real environment. Having a smaller "physical circle" instead of a large "cyber circle" is more appropriate for both one's own psychology and the social psychology of society.

22.9 Conclusion

The process of socialization has changed considerably since the recent past. Along with socialization taking place in a wider form in the virtual environment, the concept of living in the virtual environment has also emerged. There are some types of social processes that reflect the relationships between people in a real environment, and these processes are already taking place in the virtual (cyber) environment. That is, the processes of cooperation, competition, conflict, accommodation, and assimilation between people also take place in the virtual environment – mainly in social media (Khang & Shah et al., 2023).

Currently, socialization is generally divided into two types: Real and digital socialization. Socialization in the real environment allows people's social skills to develop in a positive direction. However, it is slightly different in the digital environment. It should also be noted that people are more confident in relationships in the virtual environment. With the development of smart technologies, cyber, physical, and social environments have separated, and socialization is no longer limited to human-to-human relationships. So, relationships have already started to include human–human, machine–machine, and human–machine relations (Khang & Muthmainnah et al., 2023).

The Smart Society model, one of the projects of the future, will cover all three relationships, combining cyber, physical, and social environments. This Smart Society model is based on the coexistence and development of people and smart technologies. However, the Smart Society puts the human model at the center of all processes. In the last part, the influence of social media and smart technologies on people's socialization and some suggestions that should be made to turn this influence into a positive direction are mentioned. These are suggested by experts (Khang & Kali et al., 2023).

22.10 Future Scope of Work

According to Shah and Khang et al. (2023), while Industry 4.0 presents exciting opportunities for growth and innovation, there are still research problems that need to be addressed to realize it's full potential. One such problem is the lack of standardization in IoT devices and data analytics, which can result in compatibility issues and hinder seamless integration across various systems (Khang & Quantum, 2023).

References

Baker, Laura A. "The Biology of Relationships: What Behavioral Genetics Tells us about Interactions Among Family Members." *De Paul Law Review*, 56, no. 3 (2007): 837–846. https://www.ncbi.nlm.nih.gov/pmc/articles/PMC4685725/.

Bingöl, İ. "Sosyolojik Suç Teorilerine Kuramsal Bir Yaklaşim: Sosyal Süreç Teorileri." *Bingöl Üniversitesi Sosyal Bilimler Enstitüsü Dergisi*, 24 (2022): 640–652. https://doi.org/10.29029/busbed.1119294.

Durkheim, E. *Suicide, a Study in Sociology* (1951 Edition, J. A. Spaulding, & G. Simpson, Trans.). London: Routledge, 1897. https://www.frontiersin.org/articles/10.3389/fpsyg.2021.621569/full.

Hirschi, T. 1967. https://www.simplypsychology.org/social-control-theory.html.

Hirschi, Travis, & Gottfredson, Michael R. "Punishment of Children from the Perspective of Control Theory." In Michael Donnelly & Murray A. Straus (Eds.), *Corporal Punishment of Children in Theoretical Perspective*. New Haven, CT; London: Yale University Press, 2005. ISBN 0-300-08547-8. OCLC 144609343.

Kempf-Leonard, K., & Morris, N. A. *Social Control Theory*. Obo in Criminology, 2012. https://doi.org/10.1093/obo/9780195396607-0091.

Khang, A. *AI and IoT-Based Technologies for Precision Medicine* (1st Ed.). IGI Global Press, 2023a. ISBN: 9798369308769. https://doi.org/10.4018/979-8-3693-0876-9.

Khang, A. *Applications and Principles of Quantum Computing* (1st Ed.). IGI Global Press, 2023b. ISBN: 9798369311684. https://doi.org/10.4018/979-8-3693-1168-4.

Khang, A., Abdullayev, V. A., Alyar, A. V., Khalilov, M., & Murad, B. "AI-Aided Data Analytics Tools and Applications for the Healthcare Sector." In *AI and IoT-Based Technologies for Precision Medicine* (1st Ed.). IGI Global Press, 2023. ISBN: 9798369308769. https://doi.org/10.4018/979-8-3693-0876 -9.ch018.

Khang, A., Muthmainnah, M., Seraj, P. M. I., Al Yakin, A., Obaid, A. J., & Panda, M. R. "AI-Aided Teaching Model for the Education 5.0 Ecosystem." In *AI-Based Technologies and Applications in the Era of the Metaverse* (1st Ed., pp. 83–104). IGI Global Press, 2023. https://doi.org/10.4018/978-1 -6684-8851-5.ch004.

Khang, A., Rani, S., Gujrati, R., Uygun, H., & Gupta, S. K. *Designing Workforce Management Systems for Industry 4.0: Data-Centric and AI-Enabled Approaches* (1st Ed.). CRC Press, 2023. https://doi.org/10 .1201/9781003357070.

Khang, A., Rath, K. C., Satapathy, S. K., Kumar, A., Das, S. R., & Panda, M. R. "Enabling the Future of Manufacturing: Integration of Robotics and IoT to Smart Factory Infrastructure in Industry 4.0." In *AI-Based Technologies and Applications in the Era of the Metaverse* (1st Ed., pp. 25–50). IGI Global Press, 2023. https://doi.org/10.4018/978-1-6684-8851-5.ch002.

Khang, A., Shah, V., & Rani, S. *AI-Based Technologies and Applications in the Era of the Metaverse* (1st Ed.). IGI Global Press, 2023. https://doi.org/10.4018/978-1-6684-8851-5.

Krohn, M. D., Lizotte, A. J., & Howell, J. C. "The Strengths and Weaknesses of Delinquent Peer Influence." In J. C. Howell, B. Krisberg, J. D. Hawkins, & J. J. Wilson (Eds.), *Sources of Delinquency* (pp. 21–66). Thousand Oaks: Sage Publications, 1993.

Shewale, Rohit. Social Media Users – Global Demographics, 2023. https://www.demandsage.com/social -media-users.

Siegel, Larry J. "Social Process Theories (From Criminology, Seventh Edition, P 220–253, 2000, – See NCJ-185178)." https://www.ojp.gov/ncjrs/virtual-library/abstracts/trait-theories-criminology-seventh -edition-p-146-183-2000-larry-j.

Sowe, Sulayman K., Zettsu, Koji, Simmon, Eric, de Vaulx, Frederic, & Bojanova, Irena. "Cyber-Physical Human Systems: Putting People in the Loop." National Institute of Standards and Technology ● U.S. Department of Commerce, NIST Author Manuscript, 2016. https://ieeexplore.ieee.org/abstract /document/7389271/.

Chapter 23

Improving Malicious Traffic Detection with the Integration of Deep Neural Networks and Leveraging Hierarchical Attention Mechanism

Chabi Gupta and Alex Khang

23.1 Introduction

A Deep Neural Network (DNN) is a powerful Machine Learning model that can effectively learn complex patterns in data, enabling it to detect anomalous behavior associated with various types of attacks. By leveraging its multiple layers and neurons, this approach has proven to be successful in detecting previously unseen threats. In recent years, cyber threats have become increasingly sophisticated and prevalent, making it imperative to develop advanced techniques for detecting and mitigating malicious traffic. Conventional methodologies frequently prove to be inadequate in their capacity to efficiently assess intricate patterns and promptly adjust to emerging attack strategies.

Given the escalating vulnerabilities linked to security breaches in computer networks, there exists an urgent requirement for the creation and execution of resilient intrusion detection systems. In addressing this concern, conventional Machine Learning techniques like Support Vector Machines and Artificial Neural Networks (ANN) have showcased their effectiveness. However, recent advancements in deep learning techniques, particularly Recurrent Neural Networks (RNN), offer substantial potential for enhancing Intrusion Detection System (IDS) capabilities by leveraging their ability to extract intricate invasion features. Deep learning approaches like RNNs provide an advantage over traditional Machine Learning methods by enabling deeper analysis of network data. This depth allows these models to capture intricate patterns within network

DOI: 10.4324/9781032688305-23

traffic that may indicate malicious activities more accurately. Consequently, incorporating deep learning techniques into intrusion detection systems has become an area of increasing interest among researchers and practitioners alike.

This research aims to address these limitations by leveraging the power of deep neural networks (DNNs) combined with hierarchical attention mechanisms. DNNs have shown remarkable success in various domains but applying them specifically to network security tasks is relatively an unexplored territory. By incorporating a hierarchical attention mechanism into existing DNN architectures, we can enhance the model's ability not only to identify suspicious activities but also to highlight crucial features within network flows that contribute significantly toward accurate detection.

23.2 Research Objective

To analyze and assess the effectiveness of hierarchical attention mechanisms in identifying and categorizing malicious activities within a network environment integrated with DNNs, a well-established Kaggle Network Intrusion Detection System dataset is used for this study. The research is structured as follows:

- Malicious Traffic Detection with a Deep Neural Network.
- Intrusion Detection Systems (IDS).
- Deep Learning for Malicious Traffic Detection.
- Malicious URL Detection.
- Advanced Persistent Threat (APT) Detection.
- About the Hierarchical Attention Mechanism.
- Its Applications, Advantages, and Limitations.
- Issues relevant to Malicious Traffic Detection using Deep Neural Networks.
- Hierarchical Attention Model with Bi-directional Gated Recurrent Units (HAGRU).
- Attention Layers, Maximum Pooling, and Average Pooling.
- Attention Mechanisms in Joint Model for Malicious URL Detection.
- Attention-based Graph Neural Networks (GNNs) for APT Detection.

23.3 Literature Review

While traditional Machine Learning techniques have proven to be effective, there is a rising inclination toward implementing more advanced deep learning approaches. Specifically, Recurrent Neural Networks are being increasingly utilized to extract invasive features with enhanced accuracy. Deep learning methods offer unique advantages when it comes to analyzing complex patterns and extracting meaningful insights from large datasets.

RNNs, which are known for their ability to model sequential data by utilizing internal memory units, hold promise in capturing temporal dependencies present in network traffic logs or system event records. This enables them to detect subtle variations or abnormal behaviors that may indicate potential security threats more accurately. By leveraging the power of RNN-based models along with robust training methodologies and extensive feature engineering strategies specific to the cybersecurity domain, researchers aim to enhance intrusion detection capabilities further.

A prominent research paper titled "Malicious traffic detection combined deep neural network with a hierarchical attention mechanism" (Tripathi & Maheshwari, 2021) is summarized here to provide background for this study. This comprehensive study explores an innovative approach to detecting malicious Internet traffic using advanced Machine Learning techniques. The researchers propose a novel combination of two powerful models: Deep neural networks and the hierarchical attention mechanisms. By integrating these models, they aim to achieve better accuracy and efficiency in identifying malicious activities within network data streams.

The DNN serves as the backbone for feature extraction and representation learning from raw data. It enables automatic pattern recognition by analyzing various attributes such as packet size, flow duration, and protocol type. The hierarchical attention mechanism is then utilized to prioritize significant features while filtering out irrelevant information across multiple levels of abstraction. By leveraging both internal representations learned through DNNs and adaptive attentive mechanisms provided by hierarchical attentions, this approach demonstrates promising results in capturing complex patterns associated with different types of attacks. Furthermore, it exhibits robustness against noisy or incomplete packet traces commonly found in real-world scenarios.

Thus, this investigation introduces a thorough conceptual model that tackles the constraints associated with conventional approaches deployed in identifying harmful network activity. By merging deep neural networks and a hierarchical attention mechanism, this framework facilitates an enhanced understanding of network irregularities at a profound level.

23.3.1 Detecting Malicious Traffic Using a Deep Neural Network

This concept involves using Machine Learning techniques to identify and block harmful network traffic before it can cause damage. By leveraging deep neural networks, which can automatically form learning complex patterns and features from large datasets, researchers (Chao et al., 2020; Liu et al., 2018) have made significant advancements in detecting malicious network activity. The key advantage of using deep neural networks for this task lies in their ability to extract high-level representations from raw data, such as packet payloads or traffic flow characteristics.

Furthermore, by training these models on large-scale datasets that include both benign and malicious examples, they can learn to differentiate between normal network behavior and suspicious activities indicative of intrusions or attacks (Hajraoui & Merabet, 2023; Tobiyama et al., 2016). This allows for more accurate detection rates while minimizing false-positive alerts that could lead to unnecessary disruptions. Also, employing deep neural networks for Malicious Traffic Detection brings enhanced capabilities when compared to traditional methods based on rule-based systems or signature matching algorithms (Liu et al., 2018). Their ability to adaptively learn from new threats makes them well-suited for defending against constantly evolving cyberattacks (Hajraoui & Merabet, 2023).

23.3.2 Intrusion Detection Systems

These have become crucial components in ensuring the security and integrity of computer networks. The integration of deep neural networks with hierarchical attention mechanisms has further enhanced the capabilities and effectiveness of IDS. Deep neural networks allow for complex patterns to be learned and processed, enabling IDS to detect sophisticated intrusion attempts that traditional methods may miss (Amarasinghe et al., 2018; Mercaldo et al., 2023).

Additionally, the inclusion of hierarchical attention mechanisms enables IDS to focus on relevant details within network traffic data. This mechanism assigns different levels of importance or attentiveness to various aspects or features found in the input data, allowing for more accurate identification of potential intrusions (Hajraoui et al., 2018). The combination of deep neural networks and the hierarchical attention mechanisms provides a powerful framework for improving intrusion-detection capabilities by highlighting important details.

IDS systems can effectively enhance their learning capabilities by making use of the latest technological advancements. As a result, these systems can analyze substantial amounts of network traffic data and allocate resources efficiently in order to identify potential security risks. These improvements empower IDS systems to dynamically adapt and acquire new knowledge from the vast pool of information available, enabling them to stay up to date with emerging threats. By leveraging this adaptive learning approach along with resource allocation optimization techniques, IDS systems are better equipped than ever before at identifying and mitigating potential cybersecurity vulnerabilities as shown in Figure 23.1 (Mercaldo et al., 2023; Tobiyama et al., 2016).

By harnessing the power of deep neural networks, which possess the remarkable capability to automatically acquire intricate patterns from datasets, in conjunction with hierarchical attention mechanisms that facilitate targeted concentration on pertinent attributes, this technique facilitates enhanced precision and resilience in identifying intrusions within network systems. Deep neural networks possess multiple layers, enabling them to extract increasingly abstract representations of input data as they progress through the network. This capability allows them to capture intricate relationships among various features in an efficient manner.

Furthermore, by incorporating hierarchical attention mechanisms into these models, we can assign different levels of importance to different parts or aspects within the input data. This powerful combination empowers intrusion detection systems by providing deeper insights into

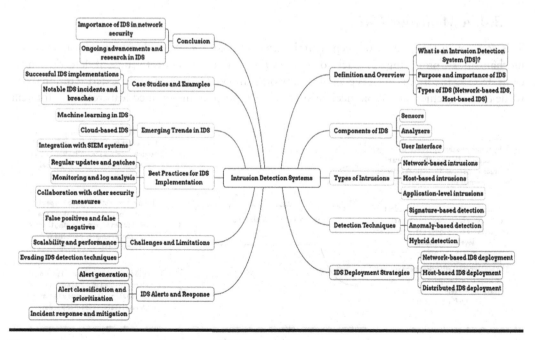

Figure 23.1   Mechanism of intrusion-detection systems.

potentially malicious activities or anomalous behaviors occurring within a system's network architecture. The enhanced depth facilitates better understanding and analysis at granular levels while reducing false positives or negatives commonly associated with traditional IDS algorithms (Chao et al., 2020; Tobiyama et al., 2016).

23.3.3 Advanced Techniques in the Detection of Malicious Network Traffic Using Deep Learning

Deep Learning for Malicious Traffic Detection makes use of deep neural networks and employs a hierarchical attention mechanism. These deep neural networks are artificial neural networks that possess several hidden layers, thereby allowing them to discern more intricate patterns and representations from the given data. The neurons within these interconnected hidden layers empower the network to extract features at a higher level from the input data, resulting in the formation of a hierarchical structure. This approach leverages sophisticated techniques in order to effectively identify malicious traffic (Amarasinghe et al., 2018; Martinelli et al., 2017).

The hierarchical attention mechanism is an important component within deep learning models used for malicious traffic detection as shown in Figure 23.2. This mechanism ensures a selective focus on different parts or constituents of the input data at different levels of abstraction. By employing this approach, the model can effectively capture relevant information and distinguish between normal and malicious traffic (Martinelli et al., 2017; Tobiyama et al., 2016).

To effectively detect malicious traffic, the application of deep learning utilizes complex neural networks comprising multiple hidden layers. Additionally, it employs a hierarchical attention mechanism that facilitates selective concentration on different components within the input data. In essence, this approach harnesses the power of deep neural networks and attention mechanisms to efficiently identify suspicious network activity.

23.3.4 A Malicious URL

This concept in the context of deep neural networks incorporated with a hierarchical attention mechanism is a promising approach to enhance the accuracy and effectiveness of detecting malicious URLs. Incorporating deep neural networks allows for more sophisticated data analysis, while the hierarchical attention mechanism enables capturing fine-grained features from different

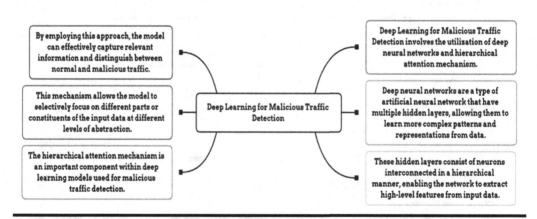

Figure 23.2 Deep learning for malicious traffic detection.

levels of abstraction (Bulut & Yavuz, 2017; Lu et al., 2020). Deep learning algorithms based on neural networks have been effectively utilized in a wide range of fields, encompassing natural language processing and computer vision. Wang et al. (2016) and Yan et al. (2021) discuss that in the context of malicious URL detection, these models can effectively learn complex patterns and representations from input data. By leveraging this capability, deep neural networks can capture both local and global dependencies within URLs.

The hierarchical attention mechanism further enhances the performance by focusing on important parts or components within each URL during model training (Abdullah & Al-Ashoor, 2020; Aversano et al., 2021). This technique assigns varying weights to different portions based on their level of importance in predicting maliciousness accurately (Hwang et al., 2019; Ullah & Mahmoud, 2022). The utilization of this mechanism boosts not only the discrimination power but also interpretability by identifying crucial indicators for classification decisions as shown in Figure 23.3. Overall, combining deep neural networks with a hierarchical attention mechanism offers an advanced solution for malicious URL detection tasks as it enables effective feature extraction at multiple levels while selectively attending to relevant information (Shenfield et al., 2018; Ullah & Mahmoud, 2022).

An et al. (2019), Kwak and Chung (2020) Shenfield et al. (2018), Ullah and Mahmoud (2022) advocate the use of a mechanism that can solve the issue by allowing the model to focus on different parts or components of a URL that are most informative for detecting malicious intent. This approach enables better discrimination between normal and malicious URLs. By employing deep neural network architectures along with hierarchical attention mechanisms, researchers have achieved significant improvements in malicious URL detection accuracy compared to traditional methods. These models not only capture complex semantic features from URLs but also accurately identify patterns associated with known types of attacks (Khang Vladimir, 2022).

Despite these advancements, it can be observed that combining deep learning techniques with hierarchical attention mechanisms requires substantial computational resources due to the large number of parameters involved, which may limit their practicality for real-time deployment on resource-constrained devices or systems (Ghaleb et al., 2022; Kwak & Chung, 2020; Luo et al., 2020).

23.3.5 Detection of Advanced Persistent Threats

The study of Advanced Persistent Threat (APT) detection holds significant importance within the realm of cybersecurity. In recent times, researchers have directed their attention toward enhancing the accuracy and efficiency of APT detection systems by incorporating deep neural networks alongside the hierarchical attention mechanism. This approach has garnered considerable interest due to its potential in bolstering both the reliability and performance of these systems. By leveraging advanced techniques such as deep learning and hierarchical attention mechanisms, there is an ongoing effort to optimize APT detection methods, ensuring they are capable of identifying sophisticated cyber threats efficiently while mitigating false positives (Ghaleb et al., 2022; Kwak & Chung, 2020; Luo et al., 2020; Patgiri et al., 2023; Wu et al., 2022).

Deep neural networks are designed to mimic the brain's ability to process and analyze logical complex patterns from large volumes of data. By utilizing multiple layers of interconnected nodes, these networks can extract high-level features that are crucial for identifying APTs within network traffic or system logs. Furthermore, integrating a hierarchical attention mechanism into deep neural network architectures allows for better resource allocation and prioritization during feature extraction (Kwak & Chung, 2020; Luo et al., 2020). This mechanism enables the model to

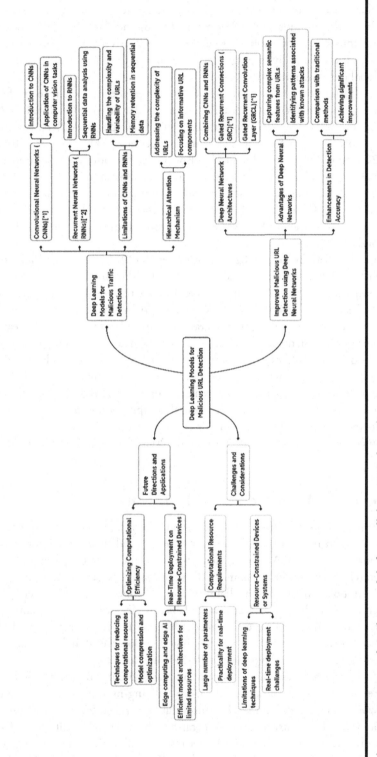

Figure 23.3 Deep learning models for malicious URL detection.

focus on relevant information while ignoring noisy or irrelevant data points, resulting in enhanced performance in detecting sophisticated cyber threats like APTs (An et al., 2019; Kwak & Chung, 2020; Luo et al., 2020). By incorporating hierarchical attention mechanisms into deep neural network models used for APT detection purposes, researchers aim to achieve improved accuracy and efficiency in identifying Advanced Persistent Threats as shown in Figure 23.4.

However, there are opposing arguments to consider when it comes to the effectiveness of this technique.

■ One argument against using deep neural networks and the hierarchical attention mechanism for APT detection is their high computational complexity and resource requirements. Training these models on large-scale datasets necessitates significant computational power, which may not be readily available or feasible for all organizations (Ghaleb et al., 2022; Patgiri et al., 2023; Wu et al., 2022).

■ Additionally, the training process can be time-consuming and may lead to delays in real-time threat detection. Furthermore, while deep neural networks have shown impressive performance in various domains, they often suffer from the issue of interpretability (Li et al., 2020; Luo et al., 2020; Shi et al., 2018).

■ The black-box nature of such models makes it challenging to understand how decisions are being made or why certain threats were detected or missed by the system. This lack of explainability raises concerns regarding accountability and trustworthiness (Angadi & Shukla, 2022; Cui et al., 2018; Ma et al., 2022).

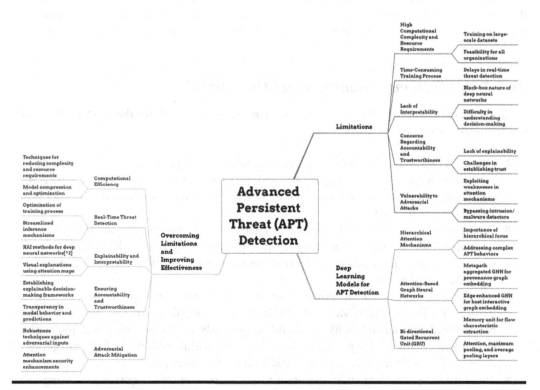

Figure 23.4   Mechanism of Advanced Persistent Threat detection (Author's data).

■ Another potential drawback is related to adversarial attacks. Deep learning-based systems can be vulnerable to carefully crafted malicious inputs that exploit weaknesses present within these complex models themselves during inference phase specifically at attention mechanism module level thereby bypassing intrusion/malware detectors altogether leading to loss opportunity cost (Catak et al., 2020; Mei et al., 2021; Xuan et al., 2020).

23.3.6 *About the Hierarchical Attention Mechanism*

The hierarchical attention mechanism plays a crucial role in the domain of natural language processing, specifically in tasks such as document classification, sentiment analysis, and machine translation. Its significance stems from its adoption of a multi-level architecture that prioritizes gathering information from various levels of granularity to improve the process of representation learning.

In essence, the mechanism is comprised of two primary elements: Attention at the individual word level and attention at the sentence level. The utilization of word-level attention allows for assigning weights to each word in a particular sentence based on its relative importance or relevance to the given task. This functionality facilitates an enhanced focus on critical words while reducing emphasis on less notable ones. Moving ahead, there is sentence-level attention which aggregates information obtained through word-level attentions across all sentences within a document or text snippet. By assigning weights to individual sentences based on their overall contribution toward understanding context or semantics, this technique effectively captures higher-order dependencies among sentences.

Overall, Swarnkar et al. (2023), Vaghela et al. (2021), Wejinya & Bhatia, 2021) concludes that by leveraging both word- and sentence-level attentions together in a hierarchical structure, the hierarchical attention mechanism significantly boosts performance as compared to traditional models.

23.3.7 *Applications/Advantages and Limitations*

The hierarchical attention mechanism approach has demonstrated tremendous potential in various application areas.

■ One such area is natural language processing, where it has been used to improve tasks like sentiment analysis, machine translation, and question answering. By incorporating hierarchical attention, models can capture all local or global semantics of text data (Catak et al., 2020; Xuan et al., 2020).

■ Furthermore, the hierarchical attention mechanism has shown promise in tasks relevant to computer vision. By applying attention at multiple levels – from individual pixels or regions to entire images – the model can effectively focus on relevant information while disregarding noise or irrelevant details.

■ Another domain where the hierarchical attention mechanism proves useful is recommendation systems (Khan, 2020; Mei et al., 2021; Quintero-Bonilla & del Rey, 2020). It enables personalized recommendations by attending not only over users' historical interactions but also aggregating behavior signals based on items within a hierarchy (e.g., categories or themes). This helps uncover more nuanced patterns for better predictions.

■ The utilization of a hierarchical attention mechanism in natural language processing tasks offers notable advantages in terms of both contextual comprehension and interpretability. By employing this approach, it becomes possible to effectively capture the intricate relationships between words at different levels of granularity within text documents. This is beneficial because it enables the model to focus its attention on specific parts (words or phrases) that are more important for making accurate predictions or understanding the underlying sentiment conveyed by sentences or paragraphs. As a result, incorporating a hierarchical attention mechanism into NLP tasks enhances the ability to grasp nuanced meanings and improves the transparency of decision-making processes (Catak et al., 2020; Cui et al., 2018; Shi et al., 2018). By employing this technique, the model can effectively capture relationships between words at both the sentence and document levels.

- The hierarchical attention mechanism allows for more granular analysis of text by focusing on different parts of the input sequence during each level of encoding. This approach enhances the model's ability to assign importance weights to key information within sentences and documents, thereby improving its accuracy in understanding complex nuances and making informed decisions (Khan, 2020; Mei et al., 2021; Quintero-Bonilla & del Rey, 2020).
- Furthermore, the use of hierarchy enables better interpretability by highlighting specific contexts that contribute significantly toward classifying documents or determining sentiments. As a result, researchers can gain deeper insights into how these models make predictions and identify areas where improvements can be made.

While the hierarchical attention mechanism approach has several advantages, it is crucial to consider its limitations as well.

- While this method enables models to capture context dependencies effectively by giving more importance to certain parts of the input sequence, it may face challenges when dealing with long sequences or in cases where important information is distributed across multiple levels of abstraction within the data (徐, 2022).
- An important limitation of the hierarchical attention mechanism approach is related to computational complexity (Panahnejad & Mirabi, 2022; Q. Wu et al., 2022; 徐, 2022). As the length of a document increases, so does the time and resources required for processing. This can make it challenging to apply this technique on very large datasets or in real-time scenarios where prompt responses are essential.
- Another limitation arises from potential information loss at different levels within a hierarchy (Coulter et al., 2022; Yu et al., 2019). Hierarchical attention mechanisms rely on attending selectively over relevant segments based on their salience scores; however, if vital details are dispersed throughout various layers, there might be instances where critical information gets overlooked or underrepresented during computation (Alshamrani et al., 2019; Tecuci et al., 2018).
- Moreover, while hierarchies provide improved interpretability compared to flat approaches due to their ability to highlight distinct characteristics at various granularities, they may struggle with capturing nuanced semantic relationships between different sections effectively (Kawaguchi et al., 2015; Tecuci et al., 2018; Vukalović & Delija, 2015).

23.3.8 Issues Relevant to Malicious Traffic Detection Using Deep Neural Networks

When considering Malicious Traffic Detection using deep neural networks, it is important to delve deeper into the various issues and challenges that may arise in this field. Understanding these complexities can help researchers and practitioners develop more effective solutions.

■ One key issue that needs to be addressed is the imbalance between benign network traffic and malicious traffic samples. Since genuine network activity greatly exceeds malicious traffic, there is a scarcity of labeled datasets for training deep neural networks effectively (Bai et al., 2020; Chapaneri & Shah, 2019; Fan & Wang, 2021). Overcoming this challenge requires collecting diverse and representative data sets with enough of both types of traffic.

■ Another significant concern lies in the interpretability and explainability aspect of deep neural networks' detection models. As complex algorithms like convolutional or recurrent neural networks are employed, it becomes challenging to understand how exactly they arrive at their decisions about classifying certain instances as malicious or benign. This lack of transparency poses difficulties in trust-building among end-users who rely on such systems.

■ In addition, robustness against adversarial attacks remains an ongoing issue within Malicious Traffic Detection research using deep learning techniques.

■ Adversaries constantly strive to find ways to evade detection mechanisms by crafting cunning attack patterns specifically designed to bypass machine learning algorithms' defensive capabilities held by these DNN-based models (Coulter et al., 2022; Panahnejad & Mirabi, 2022; Yu et al., 2019).

23.3.9 Hierarchical Attention Model with Bi-directional Gated Recurrent Units (HAGRU)

The (HAGRU) is an advanced approach in the domain of DNNs that leverages the integration of a hierarchical attention mechanism. This model aims to enhance the performance and effectiveness of natural language processing tasks, such as sentiment analysis or document classification. At its core, HAGRU incorporates both bi-directional gated recurrent units and attention mechanisms. The bidirectionality allows for capturing contextual information from both preceding and succeeding words in a sequence, thereby enabling a comprehensive understanding of sentence structures.

On top of that, the attention mechanism further refines this comprehension by explicitly focusing on salient elements within each sentence (Bai et al., 2020; Chapaneri & Shah, 2019). Integrating HAGRU into deep neural networks empowers them to effectively handle complex text data while automatically learning relevant representations at multiple levels – ranging from individual words to entire documents or paragraphs. This capability makes it particularly suitable for scenarios where nuanced understanding and accurate representation are crucial ("A Model for Malicious Website Detection Using Feed Forward Neural Network," 2022; Razaque et al., 2022; Zhao et al., 2022).

The HAGRU concept is a novel approach in the field of deep neural networks integrated with the hierarchical attention mechanism. This model combines two important components: Bi-directional gated recurrent units and the hierarchical attention mechanism, to improve document classification tasks.

On the one hand, bi-directional gated recurrent units allow for capturing both past and future information from input sequences by utilizing forward and backward processing. This enables better modeling of context dependencies within the text data (Patgiri et al., 2023; T. Wu et al., 2022). On the other hand, the hierarchical attention mechanism provides a way to automatically assign different weights to each word or sentence based on their importance for understanding the overall meaning of the document. However, it is worth considering some opposing arguments against using HAGRU in this context.

- One possible argument observed during research is that incorporating these complex mechanisms may introduce computational complexity, which can limit its practicality in real-world applications where efficiency is crucial.
- Another point to consider is potential overfitting issues when dealing with limited training data as more advanced models tend to have higher model capacity that requires larger datasets for proper generalization.
- To address these concerns, one possible solution recommended is applying regularization techniques such as dropout or L1/L2 regularization during training to prevent overfitting (Lucas et al., 2021; Martín & Camacho, 2020).

To address the challenges associated with the hHierarchical attention model combined with Bi-directional Gated Recurrent Units within deep neural networks integrated with a hierarchical attention mechanism, several solutions have been proposed. These proposals aim to enhance and overcome the limitations of this model to improve its performance.

Researches (Chen et al., 2020; Lago et al., 2021; C. Yang et al., 2021) suggest exploring alternative architectures for the hierarchical attention mechanism. Researchers have also tried to investigate different configurations or variations of this mechanism that can better capture and weigh the importance of different levels in a hierarchical structure (Erichson et al., 2020; Singhal et al., 2023; Zhan et al., 2023).

Another approach is to incorporate additional contextual information into HAGRU. This can involve leveraging external knowledge sources, such as pre-trained word embeddings or domain-specific ontologies, which can provide richer semantic understanding and improve model predictions (R. Li et al., 2020; Oliveira & Sassi, 2021; Singhal et al., 2023).

Furthermore, fine-tuning hyperparameters specific to HAGRU can also contribute toward mitigating drawbacks (Benjamin Erichson et al., 2021; Lin et al., 2022). Experimentation with varying learning rates, batch sizes, or activation functions was observed to help optimize performance by fine-tuning these parameters specifically for HAGRU-based models (Dong et al., 2020; Sharma & Agrawal, 2022).

To sum up, addressing limitations associated with combining HAGURU and hierarchical attention mechanisms requires exploring alternative architectural approaches alongside incorporating contextual information from external sources while considering fine-tuning relevant hyperparameters (Franklin & Onuodu, 2021; Prabhu & Bhat, 2020; Wang et al., 2023).

23.3.10 Attention Layers, Maximum Pooling, and Average Pooling

In the context of deep neural networks integrated with the hierarchical attention mechanism, Attention Layers play a crucial role in capturing important features and information. These layers allow the network to focus on specific parts or elements within a given input sequence, enabling it to weigh their significance during computation. Schneider et al. (2011) and Xiao et al. (2015) highlight during their research that this mechanism helps enhance the model's ability to learn meaningful representations from complex data.

By doing so, Maximum Pooling helps downsample and reduce spatial dimensions while retaining salient features that are most relevant for subsequent stages of processing (Angadi & Shukla, 2022; T. Li et al., 2020; Ma et al., 2022). On the other hand, Average Pooling computes average values within each region instead of selecting only one maximum value as done in Maximum Pooling. This technique also aids in reducing dimensionality but provides a more generalized representation by considering all values rather than focusing solely on high-value activations

(Franklin & Onuodu, 2021; Saharkhizan et al., 2020; Yang et al., 2010). Together, these components contribute toward creating hierarchical attention mechanisms that can effectively process complex inputs and extract critical information at different levels of granularity as detailed during their research (Dong et al., 2020; Sharma & Agrawal, 2022; Wang et al., 2023).

While the Attention Layers, Maximum Pooling, and Average Pooling play important roles in deep neural networks integrated with the hierarchical attention mechanism, there are opposing arguments regarding their effectiveness. One proposition is that Attention Layers can lead to overfitting. By assigning different weights to each input element based on its relevance, attention mechanisms tend to disproportionately focus on specific inputs and neglect others. This can result in a researched model (Franklin & Onuodu, 2021; Prabhu & Bhat, 2020; Schneider et al., 2011) that performs well on training data but fails to generalize effectively to unseen data. Similarly, Maximum Pooling may not always be an optimal choice for feature selection. While it helps capture the most salient features within a given window or region of interest by taking maximum values, this approach may discard potentially useful information present in other less prominent features.

Additionally, critics (Saharkhizan et al., 2020; Xiao et al., 2015; Yang et al., 2010) argue that Average Pooling might oversimplify complex patterns by averaging out diverse contextual information across dimensions. It assumes a uniform importance distribution among all elements within a pooling window and may, therefore, fail to preserve nuanced variations crucial for accurate predictions. Therefore, while these techniques have their merits in certain scenarios, they also come with drawbacks that question their overall efficacy. Considering alternative approaches such as weighted average pooling or dynamic attention mechanisms could help address some of these limitations (Heine et al., 2022; W. Lu, 2023; Pulari et al., 2023).

23.3.11 Attention Mechanisms in Joint Model for Malicious URL Detection

Attention mechanisms are important players in a Joint Model for Malicious URL Detection, particularly when integrated with deep neural networks and the hierarchical attention mechanism. This integration allows for improved performance and accuracy in detecting malicious URLs within large datasets. Considering deep neural networks, attention mechanisms enable the model to focus on specific parts of the input data that are most relevant or informative for making predictions. Ma et al. (2020), Mousavian et al. (2015), KOTEHKO et al. (2020) suggest that by attending to different levels of abstraction in hierarchical structures such as words, characters, and subwords, these mechanisms enhance the model's understanding of complex patterns present in URLs.

The hierarchical attention mechanism further enhances this process by assigning importance weights at both the document-level and word-level components. At each level, attention is applied based on contextual information extracted from previous computations. The aggregation of attentions across hierarchies provides a comprehensive representation that captures relevant features inherent to malicious URLs. By utilizing attention mechanisms within the Joint Models for Malicious URL Detection tasks alongside deep neural network architectures integrated with the hierarchical attention mechanisms significantly improves vulnerability identification capabilities while ensuring better precision and recall rates (Gamboa-Cruzado et al., 2023; Lu, 2023; Yang et al., 2010).

It is important to consider the limitations of attention mechanisms in the Joint Models for Malicious URL Detection. While attention mechanisms have shown promise in various natural language processing tasks and have been successfully applied to hierarchical structures, they still face certain challenges ("A Model for Malicious Website Detection Using Feed Forward Neural Network," 2022; Razaque et al., 2022; Zhao et al., 2022).

One limitation relates to the interpretability of attention weights. Although attention allows us to identify which parts are important during classification, understanding why these parts are crucial can be difficult. This lack of interpretability makes it challenging for practitioners or security experts to trust and validate the model's predictions (Yi et al., 2022; Zola et al., 2022). Another constraint is related to scalability and efficiency (Heine et al., 2022; Yang et al., 2010). Attention mechanisms often require calculating similarity scores between input representations, resulting in increased computational complexity as dataset size grows. Therefore, training larger-scale models may become resource-intensive and time-consuming (Saharkhizan et al., 2020; Zola et al., 2022).

Furthermore, while hierarchical architectures benefit from capturing dependencies at different levels of granularity effectively, there might still exist information loss when aggregating fine-grained details into coarse-grained representations using attentional pooling operations. Considering these limitations provides valuable insights that will help enhance future research on improving the proper utilization of Attention Mechanisms within Joint Models for Malicious URL Detection.

23.3.12 Attention-based Graph Neural Networks (GNNs) for APT Detection

Attention-based Graph Neural Networks have emerged as a powerful tool for detecting Advanced Persistent Threats within the framework of deep neural networks that are integrated with the hierarchical attention mechanism. These networks utilize attention mechanisms to selectively focus on relevant features and information, enabling them to capture intricate relationships between entities in graphs. By incorporating graph structures into traditional deep neural network architectures, GNNs can effectively model complex interactions and dependencies present in APT detection tasks ("A Model for Malicious Website Detection Using Feed Forward Neural Network," 2022; Duarte et al., 2018; Zola et al., 2022).

The hierarchical attention mechanism further enhances this capability by hierarchically attending to different levels of abstraction within the graph data. The key advantage of utilizing attention-based GNNs is their ability to adaptively learn weighted representations from interconnected entities based on relevance scores determined by the attention mechanism (Liu & Liu, 2021; Wang et al., 2020; Yi et al., 2022). This allows these models to place emphasis on informative nodes or edges while downplaying noisy or irrelevant components. In summary, Attention-based Graph Neural Networks integrated with the hierarchical attention mechanisms provide a comprehensive and effective approach for APT detection by leveraging both graph structures and adaptive feature selection (Bai et al., 2020; Fan & Wang, 2021; Usman et al., 2021).

Attention-based Graph Neural Networks have gained significant attention in the field of APT detection, particularly when integrated with the hierarchical attention mechanism within deep neural networks (Chapaneri & Shah, 2019; Jehan & Rajesh Kumar, 2023). These models aim to enhance the performance and accuracy of APT detection by leveraging both graph structure information and the attention mechanism.

One argument against using Attention-based GNNs for APT detection is that they may suffer from computational complexity issues. As these models consider not only the individual nodes but also their relationships within a graph, this can lead to increased memory usage and longer training times (Khan, 2020; Mei et al., 2021; Quintero-Bonilla & del Rey, 2020).

Further, as datasets become larger or more complex, it becomes increasingly challenging to scale up GNN architectures while maintaining efficiency (Mei et al., 2021; Vukalović & Delija, 2015; Xuan et al., 2020). Another potential drawback is related to the generalization ability across different types of attacks. The efficacy of attention-based GNNs heavily relies on capturing intricate patterns within graphs specific to known attack scenarios; however, these models might struggle when faced with previously unseen threats or novel attack techniques where existing patterns are insufficiently represented in the training data.

Additionally, optimizing hyperparameters and architecture design poses challenges for implementing attention-based GNNs effectively (Catak et al., 2020; Vaghela et al., 2021; Wejinya & Bhatia, 2021). Since there is no one-size-fits-all approach due to variations across datasets and network configurations required by diverse applications such as intrusion detection systems the process can be time-consuming and require substantial effort (Cui et al., 2018; Shi et al., 2018; Swarnkar et al., 2023).

23.4 Research Methodology

To devise a comprehensive research methodology for the proposed approach, which includes integrating a hierarchical attention mechanism into deep neural network architectures to enhance malicious traffic detection, the authors have considered various key steps.

- Firstly, an in-depth literature review on the existing methods and techniques employed for detecting and mitigating malicious network traffic have been conducted. This helps to identify any gaps or shortcomings that can be addressed by incorporating a hierarchical attention mechanism.
- Next, clear objective and research question has been defined that align with the proposed method. This includes investigating how integrating hierarchical attention mechanisms can improve accuracy rates in identifying different types of malicious traffic patterns in real-time networks.
- To ensure ample data availability for experimentation purposes, appropriate datasets representing diverse forms of malicious traffic have been selected. These datasets encompass scenarios such as intrusion attempts (e.g., distributed denial-of-service attacks) as well as malware communication protocols (e.g., botnets).
- After acquiring relevant datasets, suitable preprocessing techniques have been applied based on established practices within this domain. A packet-level analysis or feature extraction using Machine Learning algorithms like principal component analysis or manifold learning approaches. This step entails designing deep neural network architectures capable of effectively capturing complex features from raw input data while also accommodating spatial-temporal variations often encountered in the process.

To enhance the accuracy rates in identifying various types of malicious traffic patterns in real-time networks, it was considered beneficial to leverage datasets specifically designed for investigating the integration of hierarchical attention mechanisms. One dataset that is utilized in this research is the Network Intrusion Detection System dataset, which consists of network traffic data collected from diverse sources and encompasses different attack scenarios. This dataset enables researchers to assess how effectively hierarchical attention mechanisms contribute to detecting and classifying malicious activities within a network.

This dataset is a collection of simulated intrusions in a military network environment. The intention behind this simulation was to create an accurate depiction of a typical US Air Force LAN by subjecting it to various attacks. A connection within this context refers to the sequence of TCP packets that occur between a source IP address and target IP address over a specified period, during which data flows according to well-defined protocols. Each connection in the dataset is classified as either normal or anomalous, with each anomaly belonging to one specific attack type.

In terms of data representation, each record for every TCP/IP connection contains approximately 100 bytes worth of information. This includes 41 features derived from both quantitative and qualitative sources – among these are 3 qualitative features and 38 quantitative attributes. Ultimately, the class variable consists of only two categories: "Normal" for connections deemed free from any anomalies, and "Anomalous" for connections identified as being indicative of attacks. By utilizing this dataset along with techniques such as integrating hierarchical attention mechanisms, the authors increase their ability to accurately identify malicious traffic patterns on real-time networks.

23.5 Observations and Analysis

When examining the Network Intrusion Detection System dataset, it was observed that it comprised network traffic data derived from various sources, encompassing a wide range of attack scenarios. This dataset served as a valuable resource in assessing the effectiveness of hierarchical attention mechanisms in identifying and categorizing malicious activities within a network environment.

The diversity present in this dataset allowed for comprehensive evaluations to be conducted on how well these attention mechanisms contribute toward achieving robust detection capabilities. By leveraging hierarchical structures, such systems are effectively designed to capture both local and global contextual information effectively. In detecting potential intrusions or cyberattacks within networks, an understanding of the underlying patterns and relations among different elements is crucial.

Therefore, with this rich collection of network traffic data at their disposal, researchers had the opportunity not only to investigate the performance of hierarchical attention mechanisms but also to gain insights into effective techniques for improving threat identification accuracy. The Network Intrusion Detection System (NIDS) dataset was observed to consist of various constituents.

- One important constituent observed is the network traffic data, which includes packets and flows captured from different sources. This data provide valuable insights into the communication patterns between hosts and networks.
- Another significant constituent of the NIDS dataset was the intrusion detection rules or signatures. These rules defined specific patterns or behaviors associated with known attacks or anomalies in network traffic. They act as a reference for comparison of incoming network traffic against predefined patterns to identify potential intrusions.
- Additionally, metadata attributes formed another integral part of the NIDS dataset. These attributes provided contextual information about each network flow, such as source IP address, destination IP address, port numbers used, protocol type, and timestamp information.

- Metadata added an additional layer of detail to help understand and analyze detected intrusions effectively.
- Moreover, data preprocessing techniques also contributed to shaping the NIDS dataset's constituents.
- Preprocessing involved cleaning noisy data, parsing packets, and extracting relevant features. This step ensured that only necessary details are included while eliminating unnecessary noise, facilitating efficient analysis processes before feeding them into machine learning models employed by IDS system.

When analyzing the NIDS dataset, this study delves into the intricacies of the integration and explores how it impacts the overall performance of the network in detecting intrusions. By examining each layer of the deep neural network, including input layers, hidden layers, and output layers, insights were gained as to how data from different levels are processed hierarchically using attention mechanisms.

Moreover, research also considers factors such as information flow within these networks and evaluates whether there are any bottlenecks or inefficiencies. Additionally, detailing various experiments conducted on this dataset led to meaningful findings about model accuracy when incorporating hierarchical attention mechanisms compared to traditional approaches. Specifically discussing metrics like precision/recall rates helped to understand their impact on overall system performance.

23.6 Hybrid Deep Neural Network with Hierarchical Attention Mechanism

A successful technique in network intrusion detection involves combining deep neural networks with a hierarchical attention mechanism. By incorporating this hierarchical attention mechanism, the model gains the capacity to selectively emphasize meaningful attributes across multiple levels of detail. This enhanced approach allows for better extraction of flow characteristics and improved classification accuracy when dealing with malicious traffic (Khang & Gupta et al., 2023).

Data Preprocessing Techniques: Data preprocessing plays a crucial role in enhancing the efficiency and accuracy of the model. Techniques such as flow segmentation and data balancing are employed to address challenges like data imbalance and variations in traffic generation patterns. Flow segmentation allows for the extraction of relevant flow features, while data balancing ensures that the model is devoid of any bias, leading to more balanced predictions.

Performance Evaluation and Comparison: The effectiveness of the IDS model combined with deep neural networks and the hierarchical attention mechanism were assessed by analyzing real modern network communication behavior. This evaluation aimed to showcase the proposed model's ability to accurately detect anomalies in network traffic. Additionally, the viability of training a real-time IDS system that emphasizes adaptability and reliability was examined. The results from these evaluations demonstrate that the proposed models surpass traditional/classical models in terms of accuracy and detection capability.

Challenges and Limitations: Certain challenges and limitations can also be identified. Large sample categories and non-time series traffic may pose difficulties for the proposed model, which performs better in categories with small sample sizes. Moreover, the evolving nature of security threats necessitates continuous updates and retraining of the IDS models to effectively detect and classify new or zero-day attack patterns.

Real-Time Intrusion Detection System: The study also focused on the possibility of a real-time IDS using deep neural networks, particularly trained on the dataset. The system includes a feature extractor, a machine-learning pipeline, and a server accessible through an API. This demonstrates the practical application and accessibility of the proposed IDS.

23.7 Recommendations for Future Research

Malicious Traffic Detection can greatly benefit from the integration of deep neural networks along with leveraging the hierarchical attention mechanism. By incorporating this mechanism, researchers can delve deeper into understanding and detecting malicious network activities more effectively. One avenue for future exploration could be to investigate the impact of different hierarchical attention mechanisms on improving the accuracy and efficiency of detection systems (Khang & Misra et al., 2023).

Researchers can experiment with various types of attention mechanisms, such as self-attention or transformer-based models, to identify which approach yields superior performance in identifying patterns indicative of malicious traffic. Additionally, it would be valuable to explore how combining multiple deep neural networks enhances detection capabilities. Investigating strategies for integrating information from diverse neural network architectures could prove beneficial in achieving higher accuracy rates while minimizing false positives/negatives.

Another aspect worth exploring is evaluating the effectiveness and generalizability of these approaches across different network infrastructures and datasets. It would provide meaningful insights into adapting these techniques for real-world scenarios where varying challenges arise due to differences in data distributions and system configurations. Moreover, considering potential adversarial attacks against deep learning models used in malicious traffic detection is crucial (Khang & Hajimahmud et al., 2023).

Exploring robustness methods that address vulnerabilities posed by adversarial manipulation will contribute toward building more reliable defense measures against evolving threats. A list of potential research topics related to the detection of malicious traffic using deep neural networks with the incorporation of a hierarchical attention mechanism could include areas for Potential Research (author's data):

- Impact Evaluation: Assessing the effectiveness and performance benefits of incorporating a hierarchical attention mechanism into deep neural networks for detecting malicious traffic.
- Algorithm Optimization: Investigating methods to improve efficiency and speed in detecting suspicious patterns by optimizing the hierarchical attention mechanism within deep neural network architectures.
- Dataset Analysis: Analyzing different datasets commonly used in training models for malicious traffic detection to understand their limitations, biases, and generalization capabilities when combined with deep learning approaches.
- Transfer Learning Strategies: Exploring transfer learning techniques that leverage pretrained models on similar tasks or alternative domains to enhance the accuracy and reliability of detecting diverse types of malicious behavior within network traffic.
- Adversarial Attack Resistance: Investigating vulnerability levels against adversarial attacks targeting autonomous systems designed based on such hybrid mechanisms and proposing robust defense mechanisms against these threats.

23.8 Conclusion

The integration of a deep neural network model with a hierarchical attention mechanism aims to enhance the efficacy of identifying malicious traffic. By incorporating advanced Machine Learning techniques, this chapter was able to augment current methods and suggest solutions to improve accuracy in detecting detrimental activities within web traffic data.

The approach was able to analyze observing algorithms within the NIDS dataset that by utilizing a deep neural network with hierarchical attention there will be an additional improvement in accurately identifying and categorizing suspicious behavior or content. This is facilitated by allowing for better focus on different aspects or elements within each layer of the model's architecture. Through these advancements, it is expected that the efficiency and effectiveness of identification processes can be significantly enhanced (Khang & Kali et al., 2023).

In summary, the concept proves to be a promising approach for network intrusion detection systems. The models exhibit enhanced detection capabilities and accuracy, outperforming traditional methods. Data preprocessing techniques, performance evaluations using diverse datasets, and the development of real-time IDS demonstrate the effectiveness and practical application of these approaches (Khang & Shah et al., 2023).

There is some analysis that works against the integration of network intrusion detection systems. While it is true that these models have shown enhanced detection capabilities and accuracy when compared to traditional methods, there are several challenges observed with their implementation. One of the main issues is the large number of computational resources required by deep neural networks. Training such models can be expensive and time-consuming, especially when dealing with real-time intrusion detection scenarios where immediate responses are crucial.

Additionally, another observed lacuna is the lack of interpretability in deep neural networks. These complex models often act as black boxes, making it difficult to understand how they arrived at certain decisions or classifications. This lack of transparency can pose significant challenges in critical domains like network security, where understanding why an intrusion was detected or overlooked is imperative for system administrators. Moreover, due to their high complexity and data requirements, implementing these approaches may not be feasible for small organizations or those with limited resources available for cybersecurity measures. The cost involved in acquiring hardware capable enough to handle these intricate algorithms may outweigh any potential benefits gained from using them.

The effectiveness of hierarchical attention mechanisms in identifying and categorizing malicious activities within a network environment integrated with DNNs was confirmed. A considerable improvement was observed during the analysis of malicious traffic detection with an integration of deep neural networks and leveraging hierarchical attention mechanism. However, challenges remain related to large sample categories, non-time series traffic, and evolving attack patterns, highlighting the need for continuous improvement and adaptation of IDS models (Khang & Muthmainnah et al., 2023).

References

Abdullah, S. A., & Al-Ashoor, A. (2020). An artificial deep neural network for the binary classification of network traffic. *International Journal of Advanced Computer Science and Applications, 11*(1). https://doi.org/10.14569/ijacsa.2020.0110150

Alshamrani, A., Myneni, S., Chowdhary, A., & Huang, D. (2019). A survey on advanced persistent threats. *IEEE Communications Surveys & Tutorials.*

Amarasinghe, K., Kenney, K., & Manic, M. (2018). Toward explainable deep neural network based anomaly detection. *Proceedings – 2018 11th International Conference on Human System Interaction, HSI 2018.* https://doi.org/10.1109/HSI.2018.8430788

An, N. N., Thanh, N. Q., & Liu, Y. (2019). Deep CNNs with self-attention for speaker identification. *IEEE Access, 7.* https://doi.org/10.1109/ACCESS.2019.2917470

Angadi, S., & Shukla, S. (2022). Malicious URL detection using machine learning techniques. *Lecture Notes in Networks and Systems, 458.* https://doi.org/10.1007/978-981-19-2894-9_50

Aversano, L., Bernardi, M. L., Cimitile, M., Pecori, R., & Veltri, L. (2021). Effective anomaly detection using deep learning in IoT systems. *Wireless Communications and Mobile Computing, 2021.* https://doi.org/10.1155/2021/9054336

Bai, J., Zhang, Y., Huang, L., & Li, S. (2020). Vehicle detection based on deep neural network combined with radar attention mechanism. *SAE Technical Papers,* 2020-January. https://doi.org/10.4271/2020-01-5171

Benjamin Erichson, N., Taylor, D., Wu, Q., & Mahoney, M. W. (2021). Noise-response analysis of deep neural networks quantifies robustness and fingerprints structural malware. *SIAM International Conference on Data Mining, SDM 2021.* https://doi.org/10.1137/1.9781611976700.12

Bulut, I., & Yavuz, A. G. (2017). *Mobile Malware Detection using Deep Neural Network.* https://doi.org/10.1109/siu.2017.7960568

Catak, F. O., Sahinbas, K., & Dörtkardeş, V. (2020). Malicious URL detection using machine learning. In *Artificial Intelligence Paradigms for Smart Cyber-Physical Systems.* https://doi.org/10.4018/978-1-7998-5101-1.ch008

Chao, F., Yang, Z., Du, X., & Sun, Y. (2020). Android malware detection method based on deep neural network. *Chinese Journal of Network and Information Security, 6*(5). https://doi.org/10.11959/j.issn.2096-109x.2020060

Chapaneri, R., & Shah, S. (2019). Detection of malicious network traffic using convolutional neural networks. *2019 10th International Conference on Computing, Communication and Networking Technologies, ICCCNT 2019.* https://doi.org/10.1109/ICCCNT45670.2019.8944814

Chen, S., Bateni, S., Grandhi, S., Li, X., Liu, C., & Yang, W. (2020). DENAS: Automated rule generation by knowledge extraction from neural networks. *ESEC/FSE 2020 – Proceedings of the 28th ACM Joint Meeting European Software Engineering Conference and Symposium on the Foundations of Software Engineering.* https://doi.org/10.1145/3368089.3409733

Coulter, R., Zhang, J., Pan, L., & Xiang, Y. (2022). Domain adaptation for windows advanced persistent threat detection. *Computers and Security, 112.* https://doi.org/10.1016/j.cose.2021.102496

Cui, B., He, S., Shi, P., & Yao, X. (2018). Malicious URL detection with feature extraction based on machine learning. *International Journal of High Performance Computing and Networking, 12*(2). https://doi.org/10.1504/ijhpcn.2018.094367

Dong, Y., Zhang, P., Wang, J., Liu, S., Sun, J., Hao, J., Wang, X., Wang, L., Dong, J., & Dai, T. (2020). An empirical study on correlation between coverage and robustness for deep neural networks. *Proceedings of the IEEE International Conference on Engineering of Complex Computer Systems, ICECCS, 2020-October.* https://doi.org/10.1109/ICECCS51672.2020.00016

Duarte, F., Martins, B., Pinto, C. S., & Silva, M. J. (2018). Deep neural models for ICD-10 coding of death certificates and autopsy reports in free-text. *Journal of Biomedical Informatics, 80.* https://doi.org/10.1016/j.jbi.2018.02.011

Erichson, N. B., Taylor, D., Wu, Q., & Mahoney, M. W. (2020). Noise-response analysis for rapid detection of backdoors in deep neural networks. ArXiv.

Fan, M., & Wang, L. (2021). A malicious traffic detection method based on attention mechanism. *IEEE Information Technology, Networking, Electronic and Automation Control Conference, ITNEC 2021.* https://doi.org/10.1109/ITNEC52019.2021.9587109

Franklin, M., & Onuodu, F. E. (2021). An improved cyber attack mitigation model for detecting malicious network traffic using DNNs. *International Journal of Innovative Information Systems, 9*(2).

Gamboa-Cruzado, J., Briceño-Ochoa, J., Huaysara-Ancco, M., Alva-Arévalo, A., Ríos-Vargas, C., & Yllanes, M. A. (2023). A comprehensive systematic review of neural networks and their impact on the detection of malicious websites in network users. *International Journal of Interactive Mobile Technologies*, *17*(1). https://doi.org/10.3991/ijim.v17i01.36371

Ghaleb, F. A., Alsaedi, M., Saeed, F., Ahmad, J., & Alasli, M. (2022). Cyber threat intelligence-based malicious URL detection model using ensemble learning. *Sensors*, *22*(9). https://doi.org/10.3390/s22093373

Hajraoui, A., & El Merabet, H. (2023). Malware detection approach based on deep convolutional neural networks. *International Journal of Information and Computer Security*, *20*(1/2). https://doi.org/10.1504/ijics.2023.10052974

Heine, F., Kleiner, C., Klostermeyer, P., Ahlers, V., Laue, T., & Wellermann, N. (2022). Detecting attacks in network traffic using normality models: The Cellwise estimator. *Lecture Notes in Computer Science (Including Subseries Lecture Notes in Artificial Intelligence and Lecture Notes in Bioinformatics)*, 13291 LNCS. https://doi.org/10.1007/978-3-031-08147-7_18

Hwang, R. H., Peng, M. C., Nguyen, V. L., & Chang, Y. L. (2019). An LSTM-based deep learning approach for classifying malicious traffic at the packet level. *Applied Sciences*, *9*(16). https://doi.org/10.3390/app9163414

Jehan, C., & Rajesh Kumar, T. (2023). An optimal reinforced deep belief network for detection of malicious network traffic. *IETE Journal of Research*. https://doi.org/10.1080/03772063.2023.2175059

Kawaguchi, N., Tsuichihara, M., Ideguchi, K., Tanigawa, Y., & Tomimura, H. (2015). Detection of advanced persistent threat based on cascade of suspicious activities over multiple internal hosts. *Computer Security Symposium 2015*.

Khan, M. B. (2020). Advanced persistent threat: Detection and defence. ArXiv.

Khang, A., Gupta, S. K., Rani, S., & Karras, D. A. (2023). *Smart Cities: IoT Technologies, Big Data Solutions, Cloud Platforms, and Cybersecurity Techniques* (1st Ed.). CRC Press. https://doi.org/10.1201/9781003376064

Khang, A., Hahanov, V., Abbas, G. L., & Hajimahmud, V. A. (2022). Cyber-physical-social system and incident management. In *AI-Centric Smart City Ecosystems: Technologies, Design and Implementation* (1st Ed.). 7 (12). CRC Press. https://doi.org/10.1201/9781003252542-2

Khang, A., Hajimahmud, V. A., Gupta, S. K., Babasaheb, J., & Morris, G. (2023). *AI-Centric Modelling and Analytics: Concepts, Designs, Technologies, and Applications* (1st Ed.). CRC Press. https://doi.org/10.1201/9781003400110

Khang, A., Misra, A., Gupta, S. K., & Shah, V. (2023). *AI-aided IoT Technologies and Applications in the Smart Business and Production* (1st Ed.). CRC Press. https://doi.org/10.1201/9781003392224

Khang, A., Muthmainnah, M., Seraj, P. M. I., Al Yakin, A., Obaid, A. J., & Panda, M. R. (2023). AI-aided teaching model for the education 5.0 ecosystem. In *AI-Based Technologies and Applications in the Era of the Metaverse* (1st Ed., pp. 83–104). IGI Global Press. https://doi.org/10.4018/978-1-6684-8851-5.ch004

Khang, A., Rath, K. C., Satapathy, S. K., Kumar, A., Das, S. R., & Panda, M. R. (2023). Enabling the future of manufacturing: Integration of robotics and IoT to smart factory infrastructure in industry 4.0. In *AI-Based Technologies and Applications in the Era of the Metaverse* (1st Ed., pp. 25–50). IGI Global Press. https://doi.org/10.4018/978-1-6684-8851-5.ch002

Khang, A., Shah, V., & Rani, S. (2023). *AI-Based Technologies and Applications in the Era of the Metaverse* (1st Ed.). IGI Global Press. https://doi.org/10.4018/978-1-6684-8851-5

Kwak, J. Y., & Chung, Y. J. (2020). Sound event detection using derivative features in deep neural networks. *Applied Sciences*, *10*(14). https://doi.org/10.3390/app10144911

Lago, C., Romón, R., López, I. P., Urquijo, B. S., Tellaeche, A., & Bringas, P. G. (2021). Deep learning applications on cybersecurity. *Lecture Notes in Computer Science*, 12886 LNAI. https://doi.org/10.1007/978-3-030-86271-8_51

Li, R., Li, J., Huang, C. C., Yang, P., Huang, X., Zhang, L., Xue, B., & Hermanns, H. (2020). PRODeep: A platform for robustness verification of deep neural networks. *ESEC/FSE 2020 – Proceedings of the 28th ACM Joint Meeting European Software Engineering Conference and Symposium on the Foundations of Software Engineering*. https://doi.org/10.1145/3368089.3417918

Li, T., Kou, G., & Peng, Y. (2020). Improving malicious URLs detection via feature engineering: Linear and nonlinear space transformation methods. *Information Systems, 91*. https://doi.org/10.1016/j.is .2020.101494

Lin, J., Njilla, L. L., & Xiong, K. (2022). Secure machine learning against adversarial samples at test time. *Eurasip Journal on Information Security, 2022*(1). https://doi.org/10.1186/s13635-021-00125-2

Liu, A., Chen, Z., Wang, S., Peng, L., Zhao, C., & Shi, Y. (2018). A fast and effective detection of mobile malware behavior using network traffic. *Lecture Notes in Computer Science (Including Subseries Lecture Notes in Artificial Intelligence and Lecture Notes in Bioinformatics), 11337 LNCS*. https://doi.org/10 .1007/978-3-030-05063-4_10

Liu, X., & Liu, J. (2021). Malicious traffic detection combined deep neural network with hierarchical attention mechanism. *Scientific Reports, 11*(1). https://doi.org/10.1038/s41598-021-91805-z

Lu, S., Li, Q., & Zhu, X. (2020). Stealthy malware detection based on deep neural network. *Journal of Physics: Conference Series, 1437*(1). https://doi.org/10.1088/1742-6596/1437/1/012123

Lu, W. (2023). *Detecting Malicious Attacks Using Principal Component Analysis in Medical Cyber-Physical Systems*. https://doi.org/10.1007/978-3-031-16237-4_9

Lucas, K., Sharif, M., Bauer, L., Reiter, M. K., & Shintre, S. (2021). Malware makeover: Breaking ML-based static analysis by modifying executable bytes. *ASIA CCS 2021 – Proceedings of the 2021 ACM Asia Conference on Computer and Communications Security*. https://doi.org/10.1145/3433210.3453086

Luo, C., Su, S., Sun, Y., Tan, Q., Han, M., & Tian, Z. (2020). A convolution-based system for malicious URLS detection. *Computers, Materials and Continua, 62*(1). https://doi.org/10.32604/cmc.2020 .06507

Ma, L., Zhang, X., Mao, F., Cai, S., Lin, Q., Chen, J., & Wang, S. (2020). Mitigation of malicious attacks on structural balance of signed networks. *Physica A: Statistical Mechanics and Its Applications, 548*. https://doi.org/10.1016/j.physa.2019.123841

Ma, Z., Wang, Z., Wang, Z., Lin, Y., & Du, Y. (2022). Research on android malicious URL detection based on machine learning. *Lecture Notes in Electrical Engineering, 808 LNEE*. https://doi.org/10 .1007/978-981-16-6554-7_71

Martín, A., & Camacho, D. (2020). Evolving the architecture and hyperparameters of DNNs for malware detection. In *Natural Computing Series*. https://doi.org/10.1007/978-981-15-3685-4_13

Martinelli, F., Marulli, F., & Mercaldo, F. (2017). Evaluating convolutional neural network for effective mobile malware detection. *Procedia Computer Science, 112*. https://doi.org/10.1016/j.procs.2017.08 .216

Mei, Y., Han, W., Li, S., & Wu, X. (2021). A survey of advanced persistent threats attack and defense. *Proceedings – 2021 IEEE 6th International Conference on Data Science in Cyberspace, DSC 2021*. https://doi.org/10.1109/DSC53577.2021.00096

Mercaldo, F., Martinelli, F., & Santone, A. (2023). *An Explainable Convolutional Neural Network for Dynamic Android Malware Detection*. https://doi.org/10.5220/0011609800003405

Mousavian, S., Valenzuela, J., & Wang, J. (2015). A Probabilistic risk mitigation model for cyber-attacks to PMU networks. *IEEE Transactions on Power Systems, 30*(1). https://doi.org/10.1109/TPWRS.2014 .2320230

Oliveira, A. S., & Sassi, R. J. (2021). *Hunting Android Malware Using Multimodal Deep Learning and Hybrid Analysis Data*. https://doi.org/10.21528/cbic2021-32

Panahnejad, M., & Mirabi, M. (2022). APT-Dt-KC: Advanced persistent threat detection based on kill-chain model. *Journal of Supercomputing, 78*(6). https://doi.org/10.1007/s11227-021-04201-9

Patgiri, R., Biswas, A., & Nayak, S. (2023). deepBF: Malicious URL detection using learned Bloom Filter and evolutionary deep learning. *Computer Communications, 200*. https://doi.org/10.1016/j.comcom .2022.12.027

Prabhu, S., & Bhat, S. (2020). Cyber attacks mitigation: Detecting malicious activities in network traffic – A review of literature. *International Journal of Case Studies in Business, IT, and Education*. https://doi .org/10.47992/ijcsbe.2581.6942.0078

Quintero-Bonilla, S., & del Rey, A. M. (2020). A new proposal on the advanced persistent threat: A survey. *Applied Sciences, 10*(11). https://doi.org/10.3390/app10113874

Razaque, A., Alotaibi, B., Alotaibi, M., Amsaad, F., Manasov, A., Hariri, S., Yergaliyeva, B. B., & Alotaibi, A. (2022). Blockchain-enabled deep recurrent neural network model for clickbait detection. *IEEE Access*, *10*. https://doi.org/10.1109/ACCESS.2021.3137078

Saharkhizan, M., Azmoodeh, A., Dehghantanha, A., Choo, K. K. R., & Parizi, R. M. (2020). An ensemble of deep recurrent neural networks for detecting IoT cyber attacks using network traffic. *IEEE Internet of Things Journal*, *7*(9). https://doi.org/10.1109/JIOT.2020.2996425

Schneider, C. M., Moreira, A. A., Andrade, J. S., Havlin, S., & Herrmann, H. J. (2011). Mitigation of malicious attacks on networks. *Proceedings of the National Academy of Sciences of the United States of America*, *108*(10). https://doi.org/10.1073/pnas.1009440108

Sharma, R. M., & Agrawal, C. P. (2022). A BPSO and deep learning based hybrid approach for android feature selection and malware detection. *Proceedings – 2022 IEEE 11th International Conference on Communication Systems and Network Technologies, CSNT 2022*. https://doi.org/10.1109/CSNT54456 .2022.9787671

Shenfield, A., Day, D., & Ayesh, A. (2018). Intelligent intrusion detection systems using artificial neural networks. *ICT Express*, *4*(2). https://doi.org/10.1016/j.icte.2018.04.003

Shi, P., Yao, X., He, S., & Cui, B. (2018). Malicious URL detection with feature extraction based on machine learning. *International Journal of High Performance Computing and Networking*, *12*(2). https://doi.org/10.1504/ijhpcn.2018.10015545

Singhal, R., Soni, M., Bhatt, S., Khorasiya, M., & Jinwala, D. C. (2023). Enhancing robustness of malware detection model against white box adversarial attacks. *Lecture Notes in Computer Science (Including Subseries Lecture Notes in Artificial Intelligence and Lecture Notes in Bioinformatics)*, 13776 LNCS. https://doi.org/10.1007/978-3-031-24848-1_13

Swarnkar, M., Sharma, N., & Kumar Thakkar, H. (2023). Malicious URL detection using machine learning. In *Studies in Computational Intelligence* (Vol. 1065). https://doi.org/10.1007/978-981-19-6290-5 _11

Tecuci, G., Marcu, D., Meckl, S., & Boicu, M. (2018). Evidence-based detection of advanced persistent threats. *Computing in Science and Engineering*, *20*(6). https://doi.org/10.1109/MCSE.2018.2873854

Tobiyama, S., Yamaguchi, Y., Shimada, H., Ikuse, T., & Yagi, T. (2016). Malware detection with deep neural network using process behavior. *Proceedings – International Computer Software and Applications Conference*, *2*. https://doi.org/10.1109/COMPSAC.2016.151

Ullah, I., & Mahmoud, Q. H. (2022). Design and development of RNN anomaly detection model for IoT networks. *IEEE Access*, *10*. https://doi.org/10.1109/ACCESS.2022.3176317

Usman, M., Ahmad, S., & Saeed, M. M. (2021). Deep neural network-based method for detection and classification of malicious network traffic. *Proceedings of 2021 IEEE Workshop on Microwave Theory and Techniques in Wireless Communications, MTTW 2021*. https://doi.org/10.1109/MTTW53539.2021 .9607317

Vaghela, A., Patel, P., & Mane, P. (2021). Detection of malicious URLs using machine learning. *International Journal of Emerging Technologies and Innovative Research*, *8*(5).

Vukalović, J., & Delija, D. (2015). Advanced persistent threats – Detection and defense. *2015 38th International Convention on Information and Communication Technology, Electronics and Microelectronics, MIPRO 2015 – Proceedings*. https://doi.org/10.1109/MIPRO.2015.7160480

Wang, B., Su, Y., Zhang, M., & Nie, J. (2020). A deep hierarchical network for packet-level malicious traffic detection. *IEEE Access*, *8*. https://doi.org/10.1109/ACCESS.2020.3035967

Wang, H., Ma, P., Yuan, Y., Liu, Z., Wang, S., Tang, Q., Nie, S., & Wu, S. (2023). Enhancing DNN-based binary code function search with low-cost equivalence checking. *IEEE Transactions on Software Engineering*, *49*(1). https://doi.org/10.1109/TSE.2022.3149240

Wang, S., Chen, Z., Zhang, L., Yan, Q., Yang, B., Peng, L., & Jia, Z. (2016). TrafficAV: An effective and explainable detection of mobile malware behavior using network traffic. *2016 IEEE/ACM 24th International Symposium on Quality of Service, IWQoS 2016*. https://doi.org/10.1109/IWQoS.2016 .7590446

Wejinya, G., & Bhatia, S. (2021). Machine learning for malicious URL detection. *Advances in Intelligent Systems and Computing*, *1270*. https://doi.org/10.1007/978-981-15-8289-9_45

Wu, Q., Li, Q., Guo, D., & Meng, X. (2022). Exploring the vulnerability in the inference phase of advanced persistent threats. *International Journal of Distributed Sensor Networks*, *18*(3). https://doi.org/10.1177/15501329221080417

Wu, T., Wang, M., Xi, Y., & Zhao, Z. (2022). Malicious URL detection model based on bidirectional gated recurrent unit and attention mechanism. *Applied Sciences*, *12*(23). https://doi.org/10.3390/app122312367

Xiao, Y. D., Lao, S. Y., Hou, L. L., & Bai, L. (2015). Mitigation of malicious attacks on network observation. *International Journal of Modern Physics C*, *26*(10). https://doi.org/10.1142/S0129183115501089

Xuan, C. D., Nguyen, H. D., & Nikolaevich, T. V. (2020). Malicious URL detection based on machine learning. *International Journal of Advanced Computer Science and Applications*, *11*(1). https://doi.org/10.14569/ijacsa.2020.0110119

Yan, A., Chen, Z., Zhang, H., Peng, L., Yan, Q., Hassan, M. U., Zhao, C., & Yang, B. (2021). Effective detection of mobile malware behavior based on explainable deep neural network. *Neurocomputing*, *453*. https://doi.org/10.1016/j.neucom.2020.09.082

Yang, C., Xu, J., Liang, S., Wu, Y., Wen, Y., Zhang, B., & Meng, D. (2021). DeepMal: Maliciousness-Preserving adversarial instruction learning against static malware detection. *Cybersecurity*, *4*(1). https://doi.org/10.1186/s42400-021-00079-5

Yang, X. F., Sun, M. M., Hu, X. L., & Yang, J. Y. (2010). Improved HMM model based method for detecting cyber-attacks. *Tongxin Xuebao/Journal on Communications*, *31*(3).

Yi, F., Lv, S., He, P., Hu, Y., & Zeng, C. (2022). Malicious code detection based on convolutional neural network and information enhancement algorithms. *Advances in Transdisciplinary Engineering*, *30*. https://doi.org/10.3233/ATDE221025

Yu, T., Zou, F. T., Li, L., & Yi, P. (2019). An encrypted malicious traffic detection system based on neural network. *Proceedings – 2019 International Conference on Cyber-Enabled Distributed Computing and Knowledge Discovery, CyberC 2019*. https://doi.org/10.1109/CyberC.2019.00020

Zhan, D., Duan, Y., Hu, Y., Yin, L., Pan, Z., & Guo, S. (2023). AMGmal: Adaptive mask-guided adversarial attack against malware detection with minimal perturbation. *Computers and Security*, *127*. https://doi.org/10.1016/j.cose.2023.103103

Zhao, J., Li, Q., Liu, S., Yang, Y., & Hong, Y. (2022). Towards traffic supervision in 6G: A graph neural network-based encrypted malicious traffic detection method. *Scientia Sinica Informationis*, *52*(2). https://doi.org/10.1360/SSI-2021-0280

Zola, F., Segurola-Gil, L., Bruse, J. L., Galar, M., & Orduna-Urrutia, R. (2022). Network traffic analysis through node behaviour classification: A graph-based approach with temporal dissection and data-level preprocessing. *Computers and Security*, *115*. https://doi.org/10.1016/j.cose.2022.102632

Котенко, И. В., Крибель, А. М., Лаута, О. С., & Саенко, И. Б. (2020). Analysis of the process of selfsimilarity of network traffic as an approach to detecting cyber attacks on computer networks. *Электросвязь*, *12*(13). https://doi.org/10.34832/elsv.2020.13.12.008

徐志强. (2022). A survey of host-based advanced persistent threat detection technology. *Computer Science and Application*, *12*(1). https://doi.org/10.12677/csa.2022.121024

Chapter 24

Artificial Intelligence and Tourism: A Bibliometric Analysis of Trends and Gaps

Pravin Chavan, Dhanashri Sanadkumar Havale, and Alex Khang

24.1 Introduction

The world is on the verge of facing the new industrial revolution, and the revolution is driven by Artificial Intelligence (AI). AI is a branch of computer science that aims to develop algorithms and methodologies that endow machines with intelligence-like capabilities, such as learning, reasoning, and comprehension (Russell & Norvig, 2016). AI is transforming various industries, such as healthcare, transportation, and manufacturing, and improving efficiency through automating processes. The digitalization of industries results in massive data generation. With advancements in Machine Learning (ML) and Deep Learning (DL) algorithms, AI can analyze these massive amounts of data and make predictions or decisions with high accuracy (Khang & Medicine, 2023).

No doubt, Artificial Intelligence has far-reaching and complex social ramifications that may have both positive and negative effects, leading to debates on whether AI is a "curse or a blessing" (Aly, 2022). On the bright side, AI technology has the potential to significantly transform several industries via its ability to enhance job opportunities and increase production. As the various industries are riding on the high-tide of AI, the tourism industry has not remained behind the curve but has kept pace and adopted AI-driven solutions rapidly. In addition to improving the efficiency of tourist operations, the integration of Artificial Intelligence (AI) in the tourism industry plays a vital role in promoting tourism sustainability.

Exploring the potential of AI in promoting tourism efficiency is a quest of researchers in the field. This research endeavors to review the current stockpile of studies on the utilization of AI in the tourist and hospitality industry and delve into the consequences of embracing AI technologies for the advancement of sustainable tourism practices. The purpose of this chapter is to facilitate the readers' comprehension of the current research trends pertaining to the use of AI within the tourist and hospitality sector. Moreover, this study will function as a valuable resource for

DOI: 10.4324/9781032688305-24

stakeholders in the tourist sector, aiding them in identifying potential areas where AI technology might be used to enhance tourism services.

24.2 Methodology

The present research used a theme-centric review technique. In this particular methodology, the researcher assumes the role of a guide, directing the reader's attention toward the contributions made by previous publications in shaping the development of topics, ideas, or phenomena that are of interest. The first stage of the research included the selection of a thematic emphasis within the domain of AI application in the tourist and hospitality sectors. Furthermore, a comprehensive search was conducted in the Scopus Database to identify relevant material. After evaluating the chosen articles, we used a co-word analysis technique to better understand the interrelationships between the dominant study topics. The research was conducted using VOSViewer, a computer application specifically designed for bibliometric mapping as shown in Figure 24.1.

We searched the Scopus Database for relevant articles in order to conduct bibliometric analysis. Using Boolean search techniques, pertinent studies were located in databases. The articles were searched using Boolean terms such as "Artificial Intelligence" AND "Tourism" OR "Artificial Intelligence" AND "Hospitality." If an article's title, abstract, or keywords contained a particular search term, it was selected for analysis.

Our preliminary investigation yielded 1,581 documents. The year 2010 onward, Artificial Intelligence research intensified. Therefore, we began our search from 2010 to make our study as comprehensive as possible. Therefore, we restricted the publication years to 2010–2023,

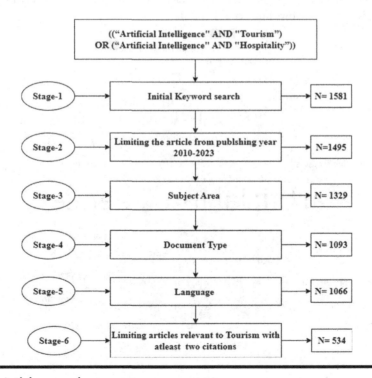

Figure 24.1   Article screening process.

yielding 1,495 relevant articles. In the third phase, we refined the search by concentrating exclusively on documents pertaining to Computer Science, Business, Management, and Accounting, Engineering, and the Social Sciences. In addition, we limited our search to the English language, which yielded 1,066 articles. In the concluding phase, the articles were evaluated manually, and tourism-related articles with at least two citations were selected for analysis. In the concluding phase, 534 articles were chosen for bibliographic analysis.

24.3 Co-Word Analysis

The importance of the theme of research identified through Co-word analysis is presented as below:

- **Artificial Intelligence (AI) is at the center of the digital transformation of the tourism industry**: AI is being used to develop new products and services, such as personalized recommendations, virtual assistants, and Chatbots. AI is also being used to improve operational efficiency and decision-making.
- **Big data is another key technology driving the digital transformation of the tourism industry**: Big data is being used to analyze customer behavior, identify trends, and make better decisions about marketing, product development, and operations.
- **Blockchain technology is gaining traction in the tourism industry**: Blockchain has the potential to revolutionize the way tourism businesses operate and interact with customers. For example, blockchain can be used to create secure and transparent payment systems, manage customer loyalty programs, and track the supply chain of tourism products and services (Khang & Chowdhury et al., 2022).

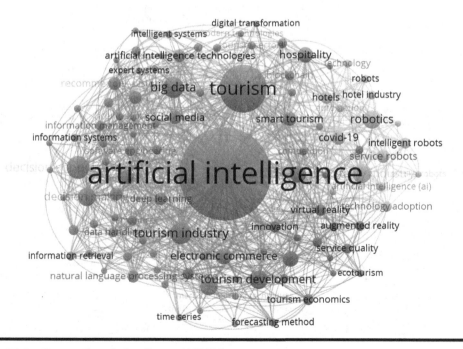

Figure 24.2   Co-word analysis. *Source*: VOSViewer.

■ **Robotics is being used to transform the tourism industry.** Robots are being used to auto-mate tasks such as check-in, customer service, and housekeeping. Robots are also being used to develop new tourism experiences, such as virtual reality tours and robotic tour guides (Khang & Anuradha et al., 2024).

24.4 Application of AI for Sustainable Tourism

After conducting a comprehensive analysis of the publications, many significant areas of AI appli-cation in the field of tourism have been discovered. The graphic provided below illustrates the determined key factors of significance. Furthermore, each area of AI application and the present state of research is discussed in detail as shown in Figure 24.3.

24.4.1 AI for Positive Behavior Change Interventions

Tourist expectations of the tourism destination are influenced by their ideals, opinions, and Interests. AI facilitates effective tourism product development that aligns with the tourist tourism expectations (Xu, 2023). The AI is being utilized to augment the personalized travel experience (Bulchand-Gidumal, 2022; Kumar et al., 2023). Personalization in tourism based on AI is a key marketing tool that allows travel companies give each traveler a unique experience based on their wants and preferences (Yang et al., 2023). AI technologies, such as the analysis of large datasets and the utilization of ML algorithms, are currently being employed in the travel industry to offer customized recommendations and curate personalized experiences for travelers, taking into account their unique requirements, inclinations, and patterns of behavior (D. Li et al., 2022; Yang et al., 2023).

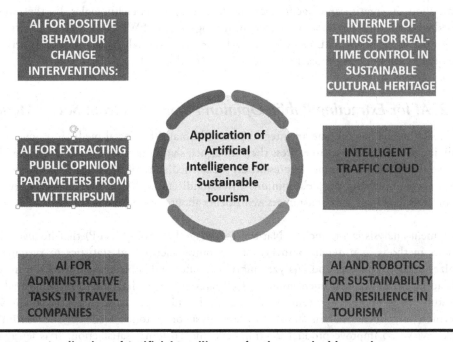

Figure 24.3 Application of Artificial Intelligence for the sustainable tourism.

AI technology is harnessed to comprehend tourist search patterns and accurately predict their requirements. Liao et al. (2010) using the association rules and clustering analysis for data mining, proposed solutions for new product development and customer relationship management. This enables travel companies to offer relevant suggestions and organize trips more efficiently (Vaidya & Al, 2021). Along with tourism product development and customer support, AI has substantial power to bring about a positive change in the behavior of the tourist (Tuo et al., 2021); (Tussyadiah & Miller, 2019).

Additionally, AI has the potential to enhance customer service in the tourism industry significantly (Bulchand-Gidumal et al., 2023). AI technology can be leveraged to improve speed, creativity, and knowledge of service, resulting in better tourist engagement and satisfaction (Dangwal et al., 2023). AI can eliminate lengthy conversations with travel agents and enable travelers to access relevant information at their convenience (Kumar et al., 2023). AI can be used for customer support in the tourism industry through technologies like Chatbots and virtual assistants (Samala et al., 2020). AI-enabled Chatbots and virtual agents can assist travelers in real time, answering their queries and providing assistance throughout their journey (Kumar et al., 2023). AI can be used to remove the language barriers between the visitors and the local community and enhance tourist engagement (Satyam & Geetha, 2023).

AI is playing a significant role in the tourism industry, particularly in customer support (García-Madurga & Grilló-Méndez, 2023). Banerjee et al. (2023) used an ML technique to develop a web interface for demonstrating a hybrid human–AI collaborative system that can handle customer queries. Koçoğlu and Yıldırım Kalem (2020) emphasized the role of electronic-Customer Relationship Management (e-CRM) for tourism companies to fulfill customer needs, safety them, and to gain a competitive advantage.

Li and Zhang (2022) developed a Smart Tourism (ST) service platform using Artificial Intelligence that allows tourists to consult and interact with intelligent machine assistants, reducing human-to-human contact during travel. The Smart Tourism design includes access control in scenic spots, integrating intelligent voice and face-recognition technologies. Furthermore, it is equipped with online ticket booking, scenic mini-programs, and WeChat public accounts to offer better tourist engagement. ML techniques are being used to analyze customer satisfaction and service quality, leading to increased revenues (Ramos et al., 2023).

24.4.2 AI for Extracting Public Opinion Parameters from Social Media

Today, social media has become an integral part of human life. Social media is a powerful tool for individuals and businesses to express their thoughts, share information, and engage with others. These thoughts and opinions expressed on social media are of immense importance for the marketers to comprehend people's opinions (Messaoudi et al., 2022). Marketers are leveraging this enormous data to evaluate customers' sentiments about their products and offerings (Sharma, 2023).

Sentiment analysis is a branch of Natural Language Processing (NLP) that involves the use of various methods in different branches of computer science and statistics to systematically recognize, extract, evaluate, and analyze emotional states and subjective information in textual data (Zad et al., 2021). Sentiment analysis facilitates social media monitoring and analysis to understand public opinion and sentiment toward a brand or product (Singh & Kumar, 2023). Furthermore, sentiment analysis simplifies the analysis of customer feedback and sentiment in product reviews to improve product development and customer satisfaction. It is leveraged to identify influencers and brand advocates by analyzing sentiment and engagement levels on social media (Ilham et al., 2023).

AI, particularly ML, is the backbone of sentiment analysis. Advanced ML models are trained on large datasets to automatically learn and predict customers' sentiments. Furthermore, with the rise of Deep Learning (DL), more advanced sentiment analysis techniques have been developed. Sentiment analysis is a subfield of Natural Language Processing (NLP), which is a branch of AI that focuses on the interaction between computers and human language. AI algorithms in NLP are designed to understand, interpret, and generate human language in a way that is valuable. Generally, sentiment analysis categorizes text as positive, negative, or neutral. Additionally, integrating it with advanced AI techniques facilitates the detection of more complex emotions like joy, anger, sadness, and more. Moreover, sentiment analysis can be integrated with AI systems, such as Chatbots, to understand user sentiment in real-time and respond accordingly.

It has been a thrust area for researchers to understand tourist sentiments using social media data. Especially during the Covid-19 pandemic, researchers have used a DL classification model to anticipate and classify people's feelings toward the tourism sector (Mishra et al., 2021). Paolanti et al. (2021) developed social media sentiment analysis, DL, and geo-location information data for managing tourism destinations. The study conducted a thematic review and identified a total of 5 topics and 27 sub-topics in sentiment analysis in hospitality and tourism. Mehraliyev et al. (2021) conducted a comprehensive review of 70 research papers on sentiment analysis in the hospitality and tourism industry.

- The first important topic identified was the use of sentiment analysis for marketing intelligence. Most research efforts in sentiment analysis centered on gaining customer insights. It focuses on consumers' experiences, emotions, and satisfaction with a tourism product, its antecedents.
- The second topic is methodological issues of sentiment analysis. Under this the researcher found the studies relating to develop new and improved methods for undertaking sentiment analysis and discuss issues pertaining to the validity and precision of sentiment analysis.
- The third topic was social media management, which focuses on understanding what comprises online review usefulness.
- The fourth topic was destination management, which embraced sentiment analysis for destination management. It primarily entails monitoring the pricing, promotion, and reputation of the tourism destination on the Internet.
- The fifth study topic was strategic management, under which sentiments analysis was harnessed for strategic management that involves scrutinizing corporate strategies and comprehending the company's position vis-à-vis its competitors.

24.4.3 AI for Administrative Tasks in Travel Companies

AI is used by travel companies for a range of administrative functions, in addition to its application in customer care. Furthermore, in addition to its application in customer service Artificial Intelligence (AI) is used in the tourist industry to facilitate efficient and precise data collecting, sorting, and interpretation (Lučić, 2022). The use of Artificial Intelligence (AI) has a plethora of prospects for enhancing productivity within the tourist industry (Lučić, 2022). The important application of AI that enhances productivity is discussed below.

- **Chatbots**: AI-powered Chatbots and virtual assistants offer 24-hour customer care for booking flights, hotels, and rental cars, among other services, without the need to wait on hold or talk with a human agent. They are capable of answering basic queries, making suggestions, and completing reservations (Zhang et al., 2023). AI-based Chatbots can provide information and assistance regarding travel destinations, accommodations, attractions, and activities. Moreover, Chatbots can facilitate personalized recommendations that resonate with the user's preferences and previous interactions, resulting in enhancing the user experience. Additionally, Chatbots can provide language translation services, allowing travelers to surmount language barriers. Furthermore, AI-based Chatbots play an instrumental role in enhancing the entire travel experience by offering suggestions for local restaurants, shopping, and entertainment options (Zhang et al., 2023).
- **Virtual/augmented Reality**: These immersive technologies provide prospective tourists with a vivid preview of destinations, hotels, and other tourist attractions. This allows them to make more informed reservations (McLean & Barhorst, 2022). The use of virtual reality enables more informed decisions that avoid any unpleasant experience and foster decisions based on their preferences and interests (Bogicevic et al., 2019).
- **AI and Personalization**: ML technology facilitates travel sites to offer customized recommendations based on an individual's data such as past trips, preferences, budget, etc., resulting in a more tailored experience (Sabet et al., 2021). Baker (2013) underscored the importance of online mapping and Global Positioning System (GPS) technology that has a significant impact on travel decisions and stimulates innovation in the travel business. Gasser (2010), revealed that the incorporation of digital technology has changed the way people travel by enabling direct customer interaction with travel services and access to user-generated travel content. Sion (2017) highlights how smartphones and digital technology foster easy and quick access to travel-related services.

Stroumpoulis et al. (2022) proposed a conceptual framework based on the resource-based view theory to explain the role of AI and Big Data Analysis (BDA) in Smart Tourism (ST) and its potential for obtaining a competitive advantage. The study recommends that the combination of AI and BDA can enable the development of innovative services and the intelligent processing of large amounts of data in the tourism industry.

24.4.4 Internet of Things for Real-time Control in Sustainable Cultural Heritage

The Internet of Things (IoT) could make it easier to keep cultural heritage safe and under control in real time(Casillo et al., 2022). IoT frameworks can gather information from many places and allow for tracking and studying of visitors' actions, likes, and requirements, which can lead to adaptable reactions and predictions (Casillo et al., 2022).

IoT apps can help protect and preserve historical buildings and cultural property by keeping an eye on and managing them more efficiently (Piccialli et al., 2020). Using IoT data along with data science and analytics methods can help the cultural legacy field by providing useful information to all parties and allowing real-time analysis (Longo et al., 2020). IoT technologies help make cultural artifacts more accessible, learnable, and safe by combining and presenting different types of data on interoperable digital platforms (Khan et al., 2020). Dwiyaniti et al. (2022) propose a secure IoT-based radiation detection and measurement system using the Waspmote platform.

24.4.5 Intelligent Traffic Cloud

Traffic congestion is a critical factor hindering tourism decisions for an individual and households. Traffic congestion reduces the amount of time available for tourist activities and may be seen as an unfavorable experience by visitors, reducing the likelihood of a return visit (Alegre & Cladera, 2006). An AI-enabled traffic management system is an effective solution to avoid traffic congestion and facilitate a positive travel experience for tourists. In tourist destinations, Intelligent Traffic Systems (ITS) can be used to address traffic problems. Implementing ITS can enhance traffic security while optimizing traffic management, enhancing transportation infrastructure, and enhancing coordination and management (Ristama, 2023). Tian and Guo (2022) suggested a cloud networking approach for intelligent transportation. Pang et al. (2015) examine the application of a fuzzy C means algorithm for vehicular traffic monitoring and management, which reduces computational complexity and time. Yu (2020) proposed a graph-based model to look at how traffic and tourists are spread out in time and space, as well as how the traffic works in each tourist draw area (Khang & Shah et al., 2023).

24.4.6 AI and Robotics for Sustainability and Resilience in Tourism

The use of AI and robots in the tourist sector has shown considerable potential in terms of enhancing sustainability and resilience (Sarmento & Loureiro, 2021). As the globe confronts increasing environmental and social concerns, emerging technology assists the tourist industry in adapting and implementing more responsible practices (Dalipi et al., 2023). Some of the key areas where AI and Robotics foster sustainability and resilience in tourism are listed below:

- **Tourism Trend Prediction and Management**: AI can analyze massive volumes of data to forecast travel patterns, assist companies and destinations in planning for peak seasons, and managing resources effectively. By reducing waste and improving resource allocation, this may support more sustainable tourist practices (Goel et al., 2022).
- **Smart Resource Management**: AI-powered systems may improve energy efficiency in hotels, resorts, and other tourist attractions. Smart thermostats and lighting systems, for example, may change depending on occupancy and consumption patterns, resulting in energy savings (Saydam et al., 2022)
- **Robot-Assisted Services**: Robots may be used in hotels to help with chores like room service, housekeeping, and concierge services, ensuring that services are supplied effectively and sustainability (Jabeen et al., 2022).
- **Waste Management**: AI-powered robots can be used for garbage sorting and recycling in tourist areas, guaranteeing ecologically sustainable waste management (Tussyadiah, 2020)
- **Feedback and Reviews**: AI can evaluate feedback from visitors to identify areas for development, ensuring that sustainable and resilient tourism practices evolve over time. By analyzing feedback from visitors, AI is able to identify patterns and trends in areas that require refinement. This enables tourism authorities and businesses to make the necessary changes and alterations to their offerings, thereby making them more resilient and sustainable. Consequently, the overall quality of tourism experiences improves, resulting in greater traveler satisfaction and the protection of popular destinations for future generations (Saydam et al., 2022b).
- **Eco-friendly Route Planning**: AI-driven systems can suggest the most eco-friendly travel routes, promoting sustainable transportation methods ("Driving hospitality and tourism to

foster sustainable innovation: A systematic review of COVID-19-related studies and practical implications in the digital era," 2022).
■ **AI for Wildlife Conservation**: With the advent of Industry 4.0, the use of intelligent, cunning technology to protect biological wildlife has increased dramatically. This includes the use of unmanned aerial vehicles or mechanized aircraft for radio tracking, GPS, and Non-GPS transmitters, and drones for radio tracking (Aarju et al., 2023).

24.5 Conclusion

Although the adoption of AI applications in different sectors of the tourism industry is still not widely used, it has been accelerating in the last three years. The use of AI in the tourism industry has brought about a fresh wave of innovation and improved efficiency. The chapter discussed how AI can have a significant impact in various areas, such as understanding people's emotions, analyzing online reviews, and predicting customer behavior.

Moreover, the tourism industry is making great progress toward sustainability by embracing AI. AI-powered technology has a potential to manage resources more effectively, provide personalized experiences that minimize waste, and implement data-driven strategies to ensure sustainable growth in the long run. Basically, when AI and tourism come together, it not only makes the traveler's experience better but also helps the industry grow in a way that is good for the environment and the economy (Khang & Kali et al., 2023).

However, the integration of AI technology in the tourism industry has raised ethical governance challenges. The digitalization of the tourist business has resulted in the generation of a significant volume of data, giving rise to issues such as data privacy that must be effectively handled. These issues highlight the significance of strategic governance via regulatory frameworks that prioritize openness, accountability, and equitable AI practices (Khang & Muthmainnah et al., 2023).

References

Aarju, Bahuguna, R., Pandey, S., Singh, R., Kaur, H., & Chhabra, G. (2023). Enabling technologies for wildlife conservation. *2023 IEEE Devices for Integrated Circuit (DevIC)* (pp. 217–220). https://doi.org/10.1109/DevIC57758.2023.10134561

Alegre, J., & Cladera, M. (2006). Repeat visitation in mature sun and sand holiday destinations. *Journal of Travel Research*, *44*(3), 288–297. https://doi.org/10.1177/0047287505279005

Aly, H. (2022). Digital transformation, development and productivity in developing countries: Is artificial intelligence a curse or a blessing? *Review of Economics and Political Science*, *7*(4), 238–256. https://doi.org/10.1108/REPS-11-2019-0145

Banerjee, D., Poser, M., Wiethof, C., Subramanian, V. S., Paucar, R., Bittner, E. A. C., & Biemann, C. (2023). *A System for Human-AI Collaboration for Online Customer Support* (arXiv:2301.12158). arXiv. http://arxiv.org/abs/2301.12158

Bogicevic, V., Seo, S., Kandampully, J. A., Liu, S. Q., & Rudd, N. A. (2019). Virtual reality presence as a preamble of tourism experience: The role of mental imagery. *Tourism Management*, *74*, 55–64. https://doi.org/10.1016/j.tourman.2019.02.009

Bulchand-Gidumal, J. (2022). Impact of artificial intelligence in travel, tourism, and hospitality. In Z. Xiang, M. Fuchs, U. Gretzel, & W. Höpken (Eds.), *Handbook of e-Tourism* (pp. 1943–1962). Springer International Publishing. https://doi.org/10.1007/978-3-030-48652-5_110

Bulchand-Gidumal, J., William Secin, E., O'Connor, P., & Buhalis, D. (2023). Artificial intelligence's impact on hospitality and tourism marketing: Exploring key themes and addressing challenges. *Current Issues in Tourism*, 1–18. https://doi.org/10.1080/13683500.2023.2229480

Casillo, M., Colace, F., Lombardi, M., Lorusso, A., Santaniello, D., & Valentino, C. (2022). An Internet of Things approach for Cultural Heritage enhancement. *Research Briefs on Information and Communication Technology Evolution*, 8, 149–161. https://doi.org/10.56801/rebicte.v8i.143

Dalipi, F., Kastrati, Z., & Öberg, T. (2023). The impact of artificial intelligence on tourism sustainability: A systematic mapping review. *2023 International Conference on Computational Intelligence and Knowledge Economy (ICCIKE)* (pp. 119–125). https://doi.org/10.1109/ICCIKE58312.2023.10131818

Dangwal, A., Kukreti, M., Angurala, M., Sarangal, R., Mehta, M., & Chauhan, P. (2023). A review on the role of artificial intelligence in tourism. *2023 10th International Conference on Computing for Sustainable Global Development (INDIACom)* (pp. 164–168).

Dwiyaniti, M., Kusumaningtyas, A. B., Wardono, S., Sri Lestari, S., & Tohazen. (2022). A real-time performance monitoring of IoT based on integrated smart streetlight. *2022 6th International Conference on Electrical, Telecommunication and Computer Engineering (ELTICOM)* (pp. 131–135). https://doi.org/10.1109/ELTICOM57747.2022.10037866

García-Madurga, M.-Á., & Grilló-Méndez, A.-J. (2023). Artificial intelligence in the tourism industry: An overview of reviews. *Administrative Sciences*, 13(8), 172. https://doi.org/10.3390/admsci13080172

Goel, P., Kaushik, N., Sivathanu, B., Pillai, R., & George, J. (2022). Consumer's adoption of artificial intelligence and robotics in hospitality and tourism sector: Literature review and future research agenda. *Tourism Review*, ahead-of-print. https://doi.org/10.1108/TR-03-2021-0138

Ilham, A. A., Bustamin, A., & Wahyudiarto, E. (2023). Customer satisfaction assessment system on transactions E-commerce product purchases using sentiment analysis. *International Journal on Advanced Science, Engineering and Information Technology*, 13(3), 1041. https://doi.org/10.18517/ijaseit.13.3.18273

Jabeen, F., Al Zaidi, S., & Al Dhaheri, M. H. (2022). Automation and artificial intelligence in hospitality and tourism. *Tourism Review*, 77(4), 1043–1061. https://doi.org/10.1108/TR-09-2019-0360

Khan, I., Oliveira, L., Amaro, A. C., & Melro, A. (2020). Internet of Things: Evolution and potential for preserving and enjoying cultural heritage. In L. Oliveira, A. C. Amaro, & A. Melro (Eds.), *Advances in Religious and Cultural Studies* (pp. 19–43). IGI Global. https://doi.org/10.4018/978-1-7998-6701-2.ch002

Khang, A. (2023). *AI and IoT-Based Technologies for Precision Medicine* (1st Ed.). IGI Global Press. ISBN: 9798369308769. https://doi.org/10.4018/979-8-3693-0876-9

Khang, A., Chowdhury, S., & Sharma, S. (2022). *The Data-Driven Blockchain Ecosystem: Fundamentals, Applications, and Emerging Technologies* (1st Ed.). CRC Press. https://doi.org/10.1201/9781003269281

Khang, A., Misra, A., Hajimahmud, V. A., & Litvinova, E. (2024). *Machine Vision and Industrial Robotics in Manufacturing: Approaches, Technologies, and Applications* (1st Ed.). CRC Press. ISBN: 9781032565972. https://doi.org/10.1201/ 9781003438137

Khang, A., Muthmainnah, M., Seraj, P. M. I., Al Yakin, A., Obaid, A. J., & Panda, M. R. (2023). AI-aided teaching model for the education 5.0 ecosystem. *AI-Based Technologies and Applications in the Era of the Metaverse* (1st Ed., pp. 83–104). IGI Global Press. https://doi.org/10.4018/978-1-6684-8851-5.ch004

Khang, A., Rath, K. C., Satapathy, S. K., Kumar, A., Das, S. R., & Panda, M. R. (2023). Enabling the future of manufacturing: Integration of robotics and IoT to smart factory infrastructure in industry 4.0. *AI-Based Technologies and Applications in the Era of the Metaverse* (1st Ed., pp. 25–50). IGI Global Press. https://doi.org/10.4018/978-1-6684-8851-5.ch002

Khang, A., Shah, V., & Rani, S. (2023). *AI-Based Technologies and Applications in the Era of the Metaverse* (1st Ed.). IGI Global Press. https://doi.org/10.4018/978-1-6684-8851-5

Koçoğlu, C. M., & Yıldırım Kalem, M. (2020). Electronic customer relationship management in tourism. In E. Çeltek (Ed.), *Advances in Hospitality, Tourism, and the Services Industry* (pp. 273–294). IGI Global. https://doi.org/10.4018/978-1-7998-1989-9.ch013

Kumar, S., Kumar, V., & Attri, K. (2023). Integration of robotics technology and artificial intelligence in the transformation of the tourism industry: A critical viewpoint. In *Technology and Social Transformations in Hospitality, Tourism and Gastronomy* (pp. 39–53). https://doi.org/10.1079/9781800621244.0004

Li, D., Du, P., & He, H. (2022). Artificial intelligence-based sustainable development of smart heritage tourism. *Wireless Communications and Mobile Computing*, 2022, 1–13. https://doi.org/10.1155/2022/5441170

Li, Q., & Zhang, Y. (2022). Design and implementation of smart tourism service platform from the perspective of artificial intelligence. *Wireless Communications and Mobile Computing*, *2022*, e3501003. https://doi.org/10.1155/2022/3501003

Liao, S., Chen, Y.-J., & Deng, M. (2010). Mining customer knowledge for tourism new product development and customer relationship management. *Expert Systems with Applications*, *37*(6), 4212–4223. https://doi.org/10.1016/j.eswa.2009.11.081

Longo, D., Boeri, A., Turillazzi, B., & Orlandi, S. (2020). *Cultural Heritage and Interoperable Open Platforms: Strategies for Knowledge, Accessibility, Enhancement and Networking* (pp. 371–382). https://doi.org/10.2495/SDP200301

Lučić, S. (2022). Digitalization and artificial intelligence: new dimensions in tourism. *The Seventh International Scientific Conference – The Future of Tourism* (pp. 564–581). https://doi.org/10.52370/TISC22564SL

McLean, G., & Barhorst, J. B. (2022). Living the experience before you go . . . but did it meet expectations? The role of virtual reality during hotel bookings. *Journal of Travel Research*, *61*(6), 1233–1251. https://doi.org/10.1177/00472875211028313

Mehraliyev, F., Chan, I. C. C., & Kirilenko, A. P. (2021). Sentiment analysis in hospitality and tourism: A thematic and methodological review. *International Journal of Contemporary Hospitality Management*, *34*(1), 46–77. https://doi.org/10.1108/IJCHM-02-2021-0132

Messaoudi, C., Guessoum, Z., & Ben Romdhane, L. (2022). Opinion mining in online social media: A survey. *Social Network Analysis and Mining*, *12*(1), 25. https://doi.org/10.1007/s13278-021-00855-8

Mishra, R. K., Urolagin, S., Jothi, J. A. A., Neogi, A. S., & Nawaz, N. (2021). Deep learning-based sentiment analysis and topic modeling on tourism during Covid-19 pandemic. *Frontiers in Computer Science*, *3*, 775368. https://doi.org/10.3389/fcomp.2021.775368

Pang, L., Ji, S., & Sun, T. (2015). The application research of cloud computing in the intelligent transportation. *2015 Fifth International Conference on Communication Systems and Network Technologies* (pp. 1100–1102). https://doi.org/10.1109/CSNT.2015.206

Paolanti, M., Mancini, A., Frontoni, E., Felicetti, A., Marinelli, L., Marcheggiani, E., & Pierdicca, R. (2021). Tourism destination management using sentiment analysis and geo-location information: A deep learning approach. *Information Technology & Tourism*, *23*(2), 241–264. https://doi.org/10.1007/s40558-021-00196-4

Piccialli, F., Benedusi, P., Carratore, L., & Colecchia, G. (2020). An IoT data analytics approach for cultural heritage. *Personal and Ubiquitous Computing*, *24*(3), 429–436. https://doi.org/10.1007/s00779-019-01323-z

Ramos, C. M. Q., Cardoso, P. J. S., Fernandes, H. C. L., & Rodrigues, J. M. F. (2023). A decision-support system to analyse customer satisfaction applied to a tourism transport service. *Multimodal Technologies and Interaction*, *7*(1), Article 1. https://doi.org/10.3390/mti7010005

Ristama, H. (2023). The utilization of intelligent traffic systems for managing traffic problems in tourism areas: A literature review. *Deviance Jurnal Kriminologi*, *7*(1), Article 1. https://doi.org/10.36080/djk.2379

Russell, S. J., & Norvig, P. (2016). *Artificial Intelligence: A Modern Approach* (Third edition, Global edition). Pearson.

Sabet, A. J., Gopalakrishnan, S., Rossi, M., Schreiber, F. A., & Tanca, L. (2021). Preference mining in the travel domain. *2021 IEEE International Conference on Artificial Intelligence and Computer Applications (ICAICA)* (pp. 358–365). https://doi.org/10.1109/ICAICA52286.2021.9498231

Samala, N., Katkam, B. S., Bellamkonda, R. S., & Rodriguez, R. V. (2020). Impact of AI and robotics in the tourism sector: A critical insight. *Journal of Tourism Futures*, *8*(1), 73–87. https://doi.org/10.1108/JTF-07-2019-0065

Sarmento, E. M., & Loureiro, S. M. C. (2021). Exploring the role of norms and habit in explaining pro-environmental behavior intentions in situations of use robots and AI agents as providers in tourism sector. *Sustainability*, *13*(24), 13928. https://doi.org/10.3390/su132413928

Satyam, & Geetha, P. (2023). Comprehensive overview of the opportunities and challenges in AI. *2023 International Conference on Sustainable Computing and Smart Systems (ICSCSS)* (pp. 420–423). https://doi.org/10.1109/ICSCSS57650.2023.10169722

Saydam, M. B., Arici, H. E., & Koseoglu, M. A. (2022a). How does the tourism and hospitality industry use artificial intelligence? A review of empirical studies and future research agenda. *Journal of Hospitality Marketing & Management, 31*(8), 908–936. https://doi.org/10.1080/19368623.2022.2118923

Saydam, M. B., Arici, H. E., & Koseoglu, M. A. (2022b). How does the tourism and hospitality industry use artificial intelligence? A review of empirical studies and future research agenda. *Journal of Hospitality Marketing & Management, 31*(8), 908–936. https://doi.org/10.1080/19368623.2022.2118923

Sharma, S. (2023). *Managing Product Reviews: A Comprehensive Guide for Brands and Businesses.* CSMFL Publications. https://doi.org/10.46679/9788195732265

Singh, S., & Kumar, P. (2023). Sentiment analysis of twitter data: A review. *2023 2nd International Conference for Innovation in Technology (INOCON)* (pp. 1–7). https://doi.org/10.1109/INOCON57975.2023.10100998

Stroumpoulis, A., Kopanaki, E., & Varelas, S. (2022). *Role of Artificial Intelligence and Big Data Analytics in Smart Tourism: A Resource-based View Approach* (pp. 99–108). https://doi.org/10.2495/ST220091

Tian, Y., & Guo, Z. (2022). A method based on cloud model and FCM clustering for risky large group decision making. *Journal of Intelligent & Fuzzy Systems, 43*(3), 2647–2665. https://doi.org/10.3233/JIFS-213216

Tuo, Y., Ning, L., & Zhu, A. (2021). How artificial intelligence will change the future of tourism industry: The practice in China. In W. Wörndl, C. Koo, & J. L. Stienmetz (Eds.), *Information and Communication Technologies in Tourism 2021* (pp. 83–94). Springer International Publishing. https://doi.org/10.1007/978-3-030-65785-7_7

Tussyadiah, I. (2020). A review of research into automation in tourism: Launching the annals of tourism research curated collection on artificial intelligence and robotics in tourism. *Annals of Tourism Research, 81*, 102883. https://doi.org/10.1016/j.annals.2020.102883

Tussyadiah, I., & Miller, G. (2019). Perceived impacts of artificial intelligence and responses to positive behaviour change intervention. In J. Pesonen & J. Neidhardt (Eds.), *Information and Communication Technologies in Tourism 2019* (pp. 359–370). Springer International Publishing. https://doi.org/10.1007/978-3-030-05940-8_28

Vaidya, P., & Al, E. (2021). Online travel companies and consumer engagement in the era of artificial intelligence. *International Journal of Modern Agriculture, 10*(2), Article 2.

Xu, M. (2023). Research on smart tourism system based on artificial intelligence. *2023 IEEE 3rd International Conference on Information Technology, Big Data and Artificial Intelligence (ICIBA), 3*, 201–205. https://doi.org/10.1109/ICIBA56860.2023.10165293

Yang, X., Zhang, L., & Feng, Z. (2023). Personalized tourism recommendations and the E-Tourism user experience. *Journal of Travel Research*, 00472875231187332. https://doi.org/10.1177/00472875231187332

Yu, Y.-C. (2020). An urban intelligence service for the impact of urbanization on National Park. *2020 International Conference on INnovations in Intelligent SysTems and Applications (INISTA)* (pp. 1–5). https://doi.org/10.1109/INISTA49547.2020.9194672

Zad, S., Heidari, M., Jones, J. H., & Uzuner, O. (2021). A survey on concept-level sentiment analysis techniques of textual data. *2021 IEEE World AI IoT Congress (AIIoT)* (pp. 285–291). https://doi.org/10.1109/AIIoT52608.2021.9454169

Zhang, B., Zhu, Y., Deng, J., Zheng, W., Liu, Y., Wang, C., & Zeng, R. (2023). "I Am Here to Assist Your Tourism": Predicting continuance intention to use AI-based chatbots for tourism. Does gender really matter? *International Journal of Human–Computer Interaction, 39*(9), 1887–1903. https://doi.org/10.1080/10447318.2022.2124345

Index

Printed in the United States
by Baker & Taylor Publisher Services